Elizabeth Singer Rowe and the
Development of the English Novel

ELIZABETH SINGER ROWE
and the Development of the English Novel

PAULA R. BACKSCHEIDER

The Johns Hopkins University Press
Baltimore

© 2013 The Johns Hopkins University Press
All rights reserved. Published 2013
Printed in the United States of America on acid-free paper
2 4 6 8 9 7 5 3 1

The Johns Hopkins University Press
2715 North Charles Street
Baltimore, Maryland 21218-4363
www.press.jhu.edu

Library of Congress Cataloging-in-Publication Data

Backscheider, Paula R.
Elizabeth Singer Rowe and the development of the English novel / Paula R. Backscheider.
p. cm.
Includes bibliographical references and index.
ISBN 978-1-4214-0842-2 (hdbk. : alk. paper) — ISBN 978-1-4214-0889-7 (electronic) —
ISBN 1-4214-0842-2 (hdbk. : alk. paper) — ISBN 1-4214-0889-9 (electronic)
1. Rowe, Elizabeth Singer, 1674–1737—Criticism and interpretation. 2. English fiction—
18th century—History and criticism. 3. English fiction—Women authors—History and criticism.
4. Women and literature—England—History—18th century. 5. Women—England—History—
18th century. 6. Social movements—England—History—18th century. I. Title.
PR3671.R4Z58 2013
823'.4—dc23
2012023931

A catalog record for this book is available from the British Library.

*Special discounts are available for bulk purchases of this book. For more information,
please contact Special Sales at 410-516-6936 or specialsales@press.jhu.edu.*

The Johns Hopkins University Press uses environmentally friendly book materials, including recycled text paper that is composed of at least 30 percent post-consumer waste, whenever possible.

For Nels Madsen

CONTENTS

List of Illustrations　　*ix*
Acknowledgments　　*xi*
Abbreviations　　*xiii*

Introduction: Locating Elizabeth Singer Rowe　　1

1　Positioning Rowe's Fiction　　46

2　Isles of Happiness　　83

3　Toward Novelistic Discourse　　122

4　The Beautiful Life　　163

Conclusion: Lifestyle as Legacy　　208

Notes　　*237*
Bibliography　　*273*
Index　　*297*

ILLUSTRATIONS

Longleat, Home of Grace and Thomas Thynne	9
Elizabeth Singer Rowe, miniature by Susannah-Penelope Rosse	15
Anne Finch, Countess of Winchilsea, miniature by Peter Cross	17
Elizabeth Singer Rowe, engraving by George Vertue	18
"Queen Jane," engraving of Lady Jane Grey by George Vertue	21
Frontispiece for *Poems by . . . Mrs. Katherine Philips*	23
Frontispiece for *Poems by Mrs. Anne Killigrew*	23
Frontispiece of Aphra Behn for *Poems upon Several Occasions*	23
Frontispiece of Eliza Haywood for *Secret Histories, Novels, and Poems*	24
Frontispiece of Elizabeth Thomas for *Pylades and Corinna*	24
Elizabeth Singer Rowe, effigy from the *London Magazine*	27
Elizabeth Singer Rowe, engraving in *Memoirs of Eminently Pious Women*	27
Elizabeth Singer Rowe, engraving for Cooke's *Devout Exercises of the Heart*	28
Elizabeth Singer Rowe, engraving for Lane's *Devout Exercises of the Heart*	28
Elizabeth Singer Rowe, engraving for *Friendship in Death*	31
Engraving of Elizabeth Singer Rowe from Killigrew engraving	31
Representation of Elizabeth Singer Rowe from J. Peaviour Johnson collection	32
Representation of Elizabeth Singer Rowe from MacDonnell collection	32
Cover illustration of Cooke's edition of *Devout Exercises of the Heart*	33
Illustration from Cooke's edition of *Friendship in Death*	37
Landscape of Jennings Park	190
Oast or "vinegar bottle" houses	230

ACKNOWLEDGMENTS

This book has been a saga punctuated by the years I spent chairing the Research Initiative for the Study of Diversity, the most fulfilling and challenging endeavor of my career. As a final salute to it, I dedicate this book to Nels Madsen, comrade-in-arms and generous spirit. Writing the book was also punctuated by my winning the MLA Lowell Prize and, for the second time, Auburn University's Creative Research Award. I dedicated those awards to my husband Nick for, as with all my books, his steady support, sense of humor, and willingness to accompany me on research trips to London make what I do possible.

The years my books have taken to write are always measured in the wonderful research assistants I've had. Benjamin Arnberg, Pamela Frank, Elizabeth Kent, Ashley Sandlin, Lacey Williams, and especially Lacy Marshalk and Ciara Smith have endlessly run down research materials, checked sources, proofread, and worked on the bibliography. I am grateful to them for their careful work and for their cheerful and engaged presences in my office.

Special thanks to Elizabeth Childs, who once again shared the final preparation of a manuscript with me, to Anya Bertolet, who shared her knowledge of reading portraits, to Devoney Looser, who gave generous advice on the Bluestockings, to Melanie Bigold and Sarah Prescott, who corresponded about Rowe's letters, and to Anna Battigelli, who has a gift for keeping me from giving up on a book project. Others who have answered random queries, given advice, or encouraged me are Norma Clarke, Joyce De Vries, Stephen Henderson, Susana Morris, Felicia Sturzer, Felicity Nussbaum, Robin Sabino, Penny Ingram, Toni Bowers, Catherine Ingrassia, and James Winn.

ABBREVIATIONS

B&I *British Women Poets of the Long Eighteenth Century: An Anthology*, edited by Paula R. Backscheider and Catherine E. Ingrassia (Baltimore: Johns Hopkins Univ. Press, 2009).

Letters The volume of *Foundations of the Novel* that collects *Friendship in Death* and all three volumes of *Letters Moral and Entertaining*, ed. Josephine Grider (New York: Garland, 1972). All citations to these four texts are to this edition, and *Letters* will be cited by volume number. With this form of citation, I am highlighting that they were commonly sold and read as a collected edition.

"Life" "The Life of Mrs. Elizabeth Rowe," which is prefaced to *Miscellaneous Works in Prose and Verse*, vol. 1: i–cxxviii.

Misc. Works *Miscellaneous Works in Prose and Verse of Mrs. Elizabeth Rowe*, ed. Henry Grove and Theophilus Rowe, 2 vols. (London, 1739).

*Elizabeth Singer Rowe and the
Development of the English Novel*

INTRODUCTION

Locating Elizabeth Singer Rowe

Few eighteenth-century writers are as familiar and as ubiquitously characterized in a single word as the "pious" Elizabeth Singer Rowe. Although she was an active, even somewhat outspoken, and sociable presence, her life is usually described as Sharon Achinstein did in an *ELH* essay: "Rowe returned to Frome where she had inherited a small property from her father, remaining there for the rest of her life, writing devotional poetry and publishing these and other literary works."[1] Norma Clarke bluntly summarizes another pervasive consensus, that her moral legacy "far from being attractive, has repelled."[2]

Although primarily known today for her poetry and for *Friendship in Death*, a book ridiculed for its title rather than read, she published three additional volumes of epistolary prose fiction, and they raise arresting questions. Editions of *Friendship in Death in Twenty Letters from the Dead to the Living. To which are added, Letters Moral and Entertaining, in Prose and Verse, in Three Parts. By the same Author* came out nearly annually through the end of the century (I shall refer to this collected edition as *Letters* throughout my book). For example, there were editions in 1735, 1736 (advertised as the fourth edition), 1738 (two), 1740 (two), 1741, 1743, 1745, and 1746, nine in the decade of the 1750s, and fourteen editions in the 1760s: 1760 (four: two London, one Dublin, and one Glasgow), 1762 (four: one London, two Edinburgh, and one Glasgow), 1763, 1764 (two), 1767, and 1768 (two). There were three in 1770 and eight more in that decade, eight editions in the 1780s, and yet more in 1790 (two), 1792, 1793, 1795 (two in New York), and 1797.[3] An enlarged edition published in London by J. & A. Archy included more of her work and Thomas Rowe's translations and sparked a new wave of editions. Prestigious publishers such as William Strahan, William Osborne, Thomas Longman, and the Rivingtons acquired the copyright. Alexander Donaldson printed it in Edinburgh, and editions were also printed in Dublin, Glasgow, Boston, and New York by the most respected booksellers.

Few prose fictions by any eighteenth-century writer can compete with this record. Just as Daniel Defoe's *Farther Adventures* was almost invariably sold with *Robinson Crusoe* as a single volume in the century, so were Rowe's four volumes of epistles, first collected and published in early 1734.[4] In comparison to the seven editions of Rowe's text in the 1730s, there were three of *Robinson Crusoe* with *Farther Adventures* (these figures include Dublin and Glasgow editions). In the 1740s, there were three editions of *Robinson Crusoe / Farther Adventures* and six of Rowe's; in the 1750s, four of *RC/FA*, five of Richardson's *Clarissa*, and nine of hers; but in the 1760s, four of *RC/FA*, three of *Clarissa*, and an astonishing fourteen of hers. By 1825, there had been at least seventy-nine editions of Rowe's *Letters*, and by 1840, eighty-nine.

In the twenty-first century, a small number of critics have begun to give Rowe's poetry serious attention, and some misconceptions about her and it have been corrected.[5] Reconsideration of her fiction, however, has lagged far behind that of her poetry, and feminists who have done so much work with the novel have almost completely neglected her prose fiction. As Sarah Prescott writes, "Rowe's significance has been read only in terms of this feminized virtuous image and she earns her place in the history of women's writing as an early example of the increasingly restrictive expectations about virtuous femininity which women writers had to conform to as the century progressed."[6] Her prose writing career corresponded with the beginning of English novel writing, 1691–1737, and, considering the long, impressive popularity of her fictions, that she has been largely omitted from serious treatment in histories of the formation of the English novel is surprising.

I begin that integration in this first in-depth consideration of her prose fictions as they were most commonly sold in the eighteenth century, as the four-part book. I will argue that Rowe's writing and her lifestyle are more influential—and differently influential—than we have recognized. I see her as a pivotal figure in the history of the English novel. As Rowe published her successive volumes of prose fiction, England entered the 1730s, the absolute low point of the production of new novels, histories, and romances. What prose fiction was published was almost entirely in backward-looking forms such as secret histories, travel narratives, and short amatory stories that were common digressions in French romances.[7] Defoe, Jane Barker, Charles Gildon, Mary Davys, and Penelope Aubin were recently dead, and Eliza Haywood had temporarily turned to the stage and political fictions such as *The Adventures of Eovaai* (1736). Franco Moretti's graph of the rise of the novel in Britain, Japan, Italy, Spain, and Nigeria shows that the severe dip in British novel production in the 1730s was strikingly anomalous. Except for Italy, in which there was a small dip in the 1840s, all of the other nations show a very steady rise in numbers of novels published per year.[8] Perhaps even more telling than numbers is the absence of texts of what we think of today as novels—reasonably long, unified narratives usually with psychological elements. The conclusion must be that style, content, quest, and reader desire needed to be rethought.

Rowe entered into this near void, and she entered using the most popular forms, but epistolary fiction, like the amatory tale, had become repetitive and in need of revitalization. In 1725, Mary Davys wrote in the preface to her *Works of Mrs. Davys* that "for some time, . . . Novels have been a great deal out of Use and Fashion . . . the chief Reason that put them out of vogue, was the World's being surfeited with such, as were either flat and insipid . . . ; or that they found them only a Circle of Repetition of the same Adventures."[9] Various kinds of epistolary fictions and collections of tales dominated publishers' lists, and both were held together in a surprisingly small and undisguised number of ways. In my first two chapters, I position Rowe's work with kinds of prose fiction common before hers were written and begin to point out what she drew upon but also how she adapted and revised them. I argue in chapter three that she developed a distinctive, modern, novelistic register, a "voice" for the novel that departed from the often wildly uneven prose found in the early novel. At every point, I contextualize Rowe and her fiction within major movements and social changes. This chapter draws upon theories of the "reading revolution" to explain some of the appeal of her texts and the ways changes in reading practices increased her authority as a writer and interpreter. The fourth chapter demonstrates major ways that she moved fiction forward by, among other things, absorbing the ideology and sensibility of another major movement, the politeness, or gentility, movement.

Rowe revolutionized the characters, plots, and quests that she inherited and shaped a major strain of novels that still have large numbers of readers. Her major focus was on creating characters who were seeking a harmonious, contented life, often in the face of considerable social pressure, and this plotline and quest became the substance of a very large number of novels beginning in the 1740s. Imitations, critiques, and varying models of the plot of a woman in difficult situations attempting to attain peace of mind and a steadfast philosophy became, perhaps, the most common kind of English fiction. Women who followed her coined names for the genres she created: "pastoral adventure" and "moral romance." Chapter four concludes with explorations of a few of these novels.

Rowe lived at a time when writers, including some women, could conceive of themselves as lifelong, professional artists, and Rowe was one of them. In addition to what we know about her writing and publication habits, she left evidence of this identity at her death. The preparation of her work for publication is nearly unprecedented in her time, and, in a small but telling sign, she left one of the very few objects named in her will, her "Picture in Wax of *Sappho*," to her beloved nephew.[10] Among women, I believe it was not until Anna Seward at the end of the century that a woman so carefully prepared her work for posthumous publication. Especially after the publicity that accompanied her death and the publication of the biography in *Miscellaneous Works*, Rowe herself became a text to be read and imitated. Many people saw her whole, knowing about her poetry, fiction, and lifestyle. At appropriate moments, therefore, I bring her poetry and fiction together as no other critics have and at other times juxtapose her personal and fictional letters.

As text, she was not a reified object but an active signifying practice, a cultural performer located in history, influencing the future, and negotiating personhood. The conclusion traces her legacies into the lifestyle we identify with the Bluestockings, women so interested in Rowe that they wrote about her and traveled to read her manuscript letters. The Bluestocking society was a movement that recast the terms and perceptions that had defined and stigmatized intellectual women and their work, and Rowe's empowering example has been overlooked. Thus, I round out my claim about the important influences of her lifestyle as well as of the revisionary writing models she left. For the first time, Rowe will be treated in both senses as one of the most read authors of the entire century.

Then and Now

During most of Rowe's life, she was known as a poet, but by the time of her death, she was more recognized for her fiction. Over a dozen obituaries read, "She has oblig'd the World with *Friendship in Death*, and *Letters Moral and Entertaining*, besides several excellent Poems in the *Miscellanies*."[11] Her poetry was appreciated for its metrical craftsmanship, beauty, and imagery. She was better known than Anne Finch, Countess of Winchilsea, today considered the best woman poet of the eighteenth century, and her works were more widely read in America than those of Alexander Pope, Jonathan Swift, or Samuel Johnson.[12] "The Life of Mrs. Elizabeth Rowe" from *The Miscellaneous Works in Prose and Verse of Mrs. Elizabeth Rowe* (2 vols., 1739) was of such interest that it was serialized in the *Gentleman's Magazine*.[13] As Chantel Lavoie observes, she was "perhaps the most popular woman writer of the eighteenth century."[14] By 1754, John Duncombe in *The Feminiad* wrote what could be said of very few other writers and their work: "The character of Mrs. Rowe and her writings is too well known to be dwelt on here."[15]

Two of the most forward-looking and profit-motivated booksellers of the time, John Dunton and Edmund Curll, published editions of her poetry. During the hiatus between the publication of the first book of her poetry (*Poems on Several Occasions*, 1696) and *Philomela: or, Poems by Mrs. Elizabeth Singer {now Rowe}* (1737 with a Dublin edition in 1738) and *Miscellaneous Works in Prose and Verse* (1739), her poetry appeared in collections published by the most prestigious and literary booksellers of the time: Bernard Lintot's *Poems on Several Occasions: by His Grace the Duke of Buckingham and other eminent hands* (1717) and Jacob Tonson's *Poetical Miscellanies* (both the 1704 and 1709 editions) and *Poems on Several Occasions* (1718).[16]

The latter is an enormous folio with beautiful engravings. She was featured in the title of *Divine Hymns and Poems on Several Occasions . . . by Philomela, and several other ingenious persons* (1704).[17] By then, she was well known as Philomela. There is disagreement over whether Rowe or Dunton chose her nom de plume, which he used in the 1696 collection of her poems. If not her idea, she certainly embraced it. She signs herself "Your Philomela" in one of her published letters to Thomas Rowe (*Misc. Works*, 2:185) and occasionally refers to herself that way in poems.

Some of the greatest poets of the eighteenth century admired her work. Pope, for instance, included *On the Death of Mr. Thomas Rowe* in the second edition of *Eloisa to Abelard* (1720). Even before she died, she was known as the Heavenly Singer.[18] Upon her death, periodicals received numerous tributes to her; the editor of the *Gentleman's Magazine* described them as arriving daily. Twelve poetic tributes preface the *Miscellaneous Works*, and poems recognizing her as an inspiration were written throughout the century. An unbroken stream of tributes to Rowe in the eighteenth century illustrates what she represented to women. Finch compliments her in *The Miser and the Poet* by putting her in the company of Matthew Prior, John Vanbrugh, Nicholas Rowe, Ambrose Philips, and others not given the appreciation they deserve.[19] Mary Masters's *Written in a blank Leaf of Mrs. Row's Works* (1755) is typical in its recognition of the subjects of her poetry and its forceful poetics: "Raptur'd I read these soft inspiring Lines, / Where *Rowe's* fair Mind in sacred Lustre shines; / *Love, Friendship, Virtue*, with full force appear."[20] In *On the Death of Mrs. Rowe*, Elizabeth Carter wrote that Rowe represented poetry's highest purposes and praises her for "seraphic fire" and "sublime passions." Above all, she finds Rowe a poet:

> Bold as when raptur'd Seraphs strike the Lyre,
> Chaste as the Vestal's consecrated Fire;
> Soft as the balmy Airs, that gently play,
> In the calm Sun-set of a vernal Day;
> Sublime as Virtue; elegant as Wit;
> As Fancy various; and as Beauty sweet.[21]

The recognition of Rowe's varied subjects and styles continued throughout the century. For instance, at the end of the century Janet Little wrote,

> To sue for the prize, fam'd Rowe did arise,
> More bright than Apollo was she:
> . . . .
> O excellent Rowe, much Britain does owe
> To what you've ingen'ously penn'd.[22]

Also years after her death, Anna Laetitia Barbauld's *Verses on Mrs. Rowe* (1773) pays tribute to her harmony of sound and image and her poetic "fire" and asks that Rowe be her muse. She praises her in terms previously reserved for Philips:

> Such were the notes our chaster SAPPHO sung,
> And every muse dropt honey on her tongue.
> Blest shade! how pure a breath of praise was thine,
> Whose spotless life was faultless as thy line.[23]

As she had been to poets before her, Rowe to Barbauld is an example as a poet, an intellect, and a virtuous, happy human being: "Smooth like her verse her passions learn'd to move, / And her whole soul was harmony and love." George Colman and Bonnell Thornton included eight of her poems in *Poems by Eminent Ladies* (1755). Until at least 1855, Rowe's poetry was regularly reprinted and anthologized in Great Britain and America. These publications and others kept her work before the public and maintained her reputation.

In contrast to the earlier period, in the twenty-first century, the only full texts in print are a facsimile of the fiction (1972) and a camera-ready edition of a representative sample of her poetry (1987).[24] In spite of recent, high-quality criticism on her poetry, Rowe's reputation even among most eighteenth-century specialists persists as a one-note, pious poet. As Sarah Prescott observes,

> Rowe's life and reputation has tended to overshadow any critical engagement with her writing. In Rowe's case, her pious and sentimental persona may have secured her a place in the history of women's writing as a modest exemplar, but it has also led to an almost wholesale neglect of her poetry.[25]

Prescott's and others' work has provided a more accurate account of her poetry. Norma Clarke, for instance, points out that Rowe existed in the cultural world of "the Augustan poet celebrating love . . . and passion" and that of the "pious moralist." She questions whether the "passionate poet" was ever lost to eighteenth-century readers and explores aspects of Rowe's influence.[26] Understanding what Clarke calls the "libidinised energies" is a project several critics have undertaken.[27] Other critics have explicated some of Rowe's political and aesthetic commitments.[28] Susan Staves's brief discussion of her religious poetry in *A Literary History of Women's Writing in Britain, 1660–1789* is exceptionally intelligent. Not only does she give the importance of religious poetry in the time its due, but she recognizes the intellectual ambitiousness of Rowe's and teases out the formal religious influences in individual poems.[29] Necessarily, journal articles and book chapters treat single aspects of her poetry, and our preference for historicizing approaches has contributed to the almost total neglect of analyses of the formal properties of Rowe's (and other women writers') prose and verse.[30] As several critics observe, Anglican and Tory women poets have received much more attention than Nonconformist women.[31] When the line of Nonconformist and Church of Scotland women that includes Rowe, Mary Chandler, Helen Maria Williams, Elizabeth Hands, and Anna Laetitia Barbauld is considered, the problem of this imbalance becomes clear. What Carol Barash did for Royalist women poets needs to be done for Nonconformist women.

The subjects of Rowe's verse actually include romantic love, politics, friendship, war, and social mores, all important subjects in her fiction.[32] She wrote coterie poems, public poetry about national events in the modes of John Dryden, Daniel Defoe, Richard Blackmore, and Matthew Prior, and, based on the thirty-five poems in *Divine Hymns and Poems* and the poems left for *Miscellaneous Works*, she deserves to be known as one of the most skilled, original religious poets in English literature. It is literary history's misfortune that Rowe wrote religious poetry when it had ceased to be a major artistic and aesthetic interest.[33] The creativity and variety of Rowe's religious poetry are unmatched in the eighteenth century, and it was surely her major literary effort in her middle years.

In the rest of this introduction, I sketch Rowe's biography, point out some significant contradictions regarding her life and reputation, and begin to make the case that she deserves an important place in the history of the development of the English novel.

Life and Times

Elizabeth Singer, born 11 September 1674 in Ilchester, Somerset, was the eldest daughter of Walter and Elizabeth Portnell Singer and their only child to survive into adulthood. Portnell met Walter when she was bringing provisions to the imprisoned Nonconformists in Ilchester. They married, and he gave up his ministry and became a successful clothier. Like so many Dissenting daughters, Elizabeth was carefully educated and also indoctrinated with their political and religious beliefs. In *Description of Hell*, she wrote of religious oppressors:

Beyond them all a miserable hell
The execrable persecutor finds;
No spirit howls among the shades below
More damn'd, more fierce, nor more a fiend than he.
. . . .
His enmity to good; once falsly call'd
Religious warmth, and charitable zeal.

On high, beyond th'unpassable abyss,
To aggravate his righteous doom, he views
The blissful realms, and there the schismatic,
The visionary, the deluded saint,
By him so often hated, wrong'd, and scorn'd,
So often curs'd, and damn'd, and banish'd thence:
He sees him there possest of all that heav'n,
Those glories, those immortal joys, which he,
. . . .
His pompous creeds, and boasted faith, has lost.[34]

Moreover, as an adult, she practiced the activism within her church that Nonconformist women, in contrast to Church of England women, were allowed. They believed that women should participate in choosing ministers, in decisions to admit members, and in speaking and voting publicly at congregational meetings, and Rowe did.[35] She took an active interest in the local school, in London theatrical news, and in colonial Georgia.[36] A thorough-going "revolution principles" adherent, she has recently been identified with the rise of a Williamite "Whiggish literary-political agenda," which "fought an aesthetic battle that was also allied to a country party, an anticourtly politics, positioning themselves against the urbane, decadent wits; they were to be the defenders of religion, nature, ethics and justice."[37] Her reading included Shakespeare, Molière, John Milton, Nicholas Rowe, Thomas Otway, Joseph Addison, John Gay, James Thomson, Colley Cibber, Henry Fielding, George Berkeley, Anthony Ashley Cooper, Earl of Shaftesbury, Blaise Pascal, Robert Law, and Abraham Cowley.[38] Her familiarity with ancient and contemporary religious and philosophical arguments informs her letters and literary texts.[39] A precocious child "doted on by her father," Rowe learned French and Italian early and "easily,"[40] and she translated and imitated a number of Italian forms, including the sonnet, throughout her life. She wrote a number of adaptations from Tasso at various times and appended her own translation of part of Pierre Nicole's *Thoughts on Death* from the *Essais de morale* (1671–1678) to *Friendship in Death*.[41]

Her mother died when she was a teenager, and her father moved to Eggford Farm at Frome, Somerset, around 1692. He became an acquaintance of Thomas Thynne, first Viscount Weymouth, of Longleat, Wiltshire (fig. 1), and his son Henry tutored Elizabeth in Italian, French, and possibly Latin. She began publishing her poetry in John Dunton's *Athenian Mercury* shortly after she returned from boarding school. In 1696, Dunton published *Poems on Several Occasions Written by Philomela*. She and her poetry made a great impression on him, and, almost immediately after

Fig. 1. Longleat, Wiltshire, the home of Grace and Thomas Thynne, first Viscount Weymouth, where Rowe made lifelong friends. From *Beautiful Britain* (London, 1894).

his wife died in 1697, he appeared at her home to propose marriage, which she declined. Other suitors included Isaac Watts, whom she allegedly declined because of his physical unattractiveness, and the American Benjamin Colman, a graduate of Harvard and the influential pastor of the Brattle Street, Boston, church.[42]

She met Matthew Prior, who was serving on the Board of Trade and Plantations with Lord Weymouth, at Longleat in 1703. Prior helped place eight of her poems in Jacob Tonson's prestigious *Poetical Miscellanies: the Fifth Part* (1704), and she and Prior carried on a flirtatious and apparently somewhat combative courtship.[43] In a previously unpublished letter to Arabella Marrow written in 1708, she recalled their wrangling over religion: "Mr. Prior's life of Solomon is at last finished; about 3 weeks since he was at Bath, and came one afternoon to drink tea with me. I could not perswade him that anything about me had an air of Devotion."[44] He seemed to test her acceptance of him by refusing to conform to her demands about his behavior. He insulted her religion and sent her his obscene reworking of the Baucus and Philemon myth, *The Ladle* (1703), and then nudged her to comment on it. He encouraged her writing, however, and helped her reputation as a poet. In a folio edition with beautiful engravings, he published her *Love and Friendship* and his *To a Lady, She refusing to continue a Dispute with Me*.[45] Indeed, the poetry that Prior published in 1703 may be a remarkable record of his hopes and frustrations with her, and they metaphorically and allegorically express experiences mirrored in Dunton's and Colman's correspondence with her.[46]

In 1709, she met Thomas Rowe at Bath, and they married the next year and settled in Hampstead. He was the son and grandson of Nonconformist clergymen and had been educated at the University of Leiden because the English universities were not open to Dissenters. He was a poet and translator, and before he died of consumption in 1715 at age twenty-eight, he was working on a series of lives of classical heroes who had opposed tyranny and been omitted by Plutarch. Elizabeth had continued to publish poetry and, after her husband's death, moved back to Frome. Her father died in 1719, leaving her substantial property and income in Frome and Ilchester. Henry Thynne's daughter Frances became her closest friend, and she visited and corresponded with her for the rest of her life.

The more carefully Rowe's career is considered, the more significant the Thynne family and especially Frances Thynne Seymour, Countess of Hertford (later Duchess of Somerset, 1748), appear. Frances was the daughter of Henry and Grace Strode Thynne, and she lived at Longleat House until her father died in 1708. Her widowed mother moved back to her family home in Dorsetshire, but she continued to spend time at Longleat with her grandparents. She married Algernon Seymour, Earl of Hertford and the son of Charles, Duke of Somerset, and they lived primarily at Marlborough, Wiltshire, in the home settled on him. They had a town house on Dover Street until 1721 (and then one on Grosvenor Street) and from 1730 a country retreat at St. Leonard's Hill near Windsor. In 1723, Lady Hertford became a Lady of the Bedchamber to Caroline, Princess of Wales. She wrote poetry and published a little of it, and her younger sister Mary and her great-aunt Anne Finch, Countess of Winchilsea, joined Rowe as part of a community of women poets.[47] One of Finch's coterie poems to Arabella Marrow mentions both "Philomela" (Rowe) and "Cleone" (Grace Thynne).[48] Finch published *Miscellany Poems on Several Occasions* in 1713, the time when Rowe was contributing to prestigious London collections.

Rowe was often at Longleat, and she visited Hertford a few times at various places; once, in 1728, Hertford visited her at Frome. Rowe occasionally praises Caroline, who became Queen in 1727 and retained Hertford; she identifies her with the goddess Virtue (*Letters*, 1:88). She also praises Anne, the Princess Royal, finding her behavior infinitely superior to the performance of a noble princess on the stage (*Letters*, 2:50–51). Rowe always came to the family when they needed her. She went to Grace in London when her daughter Mary Thynne Brooke died in 1720, and she spent part of June and all of July and August with Hertford at Marlborough after her mother died in the spring of 1725.⁴⁹ Hertford carefully copied Rowe's letters into a book bound in green leather; known as the Green Book, it contains 159 letters and attracted visitors from the time of Rowe's death. Posthumous publications of Rowe's work drew considerable attention to their friendship. John Duncombe's *Feminiad* moves smoothly from his characterization of Rowe to "Nor can her noble Friend escape unseen, / . . . / The Peeress, Poetess and Christian rise."⁵⁰

As was common in the century, a circle of writers might be mostly virtual, sustained more by correspondence than by frequent meetings. Rowe may have met Edward Young at Longleat and had quoted one of the two religious poems mentioned in her dedication in a consoling 1726 letter to Lady Hertford shortly after the death of Heneage Finch, Lord Winchilsea, her great-uncle. She includes veiled correspondence about the death in a letter by herself and one by "Cleora" (Hertford) in *Letters*, part 1.⁵¹ If she did not know Young, she knew a lot about him, because two years earlier he had been named chaplain to Princess Caroline, and Hertford surely knew him well. By then, he had an influential network of friends and Whig patrons and was publishing in a variety of genres. He had just published his two satires, *On Women*.⁵² His contribution of the preface to *Friendship in Death* had advantages for them both, as it allied Rowe with a fashionable writer whose name would attract attention and him with the publication of a book consistent with the direction his career was taking. In 1739, the year her *Miscellaneous Works* was published, he wrote to a friend that "Letters from the dead are so entertaining."⁵³

Rowe and Hertford read poetry for enjoyment and enlightenment, stayed in touch with the publishing scene, and made recommendations to each other. Rowe had brought James Thomson's *Winter* to Hertford's attention in 1726, and she quoted lines that expressed a shared sensibility:

> The year yet pleasing but declining fast
> Soft, o'er the secret Soul, in gentle Gales,
> A Philosophic Melancholly breathes,
> And bears the swelling Thought aloft to Heaven.⁵⁴

Thomson was invited to Marlborough House in the summer of 1727 and to St. Leonard's Hill in 1735. In one of her last letters to Hertford, Rowe writes that she is rereading *The Seasons* and enjoying the engravings by Kent.⁵⁵ Rowe quotes Thomson in *Letters*, part 1; in part 3, she quotes from Young's *Satire of Fame*. It is not surprising that she knew the poetry of Young and Thomson, but some of the connections to male poets are less predictable. She had the same publisher as Richard Savage, and there is a connection to Hertford with him, too. Hertford had gone to Caroline, by then the queen, to plead for Savage's pardon after he was sentenced to death for a tavern murder.⁵⁶ Savage and Thomson were at that time part of the circle of Aaron Hill, and Thomson may have appealed to Hertford.

The connections between Rowe and Hertford are deeply personal and richer than has been recognized. In addition to the consoling letter at Finch's death, Rowe wrote that Letter 14 in *Friendship in Death* reminded her of Mary, Lady Brooke, and she quotes one of Brooke's poems in *Letters*, 2:8–9. That Hertford contributed all or part of ten letters to part 1 is well known. Letter 2 to Cleora is a slightly changed version of a witty letter in the Green Book. It opens with a line reminiscent of the much-quoted (and misleading) statement by Rowe, "My Letters ought to be call'd epistles from the dead to the living, for I know nothing relating to this world" (*Misc. Works*, 2:118). What Rowe meant and what the correspondence was like are more accurately expressed in Letter 2: "I am certainly dead and buried, according to your notions of life; interr'd in the silence and obscurity of a country retreat, far from the dear town, and all its joys" (*Letters*, 1:93). Catharine Trotter Cockburn used the same trope about the same time in a letter in which she remarked that her acquaintances William Wycherley and William Congreve were dead, but, because of her residence in Aberdeen and then Northumberland, "I was in a manner dead long before them."⁵⁷ Much has been made of the contrast offered by Rowe's retirement, but letters such as these might spring from the fact that Rowe was twenty-five years older than Hertford, with the different interests and energy that this suggests.

Rowe lived through times of great change in both the political and literary domains. At age eleven, she would have heard talk of the ramifications of the ascension of James II to the throne. She was fourteen at the time of the Glorious Revolution and obviously shared her sect's joy at the coronation of William and Mary and the victory at the Battle of the Boyne, which sent James II permanently to France. Queen Mary's death and then William's, Queen Anne's sternly High Church principles, the extreme party turmoil of her reign, and the violence provoked by the ascension of George I to the throne—all events inflected by the nation's religious divisions—occurred before she was thirty-one.⁵⁸ In her *Letters*, she mentions the South Sea Bubble (1720–1721), war with Spain, and the growth of empire.

She knew well Thomas Ken, formerly royal chaplain to Charles II and a bishop, and a living history of the difficult political choices and varied fortunes of his time. He was one of the bishops assigned to tell Monmouth he would be beheaded, to stay with him in the Tower, and to accompany him to the scaffold. He had been confined to the Tower for refusing to read King James's Declaration of Indulgence from the pulpit and deprived of his bishopric for refusing to take the oaths swearing allegiance to William and Mary. Now in retirement at Longleat at the invitation of Lord Weymouth, he encouraged Rowe in a variety of ways. Her paraphrase of Job 19:26 published in the 1696 *Poems* may be the poem that he had requested and greatly admired. He had written three hymns in 1674 to enrich the devotional life of the boys at Winchester College where he was chaplain. This was before the congregational singing of anything but Psalm-based hymns, and he recommended the hymns be sung privately in their rooms. There was one for morning, one for evening, and rather oddly one for insomnia. Each ended,

> Praise God, from whom all blessings flow;
> Praise Him, all creatures here below;
> Praise Him above, ye heavenly host;
> Praise Father, Son, and Holy Ghost.

These lines are, of course, now a doxology, the most widely sung Christian verses in the world. In the 1 December 1691 *Athenian Mercury*, one of the questions asked was, "Whether songs on Moral, Religious or Divine Subjects, composed by Persons of Wit and Virtue, and set to both grave and pleasant Tunes, wou'd not by the Charms of Poetry, and sweetness of Musick, make good Impressions of Modesty and Sobriety on the Young and Noble, make them really in Love with Virtue and Goodness . . . ?" In light of her acquaintance with Ken, this question takes on considerable significance and underscores the importance of the dedication to hymn writing that she and her friend Isaac Watts came to share. His *To Mrs. Singer. On the Sight of some of her Divine Poems Never Printed* (1706) makes the same commitment to the new kind of hymn writing, "Notes of Heav'n" that "propagate the Joy" of Heaven, that her much better *The Vision* does.[59]

Born in the year John Milton published the twelve-book *Paradise Lost* and when John Dryden and Aphra Behn were already major playwrights, Rowe lived through dramatic changes in literary tastes and conceptions of the purposes of literature. The great social, reformist comedies of her girlhood, such as William Congreve's *Way of the World* (1700), transitioned to the humane comedies of the first decades of the eighteenth century by George Farquhar, Colley Cibber, and Susanna Centlivre. Charles Sedley's *Antony and Cleopatra* (1677), which she enjoyed in boarding school, could not compete with the vigor of the Exclusion Crisis tragedies. Although seldom noticed, some of the greatest religious writing in English history was published in her youth. Among these texts are all three of Milton's great epic poems, John Bunyan's *Pilgrim's Progress* (1678, 1684), Dryden's *Hind and the Panther* (1687), and Nahum Tate and Nicholas Brady's *New Version of the Psalms of David* (1696). Rowe was influenced by Ken's prescient opinions about hymns. In her childhood, the political uses of literature exploded. Within two years, Dryden's *Absalom and Achitophel*, Lee's *Lucius Junius Brutus* (both 1681), Behn's *The Roundheads*, and Otway's *Venice*

Preserved (both 1682) demonstrated the power of the most respected, traditional literary forms in political debate. In 1689 both John Locke's *Two Treatises of Civil Government* and Andrew Marvell's *Poems on Affairs of State* came out. Texts such as Behn's *Love Letters between a Nobleman and his Sister* (1684) indicated the potential of fiction to be political propaganda, and Defoe's Lady Credit and Joseph Addison's Count Tariff transformed allegorical narratives for the same purposes.

A strong literary movement was in progress, one expressed in the popular press by Addison as a call for British superiority in arts as well as arms. An impetus both for Neoclassicism and for English forms and innovations, literary nationalism produced texts as varied as Dryden's *Essay of Dramatic Poesy* (1668), Swift's *Battle of the Books* (1704), and Addison's essays on topics such as the Royal Exchange and the ballad "Chevy Chase." Translations of classic literature made Homer's epics and the works of Horace, Juvenal, Lucretius, and others available to English writers of all classes, and some, such as Horace's *Art of Poetry* by Wentworth Dillon, Earl of Roscommon (trans. 1680), propagated standards for an English republic of letters. They could be imitated and adapted widely for a variety of purposes and reached new audiences. John Dunton, Peter Motteux, Defoe, Addison, and Richard Steele revolutionized journalism. Samuel Butler, Dryden, and John Wilmot, Earl of Rochester, were replaced by Blackmore, Samuel Garth, and John Dennis, and then by Swift, Gay, and Pope. A group of women poets including Sarah Fyge Egerton and Mary Chudleigh joined women fiction writers in disputing prevailing images of the nature and capacities of women. Poetic forms that would come to rival satire in popularity by Mark Akenside, Finch, Thomson, and William Shenstone were widely circulated and reprinted. In 1731 the *Gentleman's Magazine* was born.

The Image of a Woman Poet

The contradictions between the Elizabeth Singer Rowe that we think we know and the actual woman, her life and writings, are intriguing. Before Rowe was twenty-five years old, Mary Beale (1633–1699), the first important woman portrait painter in England, had painted a miniature of her—the provincial daughter of a member of an oppressed minority. Soon after, Susannah-Penelope Rosse (ca. 1655–1700), the first important woman miniaturist, copied it. It was common practice for miniatures to be copied, and it signals the desire of friends and loved ones to possess them. In fact, miniatures were an emotionally important part of friendships. Men and women wanted these memorabilia of their most intimate friends, sometimes rather desperately. Jonathan Swift's repeated requests for Robert Harley's is a familiar example; in one, he wrote, "I have now been ten Years solliciting for your Picture, and if I had sollicited you for a thousand Pounds (I mean of your own Money, not the publick) I could have prevailed in ten days," and a year later: "I ever gave great allowance to the laziness of your temper in the article of writing letters, but I cannot pardon your forgetfulness in sending me your picture. . . . It is vexatious that I . . . should be now perpetually teasing for a letter and a picture."[60] In fiction and life, what miniatures meant is eloquently expressed; for example, Eliza Haywood's Betsy Thoughtless steals and then broods over Trueworth's, and Anna Seward wore and even slept with the miniature that John André had painted of Honora Sneyd.[61] They were collected for display and mounted in boxes as sets; Marcia Pointon quotes Goethe as saying, "thus he could collect all his friends around him," exactly what Swift was trying to do. As lockets, brooches, or ornaments on bracelets or ribbons, women were observed gazing on and pressing them to their lips.[62]

Fig. 2. Miniature of Rowe painted by Susannah-Penelope Rosse, ca. 1695, from an original by Mary Beale before Rowe was twenty-five years old. Courtesy of Bonhams.

The miniature of Rowe (fig. 2) shows a beautiful woman with a wealth of blonde hair, luminous eyes, and a cupid's bow mouth, the woman described by her suitors as "comely" in face and "shape" of medium height and slender. She had an English rose complexion—fair with rosy cheeks, and "eyes of a darkish grey, inclining to blue, and full of fire" (*Misc. Works*, 1:lv), and the eyes are blue-gray in the miniatures. Every portrait features her fine eyes. Beale was a friend of Peter Lely, the court painter, had been patronized by Charles II, and was popular with the extended Thynne family. She had painted Catherine Thynne, Viscountess Lonsdale in the 1670s; Henry Thynne; and later Thomas Thynne. Some of her earlier subjects were Katherine, Lady Kingsmill; Lady Elizabeth Percy, Countess of Ogle; Charles Seymour, Duke of Somerset; and the Duchess of Somerset. Miniatures were important to the Thynne family, and the Victoria and Albert Museum has a portrait of Mary, Lady Brooke, younger daughter of the Thynne's. It has many similarities to that of Rowe and was done by Christian Friedrich Zincke (the V&A dates it to ca. 1716).

It was common for people to order or collect sets of miniatures. They were often very small, usually less than an inch in height. Peter Cross's miniature of Anne Finch is only 7.6 × 6.4 cm (fig. 3), and that of Heneage only slightly larger. The Beale miniature of Rowe is 2¾ inches (70 mm), and the Rosse one 3 inches (76 mm). Intriguingly, both are water color on vellum, and the frames for the Rosse miniature of Rowe and the Cross of Anne Finch are the same gilt metal with pierced spiral cresting; perhaps they were once in possession of the same person. The Beale miniature is in an ornate gilt frame with an elaborate flower and ribbon top as for a brooch. Rather than the draping poet dress, Finch is in the conventional aristocratic dress. The Rowe miniature is characteristic of Rosse's work and illustrates connoisseurs' observation that she worked "with great finesse on an exceptionally small scale." Her parents were both court miniaturists, and her father, Richard Gibson, and Samuel Cooper, whose style she studied, were considered the leading miniaturists from the Interregnum forward. Later Thomas Flatman, who was a neighbor, was a friend of hers, and another neighbor, Matthew Snelling, was related to Mary Beale, while another neighbor was Peter Cross. She did a lovely set of her family and closest associates that includes two self-portraits, her husband Michael, her sister Anna Gibson van Vrijbergen, her sister-in-law Mrs. Priestman, and her neighbor Mrs. Prudence Philips.[63] Among the Thynne relatives that she did was Elizabeth Percy, second wife of the tenth Earl of Northumberland. The Rosse copy of Rowe is somewhat romanticized and not as sharp; for instance, the shoulders, neck, and jawline are not as slim and graceful as Beale's portrait.[64] The most expensive paint color was ultramarine, which added a surcharge of 10 percent, and both Beale and Rosse used it for Rowe's dress. It was made from lapis lazuli, and Charles Beale recorded

Fig. 3. Miniature of Anne Finch, Countess of Winchilsea, by Peter Cross, ca. 1690. © National Portrait Gallery, London.

paying £4.10s. for an ounce in 1674.[65] Art historians point to the growing appeal of small-format painting among the upper middle class, described as "a more modest clientele."[66] When Beale moved to Pall Mall, she had attracted a wide clientele from among the gentry as well as from the clergy and aristocracy (*ODNB*), and the sale of her husband's effects indicates Rosse's even more prolific work.[67]

Rowe's portrait anticipates what will become *the* conventional dress of a woman poet. She is portrayed in a fashionable, loose dress of heavy satin that appears almost as a drape. The neckline shows a frame made of a ruffle on her white linen shift, the garment all women wore next to their skin. The ruffle was designed to show, and a pin modestly holds the drape in place. As the seventeenth-century popularity of the loose dress waned, the Roman drape replaced it (fig. 4). The portrait in the posthumously published *Miscellaneous Works in Prose and Verse* (1739) is no less striking in that it is by the respected, famous engraver George Vertue, perhaps the best line engraver of his generation. Vertue had apprenticed with a master who engraved arms on plate, perhaps Blaise Gentot.⁶⁸ This relationship may explain the elaborate decorations engraved at the top and bottom of the frame. Crowns, leaves, flowers, and musical instruments with drapes woven in are characteristic of Gentot but more ornamental than symbolic, which is somewhat unusual for the representation of a writer. Vertue studied at the Academy founded at Godfrey Kneller's studio and apprenticed 1702–1709 with Michael Vandergucht, whose portraits of literary figures are well known. This engraving became the most frequently reprinted image of her into the present day, and Vertue was a highly fashionable engraver. All of Rowe's portraits, then, were highly fashionable because they were done by those working

Fig. 4. Engraving of Rowe by George Vertue, ca. 1725, allegedly done from life, and the most commonly reproduced image of her. Published posthumously in *Miscellaneous Works in Prose and Verse* (1739). © The Trustees of the British Museum.

in the highest, even noble, circles. Beale, for instance, had painted miniatures of King James and William III; Rosse had done Queen Mary,[69] Charles II's mistress the Duchess of Portsmouth, and Anne Palmer, Countess of Sussex; and Vertue had done George I, Frederick, Prince of Wales, and many deceased kings, noblemen, and great writers after Van Dyck, Godfrey Kneller, and others. Peter Lely assisted Beale, Kneller abetted Rosse and Vertue.

It is intriguing to speculate on the way Vertue came to do Rowe's portrait, which, allegedly, he did from the life. He did more than 120 frontispiece portraits between 1709 and 1756, including Matthew Prior, Eliza Haywood, and Alexander Pope, and almost every engraving for the Society of Antiquaries after his appointment as its official engraver in 1717.[70] Heneage Finch, Earl of Winchilsea, was president in 1725. When he died two years later, Lord Hertford paid him. Rowe had continued to see Finch with the family, and Grace Thynne wrote in 1722 that they had flirted and Rowe "coquetted much" with him and that he said he would "buy a pillion and fetch her to Leweston . . . if he did not find her there when he came."[71] Around that time, Vertue did a portrait and engraving of William Seymour, Duke of Somerset; of Heneage Finch "by his own hand from the life"; and of Henry Grove, a Rowe cousin and coeditor of *Miscellaneous Works* and author of the first part of the "Life" in it.[72] Notably, he had done "Lady Jane Grey, with emblematic devices" and "Henry VII. and his Queen, Henry VIII, and Jane Seymour," historical relatives of the Hertford family.[73] He had made line engraving fashionable again, and, because of the number and varied subjects of his engravings, he made the art familiar to the public. He included "'all sorts and conditions of men,' both contemporary and of past times," and he valued accuracy.[74]

Vertue's work with the Finch and Hertford families contributes to understanding the importance of Rowe's relationships with them. As the volumes of *Letters* grew, Rowe continued to draw from her experiences with them, and I will treat in some detail one example that reveals evidence about Rowe's inspirations and compositional practices, specifically regarding her verse epistles between Lady Jane Grey and Lord "Guilford" Dudley. A painting of Lady Jane Grey, titled "Queen Jane" and perhaps the only surviving image of her, belonged to the Hertford family, and Frances had inherited it and one of Lady Jane Grey's younger sister Katherine. She had secretly married Edward Seymour, Earl of Hertford, and had two sons; the marriage and the sons were finally legitimated in 1601. Lady Jane, who was known from her youth as brilliant, carefully educated, and pious, was a cousin of Edward VI and, therefore, fourth in line to the throne. Her father forced her to marry Guildford Dudley in an attempt to hold and increase his power. She believed she was contracted to the Earl of Hertford, but her father beat her into compliance.

When Edward died, she was crowned queen and shortly afterward executed to provide for the Catholic Mary's accession. At age sixteen, she faced the block bravely and recited the 51st Psalm before being beheaded. Over the years she became gentle Jane, a Protestant heroine and martyr (*ODNB*). The painting was the property of the Somersets at Marlborough House and passed to Algernon Seymour, Earl of Hertford, and therefore to Frances when they settled there. Vertue selected it as one of the four historical paintings he described in a short publication and made an engraving of it (fig. 5). He says that the Earl of Hertford sent it to London for him to copy. In Rowe's lifetime, the painting would have been displayed at Marlborough, where Rowe spent months in 1725.[75]

The painting, known as the Syon Portrait, belongs to the current Duke of Northumberland. In a typical Elizabethan pose and costume, Jane is painted in half length in a black dress or coat with her auburn hair pulled back severely below a black cap. As befitting royalty, there are symbolic ornaments, an ermine lining and pearls, and signs of wealth, such as a ruff trimmed in gold cording. She is unsmiling, lips pursed, and eyes rather glazed and with the irises and pupils not in the same location (the right eye appears to wander from center). The painting is in an oval within an ornamented frame and has none of the symbolic backgrounds that we see in Elizabethan paintings of royalty and nobility. J. Stephan Edwards remarks on how flat and "monochromatically black, without shadows or highlights" it is,[76] and one explanation for many of its features and its shape is that it was painted from a miniature done in Jane's last days.

In any event, the subject, not the execution, must have been the attraction for Rowe and Hertford. Vertue reproduces it accurately in his engraving, although he changes the frame and adds pearls to the central ornament at her neckline. Vertue identifies it as "from an Original in the possession of his Grace" and frames it within Corinthian columns, obelisks holding lanterns in which the flames come from hearts, and drapes. Above the portrait is a crown with five gleaming stars, the symbol of martyrdom, and a garland of flowers. The crown, globe, scepter, and sword, as well as an ermine robe, are below the portrait, and Britannia, who is leaning on the great seal of Britain, sits slightly to the right and weeps. The British lion appears in several places. Vertue has captured the martyr and propagandizes what her loss meant for the nation.

In the highly collaborative first part of *Letters*, Rowe includes the verse epistles *Lady Jane Gray, to Lord Guilford Dudley* and *Lord Guilford Dudley to Lady Jane Gray* (*Letters*, 1:82–86). Vertue produced a set of historical engravings, and Lady Jane was the fourth. The first was of Henry VII's three oldest children, Arthur, Margaret, and Henry; the second was of Queen Mary of France with Charles Brandon, Duke of

Fig. 5. George Vertue's engraving from the portrait "Queen Jane" that belonged to the Hertford family and helped inspire Rowe's heroic epistle between Lady Jane Grey and Lord Guildford Dudley. © The Trustees of the British Museum.

Suffolk; and the third was of the Duchess of Suffolk. Rowe also wrote *Mary Queen of France to Charles Brandon Duke of Suffolk* (*Letters*, 3:213–17), and Hertford wrote a heroic epistle from Yarico to Inkle. These activities seem related and suggest dating of Vertue's engraving of Lady Jane earlier than the customary 1740s. This date is probably based on the publication of Vertue's *A Description of Four Ancient Paintings, Being Historical Portraitures of Royal Branches of the Crown of England*, but the *Description* is really a sale catalog and would have required permission from owners of the paintings. The time during which Rowe was with Hertford and Vertue working with the family for the Antiquarian Society seems more likely. In 1748 to commemorate Algernon Seymour's inheriting the title of Duke of Somerset, Vertue produced a second, slightly more ornamented engraving of Lady Jane. I have reproduced the original, which is in the British Museum's Department of Prints and Drawings; the 1748 one is in the National Portrait Gallery.

Sharing observations on the portrait, giving pleasure to each other, creating conversational opportunities, and reinforcing values, at intervals long before this, Rowe and Hertford had brought Lady Jane into their correspondence, and these references are often profoundly meaningful. In 1716, Rowe was continuing to grieve for her husband, who died in 1715, and she quoted "melancholy lines" from Nicholas Rowe's recently published *Tragedy of the Lady Jane Gray* (1715), "My soul grows out of tune, . . . / . . . / And I could sit me down in some dull shade, / Where lonely contemplation keeps her cave, / . . . / And muse away an age in deepest melancholy" (*Misc. Works*, 2:37–38). In 1719, she wrote, "There is not in the *English* history a more beautiful character than that of Lady *Jane Grey*; and I am not surpriz'd to find you charm'd with the shining figure she makes in Mr. *Rowe's* tragedy. You seem to have an equal softness of temper, and a resembling delicacy in your way of thinking. Your sentiments had certainly been the same with the young heroine's, if you had the same part to act, that of a martyr, which I hope you never will" (*Misc. Works*, 2:38). Hertford had, of course, been with the court during the Jacobite Rebellion, and the women's letters reflect the fact that those at court and their friends knew they were living in dangerous times. Rowe's poems are celebrations of Protestant martyrdom, and, beyond the piety, love of learning, and gentleness, Rowe's comparison of Jane to Hertford is an easily overlooked acknowledgment that Hertford was indeed at some risk. The family's closeness to Thomas Ken and the Finch's experiences when King James was deposed also reinforced the sense of the uncertainty of court life, and Rowe's letters include many hopes for the Hertfords' safety in political life.

Vertue's portrait of Rowe replicates the shape of eyes and mouth in the miniature by Rosse, whom he knew and writes about in his notebooks. Earlier images of women writers carried more class markers, and dress, drape, and hair were more elaborate and ornamented, as are those of Anne Killigrew (painted by herself) and Michael Vandergucht's of Aphra Behn. A frontispiece portrait is an important signifier of authorial agency and gestures toward a cultured audience. The ornaments around and below the portrait, as well as the sitter's pose, speak eloquently to the reader-viewer. They are far more common in books by men than by women. Because of its wide circulation after 1739, Vertue's of Rowe surely influenced the representation of women writers and contributed to the ubiquity of the woman-poet pose. Rowe is wearing a very low cut drape with a white ruffle from her shift. Like so many women writers after her, her hair is swept up and back, her forehead is high, and her eyes are dark, prominent, and striking.

Portraits of women poets before Rowe suggest the movement toward a convention. An engraving of a bust of Katherine Philips, "the matchless Orinda," which was used as a frontispiece for *Poems of the most deservedly admired Mrs. Katherine Philips* (1667), is composed to make her look like a Roman matron with appropriate drape and hair style (fig. 6). A mezzotint of her in the popular style of showing

Fig. 6. Frontispiece for *Poems by the most deservedly admired Mrs. Katherine Philips* (London, 1667). Engraving by William Faithorne after a bust by Michael Vandergucht.

Fig. 7. Frontispiece for *Poems by Mrs. Anne Killigrew* (London, 1686). Engraving by Isaac Beckett from a painting by herself.

Fig. 8. Frontispiece for *Poems upon Several Occasions; with a Voyage to the Island of Love* by Aphra Behn (London: R. Tonson and J. Tonson, 1684). Engraving by Robert White.

Fig. 9. Frontispiece for Eliza Haywood's *Secret Histories, Novels and Poems. In four volumes.* (2nd ed.; London, 1725). Engraving by George Vertue.

Fig. 10. Frontispiece for Elizabeth Thomas's *Pylades and Corinna*, vol. 1 (London, 1731). Engraving by Giles King.

the smock made of rich fabrics as bodice and sleeves for a gown or drape by Isaac Beckett is in the National Portrait Gallery. This was the style of an aristocratic lady, one that Anne Killigrew painted in her self-portrait that became the frontispiece for *Poems by Mrs. Anne Killigrew* (1686). The engraving, figure 7, was by Isaac Beckett. The first woman whose texts were frequently published with portrait frontispieces was Aphra Behn, and Vertue's Rowe is very much like the pose in figure 8 of Behn by Robert White for *Poems upon Several Occasions; with a Voyage to the Island of Love* (1684). Although draping, the heavy satin garment on both women is not a true drape, as it is for Katherine Philips, Eliza Haywood, and Elizabeth Thomas. Other prominent printed portraits of Behn were in succeeding editions of *Plays written by the late ingenious Mrs. Behn*. In the first edition (1702) is the aristocratic pose with smock and a heavy satin gown with the sleeve caught up to show the rich fabric of the smock. The second edition is a prestigious Vandergucht engraving that is more romantic. Behn is sitting in near profile, turning her head to the viewer. Her hair is full and curly, and the sleeve of her gown is tied up with a satin bow (1716). By the third edition in 1724, the portrait is much like the Rowe and Haywood portraits from the same two-year period. By now conventional, in the B. Cole engraving, she is in an oval frame on a bust stand and the white ruffle shows above the heavy, draping gown.

By 1725, the woman-poet portrait was formulaic. As the years passed, a drape rather than a gown became conventional. As Aileen Ribeiro explains, "some idealization, either in dress or drapery, would elevate the image, making it more timeless and thus with greater appeal for posterity." The glimpse of the shift also remained and "was also 'timeless'—literally so, for the shape had hardly changed for hundreds of years. Such a garment had been used by van Dyck to depict allegorical characters and the 'careless Romance' ascribed to [the painter]."[77] Robert White's 1684 engraving of Behn served as a trend-setting model in its rather simple drape, simple hair ornament, and the single curl across her shoulder. Vertue's engraving of Eliza Haywood (fig. 9) shows his signature style but the fashion for a much lower cut dress with the same hair style. The Haywood engraving shows the style of lower cut dress and quite rounded breasts also seen in other women writers' frontispieces and in the engraving of Rowe published in the *London Magazine* in 1754. In spite of the similar pose and dress, some individual physical characteristics of the women are depicted. In general, hats and clothing came to be individualized features, not face and expression. Later in the century, a scarf was sometimes draped over the head in imitation of representations of Roman matrons and Christian saints. The 1730 engraving of Rowe's exact contemporary Elizabeth Thomas for the first volume of *Pylades and Corinna* (1731; fig. 10) shows the trend in hair styles and in portraying the woman from the waist up rather than in an oval bisecting the breasts and following the cut of the dress.[78] Vertue's was already a somewhat longer portrait of Rowe and Haywood, and the very large number of duplications of his engraving of Rowe contributed to the establishment of the woman-poet pose that reigned throughout the century. As time passed, Vertue's engraving would be modified by other engravers to follow the small variations in the pose, some of which are apparent in later representations of Rowe.

Becoming Pious

How Rowe fell from being the multidimensional woman and writer of many kinds of poetry and fiction to being dismissed as the unreadable, eccentric "pious Mrs. Rowe" who wrote *On the Death of Mr. Thomas Rowe* and spent the last twenty-two years of her life panting for death is a fascinating story.[79] One way to tell this story is through those multiple portraits and editions of her texts. Even now the life and conduct of a woman writer is news, reported along with her publications, and in the eighteenth century as women joined the republic of letters it was especially true. Just as women had a signature work, they were often assigned a signature character, as was "the great arbitress of passion" Eliza Haywood, the pudding-making Elizabeth Carter, and the Muse of Britannia Anna Seward.

By 1752, Thomas Phinn, another engraver, had reworked Vertue's portrait for a new edition of *Letters*, and Rowe was a fatter, more complacent person. Although the ornaments above and below the frame remain, with her growing reputation, the crown and manuscript now seem more appropriate. Influentially, the *London Magazine; or, Gentleman's Monthly Intelligencer* printed "A Concise Account of Mrs. Elizabeth Rowe. With her Effigy" in February 1754. Her continued appeal is affirmed on the cover, as it promises that that issue has "a Beautiful Head of the celebrated Mrs. Rowe." Collections of effigies were popular, and individuals cut them out of books and periodicals and bought them in printed books. Rowe is a somewhat sterner, thinner, more dignified woman in the *London Magazine* portrait by an unknown engraver than in the Vertue engraving (fig. 11). The hint of a smile is gone, but the drape is more prominent and the dress is very low cut, showing extremely round breasts, the fashion for women-writer engravings at that time. The text concentrates on her as a writer although it weaves salient facts throughout the one-and-a-half-column narrative. Like the early, abbreviated lives, it emphasizes her fiction over her poetry; *Friendship in Death* is identified as her "most celebrated" work. "Even her prose has all the charms of verse without the fetters, the same fire and elevation, the same richness of imagery, bold figures and flowing diction," it says. These strong,

Fig. 11. Engraving for "A Concise Account of Mrs. Elizabeth Rowe. With her Effigy" in the *London Magazine* (February 1754). Unknown engraver. © National Portrait Gallery, London.

Fig. 12. Engraving by Thomas Kitchin for *Memoirs of Eminently Pious Women*, vol. 2 (London, 1777), between pages 446 and 447. Courtesy of the Guildhall Library, Corporation of the City of London.

Fig. 13. Engraving by W. Ridley for Cooke's Pocket Edition of Sacred Classics, *Devout Exercises of the Heart* (London: C. Cooke, 1796). © Victoria and Albert Museum, London.

Fig. 14. Engraving by Francis Barlow for Lane's Edition of *Devout Exercises of the Heart* (London, 1795).

specific terms for her style set her apart from the mass of writers and are not common descriptions of women's work. Her husband is described as "a very ingenious and learned gentleman, and a poet of no inconsiderable rank," and her spending time with Thynne and Hertford after family deaths is mentioned.[80] These glimpses of her follow the portrayal that begins the second installment of "Memoirs of the Life and Character of Mrs. Rowe" in the *Gentleman's Magazine*: "What is said of Mr. *Cowley, that no one had reason to wish his Wit less*, was equally true of Mrs. *Rowe*. For with the most manly Genius, she possess'd all that Gentleness . . . of Disposition, which give her Sex such irresistible Charms."[81]

Also following Vertue's iconic image is a simple, elegant engraving (fig. 12) by Thomas Kitchin that appeared in such places as the 1772 London edition of *Miscellaneous Works*, Thomas Gibbons's *Memoirs of Eminently Pious Women* (1777), and *Collectanea Biographica, being An Historical and Pictorial Biography of Illustrious, Celebrated and Remarkable Persons* (1853). Kitchin is best known as a distinguished engraver of maps, and he did 170 for the *London Magazine* alone between 1747 and 1783. He had extraordinary technical skills and an assured manner that produced clean lines, as this portrait shows. He did many portraits and even caricatures and may, in fact, have done the engraving for the *London Magazine* above.[82] In Boston in 1782, the respected engraver John Norman copied Vertue's portrait and ornamental frame for an edition of *Friendship in Death*. It is described as having "some charm, presenting the author in dishabille, with a pleasant smile, and a long curling lock of hair."[83] Into the 1770s, then, Rowe's prestige was maintained by the distinguished engravers chosen to immortalize her writings. As portraits of later poets, including Anna Seward, Mary Robinson, and Helen Maria Williams, show, romantic masses of curls rather than the single ringlet over one shoulder shifted attention from forehead and eyes to feminine hair. Even late-life frontispieces of Elizabeth Carter by John Raphael Smith and by MacKenzie emphasize elaborately curled hair, and Angelica Kauffman's dramatization of Mary Robinson as the British Sappho had masses of hair and the Roman matron mantua. Ubiquitous copies and knock-off representations of Rowe with varying quality, often quite poor, and faddish touches show Rowe moving into the realm of popular culture.

In the last quarter of the century, a set of images and publications diverge from the writerly image of the woman described as a strong intellect with a distinctive, image-rich style. Editions of *Devout Exercises* caught up with and slightly surpassed editions of the collected *Letters*, especially in America. In the 1740s, there were eight editions of *Letters* and three of *Devout Exercises*; in the 1780s, there were eight of *Letters* and seven of *Devout Exercises*; and in the 1790s, there were another eight of *Letters* and a startling thirty-two of *Devout Exercises*. Rowe was surely one of the most popular writers of the entire century in several genres, but the trend toward categorizing her as a devotional writer began to prevail. Wide availability of her *Devout Exercises of the Heart* and her religious poetry began to revise the evidence that she was most appreciated as a prose fiction writer. For example, Cooke's *Pocket Edition of Sacred Classics* published figure 13 in *Devout Exercises of the Heart* in 1796 with a rather unattractive image of her in shift and drape with masses of curly hair cascading over one shoulder by W. Ridley. Francis Barlow did a more poetic, romantic Rowe for *Devout Exercises of the Heart* in 1795 for Lane's edition (fig. 14). In the Barlow, her hair is curling and more clearly defined, the dress is nineteenth-century, and the oval is oddly on the kind of stand featured for busts of writers. The later one increases the abundance of wavy hair.

These editions are notable because they were produced by astute entrepreneurs who advanced the book trade just as were Dunton, Tonson, Lintot, and others who printed and sold Rowe's works during her lifetime. Both Lane and Cooke made fortunes and, unlike the earlier booksellers, concentrated on mass, not elite, publications. In 1773, William Lane inaugurated the *Ladies Museum*, which carried stories on Rowe. He founded a system of circulating libraries and in 1790 created the Minerva Press as an imprint for his publications of romantic and gothic novels. Publications such as devotional literature were also branded, as this illustration is, as "Lane's Edition," an advertisement for affordable, desirable books. Charles Cooke was at least as enterprising and opportunistic. He refined and expanded serial publication; his books were often advertised as "superbly embellished," and illustrations became a signature of his series. He developed genre-specific series that included poets, novelists, essayists—and devotional authors. Some were pocket editions, and others were expensive vellum paper with hand-colored stipple engravings, and they ranged from 6p. to 1s. (*ODNB*).

In the nineteenth century, the images move farther away from the Vertue engraving. A Francis Engleheart engraving for an 1820 edition could be almost any woman, but imagination began to reign. The T. Wallis engraving for *Friendship in Death with Letters Moral and Entertaining* (1827) is the apotheosis of this movement (fig. 15). With the halo, the twigs (symbol of the nightingale's nest and eternal watchfulness), and the addition of the willow tree and urn, the print surrounds Rowe with symbols appropriate to her individual image and to Christian themes. The urn may represent her husband, with whom she was supposedly obsessed and wished to follow to Heaven. Wallis does, however, return to Vertue's image (albeit probably one of the 1750 modifications). Perhaps the most astonishing "likeness" is in the 1827 edition of *Friendship in Death with Letters in Prose and Verse to which is added Devout Exercises of the Heart* (compare fig. 16 to fig. 7 above). It places Rowe's name below

Fig. 15. Engraving by T. Wallis for *Friendship in Death with Letters Moral and Entertaining* (London, 1827). Although the portrait is based on a 1750s engraving of Rowe, she has been transformed by the surrounding iconography into the pious Rowe who longed to follow her husband to Heaven. © National Portrait Gallery, London.

Fig. 16. Engraving modified from likeness of Anne Killigrew (see figure on p. 23). With only minor changes, such as the elimination of the earrings, this portrait of Killigrew became the frontispiece with Rowe's name substituted for the 1827 *Friendship in Death with Letters in Prose and Verse to which is added Devout Exercises of the Heart* (London: Baynes for Thomas Kelly, 1827). © The British Library Board.

M.RS ELIZ.TH ROWE

Fig. 18. Printed for Richard Baldwin, unidentified engraver. Undated image in the MacDonnell collection, now in the Heinz Archive. © National Portrait Gallery, London.

Fig. 17. Undated engraving collected by John Peaviour Johnson for the extra-illustrated copy of *A Biographical History of England*, by James Granger, continuations by Mark Noble. Courtesy of City of London Metropolitan Archives.

Fig. 19. Front page of *Rowe's Exercises forming part of Cooke's Pocket Edition of Sacred Classics* (London, 1875). Engraving by W. Hawkins. © The Trustees of the British Museum.

Anne Killigrew's image. Killigrew is only slightly modified. The earrings are gone, and this "Rowe" is very slightly older and thinner. The effect of the dress is to make Rowe seem more regal, aristocratic—but also from a historically distant time.

Few of the portraits retain the sense of the woman writer, but for collectors she was. An unidentified image preserved in John Peaviour Johnson's extra-illustrated *Biographical History of England by the Rev. James Granger, continuations by the Rev. Mark Noble* in the London Metropolitan Archive shows a pensive woman with a book, but her quill and paper are ready (fig. 17). As was becoming fashionable, the state of undress was greater, as much more of the shift shows, and the breasts are round globes. The life of Rowe in the *Biographical History* lists Rowe with the poets Alexander Pope, Allan Ramsey, Aaron Hill, and Eustace Budgell, a former poet laureate, and treats her as such. In general, however, Christian symbolism increases. Another collector selected an image (fig. 18) that combines Renaissance hair ornaments with a dress suggesting angel-like wings and with pearls, the traditional symbol of purity and wisdom.[84]

The illustrations for her books drastically modify her image. A Dublin edition of *Devout Exercises* (1771) uses emblematic imagery from the sixteenth and seventeenth century, including a winged, burning heart pierced by a cross, a serpent, and a nightingale with chicks resting on the cross while tearing her breast. Heavenly light streams down. Here the allusion is clearly to the bestiary tradition going back to the symbol painted in subterranean sanctuaries of Rome by persecuted Christians rather than to the sweet-singing night bird used by Petrarch and other Renaissance poets as the figure of the lyric poet. In the Christian tradition, the bird guarded its young from a serpent in an allegory of the bird pressing its breast against a thorn in order to stay vigilant against evil through the night.[85] The pedestal on which the construction stands reads, "The Christians [*sic*] Pattern or Imitation of Christ."

Another example of an influential publication that propagated this image is the cover art (fig. 19) for *Rowe's Exercises forming part of Cooke's Pocket Edition of Sacred Classics, or Moralists Instructive Companion . . . Superbly Embellished* (1796, 1875). The woman seems to be a blend of Rowe and biblical figures like Mary who anointed Jesus's feet with oil. One hand gestures toward an hourglass, skull, and ringed serpent, symbols of mortality, while the other is an open palm receiving inspiration from Heaven as a dove, symbol of the Holy Spirit, flies overhead. Prints began to carry quotations from Rowe's poem *The Vision* and labels that fixed her image as the "pious Mrs. Rowe" that we have inherited. For example, the text under an 1825 engraving by MacKenzie reads, "The devotional Elizabeth Rowe, whose writings all excite to the practice of the most generous benevolence and heroic virtue, was found dead on her knees."[86]

These portrayals had to sift through the "Life" in *Miscellaneous Works*, which had displayed considerable pride in Rowe as a poet and unwavering respect for her lifestyle, to find sections reinforcing their emphasis on her otherworldliness. The original "Life" and early tributes to her, like the image of the woman in the formulaic poet pose, had protected her art while keeping her religion in balance. Norma Clarke points out that "indeed, it is stressed by being utterly taken for granted in formulations like the following: 'The love of solitude, which seems almost inseparable from a poetic genius, discovered itself very early in Mrs Rowe, and never forsook her but with life itself.'"[87] In fact, the rhetorical shift from "celebrated," "polite," "amiable," "accomplished," and even "virtuous" to "pious" in descriptions of her increases exponentially in the final decade of the century and largely erases the multidimensional, active woman and experimental writer. A damaging side effect is that, rather than seen as committed to rational religion, she began to be associated with evangelicals, enthusiasts, and mystics.

Yet evidence of Rowe's sustained, wide popularity as a writer of diverse texts is abundant into the nineteenth century. In 1764 Caroline Attwater's mother gave her the last volume of *Letters Moral and Entertaining*, and in 1788 Caroline passed it on to her daughter Mary Whitaker, who was fifteen years old at the time.[88] Frances Burney remarked that she had "heard a great deal of [Rowe's *Letters*] before I saw them."[89] Inscriptions from her poems appear on tombstones, as this one does in St. Vigeans Church-yard, Scotland:

> Think, vain fond heart, when on the day
> Of that tremendous awful deep
> Eternity in sad suspense I stood;
> How all my trifling hopes and fears
> My senseless joys and idle tears
> Vanish'd at prospect of the frightful flood.[90]

In spite of her changing reputation, editions of her work in the last quarter of the century suggest growing demand for varied selections of her work, especially those giving a range of her writing. The four-volume *Works of Mrs. Elizabeth Rowe* (1796; Edinburgh and London editions) is an important example of the relative appeal of her writings. Volume one is *Friendship in Death* and the first two parts of *Letters Moral and Entertaining*; volume two is the final part of *Letters* and *Devout Exercises*; volume 3 contains poems, hymns, devout soliloquies, canticles, and *History of Joseph*; and the final volume has the dialogues, letters, and, finally, the life of the author followed by tributes and elegiac verses. *The Poetical Works of Mrs. Elizabeth Rowe, including the History of Joseph in Ten Books* (1820) has the dark, curly-haired engraving redone by Charles Heath and with the legend "E. Rowe—a bright ethereal youth drew near, / Ineffable his motions and his air," a quotation from her poem *The Vision*, printed on page 19. A small, easily portable book, the collection of poems begins rather surprisingly with her Canticles, the most erotic of her religious poetry, and then the Hymn on Heaven. An 1827 edition includes fourteen of her most pious poems along with the *Letters* and *Devout Exercises*.[91]

Even as cheap editions of *Letters* multiplied, Rowe's *Devout Exercises* and other selected works came to be published in collections of pious works such as Lane's and Cooke's. "Harrison's edition" of the complete *Letters* was a slim 156 pages (London, 1786). Thomas Gibbons in *Memoirs of Eminently Pious Women who were ornaments to their Sex* (1777) abridges the "Life," inserts Pope's entire *Dying Christian to his Soul* at a point at which Rowe was ill, and adds three of the selections from *Devout Exercises*. A 1778 edition of *Poems on Several Occasions* has forty-seven of the ninety-nine poems in *Miscellaneous Works* and *History of Joseph*; the poems selected give a wide range of subjects and forms, but the collection omits some of the most difficult, such as the soliloquies, but concludes with the poems on Thomas Rowe. Many collections include *History of Joseph*, and the increasing number of narrative, biblical paraphrases published by other poets indicates their continued appeal.

At the same time, the biography published in *Miscellaneous Works* was endlessly abridged to foreground her piety.[92] Her *On the Death of Mr. Thomas Rowe* was often printed at the end of whatever version of the life was included rather than in approximately chronological order among her poems as it had been in *Miscellaneous Works*. Many of the lives precede the poem by truncating the "Life" to conclude, "She was buried, according to her request, under the same stone with her father in the meeting-place at *Frome*" and with the poor pouring "blessings on her memory."[93] In the "Life," Rowe had conversed with a friend at 8:00 p.m. and was apparently in excellent health. About 10:00 p.m., her servant heard "some noise" and found Rowe, who had been reading, fallen from her chair dying from a stroke. She was treated by a physician and a surgeon but died "a few minutes before two" (*Misc. Works*, 1:xxxvii–xxxviii). This very detailed account was rather rapidly and imaginatively modified to depict Rowe in prayer on her knees and sinking gracefully and instantly into death.

The movement toward defining Rowe as an educational writer is also discernible. The edition of Cooke's *Friendship in Death* (1797) presents distinctly middle-class country couples rather than the aristocratic men hailed by angel-like women in white Roman garb that had been included in earlier editions of *Letters*. The illustration of "Rosalinda adorning her little Companions with flowers" (*Letters*, 2:7; fig.

Fig. 20. Illustration for the story of Rosalinda by W. Hawkins from *Friendship in Death* in Cooke's Sacred Library (London, 1797), between pages 144 and 145.

20) features children now in the genre of children's book illustrations, such as those in *Little Goody Two Shoes*.

In 1969 in *Popular Fiction before Richardson*, John Richetti sketched how popular Rowe's fictions had been through the beginning of the nineteenth century but observed, "Mrs. Rowe has long since passed into the darkest corners and remotest footnotes of literary histories."[94] Shortly after Richetti's book, Rowe was usually mentioned as part of the early history of the English novel in overviews of the form. Michael Shugrue published *Letters* in the "Foundations of the Novel" series (1972 edition, introduction by Josephine Grieder). Martin Battestin included her in the

"British Novelists, 1660–1800" volume of the *Dictionary of Literary Biography* (1985, entry written by Elizabeth Napier), and she continues to be mentioned irregularly, usually on no more than a page or two in reference and critical books on the novel. Almost none of the criticism takes seriously Richetti's insistence that her fiction was extremely popular or breaks from Richetti's assessment of its content. He says, rightly, that "it was a work which was widely read and apparently highly regarded." He continues,

> In fact, among the various scribbling ladies who contributed to the mass of prose fiction which precedes the florescence of the novel in Richardson and Fielding, Mrs. Rowe was probably the most highly respected and remembered during the eighteenth century itself. . . .
>
> . . . It is hard to understand why. Her most popular work is a deadening book, written in ecstatic and inflated prose and full of the most explicit and tedious moralizing about the pains of a life of sin and the comforts of living virtuously.[95]

His conclusion, that "Mrs. Rowe's famous little book . . . is a literary polemic against unbelief," is accepted as a summary of the text.

The consensus among those who have read her fictions is, in Kathryn King's words, that *Friendship in Death* is "a work of unassailable piety," and, as Norma Clarke says, "she was the well-known author of epistolary prose fictions that dwelt on the pleasures of a heavenly afterlife."[96] Jonathan Pritchard, author of the *Oxford Dictionary of National Biography* entry, describes *Friendship in Death* as taking "sensual pleasure in the prospect of a Christian afterlife" and calls the three-volume *Letters Moral and Entertaining* "an improving, but single-minded, miscellany." Also following Richetti's assessment are those who credit her with contributing to the "moralizing of the novel," as Jane Spencer does in her important *The Rise of the Woman Novelist*. In explaining Rowe's contribution to the development of prose fiction, Cheryl Turner quotes Richetti's sources and develops some of his ideas, including applying the relationship between her popularity and the growth of a market for moral fiction.[97] Ros Ballaster categorizes Rowe as Richetti does and mentions her on two pages in *Seductive Forms*. Perhaps most telling, Richetti mentions her on a single page in *The English Novel in History* (1999).[98] These references tend to be redundant and largely unanalytical. In fact, I disagree with most of them in this book.

Unsettlingly, mentions of her are disappearing from books on the novel. She is not included in Doreen Saar and Mary Anne Schofield's *Eighteenth-Century Anglo-American Women Novelists: A Critical Reference Guide* (1996) and is not treated in books whose foci make her work a logical subject such as Ruth Yeazell's *Fictions of Modesty* (1991), Michael McKeon's *The Secret History of Domesticity* (2005), or

Elizabeth Kraft's *Women Novelists and the Ethics of Desire, 1684–1814: In the Voice of Our Biblical Mothers* (2008). Susan Staves breaks new ground by emphasizing Rowe's "*intellectual* ambitiousness," and it is helpful to demonstrate that Rowe is engaged with some of the most pressing philosophical and theological questions of her time.[99] Because Staves's book covers so many writers, however, there are teasing hints of, for instance, the ways Rowe may have been influenced by Tasso, but no real discussion of the variety of Rowe's styles and strategies. In her brief treatment of the prose fiction, she suggestively and usefully finds Rowe's to have "perhaps more kinship with the periodical essay than with the novel proper," although she recognizes the novelistic situations and links them to romance.

The wide practice of cultural criticism has led a few critics, many of them experts on Rowe's poetry, to hypothesize the need to reconsider her fiction. Some expand on John Richetti's observation in fruitful ways. In 1995, for instance, Marlene Hansen wrote, "Truly, if we are to understand the cultural climate of the years immediately preceding the appearance of Richardson's novels we cannot afford to ignore Mrs. Rowe."[100] As part of their own original historical and critical inquiries, Kathryn King and Sarah Prescott have pointed out how Rowe's career can "broaden out the accepted paradigms of female authorship" and publication.[101] Susan Staves sees "Rowe's success in developing cultural authority as a pious Christian laywoman [providing] a powerful model for later women writers and reformers like Hannah More and [pointing] forward to the ways in which nineteenth-century women in England and America claimed moral authority and justified their interventions in the public sphere by invoking the imperatives of Christian duty."[102] The project of expanding our understanding of women's compositional and publication practices and their access to print is important, and Rowe is indeed a useful and somewhat unusual model, especially as she is presented in King's "Elizabeth Singer Rowe's Tactical Use of Print and Manuscript." In most of these recent essays there is a marked shift away from treating Rowe as part of a group of moral, even pious, women writers who are in contrast to, or even in opposition to, the unholy triumvirate of Behn, Manley, and Haywood. There seems to be a trend, usually stated rather than argued, to identify her with characteristics of the novels of Samuel Richardson's period. Her *Letters*, of course, appeared eight years before *Pamela*.

In fact, Rowe exhibits the kinds of energetic experimentation with prose fiction characteristic of her own generation, the earliest shapers of the Anglo-American novel.[103] She clearly knew fiction well and was able to draw upon and adapt its major conventions and strategies while introducing some of her own. In fact, her writings are better described as "pivotal," more dramatically different than transitional texts. The distinctive elements and absorption of major social movements in her fiction determined that her writing would deeply influence a group of novels written between her death in 1737 and the end of the century.

Plan of the Book

This book integrates Rowe into the history of the English novel. In every chapter, I contextualize Rowe and her fiction within major literary and social movements and finally identify the distinctive, revisionary contributions she made that shaped a line of novels extending into our own time. My first chapter positions Rowe's fiction among the kinds of fiction being written by earlier writers and her contemporaries. While some, such as amatory and epistolary fiction, are familiar, others such as apparition and "patchwork" literature have not been used to contextualize her work and are not understood by twenty-first-century critics. This chapter demonstrates the extent to which Rowe's *Letters* draw upon fictional kinds written by Daniel Defoe, Aphra Behn, Charles Gildon, Mary Davys, Eliza Haywood, and others. It also points out that her *Letters* would have been recognized by her contemporaries as a common kind of prose fiction even as it set new directions.

Within these familiar forms, Rowe is innovative in the creation of plots, characters, and style. For example, she transforms the conflict in amatory fiction between desire and resistance born in gender education into a rational seeking of a compatible mind and sensibility that is "beautiful." Novels before her were often the means of constructing social commentary driven by moral judgment, as John Richetti illustrates in *The English Novel in History*; although there is social commentary and moral judgment, prose fiction for Rowe was a means of self-discovery and construction and therefore inward directed. This chapter lays the groundwork for my argument that Rowe reworked the amatory tale and the female bildungsroman into the plot of hundreds of novels that followed hers and continue today. Women are still besieged but threatened not by seduction and rape but by oppressive situations and misfortune, and they wage a fierce battle to establish peace of mind and the ability to maintain it.

In chapter two, I take up an even older form, an influence identified in Rowe's preface that has been, I believe, completely ignored: French women's fairy tales, especially those of Marie-Catherine d'Aulnoy. As is well recognized, lightly disguised forms of fairy tales continue to be used to transmit important kinds of romantic and feminist stories,[104] and Rowe was a pioneer in adapting them in these modern ways that are withstanding the tests of time. I am categorizing fairy tale in this popular culture way and with awareness that specialists identify them as "wonder tales" defined by their plot trajectory rather than by the inclusion of fairies. This inquiry opens a new avenue for beginning to place Rowe (and d'Aulnoy) in the history of the English novel and contributes to our understanding of the formative influences on the early English novel. My chapter brings together many English women's original fairy tales, an exercise that contradicts much current scholarship that denies the existence of a *British* fairy tale tradition. Unlike the forms in chapter one, the women's fairy tales include extended sections in which the protagonists revealed their feelings, thoughts, and aspirations, thus shifting emphasis from action to interior life.

In one of D'Aulnoy's tales, Zephyrus tells the Prince that everyone goes in quest of felicity "where they enjoy the Fruits of a Calm and Tranquillity."[105] This is the quest that Rowe puts at the heart of her stories. Moreover, imagining other kinds of worlds as well as creating an "elsewhere," a place of freedom from the limitations of imposed gender identity, conduct, and even thought, became increasingly common in eighteenth-century women's fiction, and the fairy tale was a starting point. It was a land of possibilities for alternative lifestyles and domestic situations and even, in Nancy K. Miller's formulation, a figuring of "the existence of other subjective economies, other styles of identity."[106] As my chapters cumulatively reveal, this was one of Rowe's major techniques. This chapter is especially important for understanding Rowe's distinctive style and her development of aesthetic aspects of the novel.

These chapters and each subsequent chapter are built around analyses of an aspect of form and style in *Letters*, especially as they develop a specific register that became exceptionally influential. It is important to recognize that the forms on which Rowe drew put a single, independent woman alone on center stage. The character writing a letter, the seer of an apparition, and the authorial stance of writers of patchworks are often such women. D'Aulnoy and Rowe were for most of their lives single, successful, admired women. These facts subtly broke down the power of heteronormativity with marriage as the measure of adulthood and success. Therefore, as I will do throughout the book, I will consider literary as well as lifestyle aspects that influenced her contemporaries and turned Rowe's life into a text to be read and interpreted by them.

It would be possible to see the first two chapters as forward looking because of Rowe's revisionary adaptations, and chapter three uses the forms discussed in them as the foundation for exploration of Rowe's contributions to the development of a distinct novelistic register. I use *register* rather than *discourse* or *style*, because the term simultaneously encompasses awareness of context ("field of activity/situation," in linguistic terms), tenor (an important gauge of status and highly pertinent to the development of the novel), and mode. Tenor, a sustained range (as for a singing voice), is an important determinant of status and, therefore, highly pertinent to the development of the novel. It gives access to the status, social roles, and relationships of participants. It was a meaningful concept to her contemporaries; Thomas Gray, for instance, wrote the famous lines "Along the cool sequestered vale of life / They kept the noiseless tenor of their way" in *Elegy in a Country Church-Yard*. Thus, he encompasses both class and parameters of lifestyle. Mode includes both rhetorical modes (persuasive, expository) and channels of communication (visual signals, spoken, written, monologic). Eighteenth-century writers consistently deployed mode, an identifiable method, mood, or manner such as pastoral or satiric, with telling results, and Rowe created a distinctive novelistic discourse from the parameters of field of activity, tenor, and the broader understanding of mode.[107] Content and ideology are inseparable in register, and Rowe carefully maintained one that created an authorial stance and perspective.

In this chapter, too, is the fullest treatment of poetic practices relevant to Rowe's fiction writing. Her poetry is highly, even wildly experimental, and *Letters* gave her another laboratory in which she could experiment with its aesthetics and functions. Many of the themes and language types are in the prose, but *Letters* also includes many original and quoted poems. The chapter looks at the influences and similarities between her poetry and prose, but it also points out how Rowe uses poetry for a wide variety of purposes in her stories. A little analyzed aspect of later eighteenth-century fiction is the function of poetry in novels, and Rowe, again, provided models. She released its power to allow characters to express emotions and thoughts not appropriate in prose, its ability to shift thought and experience from one realm to another, and its potential to raise the cultural capital of a text. From her poetic career she learned to domesticate both style and content, thereby creating a modern novelistic style that is still widely accepted and respected. I draw on theorists of the reading revolution such as Roger Chartier, Cheryl Nixon, Eric Rothstein, and Elspeth Jajdelska to demonstrate how Rowe assumes modern reading practices and takes advantage of them to increase her authority as a writer and interpreter. Significantly, she raises the status of the novel by creating an aesthetics of production that her readers meet with an aesthetics of reception, and character, author, and reader are drawn together into a dynamic triad. Specifically, the reader is led to construct herself from what she has experienced in the construction of author and character within the text, a strategy that would become popular in self-consciously artistic novels.

Chapter four returns to epistolarity, this time not as an inherited genre but as a technology of the politeness movement, and, as I brought her poetry into an earlier chapter, I bring her published personal letters into this one. I argue that the ideology and sensibility of this movement are woven into her fictions, and this advanced the development and status of the novel. The movement was in itself a technology of social production, and as Michel Foucault demonstrates, its everyday practices and institutionalized discourses and epistemologies are always accompanied by acceptance, adaptation, and resistance—technologies of the self. Rowe once wrote that places of retirement were where "you fortify yourself against the tyranny of custom, and the impositions of persons" and have "the most exact and impartial notions" (*Misc. Works*, 2:27–28). She seems to be particularly interested in the formation of what Ulric Neisser calls the conceptual self, that sense of self that comes from a network of assumptions and theories. She also seems to take for granted that the person is tied to her own identity by conscience and self-knowledge.

Thus, this chapter takes up how Rowe incorporates into her *Letters* some of the emergent technologies in her culture. I use *technologies* as Michel Foucault does and will concentrate on technologies of the self, the devices and techniques that make possible the social construction of personal identity. In other words, these technologies produce the knowledge of what human beings should do and who they believe they are, the conceptual self. Built in, then, are the pressures that produce a social product who knows how to act and also the need to counteract, rebel, or adapt selectively. Eric Rothstein has identified the reading revolution with the creation of "modernity" and with readers "[welcoming] continuous, directed, self-modification." As I do, he imagines readers imagining possibilities. He postulates "a sense of self that centers one's reality, that incorporates an 'enriched' personality, and that gains its stability by its agency in choosing."[108] He does not mention Rowe, but she was the pivotal figure in creating such characters and readers.

I will highlight, first, the already established politeness movement and, second, Rowe's model of a technology of the self that became a disciplining, social technology carried out through institutionalized discourses and epistemologies. The emphasis in both is on gendered self-mastery, and the second is so important because it met emergent pressures to constrict and restrict women's behavior. In Rowe's hands the quest for a satisfying lifestyle becomes dramatized technologies of the self. She created for writers who followed her novels of steadfastness in contrast to the line of novels of resignation, submission, or stoicism. The chapter concludes by tracing Rowe's influence into a few texts published very soon after hers that also create novels focused on lifestyle creation and technologies of self-mastery. I give special attention to Mary Collyer, who styled *Felicia to Charlotte* as "a pastoral adventure," and to Sarah Fielding, who called *David Simple* a moral romance, thus specifying genre and mode names that would be useful today. These novels are often associated with the gentility or politeness movement. Especially important are themes of "dear liberty" and the possibility for a code of politeness different from and parallel to the masculine one associated most strongly with the Earl of Shaftesbury. It was, as Tim Hitchcock and Michèle Cohen observe, "the main technique of male self-fashioning in the eighteenth century." Philip Carter illustrates how the politeness movement was deeply concerned with constructing and establishing a normalized understanding of masculinity, one that *used* women in a variety of ways.[109] Rowe and the women who followed her recognized the usefulness of a parallel politeness movement for women, one that came to produce a subaltern counterpublic. They "invent[ed] and circulate[d] counter-discourses to formulate oppositional interpretations of their identities, interests and needs."[110]

The conclusion extends the study of these technologies and continues the dual emphasis on prose fiction and life as text by linking Rowe's life and work to the Bluestockings. It argues that the legacy of her lifestyle may be almost as important as her influence on the English novel. The Bluestocking society was a paradigm shift that recast the terms and perceptions that had defined, marginalized, and circumscribed intellectual women and their work, and Rowe was a major empowering example for them and for women writers who followed her and wrote fiction with heroines similar to hers. In spite of the fact that the Bluestockings wrote about Rowe, referred to her frequently, and traveled to read the Green Book of her manuscript letters, even the most distinguished experts on the Bluestockings do not figure Rowe into any history of the movement. Rowe modeled a lifestyle ahead of its time, asserting values and a quest that now have been naturalized and need to be re-historicized to appreciate her accomplishments.

The conclusion then turns back to fiction and to the fact that she set a course that hundreds of novels followed and by which others were influenced. Rowe's major theme was how women might achieve a satisfying life without yielding to social pressures, and she created characters who were rational and had important interior lives. She set a course for other fiction writers that they expanded—"dilated," as critics say about Richardson's fiction—into the long novels that are familiar to us. She provided a pattern that a very large number of novels followed and then tested, critiqued, or continued to imitate. The story of her influence on women's publications remains to be traced. After her *Miscellaneous Works*, some of the best women writers of the century were empowered to collect not only their literary works but also personal letters. Examples are Mary Jones's *Miscellanies in Prose and Verse* (1750), which includes letters, and Mary Masters's *Familiar Letters and Poems on Several Occasions* (1755).

These chapters demonstrate that Rowe can be seen as a pivotal figure in important ways. Just as she metamorphosed in her readers' minds from the Pindarick Lady to Philomela to "the author of *Friendship in Death*," she drew upon the racy fiction of earlier and contemporary women writers even as she laid the groundwork for the "polite" fiction and novels of manners published after her death. Her fictions exhibit rapid, dynamic experimentation with all of her contemporaries' signature techniques and plotlines. Decades ago, Jerry Beasley pointed out that she and Penelope Aubin were "conscious innovators" who "confirmed new possibilities of form, range, and seriousness in contemporary novelistic fiction."[111] As Kathryn King says, "*Letters from the Dead to the Living* is in effect a strong acknowledgment of the new cultural authority of print."[112] It is finally time to give substance to these statements.

Rowe is also a site strongly marked by the transition to modern multivariant literary and popular culture. Bringing highly successful strategies from coterie composition and critique into a text that would appeal to a broad spectrum of what King calls "an unknown and impersonal audience," Rowe, as we shall see, skillfully combined material from what we recognize today as popular culture with what her contemporaries identified as aristocratic aesthetic practices. Most significantly perhaps, she created a conception of a lifestyle from these often opposed artistic modes, one that impelled novels of the next decades and inspired lived practices as well. My book, then, illustrates the pivotal nature of Rowe's highly influential, long-ignored prose fiction and suggests new ways that she and her writing are more significant for literary history, for the development of the novel, for the rise of modern sensibility, and for women's studies than we have recognized.

CHAPTER ONE

Positioning Rowe's Fiction

At age fifty-four after publishing only a few poems for decades, Rowe began to publish fiction rather prolifically. *Friendship in Death; or, Letters from the Dead to the Living* (1728) came out among such novels as Jane Barker's *The Lining of the Patch-Work Screen* (1726), Mary Davys's *The Accomplish'd Rake* (1727), Penelope Aubin's *The Life and Adventures of the Lady Lucy* (1726) and *The Life and Adventures of the Young Count Albertus* (1728), and a dozen of Haywood's fictions, including *The Mercenary Lover* (1726), *The Fruitless Inquiry* (1727), and *Philidore and Placentia* (also 1727). William Chetwood and Daniel Defoe were also contemporaries and published voyage literature; Chetwood's *The Voyages, and Adventures of Captain Robert Boyle* came out in 1726, as did Defoe's *The Four Years Voyages of Captain George Roberts*. And, as she did, all of these women and men used prose fiction for ideological and moral purposes. The next year (1729) she published *Letters on Various Occasions, in Prose and Verse. By the Author of Friendship in Death*. The identification of this book with *Friendship in Death* points to the first book's commercial success. *Letters Moral and Entertaining* followed in 1731, and with the re-titling of *Letters on Various Occasions* styled as part 1 of *Letters Moral and Entertaining*, the groundwork for the century-long best seller was laid.

She selected Thomas Worrall to publish her *Friendship in Death*. He had built an impressive, varied list from his shop near St. Dunstan's Church in Fleet Street that included sermons (the best-selling books of the time), practical divinity, novels, travel books, poetry, and antiquarian annals of shires. Thus, the Winchilsea-Hertford Antiquarian Society work might have brought Worrall to mind. Among books she might have noticed were William Thompson's *Poetical Paraphrase on part of the Book of Job, in imitation of the style of Milton* (1726), Aubin-like novels (long travel and adventure novels featuring women), and several poems by Edward Young, to whom she dedicated *Friendship in Death*. In the year her book came out, he also published Young's *Ocean. An Ode* and *A Vindication of Providence*, a translation of St. Chrysostom's *A Companion for the sincere penitent*, and Richard Savage's *The Bastard*, the poem aimed at shaming the Countess of Macclesfield into admitting his lineage. Rowe must have been pleased with Worrall, because he published the volumes of *Letters* and both editions of her *History of Joseph*. The third volume of *Letters Moral and Entertaining* came out in 1733 and required two editions in that year. In the same year, Worrall brought out the edition of *Friendship in Death* with all three volumes of *Letters*.

Twentieth-century critics respond to Rowe's best-known work of fiction, *Friendship in Death*, with bewilderment, and few have read any of *Letters Moral and Entertaining* or know that her long, narrative, biblical paraphrase *The History of Joseph* depends on the conventions of prose fiction.[1] As Melanie Bigold wrote, "Rowe's biographical exemplarity has been the primary legacy of her literary career."[2] Today we are likely to exclude Rowe's prose fiction from the history of the novel because the "Letters" are so short and, moreover, some of them do not include a story but are merely reflections or thoughts by a character. We must remember, however, that, at the time when she published, her Letters would not have been disqualified. Put beside texts such as Charles Gildon's *Post-Man Robb'd of His Mail* (1719), Sarah Butler's *Milesian Tales* (1719), Jane Barker's *A Patch-Work Screen for the Ladies; Or, Love and Virtue Recommended* (1723) and *The Lining of the Patch Work Screen* (1726), and Mary Davys's *Familiar Letters Betwixt a Gentleman and a Lady* (1725), Rowe's tales are not unusual. Barker's *Patch-Work Screen*, for example, opens with the well-worn device of each traveler in a coach telling a short tale, and then becomes an episodic narration of Galesia's life broken by short, sensational tales and poems originally published (although somewhat revised) in Barker's *Poetical Recreations* (1688). Young couples are separated, wicked seducers trick both innocent and scheming damsels, and Galesia's mother sets her up with a series of prospective husbands. Mary Davys's *The Cousins: A Novel* is loosely held together by the delayed gratification of Lorenzo and Elvira, while the sensational stories of Leonora, Clara, Octavio, and Alvaro make up the greatest part of the book. As Kathryn King has pointed out, "novel," then a part of many titles, was a flourishing, "distinct literary form," carried generic expectations, and might signify "novella, short story, *or even episode*" (emphasis mine).[3] Rowe's stories definitely qualify as the last two, and extended journalistic essays and interior reflections remained common in novels throughout the century.[4]

In this chapter, I want to position Rowe's fictions in relation to some of the major forms that shape and contextualize hers and begin to make incrementally the case for her place in the history of the development of the English novel. To do these things, I will explicate, sometimes at length, parts of specific texts most important as background and contextualization of Rowe's fiction, and I will emphasize the different work they did for women in the culture. One type, amatory fiction, is the most recognized and discussed. I see two unrecognized forms, patchworks and apparition literature, as equally if not more important. Patchworks, for example, resist heteronormativity and the alleged complementarity of the sexes in order to make the single life respectable through depictions of alternative patterns for women's lives. I will begin, however, with a brief introduction to them as epistolary in form, although my major discussion of letter fiction is in chapter four, "The Beautiful Life." I have divided this explication in order to begin by treating the form as I do the other fictional kinds, summarizing the state of epistolarity. In the later chapters I explore Rowe's revisionary use of the form as she participated in and contributed to new social and philosophical movements.

The Epistolary Form

It is hard for us to imagine the interest in letters in Rowe's time. Elizabeth Heckendorn Cook says that "the letter saturated Enlightenment culture" and lists such diverse forms as monthly newsletters, travel letters, and letters of classical authors.[5] Clare Brant points out that letters were the most important kind of writing in the century, and she writes chapter after chapter on kinds of letters that were written and received by all levels of society, each with its own conventions, purposes, and class markers. The market for published letters, fictional and purporting to be sent by interesting people, was growing vigorously. Rising sales of letters by famous people or lovers such as Elizabeth Thomas's *Pylades and Corinna* (1731) slightly preceded the tide of epistolary novels. Brant notes that "between 1700 and 1800, more than twenty-one thousand items were published that used the word 'Letter' or 'Letters' in their title."[6]

To compare the English epistolary collections before and after Rowe is to portray a drastic contrast. Those published near the same time as hers are backward looking and are not carriers of the emerging ideas that animate hers.[7] *Miscellanea Aurea* (1720) is a pastiche including satires, essay letters, short miscellaneous letters much like Charles Gildon's *Miscellaneous Letters and Essays on Several Subjects, Philosophical, Moral, Historical, Critical, and Amorous* (1694) and "The Garden of Adonis," made up of twenty love letters. *Love without Artifice* (1733) is actually a scandalous work based on the breach-of-promise suit between Lord William Fitz-Maurice and Elizabeth Leeson composed of a letter that quotes their correspondence. Therefore, it is more akin to the older secret history and the 1690s divorce pamphlets. Political satire in epistolary form is notable both in its prevalence and in its creativity. *Letters from the Living to the Living* (1704), for instance, plays on the *Letters from the Dead* trope but comments frankly on the War of Spanish Succession, and there are very numerous pamphlets that are strongly partisan "letters" between a Whig and a Tory or a city merchant and a country squire. Robert Adams Day finds epistolary fiction almost entirely in the categories of spy, journey, love, and scandalous chronicle, kinds that certainly persisted throughout the 1730s. Another influential, backward-looking model was manuals of letter writing. Day points out, "No very clear line, however, was drawn between collections of letters intended as instructive models and miscellanies of letters designed for entertainment, and these last bridged the gap between Emily Post and epistolary fiction."[8]

Many manuals included some literary letters including verse epistles as well as examples of practical kinds of letters such as "Business," "Duty," "Courtship," and "Friendship." Most included letters selected "to improve and entertain" taken from published correspondence.[9] As in Rowe's *Letters*, heroic epistles and other popular forms were chosen, and this practice continued through the century. *The Compleat Letter Writer* (1756), for instance, includes Lady Mary Wortley Montagu's *Epistle from Arthur Grey, the Footman, after his Condemnation, for attempting a Rape* (1747) and a heroic epistle *Flora to Pompey* by John Hervey, confidante of Lady Mary and butt of Pope's satire (*ODNB*). Another popular inclusion in the manuals was Pope's farewell to Bishop Atterbury "on the eve of his banishment, in which Pope imagined a future correspondence though neither of them could ever write to each other again."[10] *The Ladies Complete Letter-Writer* (1763) included letters by Rowe, including the letter "To Cleora, on the Pleasure of Retirement" (reprinted from *Letters*, 1:90–92) and her letter left for Hertford upon her death and then printed in *Miscellaneous Works*.[11] As Elizabeth MacArthur demonstrates, "Despite the heterogeneity of the letters in these collections and their primarily didactic purpose, brief narrative sequences appear. Any letter already involves some of the essential elements of a narrative: at least two characters, the writer and the addressee, and some sort of relationship between them."[12] Many manuals include replies, but they seldom go beyond two letters, as with Rowe's book.

Rowe's *Letters* include some common types found in manuals, such as condolences, thank-you notes, and love letters, but in drastically revised form. Her fictional letters by some of her women characters and her published letters provided a kind of manual for women. Her fictions are forward looking in relation to the epistolary form, a bridge from manual and miscellany to novel and influential in the politeness and didactic movements in both domains. Both the *Spectator* and Rowe's *Letters* had as primary aims to promote the well-being of their readers. Erin Mackie writes that the *Spectator* "sought to stock [their readers' heads] with a more worthwhile cargo of intellectual goods," and she quotes a passage expressing the desire to instill "into them such sound and wholesome Sentiments, as shall have a good Effect on their *Conversation* for the ensuing twelve Hours" (emphasis mine).[13] Rowe hoped that what she instilled into their heads and conversation would have more lasting, even eternal, influence, but she did not model conversations as obviously didactically pious as did Defoe in books such as *The Family Instructor*.

Rowe's cultured, wide reading also finds its way into the *Letters*. Some of the Letters participate with playwrights, poets, and prose writers in writing the popular fictionalizing and psychologizing lives of women such as Ann Bullen, Mary Queen of Scots, Lady Jane Grey, and Jane Shore. Among Rowe's subjects are Mary, Queen of France, to the Duke of Suffolk; Rosamond to Henry II; and between Lady Jane Gray [*sic*] and Lord Guilford Dudley. These poems contain many of the themes of the prose Letters and sometimes include a Nonconformist darting stab.[14] The fact that Lady Jane was *Protestant* and a brave martyr resigned to death is strongly asserted:

> Be *Rome*! be hell! in their revengeful pride;
> Their flames, their racks, and tort'ring arts defy'd:
> A thousand glorious witnesses have stood
> For this great cause, and seal'd it with their blood. (*Letters*, 1:83)

Forced into marriage by their fathers in an attempt to keep Elizabeth and Mary from inheriting the throne upon Edward VI's death, they were executed on 12 February 1554. Lady Jane had been proclaimed queen by the Privy Council according to Edward's will. She left letters to her father and a sister, but Rowe's poems are original and loosely based on history, John Foxe's portrayal of her in *Acts and Monuments*, and many embroidered accounts of her life in prose and drama.

In their very different ways, these writers are all offering corrective alternatives to kinds of conversations they found impolite and even unworthy of English citizens. Both Addison and Rowe reject novelty even as they point out contemporary pastimes worth enjoying. They share a style that is graceful, polished, even belletristic if not truly "literary," yet the *Spectator* essays sometimes reveal an awareness that the paper is in the midst of a diverse, changing culture with a living language while also being a fashionable commodity in an urban culture, while Rowe's consistently offer retreat. In many ways, they exemplify the country/city trope so prevalent in literature of their time, yet both strive to create characters who have mastered "the discipline of 'living both in the World, and out of it.'"[15]

The epistolary miscellany allows considerable engagement with the literary world. For instance, Rowe writes an imaginative job description for a sylph, an obvious imaginative extension of Alexander Pope's *Rape of the Lock* (1712, rev. and enlarged, 1714). Such light-hearted, fanciful play with Pope's sylphs appeared throughout the century; as late as 1796, Lady Eliza Tuite published five poems "written as a sylph" in her *Poems by Lady Tuite*. Rowe's sylph is a little prince with a glittering tiara and purple wings, and, like Pope's sylphs, he protects his lady's beauty by, for instance, screening her from the sun. Again, as in Pope's fable, mortal lovers are the sylph's rival, but Rowe's sylph has higher ambitions for her lady's sensibility and hopes she will choose the celestial world rather than the *beau monde*. In another example (part 3, Letter 9), she reworks Joseph Addison's *Spectator* essay #26 (30 March 1711) on Westminster Abbey into a poem. Styling the writer Theophilus, to whom *Luke* and *Acts* are addressed and meaning "beloved of God," Rowe writes about the categories of the dead introduced by Addison. The tones are quite different. Addison remarks that "there were Poets who had no Monuments, and Monuments which had no Poets," and she draws upon quite conventional thoughts, thoughts usually identified with Gray's later *Elegy in a Country Church-Yard*:

> There sleep the bards, whose lofty lays
> Have crown'd their names with lasting praise;
> Who, though eternity they give,
> While heroes in their numbers live,
> Yet these resign their tuneful breath,
> And wit must yield to mightier death.
> Ev'n I, the lowest of the throng,
> Unskill'd in verse or artful song,
> Shall shortly shroud my humble head,
> And mix with them among the dead.[16]

Addison is urging care in monument inscription for the glory of the nation; Rowe does much more with poets. Taken with Addison's many references to bodies "confus'd together" and "undistinguish'd in the same promiscuous Heap of Matter," she imaginatively concludes the poem by joining the great poets not on Parnassus but with their dust mingled. As it was in harmony with a later sensibility, her poem was often reprinted, usually with the title "On a Church-Yard."[17]

What differs most markedly may be the *use* to which readers put their texts, and, again, the way Rowe extends beyond being free from the fads and peer pressures of "the world" to living in an eternal "world" is a contrast. An important part of the *Spectator*'s appeal, of course, was how fully it expressed important structures of feeling and current preoccupations. Rowe develops the didactic potential in modern, more understated ways than either those who preceded or those who came immediately after her. Like Defoe, she can do this because she is conscious that she is writing to those within her faith community but also to those outside it, and, like Defoe and Addison, at some level she hopes she is improving people and bringing those "not-like-us" to become "like us." As they were, she is often exceptionally clear about "enemies without and enemies within."[18] In fact, however, she is closest to the *Spectator*, which seldom slipped into heavy-handed or verbose moralizing. In all of the politeness novels that came after hers, the *Spectator* is mentioned prominently and was also recommended reading to educate children as young as ten years old.[19] Just as Rowe's fictions went through multiple editions, so did the collected *Spectators*, and its proclaimed dedication to modeling and establishing a taste for polite writing and temperate, virtuous living kept it current. References to it became a code that allied authors, novels, and characters with it and more subtly gestured toward admirable reader communities. Writing nearly a generation later, Rowe in her epistolary fictions draws from the *Spectator* but, as chapter four demonstrates, participates in very different discourses and social movements and in multiple ways provides a revisionary foundation for the flowering of the epistolary novel that followed.

Rowe and Amatory Fiction

As has been recognized by critics, Rowe's most obvious affiliation with the fiction of her time is with amatory fiction. As early as 1756, Samuel Johnson pointed out that Rowe had employed "the ornaments of romance in the decoration of religion."[20] Richetti notes that she is exploiting the "clichés of the popular novellas and scandalous memoirs of the day." He also points out that Rowe makes "little or no attempt . . . to lay the fictional groundwork" in her stories but relies on "a kind of shorthand which enables her to refer her readers to the familiar conventional fictional situation, and then to beat the moral implications out of it."[21] In fact, she was doing what writers had in the 1720s, and the wonder is that fiction of the kind Rowe wrote was already so mature that she did not need to contextualize situations and conflicts or develop her characters. Her readers already knew them. Tellingly, the length and fullness of the seduction segment at the beginning of *Moll Flanders* (1722) disguise how formulaic it is. Rarely do the writers immediately before her take time to create a setting that enhances the mood or action, and most of them "beat the moral implications out of" these episodes.[22] Penelope Aubin in *The Life of the Lady Lucy* combines conventional setting with moral annotation: "I resolv'd to execute my wicked Design upon *Emilia*: it was Winter, the Winds blew, and the Stars gave no light; it was a Night dark as the Deed I went to execute." (33).

Rowe clearly delighted in experimenting with formulaic amatory situations, some easily identified with her contemporaries' texts, developing them, and giving them concluding twists. In one tale rather like some of Haywood's in *The Fruitless Inquiry*, a wife confesses to her sister that she spent a night with a marquis, and her oldest son is his. In a provocative twist, she charges the sister with informing the husband. Sarah Prescott's "The Debt to Pleasure: Eliza Haywood's *Love in Excess* and Women's Fiction of the 1720s" points out significant parallels between this text of Haywood's and the fictions of Rowe and Aubin. Her essay, published in 2000, is a fairly early example of the critical work correcting the old model of dividing women writers into the two separate camps of sluts and saints. Norma Clarke accurately points out that "Love was Elizabeth Singer's 'darling theme,'" and she makes a solid case for the "erotic content" in Rowe's fiction. She even concludes that "the afterlife is the stuff of erotic fantasy" and gives telling examples from the letters.[23] Susan Staves also mentions that Rowe includes some novelistic situations and ideas found in fiction by Behn, Manley, Aubin, and Haywood.[24] Although these studies point out a few of the similarities between Rowe's fictions and amatory fictions, they do not consider her to be one of the "mothers of the novel" and do not attempt to identify what Rowe found useful in amatory fiction and to what purposes she put its themes and narrative strategies.

Amatory fiction is notorious for its sensational tales of passion and signature scenes that survive in today's mass-market romances. Rowe can create jasmine bowers as well as Manley, characters who discover what true love is as well as Madame de Lafayette, and demonized aristocratic rakes as well as Haywood. In fact, when given several quotations from Rowe's *Letters* in a survey I sent out, specialists on Haywood, Richardson, and early English novelists described them as "too erotic" for Samuel Richardson and too "explicit" for Haywood. One guessed John Cleland to be the author. Sensational tales of passion are Rowe's forte. In one story, a man imprisons a fifteen-year-old in his house for his sexual pleasure, as does another of her characters, Cassander, who has become a capricious tyrant and keeps Aurelia. In the second letter of the first volume of *Letters*, a man finds his lover, "the artful Marcella," with his best friend's head in her lap and kills him. In Letter 1:1, Philario (who is married to another) bribes a servant and enters Amasia's chamber:

> Never did her charms appear to such advantage: the soft surprize, the modest confusion, the struggle between a tender inclination, and the restraint of conscious honour, gave her a thousand nameless graces: whether the yielding beauty with a gentle languishment betray'd the passion she had long disguis'd, or whether recovering her self with all the pomp of virtue she reproach'd my attempt, still she put on resistless charms. . . . I saw my own advantage, nor left the conquest unfinish'd. . . . it gave me an impious pleasure to find love triumphant over all the pride of virtue (1:4).

Any reader of Behn and Manley will recognize this classic scene of the beautiful woman intruded upon by her seducer-rapist and the prefiguring of Samuel Richardson's Lovelace in the last sentence.

Indeed, the scene is still standard in modern popular romances. Unlike these precursors, however, Rowe writes this scene from the point of view of the man, the seducer, rather than from that of an omniscient narrator whose primary interest is the woman. Haywood, for instance, writes in *Love in Excess* that Amena's "panting heart beat measures of consent, . . . and every pulse confess [*sic*] a wish to yield."[25] D'Elmont creeps into Melliora's bedchamber, where she is asleep with "all the beauties of her neck and breast appeared to view" (127). The narrator objectifies both characters. Melliora is the object of the gaze, and Haywood describes D'Elmont as an external observer rather than narrating from his point of view. Haywood writes, "He thought it pity even to wake her, but more to wrong such innocence." Melliora babbles out inflaming words about him, and he tears off his clothes "and joyned his panting breast to her's." The narration continues, "He put it out of her power either to deny, or to reproach him, by stopping her mouth with kisses, and was just on the point of making good what he had vowed" (128–29). Rowe writes for Philario: "in every transporting variety of her temper, I saw my own advantage, nor left the conquest unfinish'd." He continues, "It gave me an impious pleasure to find love triumphant over all the pride of virtue." Rowe is reworking Haywood's signature scene, and Richardson, who had printed the 1740 edition of *Friendship in Death . . . To which are added, Letters Moral and Entertaining in Prose and Verse. In three parts*, reworks hers.[26] Repeatedly, Lovelace writes of his skepticism regarding Clarissa's virtue and also of his desire to test her. He continues the tradition of using heroines as representatives of the nature and position of the sex: "Such a triumph over the whole Sex, if I can subdue this Lady!" Lovelace says. Just before the rape, he writes, "Is not *this* the hour of her trial—And in *her*, of the trial of the virtue of her whole Sex. . . . Whether her frost be frost indeed? Whether her virtue be principle?"[27]

Another dimension unites the three writers and these episodes. Haywood's scene, no less than Rowe's and Richardson's, integrates threats to conscience and enduring contentment of mind. In spite of her dreams that he is her "extatick ruiner," Melliora attempts to stop D'Elmont by arguing that he is giving up his "peace for ever" "for a few moments joy." In Rowe's narrative, Philario continues to "visit" Amasia, but she dies of a fever. Among her ravings is this very clever twist: "See yonder sullen ghost beckons me away! —another pale spectre summons me to the grave. . . . How my senses wander! . . . I am cited to the supream tribunal, —have you the hardiness to appear for me?" (1:7). Rowe's Amasia asks Philario to appear at God's tribunal for her, in effect, to atone for or expiate her actions. Haywood's rapist is interrupted and by the end of the romance reformed. Richardson's Lovelace on his deathbed babbles to Clarissa, "Look down, blessed Spirit, look down!" His last words are "Let this expiate."[28] In contrast to Haywood's rapist, Rowe's succeeds and his letter is as self-centered as Lovelace's; it is all about himself as he ends his final letter with the hope that he has excited his friend's compassion, the same response Lovelace consistently tried to arouse in Belmont.

Although most of the novelists of the early period occasionally wrote from the point of view of the opposite sex, Rowe and Behn do it most frequently and with the most damning results.[29] Behn seems an important, under-recognized influence on Rowe. The influences are large and small, and there are sometimes tantalizing similarities. For example, Behn has Sylvia write to Phiander in *Love Letters between a Nobleman and His Sister*: "I sought thee every where, but like the languishing abandoned mistress in the *Canticles* I sought thee, but I found thee not." This passage and narrative are among Rowe's most frequent poetic subjects.[30] Even if Rowe was not thinking specifically of Behn's reference, their allusions point to the significance of the Canticles as an unrecognized source for women's expressions of the experience of love. Interestingly, Rowe's husband compared her to Behn rather often, but the only critic to introduce the topic is Clarke, and her interest is heavily biographical.[31] Rowe's Philander writes bluntly of the woman with whom he expected lasting happiness but seduced: "The yielding beauty, by granting my desires, lost my esteem; her charms vanish'd, her wit was impertinence, and her artifice disgusted me" (1:60). The archetypal scene is, of course, Behn's when Philander in *Love Letters between a Nobleman and his Sister* clasps Sylvia, "the untouched, unspotted, and till then, unwishing lovely maid."[32] He writes to her later, "I beheld thee extended on a bed of roses, in garments, which, if possible, by their wanton loose negligence and gaity, augmented thy natural charms." "I saw," he continues, "the ravishing maid as much inflamed as I; she burnt with equal fire . . . not all her care could keep the sparks concealed, but it broke out in every word and look" (52–53).

In a startling revision, Rowe emphasizes the power and erotic nature of the gaze in a scene from a six-letter tale. She reverses the signature scene of the seducer and unaware object by having Rosalinda come upon "the lovely youth reclined on a mossy bank, lost in downy sleep" in a fragrant honeysuckle bower (*Letters*, 2:11). She gazes on Lucius for a while and then slips away. These scenes, as this one does, are written to arouse all of the senses. The velvety feel of the mossy bank and the heady smell of honeysuckle are even more specific than Behn's bed of roses in *Love Letters* (52) and Haywood's gentle breezes and "various odours wafted . . . from adjacent gardens" (*Love in Excess*, 63). Rowe's description of Rosalinda gazing on the sleeping Lucius and of her later encounters with him expresses female sexuality and desire as clearly as Behn's. Rather than the languishing, blushing, trembling, and panting breast of Behn's characters, Rowe's characters control the gaze and inventory their objects' charms. By locating desire in the gaze rather than in signs from the physical body, her scenes convey the message but seem more modest. The accident of seeing the lover and the luck of being able to regard him undiscovered replace the accident of the man finding the woman unaware and in dishabille (usually with a breeze to make the garment more revealing). Behn's Philander wrote, "Consider all your charms at once exposed, consider every sense about me ravished" (54). Lucius's charms are also exposed, and Rosalinda is fascinated and desiring—"ravished."

Even more Behn-like is Rowe's story of Lysander, who discharges his *valet de chambre* because he believes he is courting his sister. At that moment, Palanty, who may have been partly inspired by the Sylvia of part 3 of Behn's *Love Letters between a Nobleman and his Sister*, confesses that she is a woman in love with *him*. "This she told me with a face unstained with a rosy blush, or the least appearance of that modest disorder so natural and becoming her sex," he observes (2:55). He recalls that Palanty "had been without constraint a witness, as well as pimp, to many of my criminal amours." A man without sensibility or ethics, he continues such affairs, allows Palanty to seduce him and gets her pregnant, and, to please "a most indulgent" mother, desultorily courts Cimene, the woman she has selected for him to marry. He falls in love with Cimene, who has modesty, wit, candor, and an ideal temperament. Like Melliora in Haywood's *Love in Excess*, he learns what true love is. Saddled with Palanty, whom he is boarding nearby, he still marries Cimene. Palanty poisons herself; as Althea does in Haywood's *Mercenary Lover*, she leaves an account of the affair. It reaches Lysander's mother and wife. Because he has always been the seducer, no one believes he was the seduced in this affair. Wracked by guilt and haunted by memories of his "debauches, quarrels, licentious amours," he imagines Palanty coming to him and leaving a letter. In these narratives, the men repent, and Rowe gives each one a poem through which to speak his new state of mind and priorities.

As feminist critics have recently demonstrated, the plots of amatory intrigue did not burn out or disappear.[33] The situations, desires, and oppressions that gave rise to them had not disappeared, and women writers adapted them and reimbued them with forceful exposures. I will briefly point out a few ways Rowe joined in continuing the work of amatory fiction. Above all the amatory plots reveal the situation of eighteenth-century women. Ros Ballaster defined the type as "explicitly erotic in its concentration on the representation of sentimental love."[34] What this definition somewhat masks is the fact that amatory fiction portrays women as wanting the fulfillment of both sexual desire and a companionate marriage. This was the ideal of marriage, of course, for the first half of the century, and its expression is especially powerful in, for instance, Henry Fielding's *Tom Jones* and *Amelia*. That Ballaster and other critics see the desire for friendship and personal satisfaction in a relationship as "sentimental" is telling, and amatory fiction before Rowe often called such thinking "romantic." Equally pervasive is the picture of oppressive tactics of domination and repression aimed at women: coercion, force, confinement, and the threat of impoverishment and even homelessness. In fact, the two pictures are inseparable. Women's common vulnerability is taken for granted in these plots; in fact, many novels include a story parallel to the heroines that says, "There but for luck/the grace of God go I." Luck saves one of the women in Haywood's *British Recluse*, and Sally Godfrey is an example of bad luck in contrast to Pamela who has been able to avoid rape in Richardson's novel. Women in the fictions tell these stories to others, and sometimes the conclusion gives the satisfaction of what Nussbaum calls "a narrative of female power" and sometimes it offers the opportunity for a combination of didacticism and also sympathy for the ruined woman.[35] Rowe weaves women's desire for personal satisfaction and the sex's vulnerable position throughout her volumes of fiction.

The fiction and books of practical divinity written between 1670 and 1740 rather sequentially engaged the problems with (1) courtship practices, including seduction, (2) forced and arranged marriages, and (3) women's status and possibilities for happiness within marriage. All of these situations allowed writing about economic realities, female desire, and identity formation. Rowe writes about all of these things in revisionary and influential ways. She, like the other women novelists, often exposes patriarchal and libertine opinions and behaviors as sources of misery and evil. Fathers assume the right to marry off both their daughters and their sons. Philario has been forced into an economic marriage at age twelve (his wife is ten years old) (*Letters*, part 1, letter 1). Lemira's father opposes her marriage to Valerius because he is a citizen (3:13). Rosalinda's father tried to marry her to a French Catholic. Many of Rowe's male characters, like the stage libertines, are willing to seduce any woman regardless of rank and view the gullible as failing a test. The women can, then, be cast aside without remorse. The volumes have many examples of such men. In one of the more old-fashioned tales, Cassander has driven his wife into a nunnery and is in league with Leonora's brother to force her into a bigamous marriage (*Friendship*, Letter 11). Sisters, such as Laura in the final section of *Letters*, "Six Letters from Laura to Aurelia," describe their brothers' "criminal Amours."

A little-noticed alternative pattern for women's lives is the threesome, which can be composed of the husband, wife, and her close female friend. Rooted in households that included single relations and in seventeenth-century honeymoon trips that included a woman friend, the narratives written in the eighteenth century came to be ones often marked by tense negotiation and coercive resolution. As Christine Roulston has noted, "It is female bonding that generates the desire for narrative, whereas marriage is presented as a well-worn trope."[36] This is true in women's writings, while in men's, as in *Clarissa*, the friend must be expunged for a successful marriage to take place. Barker's "The Unaccountable Wife," the story of the wife who chooses to leave and experience destitution with her servant maid rather than fire her and remain with her husband, has received considerable attention.[37] Some of these stories are pointedly disruptive and even deliver revenge. In Sarah Scott's *Millenium Hall*, Mr. Morgan has separated his wife from her beloved, lifelong friend for many years, but he suffers a stroke and is nursed by his wife and her friend. Unable to leave his bed or even feed himself, he falls "into violent passions, which he had not words to express (for he was almost deprived of his speech)," when he misses Mrs. Morgan. Helpless, he must listen to the two women converse freely and happily in the sick room during his periods of "stupefaction."[38] These women are, of course, the founders, with another friend, of Millenium Hall.

As Rowe's leading women characters seek a satisfying life, the guidance of reason plays an unusually prominent part. Melinda understands that Henry would not court her because of the company she kept, and important to her character is that she developed "a habit of thinking." As her story unfolds and she settles into a single life with the wife of a sea captain, the power of her mind and calm, rational thought define her (*Letters*, 2:76–84). The resolution of her story is a threesome. Deliberately writing for both sexes, Rowe also creates mature men who are guided by reason. What Rowe does—and this is significant—is write story after story that emphasizes that marriage is *the* decisive moral act of women's *and* men's lives, and that it is their responsibility.[39] Thus, although they feel the social and economic pressures that are emphasized in other writers' plots, her characters' thoughts and actions foreground individual *moral* actions and their link to earthly and eternal happiness. When Polidore encounters Aurelia, once a woman he loved who had had an affair with her best friend's husband, he sees that she needs help but observes, "I heard this account with a heart full of compassion. . . . But I had too much value for my own peace, and too great a contempt for a woman of *Aurelia's* character, to make any particular proposals for her freedom; and bidding her adieu, hasted back to the Earl's, without saying one word of my adventure" (*Letters*, 3:207–8). Such men usually play bit parts in the fiction of the time, even Defoe's, thereby seeming to be representative of a small minority of men. The Dutchman in *Roxana*, Henrick in Behn's *Fair Jilt*, and Worthly in Haywood's *British Recluse* are examples.

Even when the good attain a satisfying life, the world of amatory fiction remains one of lust for sex, money, and power. As countless critics have argued, a major purpose of amatory fiction is to caution readers to be wary of seduction, their own feelings, economic predators, and appearances. For instance, Haywood's most frequent admonitions to both sexes are directed at illusions and wishful thinking; as she does in *The British Recluse*, she warns against actions based on "no other Foundation for belief in what her Lover says . . . than the good Opinion . . . *Passion has made [her or him] conceive*" (emphasis mine).[40] Aubin writes in the preface to *Lady Lucy*, "I intreat all marry'd Men . . . not to give credit to Appearances, but to examine well into the Truth of Things" (xi). In all of these fictions, including Rowe's, the women are economic units, always on the verge of being cultural or exchange capital and available to men to raise male value. Manley's *Happy Fugitives* gets to the point on the first page: "alas the Time! we speak only of Interest, Potion, Joyntures, Settlements, Separate Maintainance, now a-days! with other worldly Considerations; which clearly proves, that *Cupid* has either blunted his Darts, or makes them of quite another sort of Stuff."[41] As Sarah Prescott notes, "Amatory intrigues are always framed by the moral and social issues inherent in the representation of heterosexual relations"[42] and, therefore, of the sex-gender system.

From the time of the earliest English novels, writers sometimes used the death scenes of heroines to close their texts, to determine interpretation. Penelope Aubin writes (and illustrates in her fictions), "Let [the vicious woman's] Station be ever so great and high in the World, nay, let her Crimes be ever so well conceal'd from human Eyes; yet . . . her Death . . . will be accompanied with Terrors, and a bitter Repentance shall attend her to the Grave: Whilst the virtuous shall look Dangers in the face unmov'd, . . . dying with comfort, be freed from the Miserys of this Life, and go to taste eternal Repose."[43] More than any other early writer, Rowe developed the death scenes of women into a powerful sign system that went beyond exemplary women characters' beautiful deaths and the fallen dying terrified and desperate.[44] In contrast to the multiple meanings and possibilities generated by the ending of Defoe's *Roxana*, the death of Rowe's Amasia and the contrasting peaceful death of the beautiful, serious woman treated by the physician Leander (1:65–72) seal the moral admonitions of the stories. Amasia is similiar to Eliza Haywood's Althea in *The Mercenary Lover*, who dies a horrible, repentant death in that she was seduced but held responsible for giving in. More often, like Aurelia, the women who sinned (and they were never just "fallen" women but were women who had chosen to, for instance, seduce a friend's husband) were doomed to play out a life of misery, one impoverished economically, socially, and even aesthetically. The bad death is sometimes eroticized in striking ways, as Amanda orders a new, fashionable wardrobe from France for her dying (*Letters*, 2:35–36), while what might be the sentimentality of the good death of a young person becomes an example of rational religion. Letter 1:8 in the section "By another hand" combines both. Teraminta dies in Emilia's arms, describing not only her passionate love for a man not her husband but also their three-year struggle to repent and be virtuous.

Rowe and Apparition Literature

A standard reference book, the *Dictionary of Literary Biography* points out that the convention of letters from the dead can be traced back to Lucian's *Dialogues of the Dead* and its imitations, such as Fontenelle's *Dialogues des morts* (1683; with translations available in 1708 and 1721 titled *Fontenelle's Dialogues of the Dead, in Three Parts)* and Fénelon's *Dialogues des morts anciens et modernes* (1718) styled significantly in English translation as *Fables and Dialogues of the Dead* (1722, requiring a second edition in 1723). All three were considered classics, and others, such as Tom Brown's *Letters from the Dead to the Living* and its *Continuation* (1702–1703), were fashionably popular.[45] The identification of Rowe's works with this tradition, although valuable, is also misleading. Only the letters in *Friendship in Death* are styled as from the dead, and her texts have more in common with books such as Daniel Defoe's *An Essay on the History and Reality of Apparitions* (1727), notably published the year before Rowe's *Friendship in Death*. A glance at some of the texts that identified themselves with Brown's makes the contrast between contemporary apparition literature and the low and ephemeral category stark: *Advice from the Shades-below: Or, a letter from Thomas Hobbs . . . to his brother B[enjamin] H[oa]dly* (1710); *Sheppard in Ægypt, or News from the Dead. Being a letter from John Sheppard to Frisky Moll* (1725); and *A Lecture from the Dead, concerning Modern Patriotis. With a dedication to the late L[ord] V[iscount] Bol[ingbroke]* [1728].

Nevertheless, Rowe's *Letters from the Dead to the Living* was the basis of the demand for subsequent volumes of her fiction. Dialogues of and from the dead were a classical genre, and they were quite popular and even common in the eighteenth century. Frederick Keener lists seventy-eight dialogues published between 1641 and 1800, and he makes no effort to include dialogues with the dead and admits that his list is incomplete.[46] He identifies some written by eighteenth-century writers but not published until later, such as Elizabeth Montagu's three in George Lyttelton's *Dialogues of the Dead* (1760) and Matthew Prior's, which he dates to 1721 (publication 1907 but read by Pope and others in manuscript). Near the end of the century, both Hester Thrale Piozzi and Anna Laetitia Barbauld published dialogues with the dead. It seems that it was common to circulate these imaginative dialogues in manuscript; the second volume of *Miscellaneous Works* has three dialogues on the subjects in *Letters*; in one Rowe quotes a quatrain by Mary Barber that was not published until 1734 (from *Verses sent to a Lady, who took Delight in ridiculing a Person of very weak understanding* in her *Poems on Several Occasions*).

Most modern critics of Defoe's work have described it as "irritating" and bewildering, as they have Rowe's.[47] His book is largely composed of fifty-one anecdotes, which come from a mixture of sources such as the Bible, histories, and experiences he heard or read about.[48] Although most are quite different from Rowe's, some are highly similar. In one of Defoe's, a husband experiences the return of his dead wife who asks, "What is the Reason that you mourn thus for me?" She tries to persuade him to remarry and go on with his life. In Letter 3 of *Friendship in Death*, Rowe has a dead toddler come back to comfort his mother and inquire into her reasons for protracted grief.

The juxtaposition of reason and kinds of intense faith found in these books by Defoe and Rowe is seldom encountered today and confuses readers and can even appear contradictory. Jennifer Frangos argues persuasively that "early science takes a great deal on faith" and quotes contemporary texts in which authoritative characters pronounce that there is room for "belief in things for which 'we have no certain or demonstrative Notions,' or that may not be explainable in logical ways."[49] For these writers, reasoned evidence included faith and religion and might be substituted for empirical evidence or kinds of classical argument; this thinking was questioned in their time, of course, as well as ours. Rowe's writing includes numerous mystical passages and texts, and Rowe and Defoe sometimes present God as potentially intervening directly in human life. Both admit the possibility of guardian angels. In the account of Mrs. Veal returning to visit her friend Mrs. Bargrave that Defoe may have written, she says, "If the Eyes of our Faith were as open as the Eyes of our Body, we should see numbers of Angels about us for our Guard."[50] For many people, as in this quotation, apparitions made the world a safer, friendlier place. In an early letter, Rowe writes to Hertford, "I often please myself with the thought, that departed spirits supply the place of guardian angels to their friends; that they delight to follow them in their solitary walks, and watch their nightly slumbers, and make impressions on their sleeping fancy, to warn them of approaching dangers" (*Misc. Works*, 2:72).

The belief in a spirit world gives an urgency to the use of reason to determine when God is sending a message and when humans are falling into superstitious or wishful thinking, an endeavor we are likely to find quite foreign.[51] Rowe asserts the moderate, reasonable position between superstition and skepticism inclining to atheism through the content of her letters, especially as they advance through the four volumes. Some characters express skepticism, but each letter concludes with the moderate position and the possibility of spirits as guardian angels or conscience replacing actual appearances. In contrast, Defoe struggles with conveying a firm position, and his registers include satire, parody, polemic, and testimony even as he consistently, in George Starr's words, sees "his belief in the 'Converse of Spirits' as part and parcel of Christianity."[52] Defoe says that spirits communicate by "Dreams,

Impulses and strong Aversions,"[53] and Rowe and other writers increasingly incorporate impulses and strong aversions as promptings and guides along with conscience. In her introduction to Defoe's *Essay*, Kit Kincade points out that "arguments concerning the nature and reality of apparitions [had] actuated a theological and philosophical crisis of the later Seventeenth Century."[54] Wolfgang Neuber in his historical account of thinking about spirits, poltergeists, and messages in dreams notes, "The more widely and often spirits could be experienced, the more important was it to understand whether they came from God or the demons." He also gives examples of European anecdotes like Defoe's and Rowe's that are contemporaneous with them.[55]

In the 1720s interest in superstition, folklore, and magic was high.[56] Kincade argues that Defoe "felt it necessary to write about apparitions" because of "his clear sense of religious philosophy," one she identifies with his Presbyterianism and "basic" Puritanism, a faith and a heritage that Rowe shared. Through his Oxford-educated teacher Charles Morton and through her acquaintance with the work of John Norris and the Cambridge Platonists, Defoe and Rowe gained broader philosophical awarenesses and sought a balance that would accommodate both modern reason and their inherited religious beliefs. As most Presbyterians believed and as *Robinson Crusoe* shows and Rowe's fictions imply, reading the Scriptures, human experience, and reason could teach the nature of God better than the doctrine of the Church of England.[57] The didactic thrust and tactics in Rowe's and Defoe's work ride upon an insistence that rational creatures can learn from others' experiences, especially when those experiences are glossed by observations delivered in tones of common sense. Some critics have argued that dreams, visions, and apparitions are often examples of individualized piety that could challenge institutionalized doctrine,[58] and perhaps that was part of the appeal for both Rowe and Defoe who had lifelong objections to the Church of England. Somewhat in this line of reasoning is Frangos's argument that "ghosts come to reflect a growing cultural emphasis on the emotions of the living and perhaps empirical limits to the study of death."[59]

Defoe's *Essay on . . . Apparitions* collects stories about angels, dreams, omens, phantoms, and spirits, describes the workings of conscience and imagination, and offers some help in "one of the greatest Difficulties of Life": "to distinguish between . . . real Apparitions, and such as are only the Product of an incumber'd Brain, a distemper'd Head, or . . . worse, a distemper'd Mind."[60] Defoe writes that he is attempting to separate the legitimate from the superstitious, and he includes in the first category not only serious, pious beliefs but also things deserving respectful consideration. In the second category are events that arouse considerable skepticism or even ridicule. Statements of belief in spirits were common in the first half of the century; Addison, for instance, expressed his in the *Spectator* repeatedly. "I

... believe that all the Regions of Nature swarm with Spirits," he wrote, and he depicted the same continuity between earth and Heaven that Rowe did.[61] Even his unsuccessful stage comedy about the supernatural, *The Drummer* (1722), went into a second edition. These essays and books show that interest in the possibility of seeing spirits and receiving messages from them remained general, but they are skeptical, exploratory, and have distinctly modern elements, as suited the spirit of their time. Christine Göttler notes that "the divisions between what was perceptible and what was not were not clearly defined; moreover, there were contradictory ideas about the actual 'substance' or nature, the properties and virtues of spirits."[62] As late as 1764, John Wesley noted in his journal that he had been reading Richard Baxter's *The Certainty of the Worlds of Spirits* (1691) and mused, "How hard is it to keep the middle way; not to believe too little or too much!" Like Defoe, Wesley tried to amass evidence, and his journal from 1739 to 1742 included over sixty reports of visions, ghosts, message-dreams, and providences and at least ten in each year of the 1750s.[63] Anne Bannerman's *The Genii* (1800) is a typical portrayal of continual belief in communications from the dead:

> Benignant spirits! ye, who range the air,
> And bind the wounds of sublunary care!
> . . . .
> — Say, that the parted soul shall pierce the gloom,
> Which lowrs [sic] tremendous o'er the sullen tomb,
> And come by night, the messenger of peace,
> To speak of joys, that never shall decrease.[64]

Rowe's spirits in *Friendship in Death* are usually guardian angels or the equivalent of a rational person's moral attitudes; over the course of the volumes of letters they are replaced by the promptings of conscience. In Letter 8 of *Friendship in Death*, for instance, Amintor tells his love, who has been captured by pirates and sold to a Bassa, "The heavenly *Genii* that attend you have made a thousand Impressions on your sleeping Fancy to warn you from [suicide]" (27). Silviana's letter in part 3 describes the "inward Remorse" she felt after thoughts and actions she knew were transgressive, and even in dreams there are no spirits or genii. Defoe writes, "CONSCIENCE, indeed, is a frightful Apparition itself." He goes on to say that it "haunts an oppressing Criminal into Restitition," "shows us many an Apparition that no other Eyes can see, and sets Spectres before us," and "works upon the Imagination with an invincible Force; like Faith, it makes a Man view things that are not."[65] Defoe treats apparitions similarly as representations of conscience and "Angelick Guards." For instance, in one tale, a girl on her way to meet her lover meets the apparition of her parson. In this tale, as in many of Rowe's, a gentleman is highly skeptical but comes to be reformed.⁶⁶

An incident in Penelope Aubin's *The Life of the Lady Lucy* (1726) brings together most of the discourses about apparitions. A hermit with a terrible secret describes the appearances of the people he has murdered:

> I know . . . that these kind of Relations of Apparitions are look'd upon by a great Part of the World as Fictions, and the Product of weak Brains; nor shall I pretend to determine whether they be the real Spirits of the Persons who appear, or their good Angels who assume their Shapes by the divine Permission, to discover the Murders of such Persons as were in their care, or to awaken the Consciences of such wretched harden'd Sinners as I was to Repentance; or whether the Almighty causes such Forms to appear to the Imaginations of such Persons: This is a Search too curious for our finite Understandings; but this is most certain from the Testimony of all Ages, that such things have been frequent in all Times; and that even at Mid-day, Apparitions have been seen by Persons of the greatest Courage and Integrity; and that such Secrets have by this means been discover'd, as could never have come to the knowledge of those to whom they appear'd, any other way (40–41).

Defoe, Aubin, and Rowe work with the dead's relationship to the living. Defoe denies the possibility of their returning but leaves open the other possibilities that Aubin lists. Kincade argues that Defoe is trying to provide "rational and doctrinally sound proof of their [apparitions'] reality,"⁶⁷ but Rowe's lighter, more fanciful tone produces an imaginative style with different, albeit equally serious, intentions. Rowe's framework and tone indicate that it is a device; there is no explanatory argument. It is available to her, neither absolute belief nor superstition, and the emphasis is on relationships between people, on intimate emotional bonds, and on the here and now.⁶⁸ Although there are brief descriptions of Heaven and the state of mind of the dead, the focus of the stories is on the situation and possible courses of action for the living. Defoe's most serious work in *An Essay* is with dreams, and, as in the Amintor story and in her *History of Joseph*, Rowe represents dreams as a means of receiving spiritual communications.

Defoe's stories jog along with many repetitions and extrapolations; they are about the middling and even lower classes who might be suspected of superstition. Talking and trying to reason out what an apparently supernatural experience might mean composes most of each tale. As he writes of the couple visited by the ghostly parson: "They had a long Dialogue upon that Head" (106). The contrast between Rowe's tight, elegant, little stories and Defoe's narratives (including his novels) underscores her different allegiances and sense of audience. In fact, Rowe does not specifically identify *Friendship* with these books, and the four volumes of Letters demonstrate a fascination with most of the kinds of her contemporaries' prose fictions.

The twists she gave these forms, including apparition literature, do far more than turn them into narratives on the joys of salvation. Rowe's texts show nearly the full range of the rich, varied literary and extra-literary strains that flowed into the early novel and that have been identified in books such as J. Paul Hunter's *Before Novels*. For example, although "news" is not usually a category associated with her work, she comments on the South Sea Bubble, on Spanish and Mediterranean pirates (then costly dangers to British shipping), and notes such things as the controversies over the actresses playing Polly in the first run of John Gay's *Beggar's Opera* (*Letters*, 1:60–61). News and apparition literature come together in Letter 1 in *Friendship in Death*. Gilbert Burnet, who was at John Wilmot, Earl of Rochester's side at his death, repeated the story that he and a shipmate, George Wyndham, had promised to return after death to give an account of the hereafter. Rochester had joined Lord Admiral Sandwich's fleet as a volunteer during the Second Dutch War, and, faced with battle, his friends, Sandwich's cousin Edward Montagu and the brother of a classmate at Oxford, Wyndham, had premonitions of their deaths. Wyndham and Rochester swore the oath; Montagu and Wyndham were killed by the same cannonball. When Wyndham did not return, according to Burnet, it was "a great snare to him, during the rest of his life" and a major obstacle to belief in God.[69] In Rowe's letter, "To the Earl of R—, from Mr. —, who had promised to appear to him after his death," R— receives a letter from the friend (Clerimont in Rowe's letter), who apologizes for not returning immediately and says it "was not in my Power to give you the Evidence of a future State, which you desired, and that I had rashly promised."[70] Burnet wrote,

> Though when he told me this, he could not but acknowledge, it was an unreasonable thing for him, to think, that Beings in another State were not under such Laws and Limits, that they could not command their own motions, but as the Supream Power should order them. (18–19)

The friend's letter in *Friendship in Death* goes on to say that "Happy Minds in this superior State are still concern'd for the Welfare of Mortals," a claim found in numerous texts of the period. Thomas Ken, resident at Longleat, had written in a catechism, "I believe, O most holy Jesu, that thy Saints here below have communion with thy Saints above, they praying for us in Heaven, we here on Earth, celebrating their memorials, rejoycing at their bliss."[71] Letter 2 is also from a dead friend to a living one and gives an exhilarated account of Heaven. Several other letters in

Friendship use the same strategy to comfort the bereaved or to assure them of the reality and joy of Heaven. Over the four volumes, here, too, we can see the movement in the letters toward more modern presentations; in part 2, rather than the spirit returning to deliver a letter, Leticia dreams that her brother sits down beside her and describes the afterlife in very much the same terms as the letter (*Letters*, 2:46–48).

Some of the letters in *Friendship* are like many Nonconformist death stories, including James Janeway's *Token for Children: An Exact Account of the Conversion, Holy and Exemplary Lives, and Joyful Deaths, of several young Children* (1671; pt. 2, 1673). Janeway, a Presbyterian minister educated at Oxford before the university was barred to Nonconformists, saw his conventicle in Surrey destroyed by the government and narrowly escaped arrest on several occasions. His *Token*, with its stories for and about children, is important to the history of literature for children. In these stories, children die young, often after a time of suffering from their illnesses, with a joyous vision of Heaven at the moment of death. Their unshakeable faith serves as an example for all. In fact, children are often spokespersons of Christian truths in the literature of the period and, as innocent and as yet unsocialized witnesses, naively admonish those around them. In Daniel Defoe's *Family Instructors*, children draw out the contradictions between their parents' statements and actions, such as regarding church attendance on rainy days. They are even the instruments of criticism of social practices, as is the little boy who pities Tobey, the African servant. The practice continued; for example, in *The History of Little Goody Two-Shoes* (1762), little Margery chides another little girl for resisting praying for her enemies.[72] As Janeway wrote, "Christ doth not slight them; they are not too little to dye, they are not too little to go to Hell, they are not too little to serve their great Master, too little to go to Heaven; *For of such is the Kingdom of God*."[73] In his "Example III," Mary reminds her Mother of the greater value of "grace and the love of Christ than any thing in the world" when the "Mother had been somewhat solicitous about any worldly thing" (32). Rowe's Letter 1 has the returning spirit describing the brave, exemplary death of the Earl of R—'s brother, and there are a few accounts of the deaths of small children, some with moral judgments based on her Dissenting ideology. In Letter 3 of *Friendship*, she has the dead child learn that the protracted grief his mother feels is because his "vast estate" was entailed and the title endangered. In contrast to this very Anglican family, the child now sees the coat of arms as a toy and the land as proper for the grazing animals rather than a possession ornamenting the family.

In spite of our ridicule of Rowe's "letters from the dead to the living," every week people in churches all over the world say, "I believe . . . in the communion of saints." In the wake of Steven P. Jobs's retirement from Apple, a church vicar interviewed shopping at an Apple store said that Apple is "more like a family, a movement. I'd like to meet him in heaven and say, 'Thank you.'"[74] Keith Thomas has amassed a number of quotations to argue that early modern theologians tried to make Heaven seem a happier place by laying "increasing emphasis on the idea of heaven as a sociable place where one could catch up with old friends, as well as possibly—for the point was disputed—making new ones." Among his examples are

> Richard Baxter envisaged living for ever in the company of Old Testament worthies such as Noah and Moses, and Reformation heroes like Luther and Calvin. The learned Catherine Talbot, in contrast, assumed that the circle of heavenly friendships would be confined to those one had already known on earth: "the more connections we make here," she wrote in 1749, "the more friends we shall have to rejoice with hereafter in a permanent state of felicity."[75]

Rowe was joined in all of these kinds of ideas. She imagines an "august and sparkling assembly" and writes, "I am exceeding pleas'd with the thoughts of that numberless concourse of the great immortals, join'd together to pass an endless duration" (*Misc. Works*, 2:118). On a less speculative note, it might be said that Rowe created the aesthetic death and released the expression of the belief in reunion in Heaven—or, at least, a frequently used trope. Richardson uses it in *Clarissa*. As Rowe had written of meeting Hertford in Heaven, Clarissa writes poignantly to Anna Howe: "In God's good time we shall meet in a blessed Eternity, never more to part!" (7:408). In fact, the collection of letters Clarissa leaves to be sent after "*she arrived at her Father's house*" is reminiscent of the letters Rowe left to be opened after her death, most of which had appeared in print quickly.[76] As one of those who don't understand Clarissa's reference to her father's house, Lovelace ponders what Clarissa meant by writing that she will send him a letter after she is in Heaven and exclaims, "The devil take such *allegories*" (7:304). Clarissa writes to Lovelace that she is "as one speaking from the dead," an echo of Rowe's famous, more than half-humorous comment to Hertford that her letters "ought to be call'd epistles from the dead." As some of Rowe's characters had, Clarissa writes, "Reflect, Sir, that I can have no other motive in what I write, than your good . . ." and "Set about your repentance instantly."[77]

In fact, I question whether readers would put up with the hundreds of pages of Clarissa's preparation for dying and the other characters' reflections on that dying without the narrative that Rowe's life and works had become. After all, letters selected to be printed in *Miscellaneous Works* included some in which she chides others for wishing her life longer or accusing her of morbidity. In one letter, she writes, "I desire your Ladyship to speak to Mr.— that, when he prays for long life for himself and his friends, he'd be pleas'd to leave me out of his petitions" (*Misc. Works*, 2:30).

Theophilus Rowe, her brother-in-law, reports, "When her acquaintance expressed to her the joy they felt at seeing her look so well, and possessed of so much health as promised many years to come, she was wont to reply, *That it was the same as telling a slave, his fetters were like to be lasting; or complimenting him on the strength of the walls of his dungeon.*"[78] Such drawn-out deaths seem to have become something of a convention, and Clarissa's death is deliberately constructed as an aesthetic event.[79] The number of poses in which she wears shimmering, dazzling white dresses and over which Richardson lingers sets the stage for the elaborate coffin and then the more elaborate and symbolic funeral processions, viewing, and burial. Sarah Fielding's David Simple in *The Adventures of David Simple. Volume the Last* (1753) is another familiar example. Indeed, the trope of the spirit looking down from Heaven and the narrative and didactic possibilities have never burned completely out, as indicated by the best-selling *The Lovely Bones* (2002) by Alice Sebold in which a girl in Heaven describes the aftermath of her murder; she even has special communication with her best friend and returns to earth at least once.

Patchworks

We are most familiar with two kinds of early novels: First, with the unified fictions most like our own, including Barker's *Love Intrigues*, Davys's *Reform'd Coquette*, and Haywood's stories such as *The City Jilt* that have at most two or three interpolated life histories within a plot that concentrates almost exclusively on the protagonist. Second, those that followed the pattern of seventeenth-century French romances in which numerous characters' stories were strung along what Josephine Grider once called "the narrative clothesline" of a unifying plot, one that would be a very short story if told alone.[80] Haywood's *Love in Excess* has become a familiar example; another is Aubin's *Life of Charlotta Du Pont* (1723), which by page seventy-seven has six life stories, not counting the "history" of Charlotta's parents and incidental relatives.

Yet a third type was very common. Bringing together old tales; comments on current events; poetry; essays; translations; jokes; amatory fictions; religious, political, or philosophical lecturing; and multivalent, experimental presentations of a controversial topic, they gained their last traction around 1720, the time when Charles Gildon's *Post-Man Robb'd of his Mail* and Delarivière Manley's *Power of Love* (1720) were published. Earlier Manley had published *The Lady's Pacquet of Letters, Taken from Her by a French Privateer* (1707). Norma Clarke points out that Manley's books "had been the talk of London during the years that Elizabeth Rowe lived there with her husband,"[81] and women writers known today for their substantial, unified prose fictions were at least as well known in their time for this kind of text. Mary Davys's

Reform'd Coquette can be balanced by *Familiar Letters betwixt a Gentleman and a Lady*, and Jane Barker's *Love Intrigues* by her two *Patch-work* volumes. The writers themselves contrasted their books to the other two types and variously assessed what was in fashion and what fading.[82] Robert Adams Day remarks that Davys's *Familiar Letters* includes "brief references to everything under the sun."[83] Occasionally referred to as "olios," literally a heavily spiced stew of meat and vegetables, but used to refer to a miscellany or any hodgepodge or unexpected mixture, they delivered a variety of pleasures and often unexpectedly spicy opinions or stories. In structure, Rowe's four volumes of prose belong with these books.

Gildon's 1706 *Post-Boy Robb'd of his Mail . . . Consisting of Letters of Love and Gallantry, and All Miscellaneous Subjects* explains in the preface that "while your *Virtuosi* are poring over the Unaccountable Secrets of *Dame NATURE*, we are busie in searching into full as intricate a Subject; The Humours and Nature of Men . . . our Delights are more profitable, and more to the *Purpose of Living*."[84] The texts in this category of fiction follow this pattern. They bring together anecdotes and tales in categories or, in some cases, unified by an aspect of human nature or experience. Some of these books are descendents of the framed-novelle, a genre traced to Giovanni Boccaccio's *Decameron* (1353), Christine de Pizan's *Livre de la cité des dames* (1405), and Marguerite de Navarre's *L'Heptaméron* (1549).[85] Increasingly, however, in the eighteenth century the frame changed in importance and the form became epistolary, often with as few as two correspondents. Gildon's *Post-Boy* anticipates the *Tatler-Spectator* device of a club; in his text the nine men rob post-boys of their mail bags, mingle the contents of the packets on a table, read, and comment. The device leads to many kinds of voices and subjects, and various kinds of letters and poetry are enclosed in other letters. The club's witty and often moralizing comments further develop the illustration of the intricacies of human nature and of different belief systems alive in the culture of the time. In multiple ways, they are an important part of the evolution toward the midcentury flowering of the epistolary novel.

Declaring *Post-Boy* a success, Gildon wrote *The Post-Man Robb'd* and used a more respectable device than robbing post-boys: the friends find mail bags in ditches where thieves had thrown them and read and comment on them. Gildon, a playwright and critic, wrote primarily about literature, and letters in *Post-Man* include poetry, a letter identified as "On little *Sawny* [Pope] the Poet," and several on the theatre, one comparing the time's "farcewrights" to the better fare and audiences 100 years earlier. One letter is even addressed to Gildon from the playwright George Sewell and comments on Gildon's *Complete Art of Poetry*. Although he touts the "passionate Love-Letters of the fair *Stremunia*" and occasionally addresses women, he admits there are few letters with love interest for the ladies, and his books are more masculine-centered than the *Tatler* and *Spectator*. Some of the essays are moralistic and witty, as is the letter on gambling as a profession, in which gamblers are decided to be as moral as businessmen at Exchange Alley, as lawyers (of course), and as the recipient's father, who made his money "squeezing the poor," the underpaid wretches who made the belts he sold (41).

Compared to the patchworks by women, Gildon's seem old-fashioned and without energy. Clearly more comfortable with other genres, he concludes *Post-Man* with six letters proposing an Academy Royal for Sciences. In contrast, in Barker's *Patch-Work Screen*, Galesia is rescued from a capsized coach and her recovered luggage is discovered to contain "nothing but Pieces of *Romances, Poems, Love-Letters*, and the like."[86] She and her hospitable rescuer read them and select most to construct the screen. This dominant part of the text is preceded by the convention of travelers in a coach taking turns telling tales and by a more novelistic interval about Galesia's brief adventures between the capsizing and the lady's rescue. In *The Lining*, Galesia has "rambled" to London, and, in the preface "To the Ladies," Barker writes that she often has been in Galesia's company and will use accounts of her adventures to make a lining for the patchwork screen. In both texts, the letters and patches are exceedingly miscellaneous, but themes develop, as the evils that result from forced marriages do in *Patch-Work Screen* and criminal marriages do in *Lining*, both facilitating woman-centered plots.

Mary Davys's *Familiar Letter betwixt a Gentleman and a Lady* is a transitional text in this tradition, one with varied subjects like Gildon's and Barker's but unified by its two letter writers. Unlike Barker's, it has a sturdy, single plot that looks forward to the epistolary novel form that became so popular later in the century. Having recognized how the epistolary form, either as inserted or entirely letters, allowed the expression of thoughts and opinions, comments on news and things read, and acceptable ways to escape social strictures on what women could express, Davys, Rowe, and others modernized the form. Also without the signs of the strong influence of *Five Love Letters from a Nun to a Cavalier*, their epistolary style is decidedly eighteenth, not seventeenth, century. Gildon includes some earthy and some witty anecdotes and remarks; however, his letters are largely serious, rather formal essay letters. Barker's text is more like a collage, intermingling poems, the narrative of Galesia's life, and miscellaneous letters, recipes, and other prose. Davys's letters lead into those of other women writers in both tone and content, and all of the texts in this group foreshadow the rise of the gendered marketing of books.

It is misleading to characterize Rowe's prose fiction by *Friendship in Death*, and to look at the four volumes as a whole is to see how they conform to and advance the patchwork literary kind while capitalizing on the epistolary form. She remarkably manages to retain the sense of coterie writers and readers. The four parts are composed of 101 letters, and she unself-consciously claims authorship of them—there is no narrative frame. The second volume, originally published as *Letters on Various Occasions, In Prose and Verse. By the Author of Friendship in Death. To which are added Ten Letters by Another Hand* (1729), has no prefatory material at all—it simply begins with the first letter, an engaging one "From Philario . . . relating his unhappy Amour with Amasia." It is the most miscellaneous of Rowe's four volumes, with eight letters to "Cleora" and ten by her appended to eighteen that are somewhat evocative of *Friendship in Death* but that look strongly toward the two volumes of *Letters Moral and Entertaining*. The final volume has eighteen letters in the body of the text and "Six Letters from Laura to Aurelia" closing the volume. Running commentary on the intellectual and philosophical discussions and debates of the time is a consistent dimension in all four volumes.

Fifteen of the twenty letters in *Friendship in Death* are presented as written by men, and they are to sisters, brothers, parents, friends, and lovers in almost equal numbers. Clerimont, the friend of Lord R—, writes two more letters. Characters with Greek names write more philosophical or learned letters than those with pastoral names, as in part 1 where Philander, the Deist, writes to Eusebius. In a text dedicated to brevity, such details help create the variety of styles, tones, and points of view. The first letter in part 1 of *Entertaining Letters* signals the shift. It is from Philario to Chamont, and the subject is his unhappy love with Amasia; it includes a letter from Amasia to Philario. The letters in this volume are from living people, although one writer is on his deathbed and another writes to Clerimont, the dead friend in *Friendship*. They are almost entirely amatory fiction, and thirteen of the sixteen are by men.[87] In part 2, twelve of the letters, including the first nine, are by women, a definite shift. In fact, there are two tiny epistolary fictions, a set of letters from Rosalinda to Lady Sophia (of which there are three more in part 3), and the first exchange between two characters, four letters between Emilia and Leticia. Clerimont and Eusebius reappear, and there are continuations of stories begun by men in earlier volumes. Several of the letters by male and female characters describe other people's deaths and, thereby, continue some of the deeper themes about life choices, experiences, and kinds of deaths. Part 3 includes thirteen letters by female characters, including six by Laura to Aurelia; Amintor, Eusebius, Alcander, and Carlos from earlier volumes reappear and write or receive letters. Suggestively for relating the forms of "novels" being written, Haskell Hinnant points out that "Defoe's fictions are constructed around a sequence of interrelated episodes in which characters appear, disappear, and reappear again in the lives of Moll and Roxana."[88]

Rowe's last two volumes are more like Barker's patchworks, in that miscellaneous insertions, often poems, are unmotivated and sometimes neither numbered as letters nor inserted in letters, but they may be even more like Defoe's in that characters are figured back into texts with their stories or philosophical explorations continued. A number of important epistolary poems by Rowe are included in the three volumes of *Letters* and, along with essays by different characters on a variety of philosophical topics, add variety to the tales of love, political intrigue, and remorse or celebration.

The small number of critics who have worked on the patchworks clarify its attractions. Misty Anderson identifies the patchworks "as tropes of the narrative work of women," as a narrative space that is feminine in nature and appealing by their structural design. Anderson points out that Barker specifically contrasts her novels to the "histories at large."[89] Kathryn King has identified the patchwork technique as an "innovative hybrid narrative method" and later one in which Barker's patches are "derived from the shared materials of female life" and, when woven into a book, "assert a larger unity with other writing women" and "affirm connections between authorship and shared female experience." King has teased out the many ways Barker does this, finding evidence even in small touches, such as Barker's giving Galesia's friend the name Lucasia, which was "used by Katherine Philips to address her best-known female friend."[90] As Barker develops the Barker-Galesia duality, she goes beyond what Jorge Casanova has identified as a strategy developed through her poetic persona "which systematically re-launches different aspects of life as women."[91] The variety of ways, then, that women's experiences and situation are introduced and cumulatively developed into a presentation of woman as a political category multiplies and becomes more sophisticated in her career, leaving a powerful example for other women that may be identifiable in, for instance, Jane Austen's narrative voice and is certainly a characteristic of Rowe's fictions.

While Haywood shifts discourses even within short texts, as she does when characters begin using "thee" and "thou," Barker and Rowe are embryonic examples of the ever-present creative and judgmental consciousness that Austen perfected. Barker's titles and many addresses "to the ladies" target an audience as no text before hers had, while Rowe repeatedly creates a unified triad of author, letter writer, and reader/recipient. Barker's first poetry was coterie,[92] but she became part of the new print culture, as Rowe moved between the two forms of publication. Barker's texts seem to move, sometimes smoothly and sometimes with jolts, from speaking to an intimate coterie circle to addressing the new audience of miscellaneous strangers, somehow individual and yet united by their sex. Rowe's *Letters* do the same, and, in fact, as we have seen, they remain closer to coterie production than has been recognized. *Patch-work Screen* uses that as a device, as she confides to the lady about her experiences and feelings but gives the patches a different tone and assumed audience.

Although most critics identify such shifts as part of the transition from a primarily manuscript culture to one dominated by print, I believe that it was an important strategy for exploiting the strengths of various literary kinds. Selection and juxtaposition of genres is almost always strategic, and in women's writing of the period, it is especially so. For instance, in Eliza Haywood's *The British Recluse*, the first woman tells her story as a romance and the second as a novel. While the content in an olio is largely original, patchworks are aptly named, because they collect material from other sources and recycle, sometimes with significant revisions, the authors' own work. Manley's *Power of Love* (1720) has seven novels, two of hers and the rest revised from William Painter's *Palace of Pleasure* (1566–1567). In her dedication, she writes, "These Novels, Madam, have Truth for their Foundation; several of the Facts are to be found in Ancient History." As precedent, she mentions Dryden's "Tales from *Boccace* and *Chaucer*" and says that she, too, wants to draw them out of obscurity.[93] Barker includes "stories" from "old books," including Behn's *Fair Vowbreaker*, a sequel to *Lettres portugaises*, and many of her own poems. Gildon writes an imitative series of letters from an Oriental spy in *Post-Boy Rob'd*.[94] Like the other authors, he includes poetry, and, like Barker, Rowe prints many of her own poems. *Friendship in Death* has only three short pieces of poetry, two of them hers (21–22, 25, 35).

The number increases significantly in *Letters on Various Occasions*, a volume that seems to have been something of an efficient, relatively fast composition. Four to eight lines of verse appear in most of the letters, much of it quoted. Among those quoted are Addison, Blackmore, Cowley, Dryden, Otway, Milton, Pope, Shakespeare, Thompson, and Tickell. Her paraphrase of Crashaw's *Hymn to the Name of Jesus* takes up all but an introductory paragraph in Letter 15, and Letters 16 and 17 are the epistles between Jane Grey and Lord Guildford Dudley, first published here. Each of Rowe's last two volumes took longer to bring into print. More than half of four letters in the third volume are composed of her poetry, and she includes her translation of Tasso's story of Olinda and Sophronia (*Jerusalem*, bk. 2). There are very few quotations—one from Milton, one from Isaac Watts, and a few unidentified. Another seven of the twenty-two letters include some poetry. The final volume has the most poetry and includes a set of narrative poems, some of which are paraphrases of Michael Drayton's *Englands Historicall Epistles*. Among the significant poems are her *Pastoral: Henry and Lucy, On Happiness, Rosamund to Henry II, Penelope to Ulysses* from Ovid, and a translation of Tasso's *Enchanted Forest* (*Jerusalem*, bk. 18). Milton is quoted four times, and Pope and Addison once each. The majority of the letters in all four volumes tell a story, some continue a narrative through a series of letters, some grouped and some widely scattered in the manner of serial publication. In each volume, there are letters that are little philosophical lectures, but they always develop the character of the fictional writer or contribute to the dynamic between characters. Some themes and issues are constant through the volume, but there are also changes and developments in both content and style.

Rivka Swenson writes, "The patch-work, neither naive nor technically deficient, is a layered event in which boundaries between categories are elided." In a detailed working out of the structure of the Galesia trilogy, she finds an allegory of Jacobite history, a belief in the cyclical nature of history, and a carefully wrought structure to the fictions including movement through the seasons.[95] In many ways, "olio" is a better description of these texts because they discreetly add plenty of spice. Even Barker's recipes may carry political messages, as they come from various countries. "The *Czar's Receipt* to make *Punch*," for instance, begins, "Take Three Bottles from *Spain*, and one from *France*, / Two from the *Rhine*, and one from *Nance*," a concoction with as varied and competing sources as her description of her "Set of Ladies together." She casts them in political terms: "their *Sentiments* are as differently mix'd as the *Patches* in their Works: To wit, *Whigs* and *Tories*, *High-Church* and *Low-Church*, *Jacobites* and *Williamites*, and many more Distinctions."[96] Another recipe is from Castle Montgomery, Wales, which was destroyed in 1649 by parliamentary forces (144). Tapping into a nation with a tragic history and a castle that, like Galesia and Barker's family, had paid a drastic price for being Royalist, the recipe is for the modern kind of flummery, a sweet dish with milk and eggs rather than the older coagulated wheat flour or oatmeal. Suggestively, "flummery" could also mean "mere flattery or empty compliment" (*OED*), and it is served while musicians entertain the company with "wild Notes, in different Strains" (149). With a writer who enjoyed puns as much as Barker, this play with recipes is commentary. As Kathryn King says, these early fictions carried traces of the seventeenth-century romances and "as updated versions . . . they were in effect generically predisposed toward political commentary."[97] As she found, the more I worked with these fictions, the more political commentary emerged.

The women came to political cynicism and commentary from experience. As Swenson says of Barker, they presented not "verisimilitude realism, but the fragmented real."[98] Not only were their own lives broken up, even fragmented by the changing political fortunes of various groups, which influenced their view of reality, but their experience with political events taught them the power of print and especially the stakes in controlling interpretation. Davys was Anglo-Irish and at least once misrepresented her place of birth, Barker was a Jacobite Catholic who experienced the full consequences of "ruinous national events,"[99] and Rowe was a Nonconformist whose parents and husband had experienced serious discrimination. Politics was part of their lives, an unavoidable shaping influence. Experienced, remembered, bred in the bone—it was there. It is easier to find examples of it creeping in than texts uninflected by it. Barker, for instance, writes of "two large banners spread"

> On which heav'ns conquest were imbrodered [sic],
> For which those maids their due thanksgiving paid.
> And those who were the banners for that day,
> Were Sedge-more fight, and how Gray ran away.
> How the Kings guards, made there the Rebells bleed.

This poem, "The Virgins paradise / a dream," is referring to the Battle of Sedgemoor, where the Duke of Monmouth was defeated and Lord Grey of Warke was "easily routed."[100] The pirate in Penelope Aubin's *Life of Charlotta Du Pont* is an Irish nobleman driven to piracy by William III's Irish campaign.[101] Although sometimes the ideological darts are easy to miss, as with Rowe's poem on Lady Jane Grey, the child comforting his mother, or a father arguing that, should his son duel against his friend, he will betray "the *Protestant* Cause, the Rights and Liberties of human Nature" (*Friendship*, 65), as Kathryn King says, "many early novels came in encoded packages intended to convey their political tendency at a glance."[102]

The olio form allowed expressions of fierce partisanship in, among others, satiric portraits, textual frames, tragic stories, and allegorical characters and plots. Judgmental and often acerbic, they take up broader concerns than are usually recognized. *Familiar Letters*, for instance, begins with a couple's surprisingly vitriolic exchanges over politics and displays the potential of the epistolary form as it combines political partisanship and courtship. Set in George I's reign, Artander is an embittered Tory and Berina a Whig who is quite willing to rehearse the atrocities of the Irish rebellion.[103] Davys's novel finally includes a statement of loyalty to King George I by Artander and, given his strong Tory character, a strangely Whiggish view of vows: "no Man lies under a Necessity of keeping a Promise any longer than he has it in his power" (302). Berina's last letter is an endorsement of a patriarchal view of marriage, albeit one about which she expresses resistance, thereby creating what Toni Bowers has styled an "allegorical moment," for in the expression of these crossover beliefs and the possibility that Artander and Berina will marry is the reconciliation of Jacobite and Hanoverian partisans.[104] Probably written between 1716 and 1718, shortly after the Jacobite Rebellion of 1715, Davys asserts her loyalty to George I, as she had in the dedication to Princess Anne, granddaughter of the king, in *The Northern Heiress* (1716).[105] Rather than closure, however, Artander's and Berina's story ends with his hurrying to London to press her to marry him, while she continues to argue that he has broken his vow to maintain their relationship as a friendship. As allegory, then, this romance is true to its culture, one in which most major political issues were far from resolved.

While amatory fiction concentrates on couples, a major project for the patchworks is to depict alternative patterns for women's lives and, especially, to make the single life respectable. Within books that consistently show pressures to marry and the force of heteronormativity are dozens of counterstories.[106] Galesia is the best-known example of a character who does not marry—sometimes seeming to desire the "normality" of marriage, sometimes resisting it, sometimes embracing the single life, sometimes depicting herself as destined for the single life, she also tells numerous cautionary tales. Berina is clearly part of this narrative category, as are several of Rowe's characters. Tonya McArthur demonstrates that the monastic life is important in Barker's fictions and that convents were "an alternative to marriage and motherhood" and served "as spaces within which single and married women found fellowship and retreat, education and spiritual direction." This point needs to be generalized as it is an important alternative use of convents, which are usually treated by critics as if they were monolithic sexualized spaces from which women escaped.[107] In fact, as subsequent chapters in my book demonstrate, the trope of the retired, regular life became increasingly important in Rowe's and later fictions.

Carol Shiner Wilson sees Galesia's name as the feminine form of Galaesus, son of Apollo, god of poetry and medicine. If so, then Barker is underscoring the idea that destiny played a part in shaping the identities that Barker has Galesia assume. Berinda is even more resistant to marriage. The courtship letters take up the last quarter of the text and begin with Berina describing her dream: "I thought I saw *Artander* blind; and when I wou'd have led him, he pull'd out my Eyes too" (296). She mentions the pressures from being called an old maid but repeatedly associates marriage specifically with risk, blindness, and slavery. She tells Artander she will "make you happy against your own Will, and keep you in a State of Life, where Freedom and Liberty may be enjoy'd. Marry'd! that were to be both blind indeed" (302–3).

Her willingness to violate convention and write to him (discussed in the second letter) and her frequent, free discussions of politics go along with the contrast between the anecdotes she tells and Artander's. She tells the stories of the man who rejects the good woman over the coin (p. 80), of a "Maiden Lady of sixty-five, who has poison'd her self for Love," and of the dying gambler. Artander comes across as something of a figure of fun. He is tripped on the stairs by a woman's petticoat, slips on bacon and falls, and is ridiculed for his language. The anecdotes he tells, however, reveal his basic misogyny. The stories of the woman with the hoop skirt, the jealous women at the party, and the woman jilted at the altar are his. It is after he finds Delia, the woman who aroused envy in other women, equal to Berina that he begins to court her; his action, then, is part of the masculine world of competition and possession. He can read only one way, as he does with the woman who resisted marriage, "relishing," as Riley says, her humiliation at the altar,[108] while Berina is offended, "pitying" her, and perhaps recognizing reluctance like her own. In libertine literature, women who resisted marriage were universally depicted as flirts, jilts, hypocrites, and appropriate objects of punishment and conquest. Although most of the men in the anecdotes in the patchworks are not libertines, there still seems to be an ingrained, unquestioned "expectation that true masculinity almost requires the mistreatment of women to entrench the privilege of gender."[109]

Gildon's *Post-Man Robb'd* includes another common tactic, an epistolary, secret history, "The Lover's Sighs" which is thinly disguised commentary on George I.[110] As "King Alphonso the Wise," who has been "call'd to the Throne on the Death of the last Prince of a former Race," he does not "meet with so loving a People" as he had in his home country (157). This comment in the wake of the Jacobite Rebellion of 1715 is almost comical, and Gildon also writes that the king showed a less-than-wise "fondness" for his native country. The first letters are to the king from the miserable, discarded mistress Stremunia, perhaps intended to be Sophia Charlotte, Baroness von Kielmannsegge, created Countess of Darlington by George I; she was his half-sister but was frequently mistaken for a mistress.[111] In both of these texts, as in Rowe's and other olios, a clearly discernible, sometimes overt political ideology as infrastructure is one of the strongest unifying elements. It is not surprising that the actual characters are hard to identify. Swift, too, was exceptionally careful as he skims over the fact in the Drapier's Letters that it was the Duchess of Kendal, probably the king's wife by morganatic marriage, who sold the patent to manufacture copper coinage in Ireland to William Wood for a £10,000 profit.[112]

The open-endedness also underscores the last scars of political events and the unreconciled, unforgiven aftermaths. When Berina refers to the Irish rebellion, the full force of Davys's historical memory is applied to the novel's political theme. Berina's description is of genocide: "three hundred thousand Souls murder'd in cold Blood, . . . Mens Guts pull'd and ty'd to each other's Waists, . . . Children ripp'd out of their Mother's Womb, and thrown to the Dogs, or dash'd against the Stones; crying, *Nits will become Lice, destroy Root and Branch*" (272). The Irish Rebellion began in Ulster on 22 October 1641, started by Irish Catholics who feared the loss of property rights and religious freedom. By the 24th, a popular rebellion, undisciplined, unpredictable, and primarily bent on pillage, was underway. Many of these combatants were native tenants who had been forced to move to the higher, poorer lands while British tenants replaced them on the fertile plains.[113] Freezing and starvation became major causes of death among the Protestants they robbed and stripped of clothing. Ireland had a history of violent, bloody conflict laced with genocidal pronouncements, and, since the time of Henry II, experience with English policies of conquest and colonization.[114] The polarizing response to the rebels and their own interests led the Old English to join the Catholic side, and the conflict descended into extreme ethnic, religious violence.[115] The Catholics feared invasion, the Protestants feared massacre, and both expected persecution. Catholic clergymen, as Davys notes, were viciously killed, and women were targeted for allegedly inciting violence; as is common in genocidal conflict, children joined in and occasionally killed others.[116] The drowning of settlers at Portadown in November 1641 and the burning alive of people locked in a house by rebels led by a woman in early 1642 were the kinds of atrocities that fell outside accepted standards of the conduct of war and provided grist for the propaganda mills.[117]

Everyone, it seems, contributed to the escalation of the violence; priests made statements such as "that it was 'no sin to kill all the Protestants for they were all damned already.'"[118] As Bernard Capp writes, "The Irish massacre of 1641 sent a wave of horror through the British mainland, shocking future royalists and parliamentarians alike. Refugees flooded into England, and emotive narratives claimed that as many as 100,000 or even 200,000, had been slaughtered." Davys's figure of 300,000 was not unusual.[119] The English recovered Ireland and punished the rebels with, among other things, the Act of Satisfaction (1653), which completed the confiscation of property owned by all of the Catholics east of the Shannon River. Beginning in November 1641 and continuing for more than a decade, inflammatory, sensational propaganda written to justify causes and actions kept memories alive and probably supplied the 300,000 figure that Davys cites. Ole Peter Grell summarizes:

> The rebellion of Irish catholics in October 1641 and the accompanying atrocities committed against protestant settlers in Ulster are generally acknowledged to have exercised considerable influence over the political events leading up to the Civil War in England. Fears of invasion by marauding Irish catholics, and the suspicion that Charles I would use the rebellion as a pretext for raising an army against parliament were widespread in England. Some contemporary observers, such as Clarendon and Richard Baxter, considered the Irish massacre and rebellion crucial in precipitating the armed confrontation between king and parliment which followed.[120]

Other historians have demonstrated that the majority of the publications in England on the Irish rebellion "appeared to promote allegations of Irish atrocities."

The text that Davys summarizes draws upon the earlier literature that dwelled on the attack on pregnant women and infants and especially gruesome mutilations of men.[121]

The rebellion itself, the responses to it, and Davys's account underscore the centrality of religion to political conflict.[122] She also sees how events such as this are seized upon to keep alive the Tory/Whig, Jacobite/Hanoverian divisions. "There are thousands in this Nation who decry the Martyrdom of King *Charles*, more out of opposition to their Dissenting Brethren, than any real value they have for the Memory of that unhappy Prince," Berinda writes (273). She and Rowe lived in the same world. Feelings were still high when Davys's fiction came out in 1725; for instance, Jacobite protestors seriously damaged the equestrian statue of George in Grosvenor Square, London, in 1726, only two years before *Friendship in Death*.[123] Historians agree that it was not until the Jacobite Rebellion of 1745 that the Succession was settled, and women's concern with the Protestant Reformation was widely shared. They understood religio-political alliances as important parts of worldviews that determine the relationships among people, and, as Marta Kvande observes, "the assertion of a particular political identity was key to gaining access to critical debate." Or, I would less optimistically say, at least signaling that they wished to engage in a contemporary debate.[124]

An intriguing contradiction in early women's fiction is the representation of the fruitlessness—indeed, counterproductivity—of women characters' letters to their seducers versus the authors' apparent belief in the power of the letters produced in their collections. Many of the letters in the latter category are portrayed as being written by men, often powerful, wise, virtuous, or reformed men. Eusebius reasons energetically with his son in order to dissuade him from dueling: "The boasted Beauty and Charms of your Mistress, will be but a poor Excuse for your Gallantry, tho' you should tell them in *Heroics*" (*Friendship*, 63). Evander in Letter 6 of part 1 reasons with a libertine, comparing his enjoyments and prospects with the higher-class libertine's (*Letters*, 1:31–37). Some of the letters are highly didactic, and the satiric ones take the stance made familiar by Dryden's *Discourse Concerning the Original and Progress of Satire* (1693):

> 'Tis an Action of Virtue to make Examples of vicious Men. They may and ought to be upbraided with their Crimes and Follies: Both for their own amendment, if they are not yet incorrigible; and for the Terrour of others, to hinder them from falling into those Enormities, which they see are so severely punish'd, in the Persons of others: The first Reason was only an Excuse for Revenge: But this second is absolutely of a Poet's Office to perform.[125]

Although women note that it is their duty or "office" to write or collect such anecdotes, they also present themselves as educating or warning women about human nature, especially male mores and conduct. In Rowe's stories, both men and women play this role. In a rather sensational two-letter story, Clerimont comes back from the dead to warn Leonora about her licentious brother and the husband selected for her, the already-married Cassander. He tells her that she should fear men and run from them, not from spirits (*Friendship*, 36–42). Earla Wilputte says that Galesia sees her vengeance on Bosvill "as social justice, an act of heroism for her own sex, and a deterrent to those men who might follow her lover's behavior" (32). In a culture that did not punish what they saw as crimes against women, women writers devised punishments, as Rowe does when she ends stories with miserable men wandering the earth seeking peace of mind. Haywood's Melladore loses everything to the woman he has seduced and abandoned, and she lives in his former house (*City Jilt*); Davys's drunken husband finds his wife in bed with their lodger; Rowe's Lysander seduces Palanty, then finds out what love is with Cimene, and is racked with guilt when Palanty poisons herself and Cimene finds out (*Letters*, 2:54–58). Interestingly, some characters plan to fulfill their duty to society and women by writing the story; Galesia does, and a powerful example is in Haywood's *Invisible Spy*, a book that should be considered in the patchwork genre.

The olio or patchwork content overwrites the epistolary content of these books, including Rowe's. Regardless of the miscellaneous authors of the letters, themes and ideologies assure a sense of unified purpose and text. Matters of value, definitions of it, and mistaken, often fashionable, notions of it figure large in most patchwork novels and collectively challenge dominant structures of feeling. One of Davys's follows the biter-bit pattern usually included in the patchwork novels; it tells the story of the man who jilts a good-humored, attractive, sensible woman because her father included a brass coin in the dowry and marries a Miss Hoiden, "a thing fit for no Conversation above her Maid and Footman," because her dowry is "all *Sterling*" (289–90). As in many of Davys's stories, the moral is obvious but left for the reader to recognize the irony or the joke, and all of the women's fictions hammer away at blindness, stupidity, insensitivity, and lack of perspective, qualities that are usually depicted as inculcated by society at large or fashion. Several of Rowe's women are immersed in a life of fashionable clothes and pastimes, but their states of mind are boredom or vague dissatisfaction. Although some die in this state or succumb to vice, others are converted to the country life and find this state of mind seamlessly continuous with life in Heaven. The creative and moral energy in these patchworks has only begun to be recognized and analyzed, and Rowe has never been considered as their contemporary and their legatee.

The tamer, almost unnoticed stories in these texts actually bring to the fore that the authorial stance of writers of patchworks is usually of a single, independent woman, a fact that both reinforces and complicates their project of making the single life a respectable, acceptable lifestyle. Stance and stories, as I will argue later, move the novel toward incorporating women's friendships into novels as what Roulston calls "the fantasy of an elsewhere, of an alternative domestic narrative."[126] These stories add a dimension to a recurring portrayal in the olios, that men are not good at a lot of things that determine happy marriages—or lives. Roulston says that the female pairings suggest "that only women can do marriage properly," that in them are found all of the "qualities that the companionate model aspires to: mutuality, intimacy, affection, companionship, and later [my insertion] an absence of overt sexuality" (Roulston, 289). In one of Rowe's stories, two women live happily when the husband of one, a sea captain, is at home, and just as happily when they are alone together. In fact, Emma Donoghue has argued that the women in "The Unaccountable Wife" "are subverting this [patriarchal] economy and making its rewards meaningless."[127] Although Barker's couple is destitute, many of the pairings become successful socioeconomic units offering a model that often contrasts to the division of work, the man's paid and the woman's not, of the married couple.

Once Rowe's authorship was known, the stance of single, independent woman became one of the defining characteristics of the text. Her status and lifestyle were known to many of her readers, and, after the wide circulation of the life written to preface her *Miscellaneous Works*, it became context, serving the same function as the prefaces Cheryl Nixon discusses. She does not have to say what the other women did. For example, Davys's dedication to *Rake* reads, "I now set up for an Original, my Words and Thoughts are to be entirely my own, and I alone accountable for them" (239). Barker/Galesia foreground their single status, and, while Galesia may be bedraggled (her pockets are stuffed with ballads and scraps of verse), she is never economically desperate.[128] King notes that Barker is "a supremely self-regarding writer, mindful of her gendered singularity and fascinated with the many ways to tell her own story."[129] The preface was then and came to be an even more important place for the woman writer to carry out a complex authorial act that served her personally and professionally. Nixon explains,

> This marginal space encourages self-definition that blurs the distinction between author and character, fact and fiction, and text and pre-text. The formal strategies used to construct the character of the woman author within the preface are used to construct the female characters within the text and, it is implied, should be used by the reader to construct herself outside the text.

This three-part movement played a major part in locating the text along a continuum within the sex-gender system. Moreover, as Nixon demonstrates, the preface could actually be commentary on the text.[130] The fact that many writers identified themselves on subsequent texts as "the author of . . ." reinforced the work these prefatory sections did.

These fictions were innovative in almost every way. Never essentialist or obscuring the individuality of women and the differences in their material conditions, the texts reveal deep structures and a powerfully institutionalized patriarchy. Part of the modern world rather than set in the indeterminate pastoral or French-romance past, they featured intelligent, resolute, honest heroines who did not shy away from experience. Robert Adams Day says that Davys's *Familiar Letters* has correspondents "who manage to be witty instead of passionate";[131] he recognizes this as "a refreshing innovation," and, when we contemplate the number of imitations of *Five Love Letters from a Nun to a Cavalier*, we can see how Davys's text moved the prose fiction closer to the midcentury epistolary novel. Victoria Joule also points out the original aspects of *Familiar Letters* and argues that it is intended to be a model of male/female relationships. Berina, she notes, "is the rational, stable, and socially mobile woman" in contrast to Artander.[132] Rowe in authorial voice and in what the public knew of her life functions as Berina, producing both an entertaining, instructive text and the model of a centered woman resisting fads and temptations.

Rowe's participation in the experimentation with fictional forms was not backward looking. In 1969 Richetti observed that Rowe's exploitation of the conventions "is nothing less than a sign of the crucial transformation of fiction which takes place during the first four decades of the eighteenth century."[133] Her part in this transformation, however, has never been explored. Given the accessibility of Rowe's fictions and the number of allusions to her *Letters* throughout the century, it is a mystery why she is not regarded as an important, transitional figure between the writers of amatory fiction and the authors of the genteel novels of manners. The next chapters identify her revisionary contributions to the form beginning with qualities Samuel Johnson identified in her prose: "copiousness and luxuriance" and "brightness of imagery."[134]

CHAPTER TWO

Isles of Happiness

In the dedication to Edward Young, Rowe associated *Friendship in Death* with fairy tales: "The greatest Infidel must own, there is at least as much Probability in this Scheme, as in that of the FAIRY TALES, which however Visionary, are some of them Moral, and Entertaining."[1] Notably, subsequent volumes of her fiction picked up "Moral and Entertaining." Rowe meant a special kind of fairy tale, one now forgotten, but, I believe, an unrecognized influence on the eighteenth-century English novel. In 1690, Marie-Catherine Le Jumel de Barneville, Comtesse d'Aulnoy, published the first French *literary* fairy tale, coined the term *conte de fées*, and went on to write at least twenty-four more. Rowe read d'Aulnoy with pleasure and occasionally commented on her texts, as she did on *Le Comte de Warwick* when she told Hertford that "some beautiful parts of [the Countess of Warwick's] character" reminded her of Hertford (*Misc. Works*, 2:116). D'Aulnoy's carefully wrought tale "L'Île de la félicité," or "The Island of Happiness," was told by the hero in d'Aulnoy's first novel, *Histoire d'Hypolite, comte de Duglas* (1690), and it was quickly translated into English and published as *The History of Adolphus, Prince of Russia; and the Princess of Happiness With a Collection of Songs and Love-Verses. By Several Hands. To which is added, Two Letters in Verse from Sir. G.E. to the E. of M. with Mr. D.* [sic] *Answer to them* (1691).[2] As Nancy and Melvin Palmer write, d'Aulnoy's tales had none of Perrault's "lower-class characters and menial tasks, their poor cottages, their ugly clothes."[3] And she certainly never styled herself anything approximating "Mother Goose" as Perrault did.[4] *The Isle of Happiness* set the pattern for the literary fairy tale. It is longer than popular culture fairy tales, more complex, stylistically distinctive, highly intertextual, filled with plot twists, and was originally published as an interpolated, thematically enriching narrative.[5] Moreover, like Rowe's and Sarah Fielding's fairy tales, it is a "complex" tale, one contained in a larger text and not intended to stand alone. In addition to *Prince Adolphus*, eleven of d'Aulnoy's other tales were in her novels.[6] In France and England she was one of the most read writers in all three genres in which she excelled: novel, travel memoir, and fairy tale.

D'Aulnoy's fairy tales inaugurated a fad that quickly spread to England and paved the way by the end of the seventeenth century for something of a rage for the multiple collections of her fairy tales.[7] The popularity of her texts is truly arresting, and, although there were other *conteuses* (female fairy-tale writers), her unmatched popularity allows me to concentrate on her in this chapter. At least thirty-six editions of her work were published in England between 1691 and 1740, and her *Travels into Spain* required more editions than even *The Arabian Nights*.[8] *Les contes des fées* (4 vols., 1697; fourteen tales) and *Les contes nouveaux ou les fées à la mode* (4 vols., 1698; nine new tales) followed. The first volume of *Les contes des fées* was translated and published as *Tales of the Fairies* in 1699[9]; volumes 1 and 2 of it appeared in volume 4 of *The Diverting Works of the Countess d'Aunois* in 1707, providing a total of twenty tales, nine tales from *Contes des fées* and the rest from her novels. Volumes 3 and 4 of *Diverting Works* combined with volumes 1–4 of *Contes Nouveaux* appeared as *A Collection of Novels and Tales, written by that celebrated wit of France, the Countess d'Anois* (2 vols.) in 1721. It eliminated a few tales but brought together the fairy tales from the framing novels. A third volume came out in 1722, and they would be sold together as *A Collection of Novels and Tales of the Fairies, Written by the Celebrated Wit of France, the Countess D'Anois* as a three-volume set in 1728, the year that *Friendship in Death* first appeared. The first translation of *Hypolitus* came out in 1708, thereby providing a much better translation of *Isle of Happiness* (2nd edition, 1711). Numerous editions of her fairy tales, then, appeared before the publication of *Friendship in Death*. In fact, her fairy tales were more widely available than the six editions suggest. Several were interpolated in her novels, which were frequently reprinted, and the fairy tales were repeatedly published in different combinations; *The History of the Tales of the Fairies. Newly done from the French* (1716), for example, includes seven of the most artful, literary tales (*Graciosa and Percinet*, *The Blew Bird and Florina*, *The Golden Bough*, and *The Orange Tree and its Beloved Bee*, for instance). By 1799 there had been at least twenty-two English editions of d'Aulnoy's fairy tales.[10]

For decades scholars have identified sources, influences, and origins of the English novel, and studies by Ian Watt, William Warner, Lennard Davis, Jane Spencer, Michael McKeon, and J. Paul Hunter are especially familiar. Because they were available so early and reprinted so frequently in the period during which English women began to write novels, d'Aulnoy's fairy tales merit inclusion but have not been. Hunter, for instance, asserts that fairy tales "disappeared from the English public consciousness" and calls it a mystery. His emphasis is on what he calls "the old oral culture of the English countryside,"[11] but, as we know, the inherited fairy tales of cultures are blends of the oral and the newly written that flow together and would not survive without writing. Specialists in French literature have raised questions about the history of the English novel since at least 1974. That year the Palmers had mused, "One wonders if English fiction would have taken quite the form it did take had it not been for such *conteurs de féerie* as Mme d'Aulnoy, Mme de Murat, and their followers."[12] In an essay that argues that the country of a writer's birth is not the "sole determinant of national affiliation" and that the transnational nature of the eighteenth-century novel problematizes identifying an author, such as Samuel Richardson or Madame de Lafayette, with a single nation, Joan DeJean raises the question that I addressed, "Does [d'Aulnoy] . . . belong . . . to an extent worthy of some form of official recognition, to the English tradition of prose fiction?"[13] Anne Duggan points out that d'Aulnoy's tales and *Histoire d'Hypolite* were very popular between 1740 and 1770 and influenced Ann Radcliffe.[14] Like Beasley's and Richetti's speculations about Rowe's fictional influence, these hints about fairy tales were ignored.

How many and what kinds of fairy tales eighteenth-century English women wrote are yet unknown. A beginning survey locates them in every genre and with surprisingly prestigious, literary origins. The best-known fairy tales by an eighteenth-century woman are unquestionably the two embedded in Sarah Fielding's *The Governess* (1749), and this text has attracted specialists across a range of disciplines and national literatures. Writers like Rowe and Fielding lived in a culture with as much if not more knowledge of a literary history of fairy tales as of folk fairy tales. Edmund Spenser's *Faerie Queene* (1590), William Shakespeare's *Midsummer Night's Dream* (1600), and Ben Jonson's *Oberon, The Faery Prince* (a masque performed at court in 1611 and later printed) were among the best-known *English* sources of fairy literature. Two years before the publication of *Friendship in Death*, Jane Barker, who had lived in France, included a fairy tale as a dream in *The Lining of the Patch Work Screen*. Also earlier is Jane Wiseman Holt's *Sent with a pair of China Basons* (1717). It is a delightful poem with most of the favorite English portrayals of fairies:

> *Titania* Queen of Fairy-land
> Who Crowns the Dance and leads the Band,
> When o'er the Hills and Lawns they pass
> In wanton Circles on the Grass.[15]

Titania's favorite elves are banished to India by Oberon for mischievous pranks. They learn Eastern arts and produce the magic basins, which a mortal "In Honour of our Queen and Kind" can give to her dear friend: "Ten Thousand Graces let her Wear/ . . . /Who shall call this Bason hers" (13–14).

The literary fairy tales of the French feminists are an intriguing, neglected influence on British fairy tales and, in fact, on the mid-eighteenth-century English novel, one no one has taken seriously as an important strain flowing into the novel form. Rowe's *Friendship in Death* with *Letters* was an important conduit for adaptations of their sensibilities. She was publishing her later volumes at the very beginning of the third wave or vogue for fairy tales (1730–1758), the period Jean-Paul Sermain calls

"*Diversifications.*"[16] We now know that in spite of her retirement Rowe was attuned to happenings in London, perhaps especially literary events. There is some possibility that d'Aulnoy spent time in England, and the rapid translation and strong sales of her work led critics such as Joan DeJean to conclude that she "attained impressive status in England" and Victor Watson to say that most "well-read" women of the eighteenth-century were familiar with her tales.[17] As British women so often did with French literature, Rowe "englished" d'Aulnoy's fairy-tale style, making it appealing and appropriate in style, content, and fantasy. She included at least five fairy tales and numerous references to fairies in her fiction.

Influential critical voices praised the literary fairy tale, which had quickly become a recognizable genre. As knowledgeable modern critics argue, "The framework of fantasy is used to mediate fundamental truths or painful realities. . . . They are essentially adult stories using fantasy."[18] Jonathan Swift, for instance, wrote to Stella that he had been reading *Conte des fées* "for two days, although I have much business upon my hands."[19] Joseph Addison noted that "the Fairie way of Writing" was "more difficult than any other" and required "an Imagination naturally fruitful and superstitious."[20] His phrasing suggests that he knew that the *conteuses* referred to themselves in the salons as fairies or sibyls. Murat had dedicated her *Histoires sublimes et allégoriques* (1699) to "modern fairies," her friends the salon writers.[21] Fairy tales delighted his "Imagination with the Strangeness and Novelty of the Persons who are represented in them" (*Spectator*, 3:571), and literary precedents of fairy appearances from Shakespeare and Milton further gave legitimacy to Rowe's employment of them. As late as 1770, catalogues of very small libraries, public and private, included fairy tales and Rowe's *Letters*, as did that of Eliza Fletcher, daughter of a "yeoman farmer" in Yorkshire.[22]

The frontispiece to the 1716 English edition of d'Aulnoy's *History of the Tales of the Fairies* is dominated by the king and queen of hearts looking down upon a small circle of tiny dancing folk. Although probably not intended to be so, the proportions symbolize the literary fairy tales—they are about love, and fairies and magic often play small parts.[23] The tales relate the adventures and trials of a hero or heroine and, therefore, had many similarities to the brief tales in French romances but, as John Hawkesworth remarked in a 1752 essay on the pleasures of various genres, had the added attraction of new scenes and surprising possibilities.[24] The only author Hawkesworth mentions is d'Aulnoy as he expands upon the pleasures of fairy tales, contrasting them to the novel. He wrote that "the most extravagant, and yet perhaps the most generally pleasing of all literary performances, are those in which supernatural events are every moment produced by Genii and Fairies; such are . . . the Tales of the Countess d'Anois, and many others of the same class." Of the novel, he writes, "The narrative often stands still; the lovers compliment each other in tedious letters and set speeches, trivial circumstances are enumerated with a minute exactness, and the reader is wearied with . . . impertinent declamation."[25] Implicit in Hawkesworth's complaint are the inclusion of essays within novels and the kind of "dilated" conversations found in Defoe's *Religious Courtship* and Richardson's *Clarissa*.

I am categorizing fairy tale as many specialists do as "wonder tales" defined by their plot trajectory rather than the inclusion of fairies. Disguises, shape changing, and "magic" characterize the literary fairy tales as much as appearances by fairies, but the amount of these things varied tale by tale from none to being one of the most significant plot elements. Magic might be, among other things, an unlikely event, coincidence, or a sudden appearance. The characters' and, therefore, the readers' openness to "magic" possibilities was the real common denominator.[26] Polidore, the author of one of Rowe's *Letters*, hopes—as Hawkesworth says readers did when reading such tales—that a beautiful child he spies adorning a lamb with flowers is a fairy or "some pretty phantom" (3:203–4). The child's youth and beauty contrast with the gothic setting, and Polidore hopes for a pleasing encounter and adventure. Most commonly, the protagonist is driven away from home, experiences adventures and hardships, and is finally returned to his/her "just social, economic, and political position."[27] In stories like Cinderella and Pamela, the character's merit (ability, virtue) replaces birth or rank. The literary fairy tale is significantly different from the fairy tales we know today. Charles Perrault, whose *Histories of Past Times with Morals* (1697) was not published in translation until 1729 and the second edition not until 1737, has overshadowed d'Aulnoy and has come to be believed the more popular and, with the Grimm brothers' collections, to epitomize the genre.[28] This opinion needs correction and the differences recognized in their reception and "use" in the early eighteenth century in England. "Approximately two-thirds of the seventeenth-century *contes de fées* were written by the *conteuses*," and all over Europe women's work took up more than half of collections such as the forty-one-volume *Le Cabinet des fées*, a title that would have reminded most readers that Hypolite tells the tale of *Adolphus* in the abbess's cabinet (English "closet"; small, private room).[29]

We need to imagine the time before Perrault's versions triumphed and before they and abbreviated versions of the women's tales came to be widely sold in England as chapbooks and corrupt collections, as d'Aulnoy's were as *Mother Bunch's Fairy Tales* (1776 and many subsequent editions).[30] The third edition of Perrault's tales in English was not needed until 1741, and the seventh was not until 1796. Specialists are correcting history; Jack Zipes's anthology *Beauties, Beasts and Enchantment: Classic French Fairy Tales* (1989) prints ten of Perrault's and fifteen of d'Aulnoy's tales, giving them, respectively, 53 and 299 pages. D'Aulnoy is part of the history of the novel, and Perrault, although some of his tales are like d'Aulnoy's, found a place in the canon of what the British called nursery tales, the stories allegedly told by old women and nannies that terrified little children and lingered in the mind. As Hannah Cowley had the hero of one of her plays say, "The tales . . . that did awe / My infancy, all rush upon my mind, / And, spite of haughty reason, make it shrink."[31] In "Fairy Tales about Fairy Tales: Notes on Canon Formation," Elizabeth Harries describes the propagation of the nostalgic myth of fairy tales preserved from the oral with "the flavor and purity of the true folktale." She quotes critics who complain about the *conteuses*: "They made them so long, and the style so sophisticated, that children themselves would have been bored." The canon, she says, was built on what the Grimms wanted fairy tales to be: "simple, 'naive,' economical, a reflection of their ideas about the folk, and appropriate for the social education of children."[32] This conception of the genre is constantly reinforced now in Disney films and children's books. Jack Zipes points out that the Grimms may have omitted some tales because they were "too much within the French literary tradition or too commonly known as a literary tale to be considered a 'true' folk tale."[33] Either category would have worked against d'Aulnoy. Zipes describes Disney's *Puss in Boots* as "an attack on the literary tradition of the fairy tale" (190–91), a strong indication of the loss of favor for d'Aulnoy-style tales.

Many of d'Aulnoy's fairy tales were *literary* creations, and everything about them drew their readers into an elegant, magic world.[34] D'Aulnoy plays extravagantly with the marvelous. Lewis Seifert explains,

> In several respects, the marvelous employed by the *conte de fées* resembles that proposed by theoreticians of the *merveilleux chrétien*. Like the Christian epics, the vogue of fairy tales is a recognition and exploitation of a culturally specific type of marvelous. . . . Furthermore, both fairy-tale and Christian epic forms of the marvelous depict literal (rather than allegorical) supernatural characters and events. And in both cases, this emphatic use of the *merveilleux* strains and often transgresses the generally accepted bounds of *vraisemblance*.[35]

Seifert goes on to point out that, unlike the French fairy tales, Christian writers carefully contained their inclusion of the supernatural and concluded texts with verisimilitude. Rowe's character Rosalinda writes of the magic of staying awake when all of "the calm creation seems lull'd in a peaceful slumber; except elves and fairies" (3:127). She relates how the dairy maids and other servants have led her to fairy circles, and her reaction is in line with the connection Seifert makes: "I am no great infidel, some times I believe, and *always wish* the pretty stories they tell me were true; but I dare not object against any of those relations, for fear of being thought a heathen by the whole village" (3:127, emphasis mine). In her own letters, she had written to Hertford, "If there are fairies, (as I am not such an infidel as to deny) they are certainly very happy beings, and possess'd of a great many privileges which unhappy mortals want" (*Misc. Works*, 2:69). An interesting analysis of the appeal of Young's *Night Thoughts* suggests an affinity with Rowe's sensibility and the style of some of d'Aulnoy's tales. John Louis Kind describes Young's *Night Thoughts* as having "the chaotic preponderance of the imagination, and the implicit acceptance of the mysterious and marvellous."[36] Comparisons of motifs make the contrasts between kinds of tales stark, as Harries demonstrates with Perrault's "Cendrillon" and d'Aulnoy's "Finette Cendron" ("The Story of Finetta the Cinder-Girl"). She points out d'Aulnoy's much greater development of psychological interest, telling use of contemporary detail, and elaborate descriptions intended to be enjoyed for themselves as well as for what they reveal about character.[37] An obvious difference is the treatment of women. Perrault's Little Red Riding Hood climbs into bed naked with the wolf, the moral at the end styles all men wolves, and, as Elizabeth Marshall says, "Perrault's victim possesses a female body responsible for its own violation."[38]

The first English publication of *The History of Adolphus, Prince of Russia; and the princess of happiness* was styled as "By a person of quality," and the title page associated it with love poetry and wit. With *Adolphus*, this book, actually a collection, included poems by the youthful George Granville, who was already known for his courtship poems to the mythical Myra; John Howe, one of the best-known rakes in Charles II's court; and Aphra Behn, as well as a poetic exchange between the playwright George Etherege and the Earl of Mulgrave with John Dryden's "Answer."[39] Two of the poems by Behn came from papers she left at her death, one continuing a lover's *Dialogue for the Entertainment at Court*, and the four others from *The Lover's Watch: Or the Art of Making Love*, a set of letters describing the experience of romantic love, one for each of the twenty-four hours in a day, from Iris in the country to Damon at court.[40] They include *Advice for a Lover, On a Lover beginning to Love*, and *On Jealousy*. The obviously coterie translation included references to other playwrights, including Nathaniel Lee, and witty jokes typical of their circle enlivened the translation, as when the narrator remarks that the mother of winds "(like all other old Women) was not to be interrupted" (7). Highlighting the coterie nature of the collection are Edmund Waller's response to one of Granville's poems; a witty six-line tribute to Behn comparing her to Diana, Cybell, and Pallas Athene by Granville; and libertine freedoms with d'Aulnoy's text, such as Zephyr's description of his time with the Princess: "I peep . . . under a Petticoat, I see all, and I feel all, I please my self where I will, and with what I will" (11). Published as an elegant folio as well as an octavo edition and sold "near" Stationers Hall, its prestigious presentation associated it with a line of high-culture fairy stories such as *Faerie Queene* and *Midsummer Night's Dream* and with the fairy poetry enjoyed at the French court.[41] It is also an example of the fairy tales as pallets for the imagination and continued coterie participation.

Rowe's Fairy Tales

The plot of *Isle of Happiness* is leisurely and each section carefully elaborated. Prince Adolphus of Russia (then an exotic, intriguing country) becomes lost on a hunting chase and is caught in a violent night storm. He takes refuge in the cave of Eolus, God of the Winds. Zephyrus, the West Wind, describes the Island of Happiness from which he has just returned and agrees to take the prince there. Adolphus and the princess are charmed with each other and live an idyllic life together "inebrietated [*sic*] with Pleasures" (190). However, after a magic three hundred years in the princess's kingdom, he feels he must attempt to fulfill his ambition to "perform great Actions" and attain fame.[42] The princess tries to dissuade him but finally gives him a magic horse and warns him not to dismount; Time, however, disguises himself as a poor driver trapped by his overturned cart. When the prince dismounts to help him, Time springs up and beats him to death. Zephyrus brings his body back to the princess's grotto. She closes her gates forever, and her story teaches the world that happiness is impossible because of *man*kind's ambition and restlessness (195–96).

The sharp contrast between the prince's and the princess's sense of time and value are part of the narration, but they come fully to attention in the tragic conclusion. At the beginning, after falling asleep from fatigue on the island, the prince awakens, "much vex'd he had lost so much time in vain" (186), and, after discovering he has been on the island for three hundred years, he exclaims, "How must the World stand by this time?" "Who will know me?" "My Dominions are, doubtless, fal'n into the Hands of some strange Family?" She asks a profound question: "What is it you repine at?" (191). Expressing the values of earth, he responds, "I should perhaps have perform'd such great Actions as would have render'd my Name famous for ever to Posterity; I can't without shame, see my Courage to lie dormant, and my Name buried in Oblivion" (192). The princess reasons with him and cries, but he "could not forbear upbraiding himself for having spent so much time with a Mistress without any thing that might raise his Name among the Rank of the Great Heroes" (192). He finally uses the argument that several of d'Aulnoy's heroes do, that "Glorious

Actions" will make him more worthy of her (193). Condemnation of ambition is common in the century, and the women's tales associate it with masculinity. Hertford's Inkle is strikingly similar to the Prince:

> Reflecting now upon the time he past,
> Deep melancholy all his thoughts o'ercast,
> *"Was it for this,* said he, *I cross'd the Main*
> *Only a doating Virgin's heart to gain?*
> *I needed not for such a prize to roam,*
> *There are a thousand doating maids at home.*[43]

He sells Yarico, raising the price when he discovers she is pregnant, for investment capital. Crass ambition has consumed Rowe's Philander, who has attained a "splendid post in the government" and always been successful in work and love. "Ambition took full possession of my soul," he writes to his friend. He has lost his happiness and his ability to enjoy both nature and society. As for Adolphus, ambition seems the road to destruction, but an illness and a retreat save Philander. Finding a natural paradise of uncultivated woods and meadows, he also finds God and contentment. The letter ends with a poem praising God: "I hear him, I perceive him all around; / In nature's lovely and unblemish'd face, / With joy, his sacred lineaments I trace" (*Letters*, 1:59–64).

Most fairy tales manipulate senses of time and depend upon readers' imaginations to fill in the experiences during periods when time stands still. Some sections have elaborate detail in setting and plot. The prince's bravery, his struggle at the beginning of the tale to find shelter after becoming lost in the forest, his introduction into the cave, and the discourse styles of the winds and their grandmother are as elaborate as the core of the tale. The grandmother calls Zephyrus "you little Libertine," and Zephyrus describes how he "play'd all round about [the princess], and I now and then gently lifted up her Veil" (180–81). Similarly, the thoughts and movements of Rowe's characters are traced in detail, but then, just as with the prince and princess, periods of peace and happiness pass in a few sentences. Some of Rowe's characters' virtuous decisions are hard-won and sometimes won again in the face of repeated temptation, but the formulaic nature of the physical movement and the readers' familiarity with, for instance, a long, arduous walk down poor roads allows the compression of parts of the narrative.

Settings in the fairy tales always include exterior and interior scenes that are luxurious, elegant, and, above all, aesthetic. The first description of the garden includes beautiful sounds and scents as well as sights, and the palace walls are of diamonds with precious stones for wainscoting. The tale assumes readers' familiarity with Apuleius's story of Psyche and with Tasso's of Armida, whom the princess resembles (in *Jerusalem Delivered*). Notably, like d'Aulnoy's *Adolphus*, both of these were interpolated tales. She also builds in prefigurings that in retrospect or second reading become clear and give pleasure to the reader. A song the prince hears has the refrain "Time brings every thing to pass" and a line promising, "if your cruel Destiny shortens your happy Moments, you must hope for fair Weather" (187). The moral at the end is "Time brings every thing to pass, and that there is no Felicity in its full Persec[u]tion" (196). It has allegorical resonance, as Zephyrus tells the prince before he takes him to the Island of Happiness: "tho' every one goes in quest of it; for such is the Fate of Mankind, that they are not able to find it out . . . and some flatter themselves to be there, because they are cast sometimes into some neighbouring Ports, where they enjoy the Fruits of Calm and Tranquillity" (181). In the male mind, immortality comes from great deeds worthy of being recorded in history; in the princess's world, they already have immortality.

Fairy tales obviously create an alternate world, but for the women who write them they become an elsewhere, a place of freedom from the limitations of imposed gender identity, conduct, and even thought. Throughout her life, Rowe enjoyed imagining various kinds of other worlds, often with considerable material detail. Some in fiction and personal letters are pastoral, while others stretch into the realm of pure imagination. For instance, Junius in *Friendship in Death* reports that "the unlimited Creator had made and peopled millions of glorious Worlds" and that they are enchanted, making fables and fairy scenes "real" (16–17). A letter Elizabeth Montagu once wrote to Elizabeth Carter captures the concept of elsewhere: "My imagination . . . oft mounts aloft, rises into the Regions of pure space, & without lett or impedement bears me to your fireside, where you set me in your easy chair, & we talk and reason . . . of high and important matters."[44] Arabella in Brooke's *The History of Emily Montague* refers to Canada as fairy ground and describes it as this kind of elsewhere: "I am delighted with the idea of revisiting dear England . . . : yet I feel a regret, which I had no idea I should have felt, at leaving the scenes of a thousand past pleasures; the murmuring rivulets to which Emily and I have sat listening, the sweet woods where I have walked with my little circle of friends."[45]

By contrasting these elsewhere spaces to the ordinary world and the society in which they lived and by peopling them with like-minded individuals, these authors created islands—islands of happiness and freedom. When d'Aulnoy and Rowe create such conversations on the isles of happiness, they never provide specific dialogue but rather a fantasy of perfect harmony and communication. They allow characters and readers to glide smoothly from the world they know to the utopia of freedom, communication, and perfect harmony. A. S. Byatt wrote, "My own fairy stories are written primarily for the pleasure of entering that other world, a world of imaginary apples and forest paths, greener and darker than any encountered in everyday life, a world of powerful beasts and satisfactory endings."[46] Fairy tales like these give permission for kinds of stories and endings that join women's fictions in imagining alternate worlds but in less threatening, perhaps more liberating ways. One fairy tale explained, "Fairy Land is neither a continent nor an island; and yet is both, or either; it exists in the air, at the distance of about five feet and a half or six feet at most from the surface of this earth which we inhabit; and is of all other countries the most agreeable." Like Rowe's spirits, "the inhabitants of this country frequently condescend to visit mortals," and, as with Heaven, "whenever any man can so far divest himself of the gross incumbrance of human nature, as to take a flight to these sublime regions, he is sure to meet with an agreeable reception."[47]

As in many fairy tales, contentment, virtue, and harmony with a beautiful setting contrast to city and court lifestyles and ambitions. Men are admitted into a woman's magic world of tranquillity, erudition, and beauty. The rhythm is replicated in d'Aulnoy's and Rowe's stories. Narration gives way to a sense of time standing still, of contentment and yet of anticipation, and then the magic suspension of time gives way to the imposition of ordinary time. Time, selfhood, and then love become intertwined thematic interests. Adolphus says, "When I consult my Heart, and think of the satisfaction I feel within my self, I am almost apt to believe, I have not been here above a Week" (191). "Satisfaction . . . within my self"—alone or in company, Rowe's characters, too, experience this suspension of time and restraint.

When Hypolitus tells his tale, he chooses one "not unlike one of the old Tales of the Fairesses" (176), "un conte approchant de ceux des Fées," and he is trying to gain admission to a convent, a female world. Because of his tale, he succeeds, and he and Julie have months of tranquil happiness. Similarly, in the tale, Prince Adolphus enters the princess's kingdom and, temporarily, her state of mind. In the happy fairy tales, this is the norm, as Rowe's will demonstrate. The prince is charming, eloquent, and, as time passes, shares his education with her. Bakhtin insisted that the test of a hero was his discourse, and in some of the tales and especially in the frames for them, d'Aulnoy applies this standard.[48] Her narratives were part of an aristocratic culture, and when characters like Hypolitus are judged worthy and given free access to the community as he is by his tale, d'Aulnoy is positioning her tales by this Bakhtinian standard and, of course, within the social and literary values of her circle.

Among Rowe's true fairy tales are the stories of Rosalinda, of Bellamour and Melissa, of Melinda, and of Silviana. Although Hertford may have collaborated with Rowe throughout the *Letters*, the Bellamour story is believed to have been written by her. "Six Letters from Laura to Aurelia" concludes the last volume and brings together with the themes of the earlier tales. Robert Adams Day rightly argues that it turns "the miscellany of short stories in letters . . . another way."[49] As is typical of the second-wave fairy tales, folkloric borrowings and styles are rarely deployed, and the genre has moved decidedly away from the *romans héroique* that strongly marks many of d'Aulnoy's tales. A wide variety of literary devices, including satire, parody, and realism, are used in stories that are far more heterogeneous in content and function.[50] Interestingly, the first developed fairy tale begins with the last letter in *Letters on Various Occasions*, the book that would become the first volume of *Letters Moral and Entertaining*. Of all the tales, this one has both the most magic detail and the most economic specificity, both defining characteristics of fairy tales. It has added interest because it is collaborative and contributes to our understanding of how women writers worked.

Hertford seems to have suspected that Rowe was the author of *Friendship in Death*, but Rowe would not admit it. When her authorship was known, Hertford felt betrayed and even refused to accept letters from her. The outcome of the reconciliation was the more collaborative first volume of *Letters. To which is Added Ten Letters by Another Hand* (1729).[51] Prefacing these ten letters are eight "Letters to Cleora," the ones revised from Rowe's actual letters to Hertford. The final ten have been, therefore, attributed to Hertford, including the beginning of the story of Bellamour and the cultured ladies. The first part of this story, the letter with the description of the house and the ladies' occupations, is probably collaborative with rather than by Hertford, and the second part, the one about money, is attributed to Hertford by Bigold. Single authorship of eighteenth-century texts has always seemed overstated to me, and I believe the letter collaborative. Their story ends the volume, and readers' curiosity is not satisfied until the conclusion in the middle of the second part of *Letters*.

In this collaborative fairy tale, although Bellamour is on his own property, he comes upon "the most beautiful valley imaginable" and in it an unknown cottage whose interior is in complete contrast to its unimposing exterior. As is typical in the literary tales, Rowe lingers over descriptions. Bellamour has difficulty descending a steep hill, finds a beautiful plain, names the trees, and follows a river before reaching the neat little house with its open wicket (*Letters*, 1:131–33). Since he assumes that no "persons of distinction" live there, he just walks in—all the way upstairs, where he opens a door and finds a mother reading to two beautiful daughters who are wearing white and embroidering flowers on white silk. In a suggestive parallel, Prince Adolphus uses a magic cloak that makes him invisible to gain access to Princess Felicity's private apartments in d'Aulnoy's *Isle of Happiness*. He walks through them admiring the rooms and groups of nymphs and their music. The house in Rowe's fiction is a magic kingdom filled with cultural articles, such as a harpsichord, globes and folios of maps, fine furniture, and books on topics such as history, divinity, travel, and opera music. Basins of flowers contribute to an ambiance that leads him to observe, "I began to fancy my self in an enchanted habitation" (*Letters*, 1:134).

Improbably, the family is neither angry nor frightened at the intrusion; in contrast, the princess mistakes Adolphus for a beautiful bird, a kind that would make a "glorious Shew" like peacocks in her garden (189). Although men can be threatening in Rowe's stories, in d'Aulnoy's they often seem almost of a different species. Over several letters scattered in volumes 2 and 3 Rowe's stories of the sisters Rosella and Melissa and the gentle men who love and respect them unfold. In many ways Bellamour's story is an archetypal fairy tale. Fathers are often problems, especially where money is concerned. They are either greedy and likely to rush into marriage, as in d'Aulnoy's "The Tale of *Graciosa*, and Prince *Percinet*," or, as in this story, irresponsible and profligate. Rosella's and Melissa's father died in debt, and his family refused to help the widow and children. The exemplary widow, Honoria, has paid the debts and lives frugally but beautifully. Thus, like many of the damsels in fairy tales, they are distressed and appear of a lower class than any prince (like Bellamour) who may appear. Moreover, Honoria refuses to let Rosella marry Alphonso because he is of a lower class and from a "wicked" family. In amatory tales, fathers tend to be the obstacles, but in fairy tales, as in this story, mothers and stepmothers often take this narrative place while fathers are neglectful, immature, or exercise bad judgment.

Bellamour cannot forget Melissa, although her dowry is only £3000, and he has £4000 per year and is "in the gayest bloom of life" (*Letters*, 2:68–69). Four years later, he decides to propose, to give her dowry to her mother, and to settle on Melissa £1000 per year rent-charge for her life "in case she should survive me" (2:69). In the meantime, Alphonso has inherited fortunes from his penitent father and a clergyman, and he and Rosella marry. From the clergyman he received "his estate, which was about an hundred and eighty pounds a year; and two thousand pounds in Money; which, added to about two hundred and fifty pounds a year, and some money which his father left him, makes their fortune very easy" (2:71–72). Although emphasis is usually on the happily-ever-after union, fairy tales just as consistently end with the sudden acquisition of over-the-top wealth. The symbolic adoption by the clergyman compensates for the "wicked family," and a magic, happy ending results for both men and the daughters.

In collected volumes of d'Aulnoy's tales, the stories were continued from volume to volume, as they are in *The History of the New Gentleman-Citizen* in *A Collection of Novels and Tales of the Fairies* (3 vols., 1728). Highly intertextual, as d'Aulnoy's were, Rowe includes references to Henry Glapthorne's *Argalus and Parthenia* (1639), a Neoplatonic, pastoral play based on an episode in Sidney's *Arcadia*; to Paris disguised as a shepherd on Mount Ida (then married to a nymph); to Pope's *Messiah*; to various poems by Milton; and to *Count Gabilis* (1680), the English translation of *Comte De Gabalis* (1670), the highly popular collection of five discourses between the count and a priest by Abbé Nicolas-Pierre-Henri de Montfaucon de Villars (it has been described as reading like a fairy tale, and one discourse is styled in the 1714 English edition as "An Account of the Rosicrucian Doctrine of Spirits, *viz. Sylphs, Salamanders, Gnomes*, and *Demons*").[52] With its persecuted, disguised heroine and romantic, improbably happy ending, it is also highly imitative of fairy tales. Rowe's story of Rosalinda is also told over several letters and in two different volumes of *Letters*. Letter 2 in the third part is attributed largely to Hertford by Bigold. Rosalinda runs away from the father who would marry her to "a bigoted Papist" and becomes an upper servant.[53] She trades her brocades, jewels, and "fine China on an Indian cabinet" for "flowers in my bosom" and helping her mistress arrange "a set of Delft dishes on a free-stone chimney-piece" (*Letters*, 2:12–13). The mistress treats Rosalinda like a sister as they chat and decorate the house, and her only work is with her needle in "some verdant retreat." She encounters a "gentle youth" in an "Arcadian" setting reading *Pastor Fido*: "you would believe him some poetical form: he is so elegant, so beautiful" (2:8). This tale is also economically specific. This "prince" is from a noble family, one "remarkable for heroes and beauties," but his extravagant ancestors have reduced the estate to a mere two to three hundred pounds a year.

The "Arcadian" or pastoral settings do not confine the characters to a mythic past but enhance both the aesthetic and spiritual elements that constitute the harmony of the created lifestyle. Hers is a powerful, revisionary use of these heavily allusive, respected value-carriers to reinforce an ideology. A letter from a physician illustrates the effect of the blending of elements. The writer describes himself as in a "visionary temper":

> I had wander'd about a mile from the Earl of *****'s gardens and park, 'till I enter'd a winding valley, green and flowery as the *Elysian* fields; a silver stream ran murmuring along the middle, and willows in equal order adorn'd the banks: It was not perfect nature, something of art appear'd. . . . I . . . lost myself in a pleasing contemplation, 'till the sight of the most charming object I ever beheld, surpriz'd me: She seem'd
> > Fairer than feign'd of old, or fabled since,
> > Of fairy-damsels, met in forest wide. —Milton
>
> Her shape and features were perfectly regular. . . . But I might as well paint virtue or harmony, as describe the graces of her mein and aspect. . . . She advanc'd 'till

she came near the arbour that conceal'd me, and then seating herself on the bank of the river, in a pensive posture, leaning her cheek on her hand, white as the new fallen snow, with a soft and graceful accent, she repeated . . . lines out of *Sir Richard Blackmore*'s fine poem on the creation. . . .

. . . a spruce footman came to tell her supper was ready, and her father waited for her: She rose immediately, and follow'd the man. (*Letters*, 1:66–67)

In this magic scene, the setting, the appearance of the beautiful woman, quotations from elite poetry referring to other worlds, and his sensibility, which colors and transmits the encounter, turn her into a damsel from a fairy tale. She actualizes the blend of the aesthetic, spiritual, and pastoral that creates the aura and ambiance of this idealized state of mind and lifestyle.

As is common, the forest and nature provide a place of enchantment and re-enchantment. As Sylvia Bowerbank remarks, "The view of nature which predominated in the West down to the eve of the Scientific Revolution was that of an enchanted world. Rocks, trees, rivers, and clouds were all seen as wondrous, alive, and human beings felt at home in this environment. The cosmos, in short, was a place of belonging." She continues by describing the longing for re-enchantment, for reformulating harmony,[54] and as Rowe creates fairy tales she actualizes a means of re-enchantment. She uses the same technique for some of the descriptions of Heaven. In the second letter in *Friendship in Death*, Alamont celebrates Heaven as "this fair, this fragrant, this enchanting Land" with "delectable Vales and flow'ry Lawns, the Myrtle Shades and rosy Bowers, the bright Cascades and chrystal Rivulets rolling over orient Pearls and Sands of Gold . . . they break with rapid Force through arching Rocks of Diamond and Purple Amethist" (7–8). The gradual introduction of crystal, pearls, gold, diamonds, and amethysts is clever and acts to transmit the reader from lawns and bowers to the aesthetics of Heaven, to make the worlds inseparable and continuous. Peter Walmsley refers to such scenes as "intensified pastoral" that make Heaven "imaginatively available."[55]

As John Brewer says, "aestheticizing nature and finding personal solace in rural life" created a countryside that "could be a place of arcadian rest, . . . the home of social harmony . . . , a site of aesthetic pleasure, or a place in which to realize oneself through confronting 'nature.'"[56] Again, the elements of pastoral, nature, self-realization, sensibility, and aesthetics are an inseparable blend. Rowe is an early transmitter of what came to be an understanding of sensibility as an amalgamation. As Hannah More explains,

Sweet Sensibility! thou keen delight!
Thou hasty moral! sudden sense of right!

Thou untaught goodness! Virtue's precious seed!
Thou sweet precursor of the gen'rous deed!
Beauty's quick relish! Reason's radiant morn.[57]

As in fairyland, this is a world where sensuous pleasure, all the pleasures of the senses, is honored. The countryside as "pastoralized aesthetic object" is critical to creating this effect.[58] In turn, this leads to release of greater sensibility in the characters, a characteristic of d'Aulnoy's tales with pastoral elements, which critics say have protagonists with more sensibility and also more devotion to virtue.[59] As Margaret Doody notes, the fairy world is associated with water and air, "those two elusive elements"[60] and the elements most associated with God and with life. Rosalinda describes the setting of the farmhouse as bringing together "Mr. *Thomson's* Spring and Summer Seasons" in one "enchanting prospect," and, as with Philander, she finds the nature of God revealed in the setting. Once married, she describes the prospect on one side of the country house: "I fancy myself in Fairy-land; it looks all like the effect of enchantment, and beyond human contrivance" (*Letters*, 3:134). A cultured, educated woman, she spontaneously recites part of Milton's *Morning Hymn* in Italian (*Letters*, 2:7 from *Paradise Lost*, book 5, lines 153–56), and one of the letters closes with a poem she is portrayed as composing, *A Pastoral. Henry and Lucy*, a skillful dialogue in heroic couplets. Intertextuality is essential to the setting and creates the register. She gives us what McKeon has styled the lasting pastoral preoccupation: "the dream of a direct apprehension of nature" *and* an awareness that she is giving us an imaginative composition of nature and humankind dwelling in it.[61]

Addison wrote, "In Courts and Cities we are entertained with the Works of Men, in the Country with those of God" (*Spectator*, 23 August 1712, 4:143–44). Michael McKeon has argued that pastoral "works both to affirm and to suspend such oppositions" and says that most poets of the eighteenth century "self-consciously determined to disclose the underlying 'reality' of the contemporary English countryside."[62] Rowe might have agreed with Addison, and the kinds of economics McKeon brings to the surface are present in her fairy tales. However, she embraces the artifice of pastoral aesthetic fairy tale, and her purpose is to suspend time. Pastoral becomes an ambiance suffusing settings not usually apprehended as pastoral. Because she found harmony and even identification among Heaven, beautiful settings, and the tranquil, virtuous life, she occasionally has characters create strikingly aesthetic settings in woman-centered homes. The stands holding basins of flowers, the decorated mantels, musical instruments, and polished tables create a signature ambiance of beauty and order. Such scenes are knitted from Rowe's own life and aesthetic. Honored by a visit from Hertford, Rowe wrote of the preparations, "If you don't come in a very little while there will be no laurels nor holly-oaks left in the country, for my waiting-gentlewoman has ingross'd them all to adorn her chimneys. . . . There is a cupola and arch'd windows."[63]

D'Aulnoy creates palace after palace composed of or encrusted with carbuncles, diamonds, and semi-precious stones; when Rowe writes a similar scene with the same stones, her referent is the Bible, as to Isaiah 54:11–12 ("Behold, I will lay thy stones with fair colors, / And lay thy foundations with sapphires. / And I will make thy windows of agates, / And thy gates of carbuncles"). As early as the fifth letter in *Friendship*, Rowe establishes a continuity between fairyland and the "millions of glorious Worlds" God made before the earth. Junius pauses in his "Tour of the Skies" and describes one of these worlds: "Whatever you have heard fabled of Fairy Scenes, of vocal Groves, and Palaces rising to Magick Sounds, is all real here" (17). In both cases, sumptuousness in such magnitude with these sources bestows a kind of authority and prestige on the texts and their authors. As Duggan demonstrated, an important relationship existed between the French fairy tales and opera, and tales including d'Aulnoy's *The Fair One with Golden Locks* (*La belle aux cheveux d'or*) and her uses of images associated with Versailles replicated the atmosphere of opera.[64] Rowe's Rosalinda describes herself "as fine as any shepherdess in an *Opera*" (2:8). The White Cat's court offers theater, carousels, hunting, fireworks, ballet, and music as entertainment. The high-culture aesthetic survives in the ballet of *Blue Bird* made famous by Ballets Russes, John Ashbery's "elegantly translated" *The Story of the White Cat*, and Errol Le Cain's 1979 illustrations for *The Story of the White Cat*, described by David Blamires as "subtle in colouring, varied in mood and elegantly composed."[65]

Fiction of the first half of the century usually depicted true love with sexual attraction, as well as intellectual and temperamental harmony. Rowe's tale includes the scene in which Rosalinda gazes on the sleeping Lucius, an echo of the scene in which Psyche spies upon her sleeping monster husband and discovers Cupid, a scene repeated in several of d'Aulnoy's fairy tales.[66] Rowe's narrative progresses to a representation of complete compatibility, the kind the princess and Adolphus had on the Isle. Rosalinda describes their "delicacy of thought," modest reserve, and innocent delight in each other's company. After marriage, they enjoy books, the beautiful gardens, charitable works, and evening prayers. Throughout these six letters, Rowe maintains the milieu of fairy tales. Rosalinda writes to her friends, "If he is, as you flatter me, some bright inhabitant of the air . . ." (*Letters*, 2:11). In spite of the concreteness of his fortune, there is always something magic about her unexpected encounters with him and about his person conveyed in phrases such as "inhabitant of the air" and "one of Count *Gabalis's Sylphs*," perhaps evidence of her reading d'Aulnoy. Then he inherits an additional £6,000 a year and a "noble seat." Once married, Rosalinda continues to drift around the gardens, ornamenting the estate as it provides a beautiful setting for her, while her husband's grandmother manages the stately home. In true fairy-tale style, he has believed her beneath him in rank, but she is an earl's daughter and the rightful heir to £80,000. She hears that her father is pleased with her noble marriage and hopes for reconciliation. The "Papist" father, the escaping daughter, her disguised life, and the happy ending with augmented wealth are the conventions of fairy tales.

Specific economic details, while characteristic of the tales, are important bridges to the real world. Rosalinda tells us how Lucius budgets his annual income and includes the fact that she is given £1,000 pin money. In spite of his enormous wealth, Lucius, not a steward, is described as paying "his bills once a month with great exactness" (*Letters*, 3:134, misnumbered in text). Bordering on the ludicrous, this episode teaches a kind of middle-class morality in that the concern is for "honest tradesmen." Rowe is one of the first fiction writers to use the magic restorative of money from a returning merchant. This repair of fortune and status is a modern conversion of the kinds of restoration found in d'Aulnoy's *Fair One with Golden Locks* (by accidental poisoning of a king) and *The Story of the White Cat* (she owns enough kingdoms to provide one for everyone). Karen Rowe has identified the fact that in the fairy tales we know best, women gain wealth and status only through marriage, which she sees as reinforcing the subordination of women. D'Aulnoy's and Rowe's tales are obvious exceptions, and Rowe has her heroines gain wealth in a variety of ways. That alone is liberating—they have it, inherit it, or marry it, and some have quite original twists. In the fairy tale of Melinda, the heroine has lost her money in the South Sea Bubble. Tired of living in her brother's raucous house, she goes to work disguised as a servant. She had fallen in love with a man she saw at the theatre, but, because of "the scandal of the house" where she lived with her brother, he would not court her. He has become a rich East India merchant and married the woman for whom she works; they recognize each other. He has become a model benefactor, and his flame for her has died. He finally goes to her, tells her that he admires her escape from the licentious place in which she was living, gives her £10,000 in bank bills, and returns to sea. The wife invites Melinda to stay with her, and she gratefully accepts. The happy ending to this story, then, is the restoration of Melinda's fortune and a union of two women of harmonious temper and cultivated minds.

In a kind of Cinderella story, Silviana, daughter of a country clergyman with a "sprightly temper," inherits £20,000 from an uncle who had been a Turkey merchant (*Letters*, 3:168–76). Before that, she has left her sisters to help her mother and spends her time with Lady Worthy's youngest daughter reading plays and novels. The advance in fortune leads to an invitation to be painted as a nymph in Lady Worthy's history painting. This picture attracts Lord ——, and they marry. Silviana is a typical heroine in that she is an avid reader and refers easily to classical literature, in this case Ovid's Oenone, a nymph on Mount Ida. Silviana's story comes near the end of volume 3, and the voice is more distinctive. It includes a pastoral interlude and some of the best satire in the *Letters*. Moreover, the tale's subject is the contrast between her happy life, unmarried and married, in the country and her "illustrious bondage" in the city. In contrast, Laura, the last heroine in the text, misses the city and begs her correspondent Aurelia to tell her everything "the dear, bewitching, busy world is doing" (*Letters*, 3:223).

Rowe had remarked in her dedication that "there is at least as much Probability in this Scheme [letters from the dead to the living], as in that of the Fairy Tales, which however Visionary, are some of them Moral, and Entertaining." Adding the word "visionary" to the standard invocation of moral (instruction) and entertaining (delight) connoted both "imaginative" and "prophetic." Therefore, at the time, it fit both the fairy tales and Rowe's fictions, especially as they developed in the next three volumes of her *Letters*. Rowe carries over the allusion to fairy tales from her dedication into the first letter in *Friendship in Death*. In it the Earl of R— is "singing an Idle Song you had got out of the FAIRY TALES," perhaps "Time brings everything to pass" from *Adolphus*.[67] Rowe establishes the mode of fairy tales with the evening setting and the mood of the earl, who enters the garden "with a careless incredulous Air." Rather than being an unbeliever or skeptic, he has an "air" of being so. The narrator remarks tartly, "By the Gayety of your Temper you seem'd pleas'd, my Lord, with a new Proof against a Future Life, and happy to find yourself (as you concluded) on a level with the Beasts that perish" (2). Rowe contrasts him (and beasts) to those who already believe or can be "impressed" with "the Notion of the Soul's Immortality," thereby illustrating the goals of her dedication and preface again within the tale. As in Rosalinda's humoring the dairy maids, there is no tension between the possibility of fairies and the reality of spirits. In Letter 5, Junius describes the many worlds "the Creator" had "peopled," and the description is highly similar to many of d'Aulnoy's scenes unfolding before her travelers:

> Whatever you have heard fabled of Fairy Scenes, of vocal Groves, and Palaces rising to Magick Sounds, is all real here. . . . I have in an Instant seen Palaces ascend to a majestic Height, sparkling as the Stars, and transparent as the unclouded

Æther. I might describe them like the courtly Prophet; *Their Walls were fair Colours, their Foundation Saphire, the Windows of Agate, and the Gates of Carbuncle.* (*Friendship in Death*, 17)

On the Isle of Happiness, the castle walls are diamond, and the princess's throne is made of a single carbuncle stone, "brighter than the Sun itself" (188). The gates to d'Aulnoy's White Cat's palace are gold covered with carbuncles, and precious stones encrust the walls in both palaces (*The Story of the White Cat*). In other tales in the twenty letters in *Friendship in Death*, fairyland is described, and one spirit assumes the shape of a fairy in an attempt not to scare a mortal (35). Perhaps following Rowe, Eliza Tuite creates a sylph, "a mortal once," as the voice and guiding spirit of her five poems "Written as a Sylph to a Young Lady." The sylph begins by hoping that her shape will prevent raising "in thy mind involuntary fears" of a creature returned from the dead.

There was much in d'Aulnoy's work that harmonizes with Rowe's and her circle's opinion about literature, aesthetics, and the use of time. D'Aulnoy would later publish three volumes of her devotional meditations and two paraphrases of Psalms, both genres in which Rowe published.[68] Even Tasso's *Jerusalem Delivered*, from which d'Aulnoy drew ideas, was a favorite with Rowe. Among Rowe's poems translating or adapting Tasso's are *The Story of Erminia. Translated from the seventh Book of Tasso's Jerusalem*, *The Beginning of the Fourth Book of Tasso's Jerusalem*, *A Description of the enchanted palace and garden of Armida* (from the sixteenth book), *The Description of the Drought* (from the thirteenth book), and another part of the thirteenth book. Robert Adams Day has argued the important influence of d'Aulnoy's *Ingenious and Diverting Letters* (1692) for epistolary fiction such as Rowe's. Day calls d'Aulnoy's one of the most popular models, describes the miscellaneous content, and identifies some of the texts "based on" it.[69]

Just as d'Aulnoy's fairy tales were highly original and filled with surprising plots, events, and conclusions, Rowe's show her confidence and liberty with the form. She uses them for both grim and magic purposes. The little child whom Polidore discovers and hopes is a fairy or phantom turns out to be the daughter, the absolute image, of Aurelia, a ruined woman who had this child by her best friend's husband. Most of the references to fairies are unlike this one. The earl's song is one of several other allusions to fairy literature as part of the fashionable knowledge of the *ton*.[70] More commonly, Rowe refers to fairies as an enjoyable, imaginative part of bucolic settings. Rosalinda describes the early morning as the domain of elves and fairies and her husband's seat as so exquisite that she fancies herself in "Fairy-land" (3:134). She says that a nurse in the family is "intimately acquainted . . . with these sprightly phantoms" and has led her to the beautiful circles where they dance. The dairy maids in the family also insist they have seen them, too, and Rosalinda concludes, "Some times I believe, and always wish the pretty stories they tell me were true" (3:127, 134). Her characters are open to such experiences and to finding fairy circles, as, for a moment, Laura in the last story in the collection believes she has (*Letters*, 3:235). Rowe provides these small, imaginative moments in a number of tales to please her readers but always privileges the rational, as gothic writers would later convert supernatural horror into explanations derived from human actions.[71]

The Fairy Way of Writing

Rowe's fairy tales had influential differences from the amatory narratives written between 1685 and 1730. Although that true fairy tales almost invariably have happy endings seems like a minor detail, this fact empowered different themes and outcomes in Rowe's fictions. Both kinds of fiction often begin with a heroine who is threatened by an authority figure and either immediately or later by a seducing or highly unattractive suitor. The restrictions and limitations on women's actions, and therefore on the realization of their selfhoods, by fathers, brothers, and husbands is conventional. This is an important theme in d'Aulnoy's tales and, in fact, is the plot of *Hypolitus*, in which Julie disguises herself as a lower-class woman and then a male pilgrim. Rowe's Rosalinda and Melinda disguise themselves as lower-class women, and all of her heroines are threatened by evil or inadequate authority figures. By sabotaging attempts to situate the women by their rank, the disguised characters commit acts of anti-authoritarianism that oppose patriarchal praxis.

Amatory fiction sets up situations in which the powerless must outwit established authority, but the conclusions tend to prove that the women are, indeed, largely powerless. In contrast, in fairy tales the powerless escape or triumph over authority, as children, the poor, and the scorned do in the New Testament. In d'Aulnoy's and Rowe's tales the women are courageous, daring, highly intelligent, and manage to establish power over themselves and others. D'Aulnoy's Belle-Etoile, for instance, dresses as a knight, captures the green bird, and rescues her brothers, Chéri, and three hundred knights who have been frozen into statues shelved in crystal niches (*The Story of the Princess Fair-Star, and Prince Chery*). All of Rowe's heroines are good and arrestingly beautiful, but she does not use the hierarchy of beauty to which feminists have objected[72] to signal a hierarchy of virtue. Balancing the emphasis on beauty is that in fairy tales heroines take the initiative and never relinquish at least some degree of control over their destinies. Even Perrault's Cinderella thinks of using a rat for a coachman and goes to check the trap. D'Aulnoy's Belle-Belle goes to fight in her aged father's place (*The Story of Fortunio, Belle-Belle, ou le Chevalier Fortuné* in *The History of the New Gentleman-Citizen*).

This courage and daring is frequently displayed in the kinds of calculated violations of convention that Jane Austen often portrayed. As Marina Warner says, "Fairy tale is essentially a moralizing form, often in deep disguise and often running against the grain of commonplace ethics."[73] Rowe's heroines often violate the expectations the culture had for women and, like Austen's Elizabeth Bennett, offer an alternative ethics. The moralistic Laura, for instance, defends and befriends Charlotte, the young girl her brother has brought to the country as his mistress. "Indeed she has no other refuge," Laura explains, and she keeps Charlotte in her own apartment in the country house. Many women are generous, powerful, wise, and display self-possessed calm, as Rowe's Laura and d'Aulnoy's White Cat do. The sea captain's wife confronted by a woman her husband admits to have once loved is another such example.

The number of women who escape repressive situations, situations that threaten their selfhood and moral aspirations, through disguise is striking. D'Aulnoy's tend to be more dramatic. Aimée in *The Orange Tree and its Beloved Bee* hunts and feeds her cousin Aimé; she defeats Tourmentine while Aimé, who has been turned into the tree, is helpless. Women characters tend to remain active and courted; Aimé says his flowers can give her pleasure, and she chooses to enter one. Rowe's Laura persuades her brother to release Charlotte and Charlotte's uncle to take her in, both feats considered impossible at the beginning of the sequence of letters. D'Aulnoy's Belle-Belle becomes a knight and restores a king's lost wealth; many of the tales by all of the women interrogate class and gender. Belle-Belle, for instance, is the only one of her father's three daughters who can pass as a knight because "social identity . . . [in] a gender-specific occupation is determined not only by appearances but also by actions."[74] Rowe's heroines are determined, daring, and resourceful. When these women are placed beside the heroines of other kinds of tales in which women go into solitary retreat, the degree to which they maintain autonomy and preservation of a lifestyle—interior and social—puts them in a special category. It is clear that Rowe's theme of independence is more central in her work than in fiction by other women writers before and contemporaneous with her.

At this point I want to look at three original and influential ways that Rowe developed this theme. First, she asserts the individual rights of her heroines. Some critics of the French fairy tales have gone so far as to call the princesses "selfish," and in them and Rowe's heroines there is an unapologetic dedication to a multifaceted self-preservation. The novelists before Rowe depicted truly destitute women who struggled for food and shelter, and Ruth Perry has demonstrated the lingering importance of this theme in *Novel Relations*. Some were wanderers, actually genteel beggars, in foreign countries as Aubin's *Count Vinevil* and Haywood's *Rash Resolve* portray. Others were like some of Rowe's minor characters such as Charlotte and Aurelia, "ruined," disowned, and driven to sin if not crime for sustenance as Defoe's Moll Flanders was. In harmony with the fairy-tale ambiance, the emphasis is not on the economic problem and the wandering. A variety of people help women find safe harbors, as a relation of her Protestant mother does Rosalinda and a former nurse-maid does Melinda. What Day says about d'Aulnoy's *Histoire* might be said about numerous midcentury novels, including such well-known novels as Haywood's *Miss Betsy Thoughtless*: as wives, they become submissive, "constantly preoccupied with her reputation in the eyes of the world and with her duty to the institution of marriage, which takes no account of the character of the husband or of the treatment that as a wife she receives. Consequently, duty, *le devoir*, becomes a leitmotif of the text and we detect a growing apart, on the moral plane, of the lovers."[75]

This pattern is decidedly not true in Rowe's tales, and she consistently argues that the woman's first responsibility is to herself. Instead, what Hannon says of d'Aulnoy and her fairy-tale heroines is a better fit. They "forsake at once the conjugal house and the domesticated sensuality so widely evoked in the prescriptive literature on the nature of women." D'Aulnoy's "fabulous geographies forego husband, children, family, state, and even women's celebrated chastity, in favor of a body in constant motion." The mobile, domestic body changes into speaking and reasoning, as d'Aulnoy's do into speaking and reasoning animals. "Aulnoy's enchanted bodies become a theater for self-discovery as well as a conduit for knowledge. Because the world is explored and thus known through the ever-changing body, the latter plays an active role in the quest for knowledge and truth."[76] In a less dramatic way, Rowe's women are "ever-changing" and mobile; aristocratic daughter, disguised servants, subject of a history painting, leisured wife—roles, activities, and clothing shift. Silviana, for instance, is one day sitting as one of Diana's virgin nymphs, then in a simple dress with her hair falling in its natural curls, and then adorned with fashionable clothes, jewelry, and an immense "head."

The women characters are protecting their virtue, of course, but they also believe that they have the right to think, believe, and live with integrity. Rosalinda writes *even after her marriage*, "My hours are here at my own disposal, nor am I obliged to devote them to ceremony or vain amusements. I find myself under no necessity to court the impertinent or flatter the ambitious, nor to do a thousand unreasonable things" (3:129). One of the most original features of d'Aulnoy's and Rowe's fairy tales are the ways women are able to audition men for roles in their lives. Even d'Aulnoy's more violent and folkloric fairy tales turn on the heroine's observing and testing her suitors. A letter from Rowe's Albanus, which he says was intended to be a love letter, says that his lady has transformed him "from a libertine [to] regular and consistent; from a lover, you have metamorphos'd me into a reasonable creature" (1:87). Silviana, for instance, takes her time getting to know the lord in spite of being infatuated with him. "After I knew my Lord's character," she writes, "I had a sort of vanity in owning a sense of his merit." That he spends a month after marriage in her home where "the scenes of low life were a diverting novelty to him" is further proof of his acceptability (*Letters*, 3:172). In a time when women writers were using the conclusions of prose fictions to demonstrate the implications of social practices and to emphasize that there were no satisfactory solutions to numerous situations, the fairy tale offered a fantasy of happy endings and a starkly contrasting world. In this world, women are too strong to be seduced and men are tested, sometimes at length. D'Aulnoy's White Cat negotiates her marriage and guarantees her own dowry. As Michèle Farrell observes, she "acts as her own ambassador to represent her own desire," and a consistent feature of d'Aulnoy's "heroines is that they actively engage in the shaping of their destiny."[77]

Both Hypolitus and Adolphus must be accepted in a female space. Although the tests in fairy tales are sometimes reminiscent of trials of classical heroes, they are often based on things that have special meaning for the heroines and, therefore, are signs of understanding and compatibility. In *The Fair One with Golden Locks*, for instance, Avenant is sent to recover a beloved ring she lost in a river. Alphonso in Rowe's story told by Bellamour is exiled, and his two-year virtuous life is the test that leads to marriage. He and Rosella will live in her home with her mother, and Melissa in the same story must be convinced that Bellamour's home is close enough to her mother's. Thus, the cultured, feminocentric world is preserved intact and the men are admitted on the women's terms. When sophisticated kinds of compatibility are established, the woman admits the man into her life, and, more significantly, preserves her lifestyle, as Rosalinda does. If such harmony is not discovered, no union results. Rowe has Rosalinda describe the feeling of love as "something more than the tenderness of friendship, and less than the warmth and violence of passion; and seems like the dictates of guiltless nature" (*Letters*, 2:11). For Rowe's women, as for the princess who compares Adolphus to peacocks to adorn a garden, the men they love are aesthetic objects. Their bodies are attractive and often repeatedly described, an effective way to incorporate the physical, sexual attraction the century advised for happy, lasting love.

Obviously, the fact that the women choose highlights the importance to women's happiness of compatibility, inclination, and an affective dimension. Good fortune, virtue, and the appearance of an unusually sensitive hero bring about happy endings for the virtuous heroine whom circumstances have made miserable. In "Graciosa and Percinet," a representative tale that can be related to Rowe's stories, the virtuous, beautiful princess's father, dazzled by a monstrous woman's wealth, remarries and puts his daughter under her control. Graciosa, like the other fairy-tale heroines, is highly intelligent and has been tutored by "Learned Persons, who taught her all manner of Sciences [meaning "knowledge"]."[78] Significantly, trials imposed on Graciosa are passed on to Percinet, and Graciosa tests him in a variety of unusual ways. Respect and social forms are of prime importance. After Percinet keeps her from being flayed alive, she thanks him but asks him to leave "because she had often been told, that it was not decent for young Virgins to be alone with young Men." He leaves. After each rescue, they discuss proper behavior, and she tells him that she wants time to confirm that he loves her "with a perfect Affection."[79]

Some of the women have already developed what might be called a lifestyle and personal philosophy, but as Rowe continued to write stories in this vein she increasingly depicts women developing them, as Laura does in the final series. She also shows the struggle to retain them in various settings as Silviana does when she is moved to London. Autonomy is of central importance. Rosalinda notes that her mistress allows her to choose her employment, and, in scenes of her minding the children, it is clear she is without supervision or instructions (2:5–7). Silviana is an especially interesting case as she represents the struggle for the kind of self-preservation Rowe is developing even as she attempts to conform to the expectations of a husband she loves. Rowe shows her bargaining to be allowed to read while her hairdresser spends two hours concocting an enormous "head" "with flowers, feathers, and bits of ribbon" (3:175). Silviana is "inclined to cry" and deeply regrets the loss of her "harmless freedom." Her tales define and illustrate a new, "accomplished" woman whose private and social conduct is a civilizing model that becomes normative because it posits that such women have attained woman's "natural" nature.

In the construction of the minds of the women, Rowe includes varying amounts of explicit religion. It is more exact to say that it is an important part of the constructed consciousness rather than the *raison d'etre* of the story. The *mise en abyme* so integral to the French fairy tales develops into a philosophy that seems to anticipate Martin Heidegger's concept of dwelling. "To dwell, to be set at peace, means to remain at peace within the free, the preserve, the free sphere that safeguards each thing in its essence. . . . 'on the earth' already means 'under the sky.' Both of these *also* mean 'remaining before the divinities' and include a 'belonging to men's being with one another.'"[80] In the course of her tales, Rowe comes to portray and advocate this state of being. Rosalinda expresses it, and Laura slowly and somewhat painfully develops it. One of the most original of her characters, Laura opens her story with a riff:

> My brother brought me here to see a country seat he has lately purchased: He would fain persuade me 'tis finely situated; but I should think it more finely situated in the *Mall*, or even in *Cheapside*. . . . Indeed I hardly know where we are, only that it is at a dreadful distance from the theatre royal in *Drury-Lane*, from the opera, from the masquerade. . . .
>
> . . . we are certainly at the ends of the earth, on the borders of the continent, the limits of the habitable globe, under the polar star, among wild people and savages . . . nor could I forbear asking my brother, if we were to travel by dry land to the *Antipodes*. . . .
>
> The Country is my aversion, I hate trees and hedges, steep hills, and silent valleys . . . the smell of violets gives me the hystericks; fresh air murders me. (*Letters*, 3:224).

Later she says that she has "grown fond of the country, and have acquired a relish for its harmless delights: I can . . . listen with great attention to a purling stream" (3:234). The descriptions of nature in this series mingle more artifice and uncultivated nature. The hermit has created an arbor of flowers "twisted together with a sort of elegant disorder" on a mound with turf steps and has hung gilt cages of singing birds on the lower branches of elm trees. In the last scene, Rowe anticipates Heidegger's conception, as Laura goes to a retreat "where art and luxurious nature displayed their various beauties" and "Nature seemed animated with a conscious joy" (*Letters*, 3:249).

This letter brings Rowe's four volumes of prose full circle, as Philocles appears and speaks to her. The harmony between people, between Laura and nature, between art and nature, and between this world and the eternal is complete, somehow natural and evolved. Again, there are parallels to d'Aulnoy's work; Hannon argues that her "metamorphosed characters seem to look back towards a pre-Cartesian worldview wherein the boundaries between self and universe, human and natural, are less clearly drawn."[81] In various ways, both writers collapse the boundaries between humankind and nature and between spaces.

Another somewhat unexpected effect is the license this harmony gives to sensuality. The feel of a breeze on skin, the sounds of birds, and the smell of flowers such as jasmine, woodbine, and roses noted for their rich aroma bring Rowe's characters great pleasure and a sense of being part of the natural world. One of the richest sensual descriptions in d'Aulnoy's tales is of fruit delivered by the fairies to the queen in

The Story of the White Cat: "abricots, pêches pavis, brugnons, cerises, prunes, poires, bigarreaux, melons, muscats, pommes, oranges, citrons, groseilles, fraises, framboises. . . ."[82] This technique of making lists and piling up natural images underscores the beauty and bounty of the earth but also the sensuality of the women.

The second influential way in which Rowe developed the theme of independence is that she does not insist on heterosexual love as the basis of happiness and marriage as closure. Another means of encouraging a sense of personal autonomy that flies in the face of the strong social constraints of the time is the fact that the women are not reintegrated into the family or social structure at the conclusions. In spite of Rosalinda's father's change of heart because of her favorable marriage, no reconciliation is described in the narrative. Even in these few tales, the conclusions inscribe several possibilities for the happy life. Melinda finds a home with the sea captain's wife; Laura seems committed at least temporarily to a single life with her primary commitment to "refined and enlarged" "notions of happiness" (*Letters*, 3:251). Rosalinda's and Melissa's marriages are parallel to d'Aulnoy's *The Story of the Pidgeon and the Dove* (Le *Pigeon et la colombe*), which ends with the couple choosing to remain as pigeon and dove free to live in beautiful solitude and avoid the duties of the court.

The explorations of abuses of power and a woman's need to regard men warily come together in marriage plots in Rowe's fiction. The forced marriage becomes a major plot device that portrays an actual threat to women and often symbolizes tyrannical exercise of power, as Rosalinda's story does. Years before this was a major theme in the novel, d'Aulnoy had written as the moral to *The Blue Bird*, "Doubtless the Old Sow did not understand that kind of marriage becomes deadly slavery if love doesn't shape it. . . . In my view, it's much better to be a Blue Bird, a Crow, even become an Owl, rather than undergo the death sentence of always having what one hates before one's eyes. Our times are fertile ground for these kinds of unions." Zipes translates one line as "Too many matches of this sort I've seen."[83] This concern became a more prominent theme, and its lingering representation of destructive power can be seen in three novels published around 1750, Richardson's *Clarissa*, Charlotte Lennox's *History of Harriot Stuart*, and Haywood's *History of Betsy Thoughtless*. These novels often pitted Scriptures against each other, which leaves the heroine in an impossible situation: "Honour thy father and thy mother that thy days may be long" (Exod. 20:12; Clarissa's certainly were not) versus "Be not unequally yoked" (2 Cor. 6:14). In contrast, Rowe's Rosalinda runs away from her father's "Papist" choice of husband and cites "He that loves father or mother more than me, is not worthy of me" (2:16, Matt. 10:37). As for Clarissa, the threat is to her immortal soul, but Rowe expresses a strong Protestant sentiment, one shared by most Nonconformists who had welcomed William, and then writes a happy fairy-tale ending. In contrast,

Richardson draws the two ideologies as extremes leading to inevitable tragedy. The conflict between individual and community and the demand for sacrifices for family/community were major issues as individualism grew and became increasingly important themes in the novel. Richardson's Clarissa, for instance, is expected to sacrifice herself for her family's advancement and dies for her individualism. Richardson's linking of Clarissa's stance to religion somewhat aligns his novel with the thinking of Nonconformists like Rowe.

Marriage serves as conclusion to most French women's fairy tales, but Rowe's stories are aimed at a different kind of establishment of identity and the closure that comes from it. A striking difference, and Rowe's third influential innovation, is that d'Aulnoy's characters are almost invariably reintegrated in their cultures while Rowe's are not. Several characters never marry, the primary signal of absorption into community in the fiction of the time. Only Silviana is moved back to London and the society from which the other women characters have come. Her story clearly casts doubts on the ideology of male-female complementarity and the staying power even of romantic marriages even as it sketches the more serious threat to Silviana's integrity and peace of mind. The obverse of Laura's conversion to the tranquil, carefully guarded life, Silviana pits her love against the threats all around her in high life.

In the fairy tales, material improvement is as important as marriage in the conclusions' portrayal of the idea of "present illusions of happiness to come." Although Rowe can sometimes refer to immense, almost unimaginable wealth as she does in Rosalinda's story, she always adds a vision of an autonomous, satisfying lifestyle. Like the *conteuses*, she comes to "provide social paradigms that overlap nearly perfectly with daydreams of a better life."[84] The tales are actually composed of two inextricably bound narratives, one the story's plot and the other the unfolding of the mind of (usually) the heroine, who can imagine the "daydreams of a better life." She is, of course, working toward solving the immediate dilemma in which she finds herself, but also toward a "permanent" solution, the achievement of a lifestyle that expresses an established identity and state of mind. Even in the short tales by Rowe, such as that of the two young women discovered by Bellamour, the state of the women's minds, their precautions and desires, are given. Thus, the narrative is as Patricia Hannon describes the fairy tales: "marked by the disruption of sequential narrative through self-reflexive amplifications."[85] In Rowe's stories, these two purposes are seamlessly woven together, inseparable because of the drive of the plot.

The goal in these fairy tales is the establishment of a lifestyle, one at least harmonious if not originally created by the heroine. What Jean-Paul Sermain says of the French literary fairy tale in comparison to French novels such as *La Princesse de Clèves* (1678) is true of Rowe's: "C'est en analysant les choix littéraires propres au conte classique que nous cherchons à caractériser et à comprendre son imaginaire et une vision du monde originale que les autres genres de fiction ne sauraient exprimer."[86] While recognizing that fairy tales are closer to romance and other older forms of fantasy, Hunter notes, "Fairy tales not only contract the scope of romance; they also domesticate its problems and intensify its psychological reach—in some ways very much as the novel would go on to do." Although he discusses folk fairy tales only and seems to have no knowledge of the French women's tales, what he says describes the step toward the midcentury novel that Rowe's tales are. He continues, "Fairy tales address the real world even if they do not altogether grapple with it; they are not among the species of escape literature, in spite of the elements of miracle ... and happy ending."[87]

Rowe addresses most of the problems and situations faced by women in the stories of the women writers of the 1720s, but one marked contrast is that she omits or elides the implications and sometimes prolonged suffering of women entrapped by a tyrannical father or husband or suddenly impoverished and on their own. Her heroines are not maimed as Aubin's are; women are not married to rapists as Davys's are, fighting feelings of freakishness as Barker's are, or experiencing the "resolutions" in Haywood's fiction, as exemplified by *The British Recluse* and *The Rash Resolve*. Hunter notes that, among others, oral narratives were characterized by "alertness to crucial life choices," "awareness of the individual's need to cope with cultural expectations," "willingness to portray major problems and (at least sometimes) allow satisfying solutions, and an interest in events that are strange, surprising, and sometimes inexplicable." He speculates that the novel, which "picks up where they leave off," inevitably and necessarily had "to address some of the needs that had been met by the lost tradition."[88] Traditions, however, are never lost; we just temporarily lose our ability to follow the thread, as students of the English novel have with the work of the *conteuses*.

Women and the Fairy-Tale Mode

As this section will show, Margaret Doody did not go far enough when she wrote, "Women poets often write about elves and fairies. Some of them got quite good at it." Doody went on, "Percy told Hester Lynch Thrale Piozzi that in her (unacted) verse drama *The Two Fountains* she had written better about fairies than anyone since Shakespeare."[89] As this reference to a play indicates, women included fairies in all genres. At this point, I want to survey some of the fairy writing that women did after Rowe.

The two fairy tales in Sarah Fielding's *The Governess* illustrate both the character and uses of fairy tales and also the ambivalence and growing perception of what the term meant. Both tales are read by Miss Jenny Peace, the exemplary oldest pupil at the little private school. The first is the folkloric story of sweet, little Mignon, who is the captive of an evil giant that is everything an evil giant should be. Through luck and the giant's carelessness, Mignon is able to escape, paralyze the giant, and liberate the giant's captives, thereby uniting the lovers Fidus and Amata, who happens to be his sister. Significantly, Mignon is more active and set on rescuing himself and others than the good giant, Benefico. The lesson, then, is an empowering one for the small and weak. In fact, a major moral drawn from the tale by the girls is that "*Mignon*, in the Moment that he was patiently submitting to his Sufferings, found a Method of relieving himself from them, and of overcoming a barbarous Monster, who had so cruelly abused him" (86). The second, which is twice as long as "Mignon," is very much like d'Aulnoy's tales. It is interrupted several times, thereby emphasizing the frame narrative as d'Aulnoy did in *The Gentleman-Citizen*. "The Princess Hebe" tells the story of the good queen and Hebe driven from the kingdom by the jealous, evil sister-in-law. Rescued by the good fairy, Sybella, they live safely and happily in a cottage in the woods. Sybella has been victimized and exiled by her evil sister, Brunetta. As in so many fairy tales, the father has married badly, and the evil comes about through the scheming, jealous, power-mad wife. Like Aimée in d'Aulnoy's *The Orange Tree and its Beloved Bee*, Sybella has a magic wand, which she uses for good and to rescue herself and others. After seven years of peace, in an incident similar to the old man Time tricking Adolphus, an old man tricks Sybella into going on a quest with him. Hebe is immediately tempted by a series of Brunetta's shepherdesses and is finally tricked into giving aid to a shepherdess who drags her to Brunetta's castle. Many of the trappings of d'Aulnoy's and Rowe's stories are included.[90] Sybella's setting has "many small green Meadows, with little Rivulets running thro' them, . . . the Banks of which, covered with Primroses and Violets."[91] Brunetta's castle "glittered," "sweet Music was heard in every Room," and the courtiers "omitted nothing that could amuse and delight the Senses" (136). Sybella finally rescues Hebe, and the death of the sister-in-law allows Hebe to assume her rightful throne.

Just as the community of schoolgirls is almost totally lacking in contact with men, this tale is remarkable in that, as Harries says, "it is almost exclusively a story about women."[92] This fact allows explorations of topics such as the roots of female rivalry and calls to duty outside conventional gendered life. The feminocentric tale includes the self-reflexive parallel narrative developed by d'Aulnoy and replicated by Rowe, as Hebe comes of age, develops a sense of her limits and powers, and appreciates, first, the joys of her retired life and then the duty she has to accept the crown and do good for others. Two years before *The Governess*, Fielding published

"A Fragment of a Fairy Tale" in *Familiar Letters between the Principal Characters in David Simple* (1747). This "fragment" is an important apprentice piece for the fairy tales in *The Governess* and a very good piece in its own right. A princess is on a journey to the Castle of Wishes with her dwarf and faithful servant Rosetta when she loses her way. She takes refuge with an old woman who, as an infant, at her mother's request has been given the power by a fairy to receive instantly anything for which she wishes. This power causes her nothing but unhappiness, yet she asks the fairy to renew it when it expires. Granted for one additional year as a trial, she experiences more misery. Her story is a cautionary tale to the princess, and the moral is repeated a few times: "so blind are Mankind to their own real Happiness, that it is oftner to the Gratification than the Disappointment of their Wishes that all their Misery is owing."[93] This story is also exclusively about women, and the old woman is as self-reflexive as d'Aulnoy's and Rowe's heroines. The old woman recounts her early childhood, her difficult time at boarding school, and her experiences as a teenager and young woman with her peers of both sexes, and she recounts her own reactions and thoughts at every point.

Boarding school is a horrendous place of jealousies, tattling, and manipulation of the teacher, and, regardless of the character of the groups of young people she joins, she finds callousness and superficiality. Men are definitely passing presences. Her first husband, married as the result of one of her wishes, is indifferent to her and, indeed, without tenderness. He dies within a few pages, and her second husband makes her happy, but we hear almost nothing about him. Her father was "tolerably agreeable, his Understanding not to be complained of, his Humour easy, and his Temper quiet and composed"; he dies a page after his introduction, and her mother "had not that excessive Fondness" for him and "soon got the better of her Grief" (2:228). In fact, the man about whom we learn most is the magician who rears the fairy. Given to him because he was wealthy and her parents had many children, he is a vicious, contradictory tyrant who beats her whenever she shows fear. He often beats her, sees fear, and then beats her again. Finally, he turns her into a rabbit with the pronouncement, "There, you fearful Fool, you may now enjoy your own natural Timidity; for you will immediately be transformed into the most fearful Animal in the Creation" (2:236).

This fairy tale within a fairy tale is short and has the beautiful, graceful heroine, a transition period as an animal, and then an account of the fairy's interaction with humans. The way the fairy is freed from the curse and restored to her own body is clever. Fielding makes rules for what fairies have the power to do—they cannot change the nature of individual men, for instance. Her fairy, like d'Aulnoy's, advises and even lectures humans, shakes her head in disappointment, and tries to modify granting wishes to do the least harm. This enjoyable tale is as artful as the story of the princess, which gives the tale the sobriquet of fragment. The princess listens to the old woman's tale, but just as she is about to answer whether the story has had "the desired Effect," the old woman's family returns with their friends (2:275). Thus, two aesthetically crafted stories frame the didactic, dark biography of the old woman. All three are female bildungsroman in the tradition of Rowe. The old woman knows who she is and what she needs for contentment and selfhood, and the princess is at the point of deciding. The contrast between Rowe's view of human nature and Fielding's is clear here, however. The reader cannot help but suspect that the princess is, sooner or later, going to take up her doomed journey to the Castle of Wishes.

Fairy tales often center on cardinal sins; d'Aulnoy's "The King of the Peacocks and the Princess Rosetta" illustrates the evils of envy, pride, and covetousness. The tales are 32 percent of the content of *The Governess*, and a major theme in the novel is one common to fairy tales: the prevalence and results of rivalry and jealousy between family members. It drives "Hebe," the stories of some of the schoolgirls, and the story of Celia and Chloe that Miss Dolly reads. Fielding's texts provide important information about English fairy-tale history. In her preface, Fielding established the validity of using various kinds of imaginative genres to educate by telling a fable designed to open her readers' minds to all kinds of moral lessons. The text includes other fables, the fairy tales, a letter, a housekeeper's story, the summary of a play, the story Dolly reads, and the girls-at-school frame, which includes the teacher's and each girl's life story. Fairy tales were almost universally imagined as love stories, and the first observation about the story of Mignon is about Fidus and Amata and that they were rewarded for their constancy. As is common with English women's tales, however, marriage is not consistently the reward and resolution of the woman's life; Princess Hebe, we are to believe, is happy because she is doing her duty and also helping many people. There is no mention of love, marriage, or children for her.

Fielding is writing in a line of "novels" that have not yet been fully traced; for instance, Jane Barker's full title is *Patch-Work Screen for the Ladies; or, Love and Virtue Recommended in a Collection of Instructive Novels*. By referring to differing opinions at a "harmonious Tea-Table Entertainment," she anticipates Eliza Haywood's *Tea Table*. Barker's framing narrative is Galesia's story, and some critics identify it as "anticipating the bildungsroman";[94] Fielding's story takes Jenny from her narrative of her early life past the date that her aunt comes to take her from the school. Similarly, the story of Hebe is a form of bildungsroman. That Fielding includes a folk and a literary art tale inscribes their parallel paths. Even more indicative of the discussions surrounding fairy tales in 1749 are the sections of the book in which Mrs. Teachum and Jenny discuss the proper use of the tales. Mrs. Teachum insists several times that the fairies are strictly for entertainment and that the children should learn the lessons that they teach, as the giant "is called so only to express a Man of great Power" (84). By the end of the century, writers display even more distrust of fairy tales. Sophia King writes in her 1798 growing-up poem,

> Now fairy fancies sunk away,
> For gay arose the sun of *Truth*,
> Dispersing with its genial ray
> The dear illusive dreams of youth.[95]

Martha Mary Sherwood eliminated both of Fielding's fairy tales in her revision of *The Governess* (1820) but substituted a fairy tale about a spoiled, ungovernable princess named Rosalinda. Rosalinda's mother, who desperately wanted a child, rescues a bird belonging to the fairy Serena. Serena promises her a daughter and checks on the child every year. Finally the king and queen agree to send the unmanageable Rosalinda to fairyland with Serena. Rosalinda's new governess, Soimeme, is created from her reflection in a mirror. Soimeme is a terrible tyrant, and Rosalinda becomes an exemplary woman and ruler.[96] The contrast between this fairy tale and the story of Hebe brings to the fore the greater independence of Fielding's women and the ways conservative Christian ideas of gender drive Sherwood's book.

Ruth Bottigheimer points out that when the translation of Perrault's fairy tales "did not sell well as leisure reading . . . its publishers attempted to recast the book as a French-English schoolbook." That "foundered."[97] The entertainment value of fairy tales, however, resisted all efforts to denigrate or discount them. Some of the most commercially astute and innovative publishers in Britain assured what British fairy-tale historians identify as their fourth wave of popularity. John Harris, successor to John Newbery; Benjamin Tabart, originator of the Popular Stories series; and William Lane, proprietor of the Minerva Press, published many volumes of fairy tales between 1780 and 1830. Lane, it is estimated, published 12,000 copies of fairy tales in twelve years.[98] The insertion of the fairy tales in novels of the second half of the century shows us their lasting appeal and a variety of technical strategies. Oliver Goldsmith controls the tone of *The Vicar of Wakefield* with one even as he demonstrates his ability to deploy and manipulate his time's conventions of mixing genres.[99] Moses has been sent to sell an aging horse and to buy another. He has been cheated, and the event is described as an "unforeseen disaster" that "demolished" the family's hopes. The vicar pontificates to his distressed family: "Unequal combinations are always disadvantageous to the weaker side" (chap. 13), which introduces the frame for a fairy tale that Dick, significantly a *young* child, is asked to tell to amuse the company. A Giant and a Dwarf go on the road to fight and win honor. The Giant wins these things plus a beautiful wife, but the Dwarf loses an arm, an eye, and a leg. The frame narrative resumes with a dispute about whether the daughters will be allowed to go to London with Lady Blarney and Miss Skeggs, who are perceived to be of a much higher class but are ladies of the town. The fairy tale has a sober moral, and yet it is a moment of imaginative entertainment, enjoyable for both its art and its applicability.

What happened to Hebe is labeled "the natural Consequence" first of her disobedience and then of her "Return to duty" (143). Just before Sybella and Hebe are tricked by their desire to help others, the girls have been warned against gullibly giving beggars money: "oftentimes those Fellows made up dismal Stories without much Foundation, and because they were lazy, and would not work." Whether the beggar was deserving is left undetermined. Dolly notes that he looks "almost starved," but his story of being "burnt out of his House, and from one Distress to another, reduced to that miserable State" can seem hyperbolically exaggerated (109). Fielding seems to be anticipating a common criticism of fairy tales—one of the girls, notably the youngest, asks if they would not be better off hearing a "true history," the common name for novels. That the two most admirable, knowledgeable characters explain the usefulness of fairy tales and all of the girls learn important lessons from them counters all possible criticism. Notably, later in the text the discussion of how to read plays and their value is much longer.

Interestingly, during Fielding's career, as a genre fairy tales were approaching what we think of them and identify with Perrault and the Grimm brothers. However, when people said (and say) "it's a fairy tale," they often mean what Rowe wrote —love stories with unlikely, happy endings. The story of Celia and Chloe is really a Rowe-style fairy tale, and Fielding's *History of Ophelia* (1760) includes "forms that Fielding experimented with throughout her career" and what one of her editors has called "the airy fairy-tale plot." Harries speculates that Jeanne-Marie Le Prince de Beaumont imitated *The Governess* by surrounding her fairy tales with moral dialogues between a governess and the six young women in her care. Beaumont somewhat disingenuously repudiated the earlier fairy tales for inspiring "false ideas" and, as was common as the century progressed, highlighted the educational and "civilizing" usefulness of her fairy tales.[100]

Catherine Talbot, one of the Bluestockings who visited the Countess of Hertford to absorb the ambiance of the grounds and read Rowe's letters and poems in the green leather-bound letter book, wrote a fairy tale shortly after one of her visits in 1753.[101] During that visit, Hertford (then Duchess of Somerset) had her grandson and his cousin with her, and Talbot wrote the fairy tale for them. She names the central character George for the boy she and the duchess wanted to encourage, but the good fairy disguised as an old crone is named "Instruction," and statues with names like "Flattery" and "Modesty" come to life in her castle and lecture the boys. Other names are also in the old morality play tradition. The progress literature of writers like Bunyan meets the developing bildungsroman in her tale. Parts of it are highly imaginative—Good Temper is made of sugar and is as firm and "almost as clear as Chrystal," and George is given a tiny cabinet with millions of little drawers for his collected treasures. George reaches the Top of the Mountain and the glittering Temple of *Felicity*, perhaps a name allusive with d'Aulnoy's first fairy tale. The tale is heavily didactic, and Talbot chose not to publish it, but it shows the blending together of fairy tale and English moral literary conventions.[102] Once published, it was frequently included in collections under a number of different titles. For example, John Gregory includes it in his *Father's Legacy to his Daughters* as "Education: A Fairy Tale," and as "The Story of Little George" it was included with many of d'Aulnoy's in *Mother Bunch's Fairy Tales*.[103]

Something of a unified tradition developed that is bound together by women's extraction of an aesthetic, an essence (like perfume), themes, and a shared aspiration for women's quality of life. Fairies of the trooping variety were invoked throughout the eighteenth century in women's writing to create special kinds of settings, and poetry and prose moved apart.[104] In poetry, the references are like those little moments in Rowe's texts that recall an atmosphere. Anne Finch teases her husband to leave his studies and come enjoy the day "when faery Cercles better mark the ground" than compasses used to chart battles in *An Invitation to Dafnis* (1689).[105] Poetry more often than prose brings to mind the creations of Spenser, Jonson, Shakespeare, and Milton and other dramatic and poetic fairies. Robert Herrick begins *Hesperides* (1648), "I write of *Groves*, and *Twilights* and I sing / The Court of *Mab* and of the *Fairie-King*."[106] In *Ode to Indifference* (1757), Frances Greville asks Oberon, king of the fairies, to make the nymph Indifference her guest, thereby allowing her to live a tranquil, content life. This poem was printed as often in the century as Thomas Gray's much better known *Elegy in a Country Church-Yard*.[107] Modern critics puzzle over its appeal, but part of it was certainly that the entire poem is a delightful, imaginative address to Oberon, whom she calls "Wanton Sprite" and "Fairy Elf." Like d'Aulnoy's Zephyr in *Isle of Happiness*, her Oberon is like the playful, dancing breeze. In exchange for indifference, she wishes, "So may the Glow worms glim'ring light / Thy tiny footsteps lead / To some new Region of Delight" (lines 53–55). The originality and much-admired tone spring from this fantasy and the comparison between her imagining of Oberon's temperament and the poet's representation of her speaker's brooding over disappointments. A poem that could be maudlin or lugubrious becomes playful, always interrupting descents into "the tears which pity taught to flow" with references to, for instance, Oberon's "Acorn Goblet." Intriguingly, Margaret Doody points out that fairies "do not have to be moral—a great convenience, and an enviable one to women."[108]

Greville's poem attracted numerous poetic responses for the rest of the century,[109] and the appeal of the fairy device is clear. For example, Isabella Byron Howard's *The Fairy's Answer* purports to relay an answer from Oberon. Howard, the Countess of Carlisle, mentions that she hopes to give the poem in person to Greville. Eliza Tuite also answered the poem, and she is the author of five poems in the voice of a sylph.[110] William Cowper wrote one of the poems that objected to her desire:

> Join me, amid your silent hours,
> > To form the better pray'r.
>
> With lenient balm, may *Ob'ron* hence
> > To fairy-land be driv'n;
> With ev'ry herb that blunts the sense
> Mankind receiv'd from heaven.[111]

Perhaps with Greville's poem in mind, Laetitia Barbauld wrote in *Verses written in an Alcove* (1773),

> This is sure the haunt of fairies,
> > In yon cool Alcove they play;
> Care can never cross the threshold,
> > Care was only made for day.

These lines follow the creation of a magic, natural bower where streams of soft moonlight filter through the branches. Verse after verse contrasts this fairy world to the everyday one—"soft affections" rather than passions, "Easy, blithe" rather than grief, anxiety, and ambition. Anne Bannerman in her great war poem, *Verses on an Illumination for a Naval Victory*, breaks the catalogue of horrors:

> O! for a lodge, where Peace might love to dwell,
> In some sequester'd, solitary dell!
> Some fairy isle, beyond the Southern wave,
> Where War ne'er led his victims to the grave. (lines 75–79)

In poetry *and* fiction references to fairies give writers unusual freedom of imagination.[112] The style becomes lighter, and there are often marked contrasts between things with which the writer is struggling and the verses describing escapes from them. These struggles are exceptionally varied, as they range from states of mind to difficult experiences to vexed expression. As in Barbauld's poem, Ann Murry briefly turns from the Muses to the fairies for poetic inspiration:

> Or grown perhaps quite gay and airy,
> Address bright Oberon the Fairy,
> To take me in his pygmy train,
> . . . .
> With dulcet tones enrich my song. (B&I, 766–67)

These escapes are often short-lived, thereby emphasizing the contrast. In Murry's poem, for instance, the Muse interrupts this flight: "All vain pretenders I deride" (767, line 26), and Joanna Baillie uses a reference to them to argue the universality of inspiration (*Address to the Muses*, lines 121–26).

Women continue to find fairy tales and the fairy-tale mode useful literary strategies, as Sharon Rose Wilson's *Myths and Fairy Tales in Contemporary Women's Fiction from Atwood to Morrison* with its contemporary, global coverage, demonstrates. Either stand-alone or embedded, they serve many functions for women. In the eighteenth century, with its emphasis on the benefits of reading, the moral aspects of fairy tales were often advertised (no matter how little they figured in the plots). John Newbery, for instance, advertised editions of d'Aulnoy's fairy tales as "published for the amusement of all those Little Masters and Misses who . . . aim at becoming Great Lords and Ladies" (1776, 1785, and many other reprints). Although this language invoked fantasy and the virtues of chivalry, it also suggested both upward mobility and the gentility movement. A 1733 advertisement for Rowe's collected book read, "no Book can be fitter for the Perusal of young People at our *Boarding-Schools* . . . to form their Minds aright,"[113] and Clara Reeve wrote that Rowe's works were "proper for youth" in *The Progress of Romance* (1785). In time, some of Rowe's letters were included in textbooks, including the "highly esteemed" grammar-school reader *A Collection of Prose and Verse* by Arthur Masson.[114]

As in Rowe's and the eighteenth-century women's texts, the writers whom Wilson studies continue the tradition of using embedded tales to portray transformations from alienation and imprisonment to "greater consciousness, community, and wholeness."[115] As Wilson shows, the grappling with women's needs to maneuver a terrain of sexual politics remains a consistent theme in the tales. Interestingly, critics like Wilson work with the motifs of Perrault in spite of the fact that modern women's fairy tales are more like d'Aulnoy's in style, content, and purpose. As Jack Zipes asserts, the salon women's "remarkable fairy tales set the tone and standards for the development of most of the memorable literary fairy tales in the West up to the present."[116] Their themes, exposés, and aesthetics reappear over and over, as they do in Elizabeth Barrett Browning's *Aurora Leigh*. Sandra Gilbert and Susan Gubar have identified their strands in, for example, *Wuthering Heights, Jane Eyre*, and *Villette*.[117] As A. S. Byatt in "Fairy Stories" observes,

> The literary fairy tale is a wonderful, versatile hybrid form, which draws on primitive apprehensions and narrative motifs, and then uses them to think consciously about human beings and the world. Both German romantic fairy tales and the self-conscious playful courtly stories of seventeenth-century French ladies, combine the new thought of the time with the ancient tug of forest and castle, demon and witch, vanishing and shape-shifting, loss and restoration.[118]

Donald Haase argues that the *conteuses* "provided a model for twentieth-century women writers who (re)wrote fairy tales in order to interrogate gender."[119] Certainly as their tales have become better known, adaptations of them have become more literary and intriguing. Examples are "The Great Green Worm" by A. S. Byatt, *The Bloody Chamber* (1979) by Angela Carter, and Anne Sexton's transformed fairy tales. Byatt's version of d'Aulnoy's *Green Worm* (*Serpentin vert*) includes descriptions of Hidessa's solitary contentment in beautiful outdoor settings and her enjoyment of "serious books, books of courtly love, history books" and hearing news of the world. Byatt brings out many of d'Aulnoy's signature touches, such as references to high-culture authors, performances, and texts, including Psyche, and vivid physical descriptions of characters, human and in other forms.[120] Carter's story draws upon and compliments d'Aulnoy's *The Story of the White Cat* and other stories, sometimes explicitly as when Beauty finds "a collection of courtly and elegant French fairy tales about white cats who were transformed princesses and fairies who were birds."[121] Consistent throughout history are transformations of individuals and their surroundings, and in fairy tales by women, as Sharon Wilson says, is the "search for identity, individuation, and healing."[122] Rowe's stories carry out these transformations in an understated way, and restless, seeking women find peace and often a strikingly individual lifestyle, as Melinda does.

The final story of Laura is more of a unifying technical move than has been recognized. Laura changes more than any of Rowe's other characters, and by the end she is at peace with herself and her surroundings. She says the rural setting naturally leads her to thoughts of religion—and her lack of it. With a play on fairy-tale metamorphoses, she imagines herself at death transformed not into an angel but a magpie, a reptile, or a cow. From the frenetic first letter ("I hate trees"), she moves through "some religious panicks" and then to the calm of true religion. "With the evidence I now have of a future existence, my notions of happiness are refined and enlarged, my hopes bright and unlimited" (*Letters*, 3:224, 247, 251, respectively). While in the country, she has met Philocles and fallen in love with him. He tells her of his premonition of his own impending death: "I listened to this story as to a fairy tale, or a sort of waking dream" (3:246). She laughs, but he does die. Significantly, it is labeled a fairy tale, and the connotations of "visionary" and linkage to prophetic are activated. Earlier Laura has noted that the country is giving her the vapours: "Death that ghastly phantom, perpetually intrudes on my solitude." She then invokes fairy-tale thinking that she says she has grown beyond: "Nor have I acquired any great degree of fortitude by turning free-thinker and unlearning 'All that the nurse and all the priest have taught.' Mr. Pope." This reference from *The Rape of the Lock* (Canto 1, line 30), notable for its sylphs, to fairy tales and superstition is followed by the metamorphosis fantasy, which she says her brother calls "a visionary here after" (3:226).

Like characters in *Friendship in Death*, Philocles comes back to speak with her. She says that his voice "charmed the wildest discord into calm attention; every accent breathed celestial love and harmony" (*Letters*, 3:250). His care for her and his description and assurances about the next world are like those in the first volume, but the effect on her and the rounding out of the conversion story, the only one among the tales, are new. Rowe has also developed more meaningful aesthetic touches. Philocles leans on a sundial on a marble pedestal, symbol not only of his limited time with her but of the brief human life span. Other references recall earlier letters and develop thematic, intertextual connections. Both Melinda and Laura refer to Addison's *Cato*. Philocles has been reading Young's *A Vindication of Providence: or a True Estimate of Human Life, In which the Passions are considered in a New Light* (1728), and so the author to whom she referred in her dedication is recalled in the last sequence of letters.

Specialists today recognize that the popularity and development of fairy tales are smoothly continuous rather than sporadic. It is one of the genres that has been most frequently and successfully adapted to new social uses and to changing consumer demands.[123] Karen Rowe in a much-quoted essay points out that many genres today, including popular romances, magazine fiction, and film, depend on fairy-tale prototypes.[124] Elizabeth Singer Rowe was a key transitional adapter, one of the writers that transformed it into novelistic discourse and made them conform to British demands for both realism and magic stories. While others' fiction was being ridiculed for the use of coincidence, Rowe took a more daring course by unapologetically providing modern fairy tales—stories of trial and discovery with somewhat impossibly attractive characters and uncommon happy endings.

CHAPTER THREE

Toward Novelistic Discourse

As Rowe published her successive volumes of prose fiction, England entered the absolute low point of the production of new novels, histories, and romances. The year after *Friendship in Death*, Haywood's *Fair Hebrew* and the anonymous *Life and Intrigues of the late celebrated Mrs. Mary Parrimore* and *The Life of Mr. Robin Lyn* were the only fiction titles.[1] In 1730, there were again only four titles, Haywood's *Love-Letters on all Occasions Lately Passed between Persons of Distinction* and three anonymous works, *Amours of Philario and Olinda*, *The Brothers*, and *The Forced Virgin*. Intriguingly, secret histories predominated as if the amatory tale was now required to purport to be both "true" and more sensational. In 1731, fictional memoirs, collections of tales, and travel spin-offs of *Gulliver's Travels* emerged. A sign that the forms of prose fiction were becoming too formulaic or even burning out is the parodic title *The Ungrateful Fair, a Tragi-comic Novel* (by John Stevens).

The years 1732 and 1733 saw a slight uptick, but there were only two original titles in 1734, both secret histories: Elizabeth Harding's *Masterpiece of Imposture* and the anonymous *Life, Amours, and Secret History of Francelia, Late D[uche]ss of P[ortsmout]h* (the mistress of Charles II whom the public most detested). In 1738, only translations, no original English fiction, were published. Defoe, Barker, Gildon, Davys, and Aubin were recently dead, and Haywood had temporarily turned to the stage and political fictions such as *The Adventures of Eovaai* (1736). Perhaps even more telling than numbers is the absence of titles of what we think of today as novels—reasonably long, unified narratives usually with psychological elements. The conclusion must be that style, content, quest, and reader desire needed to be rethought. Perhaps many felt as Elizabeth Tollet did in 1724:

> Methinks that reading these Romances
> Is just like dancing Country Dances:
> All in the same dull Measures move,
> Adventures brave and constant Love;
> Each Pair in formal Order tread
> The Steps their Predecessors led.[2]

Looking closely at the fiction published in England between 1720 and 1734 reveals how dominant were various kinds of epistolary fictions and collections of tales, which were held together in a surprisingly small and undisguised number of ways. Both are categories to which Rowe's fictions belong. Like the secret histories, Barker's were in many ways backward-looking forms.[3] Gildon's mailbag device to motivate tales and anecdotes and the increasingly overwhelming preference for epistolary patchworks show the recognition of the usefulness of the *Spectator*'s model and the value of epistolarity. As will become clear in this chapter and the next, Rowe's *Letters* are pivotal and contribute to the development of a new branch of epistolary fiction. Her prose fiction does not fit into any of the categories that Robert Adams Day has identified in *Told in Letters* as the fictional epistolary types: love story, spy letters, scandalous chronicle, and journey or adventure. *Five Love Letters from a Nun to a Cavalier*, Behn's *Love Letters*, and Richardson's *Pamela* and *Clarissa* are in the tradition that identified such fiction with the interpersonal self and specifically the body, usually female, and what Cook calls "the somatic terrain of the emotions"; in contrast, Rowe's are in the zone of reflection and intellect, the space of the conceptual self.[4]

Women's fictional style between 1680 and 1725 has been criticized more often than that of men primarily perhaps because their fictional preferences have become increasingly stigmatized as "popular," strongly gendered female, and even ridiculous. In his reflections on his influential *Popular Fiction before Richardson*, which is rightly seen to be about women writers, John Richetti asserted that "popular fiction is nothing less than the central and initiating line of the novel" and at one point in the text of the book described the rhetoric of love as "almost gasps and grunts" and "a series of sighs and groans." Women, popular fiction, and "incoherent" inarticulate language are locked together.[5] While male writers were choosing the discourses of travel and journalism, styles that are still familiar and approved, women found resonance in the issues, stories, and forms of, for instance, the French romances of de Scudéry and d'Urfé. The masculine forms emphasized reportage, while the romances dramatized debates among characters over, for example, motives, interpretations of events, and degrees of blame, suffering, or happiness. These dramatized debates were designed to be indulged in by readers and were. Lindy Riley writes that the struggle to conform to "'masculine' systems of representation" in spite of their experiences and refusal to be repressed made their writings "unstable."[6] By moving from the zone of the certainties of code ethics, romances deliberately portrayed the uncertainties, contradictions, and unreconcilable experiences that encourage situational ethics, or, as men often labeled it, "casuistic thinking." What Karen Gevirtz points out about eighteenth-century women critics of Shakespeare applies to the novel. Rather than narrative, it was "discourse that did them in." She works with their adherence to "criticism's discursive conventions" and points out that the closer the adherence the more forceful the rejection.[7]

Within prose fiction, the greater the *deviance* from the discourses of masculine forms also determined (and still determines) the degree of rejection. The result was a very narrow corridor of acceptable discourse. I would also say that the struggle to find ways to depict experiences new to literature, to develop novelistic discourse, and to deal with the special gender demands on expression created the varying and, to our ears today, often strange combinations of language types and levels. Women throughout the century complained of contradictory demands on their literary expression. Aphra Behn's protests in prologues, epilogues, and introductions to her plays are well known, and complaints that the subject and genre conventions demanded knowledge and language deemed unacceptable in women continued through Charlotte Smith and Hannah Cowley. The early women were introducing new subjects and experiences; as a tribute to Behn noted, she made "inarticulated strings to speak" and found "new discover'd Mines."[8] Especially in trying to express female desire, they aroused criticism. In influential books, both Richetti and Lennard Davis claimed that women's fiction created an eroticized reading process. Davis wrote that "excitations, longings, curiosities, and pleasing agitations" were the "prime satisfaction" of reading them.[9]

One of the most significant tasks for the writers of the early English novel was to develop a novelistic discourse, and Rowe advanced the transition. In fact, rather than a transitional figure, Rowe was pivotal, as the style of prose fiction before and after her *Letters* was different. Modern novelistic discourse needed to complement the purposes and uses of the developing novel, and it needed to stabilize, to avoid the wild swings, extravagances, and sudden reliances on baroque forms that marked fiction written between 1680 and 1725. Davis points out that "ambivalence is the foundation for the double or reflexive nature of the novelistic discourse" and was the result of the novel's "constitutive ambivalence toward fact and fiction."[10] The problem had been that novelists exposed contradictions and created improbabilities. What Rowe did was transmit her certainty of what was fact, her worldview and judgments of human nature, while housing her fictional stories within them. Thus, rather than ambivalence, she offered imaginative stories of the kind her readers enjoyed within a firm truth. Davis continued by theorizing that "the frame of the novel insists the work is true"; Rowe did that by creating an ideology that unified her text rather than with a frame. She demonstrated an effective way to reconcile the experienced contradictions between fact and fiction that had troubled readers and actualized the need for a new non-patriarchal ideology that the fiction of Barker, Manley, and Haywood had revealed.

In fact, her ease with gender gave a unity to her prose that absorbed the contradictions rather than exposed them. To some extent, novelistic discourse needed to *use* gendered language rather than strike the reader with authorial gender markings and to deploy discourses artfully rather than jolt the reader with shifts. Here are some typical examples of the style of prose fiction before Rowe:

> thus betwixt each ravishing minute thou would'st swear—and I as fast believed—and loved thee more—Hast thou forgot it all, oh fickle charmer, hast thou? Hast thou forgot between each awful ceremony of love, how you cried out, "Farewell the world and mortal cares. . . ." —Aphra Behn, *Love Letters between a Nobleman and His Sister* (1684), 97.

> After this Hurricane, and divers Gusts of Sighs and Tears, I began to flatter my Fancy, that all this might be a Composition, like that of *Lowland*, and no more of Truth in this his *London* Mistress, than in that of Mistress *Lowland*; who was now actually married to another Man: And when by this means the torments of my distorted Mind was a little appeased. . . . —Jane Barker, *Love Intrigues* (1713), Backscheider and Richetti, 107.

> since I die with Impatience for a Performance, 'till when, and always, I am *Dearest Berina's Faithful Adorer*. —Mary Davys, *Familiar Letters* (wr. [1717]; 1725)[11]

> Encourag'd with this Observation, I resolv'd the Next Morning to set out with the first of the Tide, and reposing my self for the Night in the Canoe, under the great Watch-coat, I mention'd, I launched out. . . . It was a dismal Sight to look at: The Ship, which by its building was *Spanish*, stuck fast, jaum'd in between two Rocks. . . . —Daniel Defoe, *Robinson Crusoe*, 1719 (Norton, 138)

> "My dear *Charlotta*, 'tis our hard Fate to be now left here alone in the Hands of Men whose obdurate Hearts are insensible to pity, from whom we can expect nothing but ill usage, did not your angelick Face too well convince me that they will spare your Life. Oh! could I find a way to secure your Virtue, tho with the loss of my Life, I should die with pleasure: but, alas, you must be sacrific'd, and I be left the most unhappy Wretch on Earth. . . ." —Penelope Aubin, *The Life of Charlotta Du Pont, An English Lady* (1723), 37

Long, baroque sentences were the norm:

> After this, the very Porter and Page believed me escaped out of that window, and there was no farther search made after me: but the Countess was amazed, as much as any of the souldiers, to find which way I had conveyed myself, when I came down and undeceived her; but when she saw from whence I came, she wondered more than before how I could get up so high; when trying the trick again, I could

not do it, if I might have won never so considerable a wager upon it, without pulling down the sconce, and the tester also. —Behn, *Love Letters*, 350.

Decade by decade, spelling became more modern and standardized, and constructions such as "never so considerable" faded. Many sentences in *Robinson Crusoe* and Defoe's other novels are as long and spasmodic as this one ("garrulous and disjointed" in Richetti's words).[12] Elspeth Jajdelska hypothesizes that writers who imagine oral reading "produce long strings of loosely attached clauses, whereas a writer who conceives of his or her reader as [silent] will write in what a present-day reader recognizes as sentences, that is, autonomous units bounded by pauses."[13] Even in 1719, however, Gildon's letters sound like Behn's and especially Manley's politico-amatory texts. Defoe, who often depicted reading circles in his conduct books, continued through his novelistic career to write long, gasping sentences. In many cases, long paragraphs are single sentences even in his last novel, *Roxana* (1724).[14] Davys drops into formulaic language at the end of her text, but Barker's patchwork novels, as well as Rowe's, show more self-consciousness about the use of the discourses around them. Although Barker's *A Patch-Work Screen for the Ladies* and *The Lining of the Patch Work Screen* are held together by a loose narrative of, among other things, Galesia's mother's abortive attempts to find a husband for her, what really unites her books and Rowe's is a unified style and controlling narrative sensibility. Rowe's contrasting prose style, as we shall see, provides evidence of Jajdelska's theory and also of Rowe's importance as a pivotal figure. In this chapter, I will explore some of the ways that Rowe advanced novelistic discourse.

The Poet in the Prose Fiction

The most important of Rowe's contributions to prose fiction was her writing style. She firmly domesticated novelistic style and produced the ease of expression and appearance of naturalness that came to be so admired after midcentury. Style was attracting increasing attention, and anything perceived as too extravagant or too idiomatic and low drew negative comment. The abbess's remarks on the style of Hypolite's story at the conclusion of "Isle of Happiness" were a harbinger of the future and became standard. For example, Mrs. Teachum and Jenny Peace discuss the style of the fairy tale "The Princess Hebe" in Sarah Fielding's *The Governess*. The aura of the *Spectator* hovers over Rowe's fiction. The polite moralism and urbane conversational discourse set a powerful example, and each essay was a kind of epistle to readers. It was familiar, and it established the triad of essayist, exemplary characters, and aspiring reader that Rowe developed and further aestheticized. In contrast,

Rowe's poetry was often exuberant, mystical, and wild, and it was characterized by experimentation and a remarkable variety of forms, including Pindaric odes, verse epistles (Horatian and Ovidian), pastorals (monologue and dialogue), fables, eulogies, songs, and elegies. However, she seemed to grasp earlier than most that novelistic language needed to be cultivated, even regularized. The ways in which Rowe's first literary career—that of a poet—influenced her as a fiction writer have never been explored but are highly pertinent.

Rowe began writing at the time when male poets and critics were united in raising the quality of their nation's poetry. They pushed for "correctness," energy, and musicality and worked to adapt the great classical forms to British themes and language, and for a time there was a dominant set of aesthetic values.[15] This drive was present in religious as well as secular poetry, and Rowe was one of the most experimental religious poets of all time.[16] Pope, the heir of this movement and only fourteen years younger than Rowe, summarized the cultural demands in *Epistle to Augustus* (1737), the year of Rowe's death:

Wit grew polite, and Numbers learn'd to flow.
Waller was smooth; but Dryden taught to join
The varying verse, the full resounding line,
The long majestic march, and energy divine.

Polite, flowing, smooth, energetic—these are the characteristics of her prose. Commitments to this project of improving and uniting meter and expression were legion during her formative years as a poet. Buckingham's *An Essay upon Poetry* (1682), Francis Atterbury's "Preface" to the second part of Waller's *Poems* (1690), Dryden's "Postscript to the *Aeneis*" (1697), and John Dennis's *The Grounds of Criticism in Poetry* (1704) are all of that time.[17]

Her poetry is both highly experimental and impressively aware of what other writers had done and were doing, just as her prose fiction is. Even as a young woman, she used quatrains, tercets, dialogues, and a variety of meters and rhyme schemes. A group of poems on any of her favorite subjects makes this point, as do poems in forms and styles not usually associated with her. For example, *To Celinda* is an ardent friendship poem, *Thoughts on Death* (published when she was twenty-two) is on the subject most assigned to her, *A Pastoral Elegy* is in a fashionable, classic form, and *To Madam S— at Court* is a lighthearted cavalier lyric:

Come prethee leave the Courts
   And range the Fields with me;

> A thousand pretty Rural sports
> I'le here invent for thee.

Verse 4 depicts the women "seated by a lovely Stream, / Where beauteous Mermaids haunt." The harmony of the women's minds is emphasized by the next two lines, which slip in a surprise:

> My Song while *William* is my Theam,
> Shall them and thee inchant.[18]

Her praise of King William delights both her friend and the magical mermaids. Kathryn King describes what Rowe has done with the form thusly: "The effect is to plant a Whig flag in the very centre of royalist poetic territory."[19] In other words, Rowe has found a way to rather unobtrusively make a poetic form already associated with competing ideologies a contemporary comment on the monarchy and what Jacobites saw as a new displacement in the line of succession. Rowe occasionally made similar political moves in her prose as when the dead child in Letter 3 of *Friendship in Death* describes discovering that his greatest value to his family was as heir "to a vast Estate and distinguish'd Title" (11).

Rowe wrote poetry throughout her life. Critics have described it as if it were largely homogeneous—that is, narrowly religious. However, it is more accurate to describe it as highly, even wildly, experimental in both content and form, and *Letters* gave her another stage on which poetry could perform. For example, Lindamor writes to Lucius that she has attempted a poem on the subject he proposed, love. The poem is a skillful ode that is a sophisticated development of ideas in such early poems as *Platonick Love* in which she tried to articulate the relationship among divine and various kinds of human love. *A Poem on Love* begins,

> Assist my doubtful muse, propitious love,
> Let all my soul the sacred impulse prove,
> For thine's a holy unpolluted flame,
> Howe'er the libertine prophanes thy name,
> Howe'er with impious cant, hypocrisy
> And senseless superstition blemish thee:
> > The pure result of sober reason thou. (*Letters*, 3:163)

As the poem turns to human love, the ode form predominates:

> > On thee the graces and delights attend,
> > > On thy propitious influence
> > > Our gayest hours depend;

> Whatever charms the soul or sense,
> Beauty and sacred harmony,
> Accomplish'd love! belongs to thee.
> To thee his shining genius *Strephon* owes
> His just ideas and expressions fit;
> To thee *Cleora* owes that sprightly wit,
> Which from her lips in easy language flows. (*Letters*, 3:165)

The poem ends with three verses on how God's love preceded "Th' immortal lovers," Venus, and all lovers as the angels "Their golden harps, and soft preludiums sung / To love, the mighty cause whence their existence sprung" (3:166–67).

While it is true that the greatest number of her poems are religious, the differences among poems and groups of poems defy critical dismissal. In this poem, the reference to "Cleora" is an almost invisible tribute to Hertford. In another example, Rosalinda ends the letter describing the pastoral idyll of her married life with *A Pastoral: Henry and Lucy*, a dialogue that reflects their life and draws parallels to "the first Pair" before the fall and to other happy biblical couples (3:137–39). Thus, isomorphic narratives are created.

Many of her poems are narrative, either as short intervals or in long poems or even in series, as her Canticles were. The construction and allegorical development of her final publication, *The History of Joseph*, suggest that it was probably intended to be in the family with Milton's and his classical antecedents' epics. *Miscellaneous Works* includes three strangely stilted narrative *Dialogues*. She revised some of these narratives, giving us a valuable glimpse into her evolving composition practices. For example, *Cant. 5, 6, etc* appeared in the 18 June 1695 *Athenian Mercury* and the 1696 collection (2:13–14), and she or her editor chose not to reprint it in *Miscellaneous Works*. Curll, however, included it in *Philomela: or, poems by Mrs. Elizabeth Singer, now Rowe* (1737). There are two changes, presumably Curll's. The opening line becomes "Oh! How his pointed Language, like a Dart" rather than "Oh! How is pointed Language, like a Dart." Her original emphasizes the power of language and recalls that of the theoretical descriptions of what her contemporaries wanted in poetry, while the change makes the line more conventionally religious and in harmony with the later period's preaching. Her *Miscellaneous Works* includes a very different treatment of the Canticle, *A Hymn. In imitation of Cant. V. vi, vii*, and an extensively revised *Canticle, Chapter V* from the one printed for the first time in the 1696 *Poems on Several Occasions*. These two poems recall another of her *Athenian Mercury* publications: her first publication of a canticle, her paraphrase of Canticle 5, verses 6–16 (June 5). Canticle, Chapter 1, reworked into what she calls a "Divine

Pastoral" in blank verse, is dated in the *Miscellaneous Works* "August, 1735," giving us perhaps some idea of when she revised the set that covers the first six chapters of *The Song of Songs*.

All of them rework the story of a disappearing bridegroom/savior and her frantic search for him.[20] Over and over throughout her life she reworked favorite passages, stories, and motifs in a variety of tones, forms, and metrics, and the revision of *Canticle, Chapter V* is an example of her growth as a poet and her engagement with narrative. In fact, there is a fullness to the development of the story and of the thoughts and motives of the speaker that is found in many of her *Letters Moral and Entertaining*. The original published version from the 1696 *Poems on Several Occasions* begins,

> The *Night* her *blackest Vestments* had put on,
> And all the *fair remains* of *day* were gone:
> When my dear Lord, as he had oft before,
> With Speed and Love approach'd the bolted Door:
> Arise, my Love, he cries, and with a Voice,
> Divinely charming, pleads his *entrance* thus;
> My *Spouse*, my *Sister*, and my fairest *Love*,
> [(]Believing, sure, that Dialect would move;)
> Arise, for loaden with the Midnight *Dew*,
> Disorder'd, all my streaming *Tresses* flew.[21]

What follows is an erotic tale. The speaker is "careless" and on "a Mossy *Bed* . . . / with *Odorous Roses* spread." Finally leaving the comfortable bed, she "Forgetting now to say, I am *Undrest*," she rushes to the door only to find him gone, although a "fragrant sweetness" fills the air where he had been. She rushes through the streets, seeking help from the Watchman and then the virgin Daughters of Jerusalem. The poem ends with her description of him to the Daughters.

The revision uses more Miltonic images, is smoother, and is less dramatic. It begins,

> The night had now her gloomy curtains spread,
> And ev'ry chearful beam of light was fled;
> This dismal night, my Lord, who ne'er before
> Had met a cold refusal at my door,
> Approach'd, and with a voice divinely sweet;
> My ears with these persuading words did greet.
> "My fairest spouse, my sister, and my love!"
> (But, ah! no more these charming names could move)

> "Arise, for thro' the midnight shades and dew
> I thee, the object of my cares, pursue." (*Misc. Works*, 1:137)

She knows "the blest design my Lord prepar'd," but the bed, which is not otherwise described, is "enticing." In this story, the Lord is "Tir'd with my cold delay, 'Farewell,' he cries." She runs to the door, seeks him, asks help from the watchman and then the Daughters, who again ask her for a description. In the 1696 version, she is the lover who tells the Daughters she is sure they understand how she feels, "Robb'd of the once kind *Partner* of my *Fires*, / And still *dear Object* of my rackt *desires*" (*Poems*, 1:49):

> I charge you, if you meet my *absent Love*,
> With all the *Rhetorick* of our *Sex*, to move
> His deafn'd *Ears*; and tell him, with a *Sigh*,
> Deep as my *Wounds*, ah tell him how I *dy*.
> . . . .
> —He's altogether — *Lovely*, This is *He*,
>   Now, Virgins! *Pity*, tho' you *envy Me*. (*Poems*, 1:49, 51)

In the revised version, at the point she meets the Daughters, it is clear that the entire poem is spoken to them, not just the dialogue at the end. The characterizations of them and her love are dramatically different:

> But you, *Jerusalem's* fair daughters, you
> That know what pity to my cares is due,
> O! if you meet the object of my love,
> . . . .
> Tell him his presence makes my heaven; and tell,
> O tell him, that his absence is my hell!
> . . . .
> He's altogether lovely— This is he
> So much belov'd, so much ador'd by me. (*Misc. Works*, 1:138–39)

Although this passage echoes the language of lover and spouse, it is largely animated by Christian conceptions. Love and adoration replace the formulaic, amatory stance of pity/envy me, and hell is the separation, exile, from God. In the conclusion to the 1696 version, angels "throng" to the "*Musick* of his *Tongue*" and, therefore, become another group of women who are erotically drawn to the Canticle's bridegroom.[22] Her late poetry, like *Letters Moral and Entertaining*, becomes more feminocentric.

Rowe's experiments were exceptionally broad and the uses of poetry in *Letters* varied and artful. Unlike most women writers, for instance, Rowe occasionally wrote from the masculine point of view, as she did in some of her fictional tales and in some of the Canticles and poems such as *Lord Guilford Dudley to Lady Jane Gray* (1729). Not counting the eighteen letters at the end of part 1 of *Letters*, fifty-two of the eighty-three letters in the four volumes of fiction are by men (the sex of some "authors" of letters and poems is not specified). Among them are letters from Philander, a name she seems to use for letters from a somewhat philosophical writer about points of view of interest at the time, including a Deist, an ambitious statesman, and a spirit who tours the depths of the ocean and the planetary universe.[23] Philander's letters usually include poetry, and in the last volume, male writers send male correspondents *On our Saviour's Nativity* and *Divine Love*. *On Happiness* is sent to Albanus by an unnamed former libertine but in a voice that is masculine in experience and easily claiming equality in rank with the recipient and superiority in philosophy. The correspondent writes after confessing to have been a "philosophick libertine" who pursued pleasure for its own sake: "my thoughts found leisure for a nobler application, my soul grew familiar with itself, and sought acquaintance with intellectual beings" (3:158). The number of letters by and about men tends to neutralize the author's and the authorial voices' gender and give a neutral authority to the text as a whole.

The strategy of putting important didactic or political points in the speeches of admirable, authoritative male characters was already well established. Rowe has Rosella's and Melissa's stories told in letters by Lysander, and the practice continued as is evident in novels such as Frances Brooke's *History of Emily Montague* (1769), in which Rivers argues that women should have the right to vote. By Rowe's time, however, the epistolary novel was well established as a place to "hear" the female voice. *She* narrated and interpreted the experience and her response to it. As Susan Lanser notes, however, the letter was almost invariably directed "to a private, usually epistolary narratee" and, therefore, "channeled female voice into forms that contained and defused it, minimizing the power of 'free speech' to destabilize patriarchal culture and undermining the potential even for white, privileged-class women to maintain an enduring literary authority."[24] Haywood certainly recognized the ways women's voices were defused or denied, and *Invisible Spy* shows her obsession with the subject. Canning's is unheard, but other female narratives are preserved and published, specifically aimed at exposing miscreants as representatives of behavior Haywood wishes to condemn. The Spy, for instance, rescues the manuscript that Alinda, who has been seduced, robbed, and confined by her tutor, has addressed to an intimate lady friend, begging her to publish it "to the world."[25] Rowe, in contrast, confers equal authority on male and female voices and skillfully and relatively unobtrusively asserts her own authorial command in a number of ways.

One of her most original and effective means of establishing her authority was her use of her own and quoted poetry. Lines from Milton, Pope, Thomson, and other respected poets raised the poems of her own that she included to equality with theirs, and poetry, a more prestigious genre than fiction, gave her texts more cultural capital. More than her predecessors, Rowe included quotations from the great poets, both earlier and contemporary. The publication of poetry, original, reprinted, and quoted, in prose fiction was common throughout the seventeenth and eighteenth centuries, and critics have identified the most common uses as part of the action, to emphasize points, to heighten the emotional intensity of scenes, to reveal the inner feelings of characters, to exhibit transcendent spiritual feelings, and to develop characters (women who wrote poetry, for instance, were often marked as more intellectual or self-aware).[26] Philip Sidney's highly popular composite *Arcadia* (1593) was a prose romance that incorporated many poems,[27] and women writers from Jane Barker through Charlotte Smith included some of their best poetry in their fictions. Margaret Ezell identified some of the major uses of poetry in women's fiction in her essay "From Manuscript to Print: A Volume of Their Own?" She observes that Haywood "incorporated verses into her fictions to heighten the dramatic intensity of a scene and to reveal the inner feelings of the characters, verses apparently written specifically for the characters rather than recycled from her dramas." She notes that Barker quotes a poem by Katherine Philips, and that her characters are "constantly bursting into verse."[28] Barker, like Haywood, uses the poetry most often to reveal intense inner feelings, often ideas uncommon in their prose. For instance, Barker has Galesia make her vow to the Muses in verse. Unlike these examples that help contribute alternative ways of thinking and behaving, when Rowe's characters reveal their inner thoughts through poetry, those thoughts are often religious. Her *To one that perswades me to leave the Muses* is comparable to Barker's vow to the Muses that she writes on a tree, but, significantly, Rowe does not include it anywhere in her fictions.[29] Typical examples of her use of verse to express inner feelings in *Letters* are when Emilia quotes Isaac Watts's "*Hark! how beyond the narrow bounds / Of time and space they run*" from his *Song of Angels* to describe her thoughts as she recovers from a friend's death (2:39–40) and when Laura adapts Satan's lines in *Paradise Lost* as she compares herself to Philocles:

—————— Abash'd I stood,
And felt how awful goodness is, and saw
Virtue how lovely in her native shape![30]

In fact, this use is more common in the letters by Cleora as "Letter I" illustrates with its three poetic interludes.

More commonly, Rowe uses the verse that gives access to characters' minds to reinforce a unified sensibility, one that is elevated by identification with the poet. Herminius, perhaps a fictionalized Lord Hertford, quotes Dryden's "I watch'd the early glories of her eyes" from *The Indian Emperour* (1.2.146) to describe how Cleora's "dawning beauty" had impressed him as a young man (1:39). Rosalinda spontaneously translates into Italian six lines of the section of *Paradise Lost* (bk. 5, lines 153–208) that was coming to be known as "Milton's Morning Hymn" (*Letters*, 2:7), and she and Sally share the same tastes (Milton, Pope). A contrasting and perhaps telling episode is when the seduced and ruined Amoret quotes Otway's Belvidera:

> ——— And oh! his charming tongue
> Was but too well acquainted with my weakness.
> He talk'd of love, and all my melting heart
> Dissolv'd within my breast,—. (*Letters*, 1:29)

Amoret is drawn from amatory fiction and is one of the most formulaic of Rowe's characters. She has been naive, flattered, and the victim of her own self-confidence and his artifices and now is distraught and deeply regretful. Belvidera speaks these lines in describing her agreeing to marry Jaffeir, a marriage that was her disobedience and his betrayal of her father and the cause of the tragedy *Venice Preserved* depicts (3.2.77–80). Rowe thus offers her readers a striking parallel between Amoret and Belvidera and gives an interpretation of the heroine of the play that many of her contemporaries probably shared.

Writers of the time also included poetry in polemical tracts, as Rowe did in her philosophical and moral epistles in *Letters*.[31] The poem from the Deist is a typical example (*To the Unknown God*). Unlike the other writers, however, Rowe includes letters that are single poems and has other letters in which entire poems are set apart so entirely from other text that they appear to be freestanding. It is not clear, for instance, if "The Story of *Olinda* and *Sophronia*. Translated from *Tasso's* Jerusalem, Book 2" is enclosed in a letter to Eusebius or an independent insertion (*Letters*, 2:85–100). Other examples are Letters 5 ("The Enchanted Forest" from Tasso), 7 (*A Poem on Love*), and 14 (*Divine Love*) in the last volume of *Letters*.

In striking ways, Rowe's four volumes of prose fiction parallel the agendas and practices of poets. The epistles are as varied in style and content as the poems she wrote for separate publication. Several poems are about different kinds of love, and the forms are selected in harmony with the subject and, in the fiction, the context. For example, as in *Letters*, *Platonic Love*, a friendship poem, is an early example of the flexibility women poets found in Philips's work. She begins with a reworking of one of Philips's best-known images: "So Angels Love and all the rest is dross" (*Poems on Several Occasions*, 1:1). Her conclusion, however, is distinctively her own:

> Nor is the greatness of my Love to thee,
> A sacriledge unto the Deity,
> Can I th' enticing stream almost adore,
> And not respect its lovely fountain more? (*Poems*, 1:2)

In marked contrast is the purely secular *The Female Passion* in which the speaker describes the romantic love that seems her "destiny" (*Poems*, 2:30–31). *To Madam S— at Court* goes beyond the homoerotic Platonism of Philips's friendship poems to indulge in gender bending found in some of Aphra Behn's poems. After inviting Madam S— to "range the Fields with me," the speaker imagines they will sit by a stream and "We'l all the charming things repeat, / That introduuc'd [sic] our loves" (*Poems*, 2:47). This verse looks forward to texts Rowe wrote from a masculine point of view and to her pastoral dialogues, *Pastoral: Henry and Lucy* and *A Pastoral*, in which Phillis and Aminta debate the best way to treat lovers, but it continues,

> I'le pluck fresh Garlands for thy brows,
>   *Sweet* as a Zephirs *breath*.
> As fair and well design'd as those
>   The Elisyum Lovers wreath.
>
> And like those happy Lovers we,
>   As careless and as blest;
> Shall in each others converse be
>   Of the whole world possest.
>
> Then prethee *Phillis leave the Courts*,
>   And range the Fields with me;
> Since I so many harmless sports
>   Can here procure for thee. (*Poems*, 2:47–48)

From gossiping about their male lovers in these pastoral poems, Rowe's women turn to other pleasures with each other, and the language is allusive, suggestive, and embedded in the sexual codes of pastoral and court poetry.

For *Letters*, Rowe writes several verse epistles, a venerable and popular form in the period, and, again, her experimental drive is evident. *Lady Jane Gray to . . . Dudley* is remarkable for the way it conflates the immediate and eternal, Dudley and Christ. "To men, to angels, be my soul unveil'd," Jane writes. The poem moves from references to their lives and situation to peaceful rural settings, of which the first reference is pastoral and the second redolent of Heaven and the Garden of Eden where "springs of joy in endless currents flow" (1:83–84). Dudley's epistle refers more concretely to the political situation and focuses on praise of Jane, especially her beauty. This poem ends with an echo of John Donne's "Death, be not proud" (*Holy Sonnet X*, pub. 1633): "O death! where is thy boasted conquest now? / Where are the frowns and terrors of thy brow?" At this point, Dudley's epistle mingles earth and eternal by describing his wife in terms that evoke Heaven:

> Thou hast an angel's heav'nly form and air,
> Pleasures and graces in thy train appear.
> Ten thousand kind transporting scenes arise. (1:86)

Whether these scenes are recollections of his brief life with Jane or imaginations of Heaven is deliberately obscure, and Rowe's strategy of creating a sense of seamless continuity of earth and eternity is successful.

The group of verse epistles near the end of the last volume of *Letters* are wildly different from each other in spite of the clear influence of Michael Drayton's popular *England's Heroicall Epistles* (1597) on two of them.[32] *Rosamond to Henry II* is a more conventional remorseful confession of an adultress. Rosamund Clifford, "Fair Rosamund," the beloved mistress of Henry II, regrets her fall, describes Woodstock, the beautiful, luxurious hide-away he built to share with her, and her premonition of being forced to drink poison by the jealous Queen Eleanor (*Letters*, 3:209–12). The story was familiar, and Addison's *Rosamond: An Opera* (1707) with its new musical setting by Thomas Arne (1733) was just one of its early eighteenth-century reworkings and a sign of engaged public interest during the time Rowe was composing her *Letters*. She begins with Drayton's second verse, which uses the trope of the woman as unstained, blank paper. He writes, "This scribbled Paper which I send to thee, / If noted rightly, doth resemble mee: / . . . / So pure was I, ere stayned by thy Hand."[33] Rowe's is slightly more dramatic: "Clean as this spotless page, 'till stain'd by me, / Such was my conscience, 'till seduc'd by thee" (*Letters*, 3:209). Everything that Rowe's Rosamond encounters tweaks her conscience. In a beautiful section, a statue of Diana seems to "dart an angry glance" at her. In an original touch, the poem ends with Rosamond's prophetic dream of Queen Eleanor appearing with "The destin'd bowl": "This dismal omen aggravates my fears, / Before my fancy still the furious queen appears" (*Letters*, 3:211–12).

Mary Queen of France to Charles Brandon Duke of Suffolk is a variant on the heroides form somewhat revised from its first publication in *Poetical Miscellanies, consisting of original poems and translations. By the best hands. Publish'd by Mr. Steele*

(London, [1714]). The revision shows Rowe's development of clarity, more mature political sensibility, and more accessible emotional and psychological force. For example, in the early version, she writes, "How oft I wish'd my kinder Destiny / Had sunk the Queen in some obscure Degree," while the later text reads, "How oft I wish'd my humble lot had been / Beneath the glorious hazard of a queen." Unity of situation and thought is also greater. The earlier version has "Then unmolested we had liv'd, and free / From all the curst Restraints which Greatness brings," while the later picks up the uncertainty of political, especially royal, life in the period: "Then unmolested had we liv'd, and free / From those unhappy turns which greatness brings."[34] This poem is identified as "An Imitation of [Michael] *Drayton's* Epistle" and adapts his story of Mary, recently freed from her political marriage to Louis XII of France by his death. Mary writes to Suffolk doubting his love since he has not rushed to her (*Letters*, 3:213–17). Rowe's poem is more dramatic and in smoother verse. Drayton writes,

> LEANDER had an *Hellespont* to swim,
> Yet this from HERO could not hinder him (2:261)

Rowe expands,

> But *Calais* from the *Kentish* strand is seen,
> A gentle current only rolls between.
> Nor needs my *Suffolk*, like *Leander* brave
> A threat'ning death in ev'ry breaking wave,
> When, guided only by a glim'ring light,
> He cross'd the stormy *Hellespont* each night. (3:213)

Rowe omits a long passage on King Henry's aged impotence ("But Age must needs have something that is warme," 264) and strips away the arousal of jealousy in a lively episode in which the queen watches a tournament when Suffolk "Carry'd the prize from all the youth of *France*" (*Letters*, 3:216). Drayton's queen finishes her epistle with the promise to take revenge for his procrastination, "But it should be with too much loving thee" (2:266). These and other changes transform the sexual tension of Drayton's poem into the story of a woman rather like Silviana who can say, "I know my rank no private choice allow'd," and conclude the poem, "This toy a crown, I would resign, to prove / The peaceful joys of innocence and love." This poem was occasionally reprinted in the century in prominent, accessible places such as *A Select Collection of Poems: with notes, biographical and historical* . . . (London, [1780], 4:79–83) and *Bell's classical arrangement of fugitive poetry* (London, 1789, 7:26–31).

Penelope to Ulysses. From Ovid, also in heroic couplets, begins with Penelope reciting a catalogue of the history of the Trojan War, a masterful exercise in classical knowledge and compression. The poem moves rapidly, as Rowe describes the celebrations of women and returned warriors, Penelope's imaginings, and her beleaguered life as an unprotected woman. An interesting comparison is Anne Wharton's *Penelope to Ulysses* in *Ovid's Epistles: with his Amours* published by Tonson the year before *Friendship in Death*:

> Whatever Stranger lands upon our Shore,
> Thither I run, wing'd Hope flies on before;
> I ask, Where is my Lord? Will he return?
> . . . .
> Then to his Hands a Letter strait I give,
> And cry, Give this to him in whom I live.[35]

Rowe writes, "*Ulysses* I of ev'ry ship require, / The sailors with repeated questions tire" (3:220). Rowe is more explicit, giving full rein to her skill with formulaic amatory imaginings. Wharton writes, "I fear all Dangers Sea and Earth can yield. / . . . / I sometimes think some crafty Stranger may / Have made thy absent wand'ring Heart a Prey" (122), while Rowe adds considerable emotional power:

> Now all the dangers of the land and seas
> Are present to my thoughts, and banish ease:
> While you alas! perhaps with pleasure rove,
> And faithless nourish a forbidden love;
> Take some deluding harlot to your breast,
> And in her arms with lawless transports blest,
> Make my dull easy constancy your jest. (3:221)

Both poems end with fears of growing old and unattractive. Wharton writes simply, "Return, and bless thy Wife, whose Youth decays / With shedding Tears at thy unkind Delays" (124). Again Rowe expands and the poem recalls how many times she tells the story of a woman waiting for her love, as she did so vividly in her Canticles:

> Will ev'ry grace, each fancy'd charm decay?
> Increasing cares, and times resistless rage,
> Will waste my bloom, and wither it to age;
> Yet at thy sight wild joys and sprightly love
> Shall dying youth recall, and ev'ry charm improve. (*Letters,* 3:222)

Again as is typical of her stories of the waiting women, rebirth and joy are possible. The final verse epistle in the set, *Hellena to Amasia*, concludes the volume and gives symmetry to the four volumes as Hellena writes from Hell to warn Amasia. This poem, like the one before it, must weave difficult names into the rhyme scheme for Hellena sees Helen, Cleopatra, Ovid's Julia, and others there. Like a number of Rowe's characters, she has led her friend to sin and hopes to expiate partially by rescuing her.

Rowe's demonstration of mastery of epistolary and poetic forms conferred authority on her text. As Ezell says of Jane Barker, "In publishing her fictions, she was also publishing her poetry."[36] Barker had also quoted Philips, and some theorists argue that this is a way to augment an individual voice with a collective or communal one. The most commonly quoted poet in Rowe's fiction is John Milton, the greatest Nonconformist writer of them all. Some writers, like Haywood, claimed a special expertise, as she did as the "great Arbitress of Passion" and then through signing her texts "by the Author of *Love in Excess*" or with titles such as *Life's Progress through the Passions*. Rowe was a respected poet, and, in contrast to Haywood, Philomela was the wondrous singer dutifully alert in her thorn nest. All three volumes of *Letters Entertaining and Moral* were identified as by "the Author of *Friendship in Death*," a very different kind of identification although it followed the convention of the print world as exploited by Daniel Defoe, "Author of *The True-Born Englishman*," and Haywood. In many ways, however, Rowe's prose fiction occupies a middle ground, a narrative voice that draws upon what the Pindarick Lady and Philomela stood for even as it claimed the narrative originality of the adaptations of prose fiction types in *Friendship in Death*. This voice laid the foundation for the creation of a revisionary space for Rowe to affirm her writerly identity, to practice her literary craft, and to express her opinions.

Author, Character, Reader

In the hands of a skillful writer such as Rowe the epistolary form offered enormous freedom; it could employ any discursive mode, could address any topic, and could vary the number and kinds of people addressed. The compression, rhetorical strategies, and polish she had developed as a poet contributed to the precision and conciseness of her prose. By demonstrating range and variety parallel to that of the subjects and styles of her poetry, Rowe becomes a visible master of discourses and subjects. In contrast to the sober reflections of many of her characters, she can create characters like Lavinia in part 2, letter 4 who reveals a lively temper, an ability to laugh at herself, and, most of all, delight in the city and its fashionable abundance.

Her element is the world of the Duke's shapely legs with clocks on his stockings and his gilded wainscots, not her ancestral home, "a Gothick heap" with bow rather than Venetian windows.

Rowe's epistles reproduced respected, effective social and textual conventions, but, as women writers were doing with many masculine forms, she opened the way for her to call into question the authority they embody. In a time when people who could write letters like those in collections had authority because the ability spoke of class, privilege, and power, Rowe's letter-writing characters and those they address are automatically empowered. An issue that is sometimes vexed for woman writers is the kinds of knowledge the authorial voice can display. Incongruities arise when characters need to have knowledge that the author should not *and* when the writer wants to "deliver sentiments and display knowledge which would not properly belong to any of the characters."[37] Rowe moved comfortably within the parameters of acceptable knowledge in both categories. Not only did the epistolary form allow a wider range of experiences and sentiments, but Rowe stretched the categories by having cultured, educated characters who comfortably moved through the world, literature, and philosophy. Even when they make numerous learned allusions, they are not responded to or described as d'Aulnoy's Laideronnette in *The Green Serpent* was.[38] What they know seems natural and easy, and because her stories are not extravagant, wild, or exotic, content and expressions flow easily. Rowe includes numerous allusions to Blaise Pascal to develop her characters' self-reflective thoughts. Her fairy tales gain authority from their discourse and from the philosophical, adventure, and historical letters and poems included in the volumes. Silviana's story is followed by the letter on Westminster Abbey by "Theophilus." It is an obvious meditation on Addison's *Spectator* piece and appropriately attached to Silviana's satiric account of fashionable life in London. Rosalinda writes to *Lady* Sophia, and her sentences, ideas, and vocabulary are graceful and sophisticated:

> A more agreeable situation cannot be imagined, nor a greater variety of sylvan scenes described in poetry, unless Mr. *Thomson's* SPRING and SUMMER Seasons could rise in one enchanting prospect. The wide landskip round is all my master's propriety. (*Letters*, 2:4)
>
> Persuasion dwells on his tongue, while he describes the gentle passion in accents calm as the midnight air. (3:132)

Following the *conteuses*, in her most important move, she created an aesthetic of production and an aesthetic of reception that unites Rowe as author, the women characters, and, finally, the reader in a project of self-construction.[39] In Rowe's fairy tales, the letter writer is a beautiful, intelligent, virtuous woman, the conventional heroine of such stories, and Rosalinda and Laura become the pastoral damsel, a kind of feminine aesthetic object. Silviana is discovered by the earl who marries her as one of Diana's nymphs in a painting, and her honeymoon is a pastoral interlude. Sylvia Bowerbank has pointed out how much cultural capital "Diana and a community of forest women" had, and Silviana's story recalls Mary Wroth's description of her Silviana, who has sworn allegiance to Diana, meeting Pamphilia in *The Countess of Montgomeries Urania* (1621).[40] Thus, Rowe orients her reader with two of the most powerful aesthetic images of the time, classical and pastoral. Over and over she creates a carefully crafted, beautiful setting, and the details are subliminal masterpieces. Silviana is in a summerhouse painting, thereby invoking leisure and wealth and encouraging readers to imagine an architecturally interesting building on a gentle hill commanding refreshing prospects of gardens and walks. It would be crude and voyeuristic for Lord— to watch her being painted, so her picture and then tea in Lady Worthy's summerhouse are the genteel introduction of the lovers. Rowe's careful artistry in delivering her philosophy is on display in the honeymoon episode, as Silviana writes,

> This period was all pastoral and romantick, the golden age seemed to be renewed with *Ovid's* Oenone: I could have wished the noble youth divested of his hereditary honours, possessed only with a snowy flock, and graced with no distinction, but that of the *Lovely Swain*.
> Then unmolested we had liv'd, and free
> From those vexatious forms which greatness brings;
> While rocks and meadows, shades and purling springs,
> The flow'ry valley and the gloomy grove,
> Had heard of no superior name to love. (*Letters*, 3:172–73)

This section has considerable cultural capital with its reference to Ovid's Oenone and the combination of pastoral and "romantick," a reference to the older literary romances "composed of the Constant Loves and invincible Courages of Hero's, Heroins, Kings and Queens, Mortals of the first Rank," as Congreve styled them in 1692.[41] Classical, pastoral, French literary romances—again she subtly allies her work with prestige genres. As Bourdieu noted, "An art which ever increasingly contains reference to its own history demands to be perceived historically; it asks to be referred not to an external referent, the represented or designated 'reality,' but to the universe of past and present works of art."[42] Nowhere is the technique of creating an aesthetic of production more obvious than in d'Aulnoy's "The White Cat," and what Rowe is doing is analogous. The cat is a powerful storyteller and one who habitually composed verses and songs. "The most elaborate fiction within the tale is the White Cat's own story, a version of Rapunzel." As Elizabeth Harries notes, "The cat's castle also mirrors her power and luminous intelligence." The tower walls depict scenes representing major fairy tales, including some of d'Aulnoy's.[43]

Silviana's allusion to Oenone is especially rich and, indeed, prophetic. Married to Paris and living in idyllic happiness, Oenone has the gift of prophecy and warns him that his voyage to Greece will destroy him and his country. At this point, the myth suggests the misgivings of d'Aulnoy's princess in *Isle of Happiness*. Paris goes to the Trojan War and comes back severely wounded. He begs Oenone to heal him, but she is angry and refuses. By the time she changes her mind, he has died. Rowe uses the myth prophetically. Silviana's story ends with their move to London and a picture of uncomfortable, extravagant dress and seduction attempts by a variety of men, including "the most intimate friend my Lord had" (*Letters*, 3:175). The story of Paris and Oenone was a favorite of Rowe's contemporaries during the time she was living in London. Aphra Behn had been chosen to contribute *A Paraphrase On the Foregoing Epistle of Oenone to Paris* in John Dryden's *Ovid's Epistles, translated by Several Hands* (1680), and Henry Carey, then a music teacher whose students sometimes performed on the London stage, had published *Cantata IV. Paris and Oenone* in his *Poems on Several Occasions* [1713].[44] Wroth's story also ends with Silviana leaving her forest sanctuary, her friend Pamphilia, and her independence for marriage. Rowe provides a palimpsestic text, one that some readers could place in a tradition of stories that contrast markedly to the happy-ever-after of marriage.

Sarah Prescott speculates that Rowe's authorship of *Friendship in Death* was widely known by the time of the publication of the first part of *Letters*, which was advertised as by the author of *Friendship in Death*.[45] Obituaries and reviews of her posthumously published works make clear that her authorship was well known and that her lifestyle and writing styles, as well as her moral content, shared an admirable reputation. As Robin Kirschbaum points out, she was "in the public eye as a writer for over four decades [and] enjoyed success in a range of literary genres and communities."[46] How much is generally known about her is a little surprising. A letter and review of *Devout Exercises* sent to Richard Hooker for *The Weekly Miscellany*, for instance, notes that she was a Dissenter and the author of *Letters from the Dead* and comments, "How strong is her Trust in God, and how strongly express'd!"[47] The *General Evening Post* called her "the Ornament of her Sex and Age" and noted her authorship and public respect for *Friendship in Death* and *Letters* "besides several excellent Poems in the *Miscellanies*." Most significantly, the writer seems acquainted with her "private Character" and describes her as exemplary in charity and "all that is amiable in Human Life" and a "Delight of her Acquaintance."[48] The *Weekly*

Miscellany elaborated on its earlier obituary and devoted almost equal coverage to her publications (mentioning *History of Joseph*, as well as *Friendship, Letters*, and her poetry), her biography, and her lifestyle. Calling her "celebrated," "extraordinary," "of distinguish'd Character," and "the Ornament of her Sex, and the Honour of the County of Somerset," it notes her amiability and that "her Conversation was the Delight of all the Nobility and Gentry in those Parts."[49]

She was news; the *Daily Post* published this item on 2 September 1737 and the *Old Whig, or the Consistent Protestant* repeated it on 8 September:

> The late celebrated Mrs. Rowe, to whom the World is already much oblig'd for her many ingenious Writings, hath left the Publication of her Devotional Manuscripts to the Care of the Rev. Dr. Isaac Watts.

Rowe's name did not appear on the prose fiction until after her death, but in the small literary community of Rowe's time recognition of her authorship was undoubtedly widespread. She had a marked authorial presence established from her published and reprinted poetry and the wide circulation of her *On the Death of Mr. Thomas Rowe*. Her lifestyle was publicized in part by her friendship with the high-profile Lady Hertford, who "was to become a well-known literary patron who cultivated her own literary circle of poets and writers which included Rowe."[50] Lady Hertford was, after all, a Lady of Our Bedchamber in Ordinary to Queen Caroline (1723–1737), and her tasteful improvements at Marlborough Castle (which Rowe visited), St. Leonard's Hill, and especially Percy Lodge were praised by her contemporaries. Lady Hertford's piety and preference for the country over court life were well known, and they were publicized by poets. David Hill Radcliffe describes her as "the unwilling focus of national attention through praises of her taste and piety in prominent works"[51] as he discusses poems by John Dalton, Moses Browne, and William Shenstone. The publicity was general; for instance, the *Gentleman's Magazine* published *To Mr Thomson, On Hearing Lady **** commend his Seasons*.[52] Thomson had dedicated *Spring* to her in 1728 and complimented her in it and in his *Hymn to Solitude*.[53] Isaac Watts deliberately echoed Pope's laudatory norm:

> Is there a Soul at Court that seeks the Grove
> Or lovely Hill to muse on heavenly love;
> And when to crowds and state her Hour descends,
> She keeps her Conscience and her God her Friends?[54]

The actual letters between the two women printed in the first part of *Letters* reinforced the kind of aesthetic author that Rowe constructed herself to be; she was herself an aesthetic creator in an aesthetic setting producing aesthetic objects—individual letters in prose and poetry. Like d'Aulnoy's White Cat, she gracefully assumed an authoritative position, one not emphasized or insisted upon, but established by association with a setting rich in symbolism and with prestige genres of aristocratic and religious writing. Moreover, the continued vigorous sale of Rowe's collected *Letters* after her death, now advertised as her work and augmented by the *Miscellaneous Works* and appreciative biographies published at her death, strengthened the authority of her writerly presence. Part of the aesthetic of production is to include allusions that only the refined readers will recognize. The *conteuses*' tales were full of them, delivered in all but invisible images of Versailles, the opera, and aristocratic, public dress. The domestic settings created for Melissa, Rosella, and Melinda by Rowe deliver a blueprint for aspiring middle-class women. Christine Jones has described what "the enduring success of [d'Aulnoy's] stories can tell us about the role ascribed to France in the formulation of bourgeois aesthetics in England."[55] This accessible aesthetics, like that of Martha Stewart, depends upon material objects and practices. Just as a taste for quesadillas or scotch or Cabbage Patch dolls can be produced and cultivated, the taste for cultural goods—for ways of living that have cultural capital—can be produced, and Rowe's fictions carried that out. Keeping things clean and orderly is more important than using them; thus, what might have had use value is moved into the category of cultural capital. Rosalinda writes of her "clean Cambrick cap, and an Holland gown wrought with natural flowers" and her "red cross-knot" as ornament (*Letters*, 2:13). What Melissa and Rosella's mother have saved from their former luxurious lives includes Indian matting, *folios* of maps, "very fine globes," and elegant furniture. The kinds of books recommended by the scene include history, music (with operas), "a few books of the best philosophy," and plays, an abiding pleasure for Rowe.

As Cynthia Wall has demonstrated, "the curiosities that adorn" rooms conveyed a great deal of information to readers of the time through implied rather than specifically detailed spaces. Rather than the kind of descriptions of objects with visual connections to each other revealing important information about characters that are found in modern fiction by, for instance, Henry James or Tom Wolfe, she notes that objects tend to be emblematic and introduced only as characters need to encounter them.[56] Anne Duggan writes,

> In many respects d'Aulnoy's tales are all about worldly pleasures and men and women pleasing each other. Part of this pleasure comes from the physical beauty of the characters, enhanced by makeup, jewels, and fine clothing. In order to please her father, Gracieuse wears a green robe lined with gold and a crown of roses and jasmine with emerald leaves.[57]

The women often sit or walk among flowers, and, as with Rosalinda and the delicate blooms of a hawthorne hedge, there are often exquisite white flowers as background. Melinda becomes part of the household of "the wife of an *East-India* merchant, who lived in great splendor" (*Letters*, 2:79). Surrounding the life of "temperance and sobriety" were "noble" rooms "furnished with all the riches of the *Indian* world" (2:80). Women arrange flowers, and men or children present them with baskets of flowers. Rowe names some beautiful objects and scenes, but she also depends on the readers' imaginations to create (or re-create) scenes they have experienced or read about. In spite of occasional displays of elegant, elite objects, the scenes dissolve into the accessible, and she appeals to all senses with color, smell, sound, taste, touch, and sight. Just as the Princess Felicity's garden was described as more neat than magnificent, Rowe's fictions are filled with scenes of neat courtyards and small natural retreats. In another historicized aesthetic move, D'Aulnoy and Rowe often compare their heroes to Adonis, and descriptions of them objectify their physiques and clothing. Silviana falls in love with "this enchanting form" when she meets the visiting lord whom she will marry. Rosalinda says that Lucius "appeared like another *Adonis*" and describes him in a ten-line poem beginning "His faultless shape appear'd with ev'ry grace" and ending "His aspect open, artless, and serene, / Reveal'd the spotless mind that dwelt within" (*Letters*, 2:8–9).

Other writers' collections of epistles vary the class and grammatical features of correspondents, but Rowe keeps her correspondents on a plane of gentility, education, and graceful expression. The letters identified as Letters to Cleora and to the Author symbolize important elements of this unity. Rowe as retired gentry and Cleora as aristocrat moving in elite cultural, court, and country-house settings fashioned cross-class, identical sensibilities. The first eight letters addressed to Hertford's Platonic name are altered from real letters.[58] The fifth letters by both women reflect on the death of Heneage Finch, and the second to Cleora is a slightly changed version of a witty letter found in the Alnwick manuscript: "I am certainly dead and buried, according to your notions of life" (1:93). In some letters throughout the four volumes, the reader watches a character construct him- or herself. This movement is somewhat true of the Cleora letters, as the first letter reads, "Without any apology, I am going to talk to myself" (*Letters*, 1:91), and the following letters give brief insights into her moods and thoughts. There are almost no exchanges of letters in any of the volumes, and what we learn about the recipients varies but is never extensive. There are four letters between Emilia and Leticia, who regrets joining with Amanda's friends and physician to deceive her about her impending death. Amanda continues in character to the extent of having plays that she can no longer attend read to her and ordering a new wardrobe "the most fashionable *deshabille* to be sent for from

France; as if she designed to expire genteely, and appear polite, even in the languishments of death" (*Letters*, 2:35–36). In reacting to Leticia's description, Emilia proves more serious than Leticia fears but also more vivacious and worldly than her friend. The friends exchange literary allusions and poetry, some of which reveal more about their minds than the texts of the letters.

In remarks about the educations, lifestyles, and manners of death of others, these letters dramatize a wide range of philosophies. They end in recognition of similarities and differences rather than the kind of explicit moralizing or directives common to more didactic fiction and conduct books. Elizabeth Heckendorn Cook points out that "the rhetorical structure of the letter always makes us ask, 'Who writes, and to whom?'"[59] But, because so little emphasis is put on the recipient and there are so few exchanges of letters, emphasis shifts to the reader as an equally important recipient. Most of the letters have passages intended to persuade and as such deliver covert, didactic messages. To send a persuasive message in a letter implies someone who may not agree or, indeed, may be markedly different in important ways; however, Rowe's constructs reinforce agreement and recognition of shared sensibilities far more often than they privilege persuasion.

For example, Silviana's letter opens, "Your curiosity is very obliging in desiring to know my manner of life, 'til I had the honour of being married to my Lord—" (*Letters*, 3:168). She then tells of her life as the daughter of a country clergyman. The parallels to Richardson's *Pamela* and the curiosity people had about her, her family, and the frequent requests that she explain, narrate, and elaborate are striking. Like Pamela, Silviana has married much above her station. During the courtship, like Pamela, she says that she "was unacquainted with all forms, but such as were the dictates of nature and virtue" (3:172). In her altered state, "I had no design in dressing but to please my Lord; it was only with regard to him, I was concerned for the figure I made in publick" (*Letters*, 3:175). Pamela's desire to please her husband is her strongest aspiration after her devotion to religion, and both are strongly aware of the change in their positions: "After this account of myself, you will not wonder to find me so little at ease in the high station to which I am raised," Silviana writes (3:176).

We learn more about Oriana, Melinda's correspondent, than about Silviana's. "You have too much candour and charity to judge harshly of my proceedings," she writes, and Melinda imagines Oriana pitying her. In this case, the women know each other well, as Melinda begins by saying she is keeping her promise to let Oriana hear from her as soon as she has found safety. But Oriana has not known everything—that Melinda is suffering from a "hopeless passion" (*Letters*, 2:76). Here the construction of the reader is stronger, as s/he is being instructed to respond as Melinda's friend will—with interest, understanding, and pity. Little prompts such as "think what was my affliction" keep the reader involved (2:80), and the conclusion invites Oriana and the reader to admire the maturity and goodness of the sea captain. All of these strategies of involvement and construction are used in the letters from Laura to Aurelia that close the book. "You have been too often of our party..." and "I have too much confidence in my dear *Aurelia*..." show their close acquaintance (*Letters*, 3:226, 229). "You pity me I know," "you will be surprised to hear...," and "You will wonder to hear me treat those subjects..." engage the reader's curiosity and prompt reactions (3:225, 234, 248).

Oddly, both authorial presence and heroines are at once active and passive, conformist and subversive.[60] Because few of the recipients of the letters reply, characters are active in writing but rendered passive because there are no dialogues, no possibility of disagreements or even occasions for clarifications. In a few cases, a writer will imagine the recipient's reaction or comment, but these quickly fade and are absorbed into the smooth whole. Richardson made the epistolary form active not only by multiplying correspondents and readers but by emphasizing the materiality of the letters as things hidden, stolen, taken by force, and read as evidence in moral trials. Rowe's texts are more monologic and her purposes harmonizing. For example, with the discovery of the rank of the woman writers, or, more revolutionarily, by inheritance, Rowe creates equality between men and women. It is interesting that it is Richardson, not Rowe, who tries to argue that virtue can balance rank as money does in Rowe (and in actual British families). Epistles ordinarily deflect attention away from a single author, but Rowe does not claim the authenticity of "found" letters or use any of the other truth-claim devices common to her time. She gains authority and her writerly presence is asserted by her manipulation of genre and setting. Unlike other authors of epistolary collections, including Addison and Steele, Rowe makes no pretense about the fact that she has written all of the letters except those by Cleora/Hertford.

Rowe's dedication "To Dr. Young" parallels her epistles even as it constructs her as she does her letter writers. Like many of them, she is literary—she enjoys Young's two poems. She is a good reader, as she has gained "Pleasure and Advantage" from them. Like her letter writers, she is not a petitioner as she is "above any View of Interest." Her women characters are often incognita, and she, like they, intends to remain "concealed." In the correspondence, Rowe hopes that "the rest of the world will continue ignorant [of her authorship of *Friendship*], except 2 or 3 who know my impertinent manner of thinking."[61] Startling parallels between Rowe and her characters hide here, most notably in the word "transgressive." Her characters run away, disguise themselves, and marry above themselves (or don't marry), and actions and thoughts by Rowe and the characters are subversive. It is only at the end of her dedication that Rowe expresses an intention different from many of the epistle authors: "if they prove a serious Entertainment to Persons whose leisure Hours are not always innocently employed, the End is fully answered." Some of the letter writers, of course, plead with their correspondents to reform, but the majority do not.

What Rowe and the letter writers share most strongly is the benevolence toward the reader; in addition to active and implied well-wishing, there are expressions of tolerance and a lack of reproof. The opportunity for the reader to construct him- or herself in the image of the recipients and letter writers is always there, invited as in Rowe's dedication. Cheryl Nixon has described the dynamic created in some women writers' paratexts in which "the formal strategies used to construct the character of the woman author within the preface are used to construct the female characters within the text and, it is implied, should be used by the reader to construct herself outside the text."[62] This dynamic was not new, as Cook describes the way Montesquieu in his popular *Lettres persanes* (1721) makes "his letter-narrative an analytical instrument that shapes its own ideal reader, a reader whose relation to the text and the society it describes is (literally) critical."[63] What was publicly known of Rowe's life is just this kind of initiation of the process, and, combined with the dedication and register of her letters, the tri-part construct takes effect. Just as she projects concern for her readers, her letter writers express the same concern for their correspondents.

In fact, Rowe is expanding the concept of the coteries in the letters that are gendered female while drawing upon other models for the letters between men. Every coterie develops a distinctive style, one that they see as coming from and establishing their identity. By continually reading each other's texts, reading aloud, and commenting, they polish, refine, and to some extent narrow the style. In the letters between Rowe and Hertford and between Hertford and the Duchess of Pomfret, they confide, but they also want the novelty, or at least variety, that their contemporaries demanded from prose fiction. They search for amusing, unusual events or experiences to share. They also display a somewhat unusual commitment to seriousness, be it philosophical or explicitly moral. In addition to refinement and polish, Rowe and her immediate circle of readers wanted a natural, modern style that also accommodated the extraordinary and marvelous (metaphysical) and displayed authorial and communal identity. Hertford clearly found the style established by Rowe in her fiction familiar and compatible with her own as shown by the letters she added. How much the women enjoyed the blending and collaboration is evident in one letter in which Rowe wrote, "I long to see [their letters] publisht as they soon will bee."[64] Especially telling is the fact that critics are unwilling to assign authorship to the five letters printed after those by Cleora: Iris to Clorinda, Emilia to Almira, Anastasia to my Lord, Diana to Leonora, and Bellamour to Lysander.

Over the four volumes of *Letters*, there are changes, but there are also signs of a sustained vision and structure. *Friendship in Death* begins with a dedication to Edward Young, and the fourth letter from Laura to Aurelia at the end of the four volumes depicts Philocles, the pious hermit, reading Young's *True Estimate of Human Life* (*Letters*, 3:239).[65] The dedication closes with a reference to "Moral, and Entertaining" reading, and, of course, the subsequent three volumes carried that title. Even small touches show structural craftsmanship. For example, Rosalinda looks out over the farm where she has taken refuge and observes that she feels as if she has entered the "scenes of innocence and plenty" on the plains of Mamre (*Letters*, 2:5). Near the end of the sequence of Rosalinda letters, in a pastoral dialogue that Rosalinda wrote as a "solitary amusement" and sent her friend, the swain tells his love that they are like the Jewish shepherds "who fed their flocks on *Mamre's* fruitful plains" (*Letters*, 3:137, 139). She tells her correspondent that she is writing of the British plains, but they can be imagined as Tempe, Arcadia, or Mamre. Mamre was the focal point of the area in which Abraham lived and was named after an Amorite, Mamre, who joined Abraham in a victorious battle. Abraham purchased a cave there for the tomb for himself, Sarah, and other patriarchs and their wives. The depth of Rowe's knowledge is evident in her easy references to Haran, Rachel, and Boaz, each bringing a story to the minds of frequent Bible readers. *Friendship in Death* is marginalized because it is composed of letters from the dead to the living and accounts of visits by the dead to the living, a device Rowe rarely employs in the three volumes of *Letters*—until the final letter in the final volume when Philocles returns from the dead to speak with Laura.

The kinds of letters in the volume change, and, in addition to broadening the subjects and styles, they incrementally weld the text into a unified sensibility. With this expansion both the authority and the artistry of the overarching author are increased. Like the *conteuses* and unlike Haywood, Aubin, and Defoe, Rowe presented herself as a sophisticated author, one conversant with the world of ideas as well as with the realities of economic, social, and legal forces that were the primary subjects of these other writers. Coterie letters, like the satire of the period, are designed to create insiders and outsiders, and Rowe's epistles continually reiterate "you will understand . . . ," "you will be interested in . . . ," and even "you want. . . ." The goal was a story like Laura's that was a new kind of modern allegory. Characters, events, and settings are ordinary and then suddenly ornamented. The story begins like the hundreds of prose fictions of the time and then reveals the "truth" it is designed to communicate. Rowe's woman-centered tales are like many midcentury novels by women that define and illustrate a new, "accomplished" woman whose private and social conduct is a civilizing model that aims to become normative because it posits that such women have attained woman's "natural" nature. Women are happiest and most themselves when they live in a private sphere idyll. If the roles and activities of these couples are strongly gendered and traditional, the relationship is not. They are alike in virtue, intelligence, discrimination, mutual interests, and respect. Some include hidden coterie references, as the "handsome hermit" of the Laura sequence may be a gesture toward Hertford's closet, whose walls were decorated with images of hermits.[66] In later volumes of the letters, Rowe begins to develop theories of charity, and the characters are shown in relation to more people of various ages and classes.

Character after character develops toward a core identity and lifestyle that mirror Rowe's and Hertford's private lives and that insistently push the reader to construct herself (or himself) by that model. As Roger Chartier observes about such fictions, "The reader . . . is projected into the narrative, and, conversely, the hero of the fiction becomes someone just like the reader him-or herself."[67] This innovation created a powerful triad between authorial presence, character, and reader. In the fairy tales, Rowe multiplies expressions of "I," thereby creating a thinking and acting speaker, one whose "I" sentences often reinforce the identity that the author is asserting and protecting. For example, Laura uses "I" ten times in thirty-two lines as she describes her identity as a relationship to the city (*Letters*, 3:229, 231), then there are more descriptive passages and quotations from Philocles, the "handsome hermit," and then ten times in thirty lines as she recounts becoming religious (3:248–49). Similar increases occur at developments in Rosalinda's identity. Émile Benveniste argues that a speaker's enunciation of "I" generates a subject identity in relation to an addressed "you."[68]

Because the recipient is addressed with respect and the rank of this person usually given, the aesthetic of production generates an aesthetic of reception.[69] Benveniste observes that the subject identities cannot be separated from the *Present* instance of discourse ("L'essentiel est donc la relation entre l'indicateur . . . et la *présente* instance de discours"), and both are defined by the I/you relationship created.[70] Because addressees within the tales are of equal or, usually, higher rank, and the women letter writers' characters' discourses remain the same even as they change their status from, for instance, titled, wealthy lady to servant, the strength and resilience of the identity that Rowe is asserting are reinforced. The reader, of course, is receiving the letters just as are Lady Sophia, Oriana, Aurelia, and the nameless "Madam." Silent reading was becoming the norm, and theorists identify the "reading revolution" with this time.[71]

Chartier's revisionary theoretical model is especially pertinent to Rowe. He argues against the model of the two styles of reading, one "studious" and one "consumerist," to posit the reader as projected into the work of fiction where "a new figure of the author" had "quasi-religious status."[72] Rowe *gave* her text quasi-religious status by her life and the publications that had kept her somewhat in the public eye. In addition to poems in such periodically reprinted collections as *Divine Hymns and Poems on Several Occasions* (1704, 1707, 1709, 1719) and Tonson's *Poems on Several Collections* (1718), her *On the Death of Mr. Thomas Rowe* had been printed in Bernard Lintot's *Poems on Several Occasions: By His Grace the Duke of Buckingham and other eminent hands* (1717) and with Pope's *Eloisa to Abelard* in 1720. Specifically by dedicating *Friendship in Death* to Edward Young, as Prescott notes, she "guides the reader into associating her text with religious verse."[73] The fact that her fiction was advertised with Young's *True Estimate* institutionalized and commodified this linkage. Chartier argues that "the most essential feature" of the reading revolution was the transferring of "sacrality to the writer,"[74] a characteristic that became more prominent in the case of Rowe and her readers because of the publication of *The History of Joseph* and the posthumously published collections of her work with their constructions of her saintliness. As Radcliffe says, Hertford, to whom Watts had dedicated Rowe's *Devout Exercises of the Heart in Meditation and Soliloquy, Prayer and Praise* (1737), was increasingly presented publicly as leading "a quasi-monastic community of polite readers and talkers" and creating "a domestic routine modeled on the ancient rituals of devout life."[75] Given Rowe's public reputation and the piety of her stories and poems, it was easy for readers to believe it appropriate for them to internalize the "truths" in the text.

Chartier gives Diderot's description of the ideal reader of *Clarissa*, one "freed from worldly exigencies," "tranquil and solitary . . . who loves to dwell in the shadows of some retreat" and is "fully susceptible to the influence of that text," the exact physical and mental location of Rowe's letter writers. Rowe gains authority by associating her texts with a specific kind of literary religious expression, just as she does with classical, pastoral, and other respected secular forms. In one letter, a statesman retired in the country says he put holy fables, "the poet's rosy bowers," and "soft *Elysian* fields" on the same level (*Letters*, 1:59), and from these different views of nature says his "mind retires within itself, where it finds treasures 'till now undiscover'd" (1:58). The correspondents sometimes write in these very terms. Letter 1 of "To Cleora" says, "Such a retreat as disengages the mind from those interests and passions, which mankind generally pursue," and this set of letters and many others dramatize the disengagement and higher thoughts in retirement. Letter 3 by Cleora describes her planting and caring for trees "at a time when my health is declining," and as the letter progresses, her involvement and identification with her plants and flowers grow until the external world fades (1:91, 110).

Chartier writes that at this time there was a "transference of an older model, that of spiritual reading, onto the text of the novel."[76] Rowe produces this configuration of tranquil, solitary, in retreat, and sacredization of the text, and it brings to mind that she was writing *Devout Exercises* at the same time, which she inscribed,

> The Reflections were occasionally written . . . I am not without Hopes that they may have the same Effect on some pious Minds, as the reading the Experiences of others have had on my own Soul. The experimental Part of Religion has generally a greater Influence than its Theory.[77]

In a good biographical overview, Elizabeth Napier observed that the prose fictions are "more devotional than fictional in tone and intent."[78] The stories within her fiction are narrated experiences and can be seen as written in another genre but with the same compositional and didactic purposes. Twenty years later, when Richardson extracted and published *A Collection of such of the Moral and Instructive Sentiments, Cautions, Aphorisms, Reflections and Observations* (1751) from *Clarissa*, he was reinforcing this author-reader-text construct and mode of reading. This kind of reader is reminded "of truths that they already ought to know," as Eric Rothstein argues,[79] and is encouraged to reflect on what they have read. Because Rowe's epistles are so short, her text accommodates the much-maligned "consumerist" reader even as it functions successfully in this quasi-religious-mediational truth-delivery mode.

Chartier argues that the revolution consisted in the "newfound capacity to read in a variety of ways."[80] It is possible, then, that the rather brief burgeoning of prose fictions made up of tales, mini-lives, and letters both contributed to developing these skills in readers and owed their popularity to rising numbers of this kind of reader. The letters in Rowe's fiction, as in Barker's *Patch-work* novels, in Delarivière Manley's *Lady's Pacquet of Letters Taken from Her by a French Privateer* (1707), in Gildon's epistolary novels, and even in Fielding's *Tom Jones*, required this kind of flexibility. In a typical clump of four letters, Rowe has a scandalous, deathbed confession of a past adulterous affair; a meditation on the sudden death of a young bride-to-be; a condemnation of dueling by a wounded combatant; and the adventures of an English merchant with corsairs and Turks (*Letters*, 2:105–25). In another group, a man who loves another woman begs to be released from a contracted marriage; a dying duke writes a reflective letter on wasted, idle time; an orphan is seduced by his guardian's wife; and a fashionable rake describes his solitary retreat (*Letters*, 1:43–64). These letters include poetry of various kinds and several kinds of discourses. Other letters require markedly different reading skills as styles, as they are poetic heroic epistles or philosophical statements by Deists, recently saved men, or ambitious mercenaries.

The most significant aspect of the reading revolution was the alleged repositioning of the reader. Chartier posits that "every distinction between the world of the book and the world of the reader" is abolished in *Clarissa*,[81] and Rowe produces a particular kind of dynamic that abolishes this distinction in a different way. Elspeth Jajdelska theorizes that the reader—now a silent reader—"conceives of himself or herself as the hearer of an internal voice, that of the notional writer." That internal voice becomes a guide to a lifestyle that is guided by both choice and conscience. She sees the dynamic between writer, reader, and text as Chartier, Rothstein, Nixon, and others do. Jajdelska notes that "if the model reader is a speaker [reading aloud], then the text is modelled around the reader's physical presence. . . . If the model reader is a hearer, then an imagined, non-embodied, and absent writer is addressing a reader who is bodily present, but who, in order to comprehend the imagined voice, is playing the part of assumed reader, distinct from the embodied reader holding the book."[82] This describes the epistolary dynamic of Rowe's work well. The letter writers are usually narrating their process of moral self-creation, which becomes identity construction. Rowe brings her authorial presence to mind by emphasizing character traits that duplicate those she was known to have. Because letter recipient and reader are cast in the same position, Rowe can define her reader "as a similarly authorial/actorial woman who can use similarly authentic/fictive behavior to define the self."[83] Although most letters travel between city and country, solitary, cultured correspondents in aesthetic clothing and settings are imagined. The shared sensibilities between writer and recipient are intended to be assumed by the reader.

Domesticating Content

Early eighteenth-century novels highlight threats to women. Beloved fiancés become seducer-rapists, as do tutors carefully chosen by fathers and the sons of women who have given safe harbor to teenagers like Moll Flanders. Barbary pirates capture women in fiction and on the seas. Women characters sometimes responded extravagantly, as Defoe's Roxana did when she was threatened into willing Susan's murder and Aubin's Maria in *Noble Slaves* did when she ripped her eyeballs out rather than witness her own rape. Davys's and Haywood's women trick men to gain economic security or out of revenge. The novels are filled with women's casuistical reasoning justifying trickery, lying, stealing, disguise, and even bigamy.[84] Rowe's heroines run away from bad situations, and her heroes take sabbaticals to change course, yet both settle down in settings where they have found peace of mind or, at least, resignation. Even the ruined Aurelia has found such a state. Because of the disguises and class crossing, the traditional plot of heterosexual love between aristocratic characters is problematized. The women leave heredity, tradition, their pasts, and their presumed destinies, but through transformation and adaptation, those defining elements of fairy tales,[85] they become epitomes of domestic femininity, even when they remain single. Unlike Galesia's uneasy and fraught "destiny" as a single woman, Rowe's evolve into that life, which appears equal to the marriages of Melissa, Rosella, and Rosalinda.

Thus, Rowe also moved fiction toward novelistic discourse by taming plots. Even when the story is sensational, as when a woman reveals that her oldest son is not her husband's, the emphasis is not on the affair, the events, or even the consequences but on relationships with her sister and her beloved but wronged husband. These relationships are presented as unsensational. Hermione writes to her sister Lady Mary that her peace with heaven is made: "Weeks, and months, and years, are past, since the date of my guilt" (*Letters*, 2:106). She tells her virtuous sister that she was seduced, "the effect of inadvertency and surprise"—what we might call rape. She asks her sister to tell her husband, because he has left his entire estate to this son. She wants "justice" for all of her children (*Letters*, 2:107). Because her death is imminent, her language is calm, and the sons are not present in any way; there is no possibility of dramatic consequences. The conclusion prefigures *Clarissa*, as she assigns her fall as Clarissa did: "From the height of self-confidence, and arrogant virtue, I was left to make this reproachful step to humble me." As Clarissa would, she now believes her repentance means that "through the Divine Redemption, my pardon is procured, and my guilt for ever obliterated" (*Letters*, 2:108). Similarly, Rowe omits the flights of passion in Drayton's *Epistle of Rosamond to King Henry the Second* in his *England's Heroicall Epistles*. Her Rosamond sounds more like Nicholas Rowe's exhausted, repentant Jane Shore than Drayton's Rosamond, who rails,

> Oh no; that wicked Woman, wrought by thee,
> My Tempter was to that forbidden Tree;
> That subtil Serpent, that seducing Devil
> . . . .
> That vip'rous Hag, the Foe to her owne Kind. (lines 51–53, 57)

Drayton's hammering alliterations become Rowe's "Perdition to herself the wretch insur'd, / When she my youthful modesty allur'd" (3:209). The passion and immediacy of Drayton's Rosamond become reflective, de-sensationalized as if years and years had colored the story in neutral colors rather than the vivid ones of Drayton. Rowe reproduces each of Drayton's episodes and transforms each in the same way. His Rosamond watches the road from the towers of Woodstock; hers walks in its gardens. His Rosamond reflects on a statue of Diana and feels pursued by her regrets as if they were Acteon's hounds; hers appreciates the beauty:

> Amidst the garden, wrought by curious hands
> A noble statue of *Diana* stands;
> Naked she stands, with just proportions grac'd,
> And bathing in a silver fountain plac'd;
> When near the flow'ry borders I advance,
> At me she seems to dart an angry glance:
> What scenes, alas, can please a guilty mind! (*Letters*, 3:210–11)

As decades passed, the extraordinary and marvelous are domesticated and become coincidence and more modern contrivances, such as the transformation of scenes through association or magic fortune-repair through the return of an East Indian merchant-relative, and Rowe was an important part of this transition. The world was not such a threatening place for her, although she shared her contemporaries' fascination with moments of crucial life choices. She domesticated common situations in early novels while expanding the characters' psychological life without losing the recognition of gender as a category of political knowledge and resistance. Before Rowe, although there were beautiful natural settings, they were often places of seduction and threat. Rowe sets her fairy tales and many other letters in idyllic meadows, forests, and gardens that harmonize with the states of mind of her virtuous heroes and heroines.

"Choice" is a key word here. As noted, Eric Rothstein postulates "a sense of self that centers one's reality, that incorporates an 'enriched' personality, and that gains its stability by its agency in choosing."[86] In most early novels men define women and their roles, and the psychic and even physical violence to enforce them continues in novels by Elizabeth Griffith and Frances Burney. Rowe's heroines have a firmer sense of self, not only of what is right or wrong but what they will or will not do. They *choose*; as Rothstein further explains, "The capacity to alter one's image and surroundings, updating rather than progressing, confirms the worth of that inner core." Rowe's characters have two modes of defense. First, they leave the threatening environment. In Rowe's stories, it is the heroine who displays courage, as she undertakes a journey beyond her familiar situation into an unknown. More like Henry Fielding's Sophia Western than the earlier women characters who encounter seducers, pirates, and charlatans, Rowe's women, unlike Richardson's Pamela, are willing to risk the dangers of the road but encounter none. Second, Rowe's women adapt. Rosalinda, for instance, writes a self as she writes her story. As is so often true in eighteenth-century fiction, changes of clothing are highly symbolic, and Rowe's characters easily slide from one style to another. As with Rosalinda, what they wear and how they occupy their time changes, but who they are does not.

Nancy K. Miller identifies one of the signs of feminist writing to be "through an insistence on [the heroine's] singularity [it generates an awareness of] the existence of other subjective economies, other styles of identity."[87] Rowe's positioning of her characters in a universe that is both metaphysical and material produces another subjective economy and "other styles of identity." Her fictions, although clearly in the tradition of English tales told by coins, saved "patches," or based on stolen bags of mail, are actually closer to the salon productions because of their polish; their intertextuality with other learned discourses, including elite poetry; and the rapidity with which they leave the ordinary world behind and engage a universe in which earth and Heaven are seamlessly joined. Rowe insistently creates this different subjective economy, and it is perhaps the most important definition of her contribution to feminist thought and the eighteenth-century novel. Instead of warning women about the world as Haywood and Defoe did or building a text on "strange and surprising adventures" as Aubin and Defoe did, Rowe domesticated these emphases in order to give women the skills to cope with the world.

In the prose fiction of the time, domestic arrangements can sometimes take bizarre flights, as one does in Jane Barker's "The Unaccountable Wife." Unlike Barker, however, although Rowe does not make heterosexual marriage the normative happy ending, she never makes unusual domestic arrangements threats to social order. Thus, she takes a critical life choice for women and makes its exploration acceptable. As Emma Donoghue argues, some partnerships could arouse uneasy feelings that "endangered the socially acceptable lifestyles of spinsters and romantic friends." Donoghue goes on to point out that Barker "masks" "its anarchic message by presenting it from the hostile point of view of the Wife's in-laws and acquaintances, as something 'unaccountable.'"[88] In Rowe's stories, women whose romantic circulation has been threatening are taken out of the market, but not in ways that elicit sometimes controversial interpretations, as Haywood's *British Recluse* has. And, of course, Rowe's are first-person letters directed to a specific "you," and readers are likely to be pleased, as the recipient apparently is, with the outcomes.

Thus, Rowe also domesticates the revenge-fantasy plot. As Earla Wilputte notes, such plots encourage women "to see their injuries as worthy of resentment and repayment." Even though Rowe has nothing as extreme as Haywood's *City Jilt*, she does construct conclusions that warn "society of the possible consequences should women refuse to tolerate their unfair treatment and finally act upon their just resentment."[89] Rosalinda leaves her father without a daughter to commodify, and the women who leave the libertine, raucous homes of brothers take themselves out of the marriage economy, a system perceived to be essential to everything from social order to war efforts.

Monetary references and transactions are ubiquitous in the fiction of the time. This passage from Mary Davys's *The Cousins* could be the opening of almost any woman writer's story before 1740. What might slide by unnoticed is that there is an economic reference in almost every line:

> Within the Kingdom of *Spain*, there dwelt a Gentleman call'd *Gonsalvo*, of a large Estate, and a very fair Character, who married the Daughter of a wealthy Neighbour; a Woman of incomparable Virtue, and the most remarkable for Wit and Beauty, of any in or about the Place she liv'd in: her Fortune was answerable to the rest of her Qualifications.[90]

Moll's and Roxana's obsessive tallying of their financial gains and losses is familiar to all readers, but in texts by Davys and especially in an allegedly rather otherworldly writer like Rowe they have not attracted attention. In a passage that could have come from a Defoe novel or Richardson's Pamela, Rowe describes the sea captain's wife giving Melinda £10,000:

> My mistress immediately came into the chamber, with goodness shining in her eyes, and gave me the bank bills, with a grace, which only virtue can stamp on human actions: She prevented my thanks. . . . And that the hopes of my staying with her, was the greatest satisfaction she proposed. . . . I could not possibly discover my sense of this surprizing benefit, by all the force of language—my silence, and the tenderness into which she saw my soul was melted, was the only evidence of gratitude I could now give. (*Letters*, 2:82–83)

The implications of "benefit" are ambiguous and double, as "improvement" is in *Robinson Crusoe*, and the passage is both mercenary and the beginning of a sentimental discourse of gratitude. Silviana, daughter of a country clergyman, inherits £20,000, an astonishing $2,400,000 in today's money,[91] from her maternal uncle, a Turkey merchant. It is four pages before we find out that Rosalinda frequented the court and was Lady Frances, an earl's daughter. These facts, as they are for the other women, are slipped in unobtrusively, even when specific sums of money are mentioned, as they are most notably in the stories of Melissa and Rosella.

Social status and money are important subjects in Rowe's novels as they are in the novels by others of her time, but, interestingly, she brings to the fore another consideration of prime importance for women: geographic location. Women's increasing demand to have, if not choice, then the power to decline a would-be husband has been frequently studied, but where a woman was allowed to live is also a fascinating and richly symbolic subject. Many women wrote about their own and their characters' separation from friends, usually by being moved to remote locations by husbands. Rowe depicts a wife moved to London, where she is separated from friends but also from the outdoors that has nurtured her spirit. Countering this geographical theme, however, is the security and continuation of the women's friendships in this and all of the other fairy tales where, of course, the pilgrim-women are separated from family and friends when they leave intolerable situations. Perhaps because of Rowe's religious philosophy, love and friendship depend less on physical presence than for other writers. Part of Rowe's domesticating of the novel is unobtrusively suggesting that the almost unimaginably spacious country-house landscapes and gentry farms somehow can be shaded into tidy entrances to homes and middle-class contemplative spaces.

Jane Barker did not create a new ideology for women but showed the need for one in her fiction; Rowe, however, created one for women and thereby brought the space of the Other to consciousness. Louis Althusser defined ideology as "the 'lived' relation between men *and their world*" and "a system of representations" (emphasis mine).[92] God gave Crusoe a material adversary and Clarissa a rigid oppositional position. In contrast, Rowe expanded "world" to include the metaphysical, a "naturalized" part of the mind as no other writer had.[93] Readers could glean information from the imagined settings, material and internal, that she created. Rather than hailing a reader who would be surprised, amazed, shocked, and called upon to judge characters and actions, she drew authorial presence, characters, and reader together. Her characters are always reasoning and speaking, discovering themselves in both senses of the concept: learning more about themselves and also revealing themselves to the recipient of the letter and, therefore, to the reader. As such, they become conduits for knowledge. As Rothstein explained, "The most important skill that one uses in learning from texts about the world—getting in place to process future possibilities and events—is then the same kind of skill that one uses in continuing to read the text itself."[94] She wrote a distinctive worldview into her narratives and, by doing so, harmonized style and content, thereby domesticating some of the sensationalism in both. While texts before hers had been dedicated to saving the body, as Haywood's had, or the soul, as Bunyan's had, she portrayed saving body, sanity, and soul. Aubin had done some of the same things but in exceptionally extravagant fictions in exotic locales, such as gothic forests and pirate ships. Because Rowe's social commentary is driven by moral judgments and a firm sense of lifestyle as an expression of identity, many elements of content and style become harmoniously inseparable.

Pierre Bourdieu speculates that "intellectuals could be said to believe in the representation—literature, theatre, painting—more than in the things represented, whereas the people chiefly expect representations and the conventions which govern them to allow them to believe 'naively' in the things represented. The pure aesthetic is rooted in an ethic, or rather, an ethos of elective distance from the necessities of the natural and social world."[95] This hypothesis can be applied to Rowe's epistles, as the lifestyle she constructs is an aesthetic one rooted in her religion, obviously an ethic. The Bible continuously reinforces the association of God with Beauty:

Out of Zion, the perfection of beauty, God hath shined. (Ps. 50:2)

He hath made every *thing* beautiful in his time: also he hath set the world in their heart. (Eccles. 3:11)

Our holy and our beautiful house,
Where our fathers praised thee. (Isa. 64:11)

How beautiful are the feet of them that preach the gospel of peace, and bring glad tidings of good things! (Rom. 10:15 from Isa. 52:7)

The transfer of "the beauty of the Lord our God" to "the work of our hands" and its transmission in the world is a fundamental concept, as expressed at the conclusion of Psalm 90. By reinforcing it with images and even short quotations from the Bible, she provides a recognizable aesthetics and ethos for her readers. As in the fairy tales, the mode of representation is more important than the content and carries more meaning. In *Distinction*, Bourdieu firmly demonstrates that aesthetic choices belong to a set of ethical choices and, in turn, to a resulting lifestyle. By associating lifestyle with aesthetics, Rowe makes her characters' choices more attractive.

Rowe seems to be refining rather than challenging women's abilities and roles. Resolutions to the early novel have often been criticized as improbable, unsatisfying, or nonexistent. Although replicating the situations of characters, Rowe provides resolutions that, like the domestic arrangements, do not always reinforce social norms but also do not seem "unaccountable" or arouse uneasy feelings. She both holds up for critique and affirms parts of patriarchal ideology, and in spite of her controlled, polished prose, she manages to produce "stories shaded across social and economic lines." "Shaded," a concept I borrow from J. Paul Hunter's description of a similarity between old oral tales and the novel, is a good word, because the kinds of aristocratic trappings and privileges are apparent and yet dissolved as the stories develop.[96] Rowe's fictions, like Mary Davys's, by their content rather than explicit comment question the authority and "rightness" of the patriarchal order.[97] Rowe is especially adept at exposing and marginalizing the patriarchy. Rosalinda's father becomes interested in reconciling when he sees what an advantageous marriage she has made. Although Rosalinda regrets her father's stance when he tries to marry her to a "Papist," she conducts her life completely satisfactorily without him. What Kathryn King says of Mary Hearne's Amaryllis and Calista in *The Lover's Week* (1718) could be said of numerous Haywood and Rowe heroines: "Retirement . . . comes to mean release from the constraints of the aged, overbearing, and foolish guardians explicitly linked with a discredited Stuart past, a severing of the old lines of authority celebrated in royalist romance that leaves these up-to-date heroines free to forge new kinds of relationships for a new kind of socio-political order."[98] Hearne's characters follow their lovers, but Rowe's take the initiative in retiring and discover men worthy of them, thus moving her fictions beyond those of the 1720s. As should be expected in a new form with new purposes, writers moved quickly beyond reproducing the visible to making systems and consequences visible.

In contrast to the incidents in which Rowe exposes the way the patriarchy works are technical moves and episodes that reveal the instability of the sex-gender system. Rowe has usually been assumed to be and described as the kind of writer who is strongly gendered in a specific way; therefore, her gender is inscribed as a distinguishing feature of authorial voice, textual production, and meaning.[99] In some of the letters, this is true. However, Bellamour tells the story of Melissa and Rosella to Lysander, and he, like other male letter writers, mentions business, responsibilities, and the need for travel. An English merchant who writes polished, elevated prose describes his adventures to Valerius; Amintor writes to Eusebius describing how he has coped with the death of his wife; and Polidore describes an adventure to Alonzo. Rowe is obviously comfortable writing as a man addressing another man. Perhaps more significantly, rather than her couples illustrating heterosexual complementarity, they discourse as equals, establish lifestyles that are similar in important ways, and also respect differences. Nonconformists like Rowe often said that all souls were equal before God, and Rowe has men and women write the same way about religion, city life, sin, the outdoors, salvation, literature, and various religious experiences. I believe an argument could be made that some of Rowe's religious poetry is strongly gendered female, but such an argument cannot be made of her prose fiction.

Commitment and the New Reader

By looking at Rowe's shading, domesticating touch, the pivotal, influential nature of her work emerges. The *Spectator* aimed at constructing a civilized, humanist society, and Rowe's epistles were sophisticated exercises in such a construction. Rowe produces an aesthetic of reception that increases the size of at least two communities of readers who had specific skills and purposes for reading: those reading fiction for moral improvement and those seeking reinforcement for their commitment to the politeness movement.[100] Like the hearers of exemplar in sermons and the readers of anecdotes in periodicals like the *Spectator*, these readers have much to teach us about the social conditions that produced these new kinds of readers. Rowe's readers are especially interesting because of their commitments to Christian morality and therefore to intensive reading and to politeness, a new social movement that was strikingly marked by consumerism. They identified proudly with their groups yet meditated privately and methodically; they desired timeless Truth and yet embraced modern "accomplishments." They delighted in finding authors whom they could sacralize, and they insisted upon novelty and contemporary relevance. Remarkably, Rowe's obituaries with their compliments about her conversation and virtue inscribe her inspiration to these readers. Rowe had acted out in her life a lifestyle and, therefore, an identity, defined in the text. The poems included in the text further blur the distinction between author and character. Thus, she created "an authorial presence by emphasizing character traits that duplicate those exhibited in the fictional text," setting up a reciprocal flow and an isomorphism that passed to the reader, who was invited to become an "authorial/actorial woman."[101] Rowe's most artistic composition was her lifestyle and constructed identity, and she uses the same methods repeatedly to construct characters and passes them on to her readers.

Rowe goes beyond writing transitional texts to being a pivotal figure. Her fiction was a new way to combine the internal and external, the metaphysical and the mundane. Novels after Rowe often included this characteristic, one Christine Roulston identified in Sarah Scott's *Millenium Hall* as a "fantasy of an elsewhere, of an alternative domestic narrative."[102] That "elsewhere" is a land not of fairies and giants but of possibility for alternative lifestyles and domestic arrangements. The elsewhere of the lifestyle is an allegory of the state of mind that would become the central strategy and quest of women's novels written after hers. Therefore, she delivered a sense of something more true than empirical, material experience. That Heaven and the earthly settings of her characters are presented aesthetically welds them into a single reality. Because her fictions are so ideological, they appeal to kindred spirits almost as political propaganda does. In her time, people holding residual, contemplative religious structures of feeling were augmented by those committed to the emergent structures of feeling associated with the politeness movement. These feelings were not mutually exclusive, and these desires prevailed in numerous groups, perhaps the majority of the population, thereby sustaining the sale of her book into the nineteenth century.

This deliberately calm, elegant style moved the novel toward a distinctive English voice, one that Richardson came to recognize and revise toward.[103] Together these things give her prose fiction books a unified style and controlling sensibility and raised the status of the novel. Aphra Behn had used the epistolary form to reveal female subjectivity and sexual desire; Rowe also portrays female subjectivity, but the desire is for peace of mind and the freedom to maintain a quite specific state of mind. The epistolary form authorized expressions of interiority and created the illusion of honest, natural feelings. Unlike more didactic texts, hers are filled with verbs that express intellectual states that are not observable and are, therefore, "private." "Think," "hope," "hear," "see," "believe," "suppose," "remember," "expect," "intend," "fear," and "imagine," for instance, occur much more often than modal verbs, such as "can," "should," and "would."[104] Rowe thus took a firm step toward creating psychologized novelistic characters. Because she creates this so consistently and it is so specific, it can become a benchmark for measuring women's happiness (and virtue), and hundreds of later novels show women besieged, threatened not by seduction and rape but by persecutions that set up a fierce battle for the establishment of this state of mind. It was nothing less than an autonomous existence. Frances Burney's greatest novels, *Cecilia* and *Camilla*, are fine examples.

Patricia Hannon argues that "ideologies and formal textual properties intersect, thus shedding light on the cultural production of meaning."[105] That is a good way to explain the way Rowe's identity, prose voice, and characters work to produce the message about total lifestyle that readers received and that later fiction writers endlessly set up as the novelistic quest. The aesthetic domesticity, guides to how to behave in various situations, and the accomplishments, temperaments, and leisure occupations of her characters are typical of the later novels. New meanings, experiences, and needs must generate new forms, and Rowe's fictions, because of the popularity of her work, had broad effects. Susan Lanser took as her subject in *Fictions of Authority* texts that "construct narrative voices that seek to write themselves into Literature without leaving Literature the same."[106] She does not include Rowe, but she could have. Rowe's fictions contributed to the uses of the epistolary form, and we are only beginning to see how varied the form was before the unified novels of Richardson, Smollett, and Burney. More significantly, writers expanded the kinds of inner quests she dramatized into unified, full-length novels, and that is the subject of the final chapter of this book.

CHAPTER FOUR

The Beautiful Life

Rowe was one of the first English prose fiction writers to incorporate the politeness movement into her texts. In this chapter, I will expand on this revisionary aspect of her work. She wrote in a letter to the Countess of Hertford, "I have been reading my Lord *Shaftesbury's Moralist*, which has fill'd my head with beauties, and love, and harmony, but all of a divine and mysterious nature" and "I have been agreeably led on thro' I know not what inchanting scenes of happiness. I wish you would read it."[1] Shaftesbury's *Characteristicks of Men, Manners, Opinions* (1711) was perhaps the key text in the movement, and his and other propagators' aim was to create a way of living. I will paint a picture of the lifestyle that Rowe created in her fiction and with her life. This concept was of the beautiful life—the life of "beauties, and love, and harmony." Hidden within it, however, was a powerful technology of self-mastery, and she left it as a legacy that later women could draw upon.

What Rowe did is especially important because she makes visible some technologies that emerged contemporaneously with her *Letters*. It seems obvious that in the century the emphasis on women's self-mastery grew and became more forceful. Therefore, I am primarily interested in what Michel Foucault described as technologies of the self, the devices and techniques that make possible the social construction of personal identity. In other words, these technologies produce the knowledge of what human beings should do and who they believe they are, the conceptual self. Built in, then, are the pressures that produce a social product who knows how to act and also the need to counteract, rebel, or adapt selectively. As a woman Rowe was especially vulnerable to socializing pressures, but as a Nonconformist she was especially equipped to resist and conscious of her responsibility to herself as an individual.

In Rowe we have an interesting case of how "individuals effect by their own means or with the help of others a certain number of operations on their own bodies and souls, thoughts, conduct, and way of being, so as to transform themselves in order to attain a certain state of happiness, purity, wisdom, perfection, or immortality." In the texts she left a record of a "set of effects produced in bodies, behaviors, and social relations."[2] That Foucault includes "souls" and "immortality" in his definition and puts emphasis on the development of ethical self-consciousness makes this method especially appropriate for study of Rowe, her texts, and her legacy. Adding interest is contrast in the time/space operations of two technologies. One is a dominant structure of feeling, and the other would prove to be emergent. The first case, that of the politeness movement, is an illustration of the operation of a structure of feeling, a generative and widely shared formative consciousness in a period that includes material practices and dominant ideas and beliefs.[3] The second case, that of the disciplining of women's behavior, is one of Rowe modeling a technology of the self largely from within and providing a model that in itself became a disciplining, social technology carried out through institutionalized discourses and epistemologies. The variety of its descriptions and the judgments of its efficacy in the work and lives of later women have been the subject of much study but have never been linked to Rowe in any meaningful way. The chapter begins with a second look at epistolarity and concludes with a description of a few novels that should be related to hers.

The Epistolary as a Technology of the Politeness Movement

Politeness became a code word for proper, polished behavior, and Lawrence Klein points out "the spread of 'politeness' from discourse to discourse" that gradually appropriated "the world of social, intellectual and literary creation" and brought "under its sway . . . gentlemen and ladies, society, learning, arts, writing and literature, nations, ages of human history."[4] Rowe, in life and posthumously, was perfectly situated by reputation and ideology to ride what had become a rising, irresistible wave. Poetry and history were "the two chief Branches" of polite studies,[5] writers agreed, and Rowe as a respected poet brought that cultural capital to her prose fiction. The biography that prefaced her posthumous *Miscellaneous Works* and that was endlessly excerpted and printed well into the nineteenth century with various selections of her writings casually described her as the epitome of these values. Typical of the scattered remarks are "The elegant *Letters* which gave occasion to remark this distinction in Mrs. *Rowe's* character as a polite writer," "This highly accomplished woman had a great share of all the personal charms that awaken love, as she had all the virtues to rivet it," and "not more admired for her fine writings by the ingenious that did not know her, than esteemed and loved by all her acquaintance, for the many amiable qualities of her heart." As for her conversation skills, she "had few equals."[6] Bayle's *General Dictionary* describes "her shining merit with the charms of her person and conversation" and her "flowing diction."[7] Her life, then, became a text that was studied and interpreted. In the abridged lives that came to preface collections of her texts, these qualities become more prominent partly because so much is missing and partly because they are placed at the beginning of paragraphs rather than being embedded in paragraphs. By midcentury, consensus about politeness reigned; Smollett wrote to Catherine Macaulay, "If I was obliged to define politeness, I should call it, the art of making one's self agreeable. I think it an art that necessarily implies a sense of decorum, and a delicacy of sentiment."[8]

D'Aulnoy's popular, influential collection came out as *Ingenious and Diverting Letters*, and Rowe uses "moral and entertaining," an obvious reference to Horace's definition of good literature. Concerned with the movement's current values of civility, "reasonableness," moderation, proper behavior, the "art of pleasing in company," "refined sociability," and "grasp of form," Rowe found important guidance in the *Spectator*. She propagated, institutionalized, and established as normative the values inherent in the *Tatler*, *Spectator*, and especially Shaftesbury's *Characteristicks of Men, Manners, Opinions* (1711).[9] She shared their opinions. For instance, she wrote to Thomas's sister Sarah, "If the *Spectator* had not told me, that the greatest friendships are least noisy and talkative, my own experience would have convinc'd me of it" (*Misc. Works*, 2:195). The literary fairy tales had dramatized these precepts first not only through the conduct of their protagonists but through the identification of an imagined audience with an author with similar values and sensibilities. Both had a highly developed taste for pleasure, what Lawrence Klein has called "capacities and interests concerned with the 'ornamental' aspects of life, such as taste, style, fashion, and politeness."[10] Although treated in different tones, all shared topics of current interest such as reading, writing, love, courtship, marriage, education, religion, finance, conversing, dressing, and even business—"the polite conduct of life in all its arenas."[11]

Klein identifies 1660–1730 as the period during which "'politeness' rose to prominence in English discourse." Rowe's fictions appearing when they did gave impetus to the establishment of these values because of what she had come to represent. A cornerstone of the politeness movement was conversation, and the familiar letter, a mode of conversation, was women's special province.[12] It is important to remember that in the 1730s Rowe published the fictional *Letters* and left 257 letters to be published as a group in *Miscellaneous Works*. Both are important in similar and different ways. Models of polite conversation are treated in some detail in Rowe's fiction, and, collectively, they represent many aspects of the movement. Rosalinda and Sally, who are from two different classes, are but one example, and the emphasis on philosophy and literature that the chief theorists of the movement identify as definitional is evident in character conversations. The letter from Eusebius to a Deist, for instance, is searching and reflective and includes the poem *To the unknown* GOD.[13] The letters are filled with records of disagreements and topics of changing opinion. Among these topics are dueling, the "right" to commit suicide, women's right to resist arranged marriages, and fashionable, rakish behavior. This aspect of her letters has not been noticed, probably because of the graceful, nonconfrontational, equitable tones and carefully maintained register.[14] They seem to be reasonable discussions, not stands on a topic upon which people were disagreeing strongly.

The first letters printed in *Miscellaneous Works* transition readers from Rowe's fictional letters to her actual letters and, because of their content, heighten awareness that she has died and had prepared in exemplary ways for that death. The first two letters are labeled "Letters under fictitious names." The first combines the discourse of politeness with the construction of an author who is deeply concerned for her friends and readers. It begins, "A Person of your merit, Sir . . ." and says that "your good humour and wit was the greatest entertainment" at a social event (*Misc. Works*, 2:17). The letter, styled as by a man to a man, continues by expressing great concern that he does not believe in the immortality of the soul. The letter stresses how rational religion is and makes a number of arguments, such as that he is "as uncertain, as you think the pious man is of all his visionary hopes" (18). The tone is one of concern and calm self-control, of reason, not enthusiasm. The second letter is a wild story from the dead. A man killed in Rome by a friar at the entrance to a monastery writes to his friend to rescue the niece of a cardinal whom he has converted to Protestantism: "you are absolutely oblig'd to attempt the rescue of my fair proselyte from the tyranny of her bigotted and superstitious guardian." More anti-Catholic and more coercive than any of the letters in her prose fiction, it includes an argument in the letter's story that few would accept: "You can but die, my Lord, and considering death abstractly as the period of human action, a violent or natural death is just the same" (*Misc. Works*, 2:21).

Rowe the writer of *Friendship in Death* and the *Letters* becomes the writer of polite, familiar letters, and the sets created in *Miscellaneous Works* are interesting both as kinds of letters and as revelations about Rowe's life and thought. On 8 October 1732 she wrote to Hertford, "I have been putting your letters and papers in order. When I die, I design to leave them in ———'s hands, as a trust sacred to friendship and virtue" (*Misc. Works*, 2:139). In their own way, each set is a record of friendship and virtue and of the ideal of conversational letters. The letters to Grace Thynne that follow the two fictitious ones begin a debate about whether or not Rowe is dangerously ill or has the spleen. Rowe imagines dying and becoming Thynne's guardian angel, and the letters turn from the more fanciful imaginings to reflections on how to live life, some admonitory: "While people are in their right senses, it cannot be an indifferent case to them, whether they are to be happy or miserable in an endless duration" (2:27). Continued veiled discord over life and death between the women continues. These seven letters, starting in 1697 when Rowe was quite young and just beginning to publish her poetry, show a human being actively constructing herself, her relation to the world, her writing style, and her ethical self-consciousness. Admiring the gentility of Thomas Rowe and Thynne, she praises his "elegant taste" and comments to her, "I never read the *Spectator*, but I apply all his characters of a fine woman to you" (*Misc. Works*, 2:33). She explains her "inclinations to solitude" clearly, denying they are "the effects of melancholy, or ill-nature, or the narrow principle of believing I was born wholly for myself.... I aspire to no character above that of a reasonable creature." She finds retirement the place of the "most exact and impartial notions" and where "you fortify yourself against the tyranny of custom, and the impositions of persons" (2:27–28). Firm in the interactions with the older, higher-rank woman, the person aware of pressures and creating ways to resist that marks Rowe's conduct and writings throughout her life emerges.

Another way that these first letters are transitional is that they refer repeatedly to other worlds. They reach back to the places from which spirits in *Friendship in Death* came, to fairyland, to Elysium (which she styles as the *poets'* fable), and "invisible regions." Imagining and imagining other worlds, worlds definitely not limited to Heaven and earth, gave her lifelong pleasure, and these early letters (in both chronology and placement in *Miscellaneous Works*) contribute to the sense of continuity and personhood. The letters become increasingly personal. She refers to her delight in "Mr. *Rowe's* elegant taste and good sense" (2:33), and the final letter is a simple, short expression of condolence written in 1720, the year Thynne lost her daughter Mary, Lady Brooke.

The next 106 letters are to Hertford, her lifelong friend and Thynne's daughter. The second letter is a touching but practical letter written the year after Hertford married at age sixteen and Rowe was widowed at age forty-one. She refers to marriage as "a just and innocent passion" and expresses concern for the couple whose fortunes are so tied to King George I, the object of the current Jacobite Rebellion. Their sensibilities are clearly more in harmony than Rowe's and Thynne's. As early as letter five, Rowe writes, "I cannot but own, I am secretly pleas'd that you find the gay expectations from this world all deluding and treacherous" (*Misc. Works*, 2:40). In contrast to her letter to Thynne upon Brooke's death, hers responding to Hertford begins simply, "I can hardly read your Ladyship's letter for tears." She agrees to come to her quickly and encloses *An Elegy on the death of the Hon.ble Mrs.*—, although she is afraid it will renew her grief (*Misc. Works*, 2:41–42). The letters quickly become exemplars of politeness practices and values. Among the most significant is the performance of a lack of ceremony and even equality. To some extent, Rowe's age balanced Hertford's rank. In fact, the Nonconformist insistence of the equality of souls intersected with the realignments of the politeness movement that ranked people by their polished sociability and their accomplishments rather than strictly by class and that insisted upon at least a pretence of the equality of participants in conversation. Purportedly, this attitude created a "zone of freedom, ease, and naturalness."[15] As Keeble notes, nonconformity was a defence of human individuality and of the variety of human experience and circumstances that led to the creation of varied protagonists with equivalent value as friends and human beings.[16]

How correspondents addressed each other in the eighteenth century revealed a great deal about their perception of rank, and theorists of early modern letter writing have attempted various ways of looking behind convention to assess intimacy.[17] Comparing Rowe's *Letters* and her personal letters shows that she respected convention in her salutations in both and represented more freedom in the discourse of the *Letters* than in her own writing, thus modeling polite conversation in the *Letters* and practicing a different style with her younger although much higher ranked friend. It is only in the letter left for Hertford at the time of her death that she writes, "I am past the ceremonies of the world, and therefore I cannot treat you with the least formality." Yet her letter begins, "To the Right Hon. the Countess of—. Madam," (*Misc. Works*, 2:46). At various times, she had addressed the topic specifically:

> 'Tis well your Ladyship has given me a full dispensation from all forms and ceremony, and that I have your permission to be as free and licentious in that point as I will. If I was writing to any other person of your quality, 'tis likely, I should be as formal as your mantua-woman . . . ; but in addressing myself to you, I . . . can't help talking in a manner perfectly unaffected and sincere. 'Tis quite different in my intervals of politeness. (*Misc. Works*, 2:50)

The letter is filled with contradictions between statement and language. Rather than "you," Rowe often writes "your Ladyship," and her second paragraph begins, "Your Ladyship will easily excuse me for venturing to let you pass a thousand times thro' my imagination, with no other circumstance of grandeur than your own innate merit." Even thinking about Hertford is something of a class transgression. Taking the letters to Hertford as a whole, it is interesting how many times Rowe "sees" her in some elevated, highly virtuous character in literature, for example, Selima in Chevalier Ramsay's *Travels of Cyrus* (1727, *Misc. Works*, 2:75). This letter and others, however, subscribe to the point that Richardson makes about virtue as elevating in *Pamela* later. In reflecting on King George's death in 1727, she writes, "All distinctions are then lost, but those which virtue gives" (*Misc. Works*, 2:70). In a few letters in which Rowe feels she has been misunderstood, she presents herself as incapable of certain ungenerous or unvirtuous thoughts or actions. The virtuous conduct and principles of the two women are the equalizing factors although rank never really fades from Rowe's mind. As in the earlier letter, she mentions "politeness," a term that also grants equality (or temporarily assumed equality) and yet controls discourse, creating a proper register that acknowledges class consciousness and the performance of free communication.

Twenty-six letters grouped as "Letters to Mr. Thomas Rowe, and to several of his relations" followed the group to Hertford, and those to the two Sarah Rowes make degrees of freedom stark. Her letters to her mother-in-law Sarah are examples of attempts to find scriptures and Christian thoughts to aid acceptance of the deaths of her husband, her father, and Sarah's son William. There is a freedom of religious expression, an immediacy that contrasts to the everyday religious seriousness in her letters to Hertford. She writes honestly in 1719, "There still hangs a dead weight on my soul, that takes off all the springs of action" (*Misc. Works*, 2:192). These letters refer to her as "you" and "my dear mother," and some phrases are the language of Dissent, as is "O may that God that has been your dwelling-place from generation to generation, confirm his covenant with the seed of the righteous; and may you find that treasure you have committed to him secur'd, when the times of refreshing shall come" (2:189). The language is more allusive and metaphorical and conveys something of the community that has experienced separateness and discrimination. N. H. Keeble points out that "conformists locate the essence of Christianity in the moral life [the substance of religious conversation with Hertford]; nonconformists locate it in the experience of grace."[18] The latter rings in this sentence to Sarah Rowe—"dwelling-place from generation to generation," "the righteous," "time of refreshing." Her letters to the younger Sarah, Thomas's sister, have another characteristic of Nonconformist writing, an eagerness to encourage her in her faith as "true to the experience of grace within" herself.[19] Her letters in this section are equally polite—they include graceful, easy references to literature, poetry, love, and pastoral scenes.

Rowe shows a fine awareness of language, one that might be expected of such a dedicated, artistic writer. In declining an invitation to Marlborough, she writes Hertford, "Compar'd to this, M— is a theatre, a court, nations, and languages." She would if she came "intrude on the *Grand Monde* so unseasonably." She and her language would be anomalous among the languages at the stately home (*Misc. Works*, 2:101). In the letter on George I's death, she writes that the Queen "is the pride and pleasure of a great and happy people" and immediately asks, "What a dialect am I got into? this is . . . wandering from my rural simplicity. The sylvan scenes are much more suited to my . . . language" (*Misc. Works*, 2:70). Because of Hertford's position at court, Rowe comments on royalty and the royal family occasionally, but sentences like this one raise the question of when women writers comment on royal people and to what ends. Rowe was also conscious of the discourse she had learned as a Dissenter and was self-conscious about it. She draws herself up when she hears it, as she does when she writes, "One would think I was writing to some sober Dissenter" and "Your Ladyship will certainly think that I am transcribing some honest Dissenter's sermon for your edification" (*Misc. Works*, 2:49 and 100). At another time she writes that she doesn't want others to think her "more partial to the Dissenters than I really am" or to have "turn'd Quaker" (*Misc. Works*, 2:68, 50).

Richardson once wrote, "Correspondence is, indeed, the cement of friendship; it is friendship avowed under hand and seal; friendship upon bond, as I may say."[20] Rowe's fictional and actual letters modeled that, too. Her women characters were loyal, discreet, virtuous, and did not display any of the behavior that maintained suspicion toward women's friendships. Novelists quickly followed the example. In Mary Collyer's *Felicia to Charlotte* (1744), Felicia writes that corresponding with Charlotte "will flatter and sooth my friendship" and imagines a delightful, "pleasing intercourse of minds" and "an open undisguised friendship" without secrets.[21] Rowe's letters gave permission for the kinds of letters that the Bluestockings wrote and, in some cases, published. Rowe's letters bridged the ideals that letters were intimate, trusting, even transparent revelations of the heart and could also be gracefully written belle lettres covering a wide range of erudite subjects, literary and political.[22] As Elizabeth MacArthur noted, "Letters . . . were the only kind of writing women were thought to be able to do well, and even women with no literary pretensions did not hesitate to write letters." MacArthur also points out that writing letters gave women an outlet for creating works of art.[23] Rowe's actual letters are highly conversational, but her fictional ones and parts of some personal ones are obvious works of art.

Clare Brant tells us that "between 1700 and 1800, more than twenty-one thousand items were published that used the word 'Letter' or 'Letters' in their title" and that the market for published letters grew vigorously and came to be an important element in the construction of "the man of letters."[24] She claims it was the most important kind of writing in the century and contributes chapter after chapter of kinds of letters that were written and received by all levels of society, each with its own conventions, purposes, and class markers. Nevertheless, epistolary fiction modeled on the polite correspondence that Rowe obviously practiced was revisionary, and the publication of so much of hers was revolutionary. Before Rowe, few women had published their letters, and the best-known examples were Katherine Philips's *Letters from Orinda to Poliarchus* (1705), Mary Astell's correspondence with John Norris, *Letters Concerning the Love of God*, and Elizabeth Thomas's *Pylades and Corinna* (1731–1732), her love letters with Richard Gwinnett. The early history of the English novel is marked by some perverse eureka moments. After Rowe, many women published distinguished collections of their letters. Lady Mary Wortley Montagu, for instance, gave her letters to the Rev. Benjamin Sowden with the intention that he publish them, and they appeared in 1763, the year after her death, as *Letters of the Right Honourable Lady M—y W—y M—e, written during her travels in Europe, Asia, and Africa, to persons of distinction, men of letters* . . . .[25] These later collections of letters branched into all the categories that Rowe's real and fictional letters represented and mingled with many established traditions. Some examples in books compiled like Rowe's *Miscellaneous Works* are the two groups of letters to friends in Mary Jones's *Miscellanies in Prose and Verse* (1750) and letters to twelve correspondents in part 1 of Mary Latter's *The Miscellaneous Works, in prose and verse, of Mrs. Mary Latter* [1759]. Collections of women's letters after Rowe's include Sarah Pennington's *Letters on Different Subjects* (4 vols., 1766–1767), which include stories and comments on current events as well as various kinds of letters; Henrietta Knight, Lady Luxborough's *Letters written by the late Right Honourable Lady Luxborough, to William Shenstone* [1775]; and Hester Ann Rogers's *Spiritual Letters Written by Mrs. H.A. Rogers, Written Before and After her Marriage* (Bristol, 1796). The advertisement with Lady Luxborough's letters described them as "written with abundant Ease, Politeness, and Vivacity."[26]

Penelope Aubin had written that Defoe had shown novelists a new way to teach morality, and, as Robert Adams Day said long ago, Rowe "turned another way" the miscellany of short stories.[27] She included the kind of short stories and fragments in Patchwork novels but also letters characteristic of later epistolary fiction, specifically with the kind of "beginning, development, and an end" and with "characters linked in a chain" with "unique combinatorial capacity, the ability to assimilate fragments into a coherent whole." From Rowe's letters to Hertford it is clear that the language that they spoke combined observations on what they were reading, predominantly literature with philosophy and history books mixed in; on poetry, snippets quoted or written by Rowe; on the outdoors, especially pastoral scenery; and on whatever religious mood she was experiencing. Books were recommended or even sent. This is the world of the letter writers in Rowe's fictions, but their letters are more leisurely, developed, and unified.

Elizabeth Heckendorn Cook quotes Montesquieu: "in the epistolary form . . . , the author permits himself to join philosophy, politics, and ethics to the story, and to find the whole with a secret and in some sense obscure chain."[28] The terms of this observation are those valorized by Shaftesbury and the leaders of the politeness movement: literature (the story), philosophy, politics, and ethics (virtue). As we shall see, Rowe's chain is the creation of a lifestyle within a seamless, harmonious world. Drawing upon Laurent Versini, Cook observes that the secret chain operates "not as a thematic element but as a methodological principle operating at a metatextual level" ("Is the 'secret chain' not the tissue of connections that the letters establish across space and time?").[29]

English epistolary collections after Rowe are stylistically like hers and are carriers of the new gentility movement. Books with titles such as *Polite Epistolary Correspondence. A Collection of Letters, on the most instructive and entertaining subjects* (1748, 2nd ed. 1751) began to appear. Although they seem to be manuals, they are also bridges between collections before and after Rowe and evidence that politeness was shifting from an ideal of sociability to "a mode of behaviour and a variety of language," "an absolute standard of prescriptivism" that could be learned.[30] As Susan Fitzmaurice demonstrates, "Polite English thus becomes synonymous with standard modern English—the uniform, codified, prescribed language of the insecure middle classes." In one example, she points out that Thomas Dilworth in his *New Guide to the English Tongue* (1751) assumes "that if the language and style of *The Spectator* is polite, then it must also be correct."[31] John Campbell's *The Polite Correspondence: or, rational amusement; being a series of letters, philosophical, poetical, historical, critical, amorous, moral . . .* (1741) illustrates how institutionalized the politeness movement and collections maintaining it had become. Campbell's book includes a set of travel letters and a twenty-nine-letter exchange among five people that Campbell describes as a novel. Eve Tavor Bannet says that *The Complete Letter-Writer, or Polite English Secretary* (1755) "came as close to becoming a standard, universally available, compendium during the second half of the eighteenth century as any letter manual managed to get."[32]

Such books continued to be published and intersected with the education market, as did *The Polite Instructor: or, youth's museum. Consisting of moral essays, tales, fables, visions, and allegories* [1768]. Some of Rowe's works took on a life of their own in such books and suggest the lingering appeal of reunions in Heaven. "A Letter from a young Lady to the Countess of Hertford, wrote not long before her Death" and part of Letter 7 in *Friendship in Death* appeared in *Bretts Miscellany: Being, a Collection of Divine, Moral, Historical, and Entertaining Sayings and Observations* (1748). The writer quotes what she imagines, "when we meet again, I hope, it will be in the Heights of immortal Love and Ecstasy. Mine, perhaps, may be the first glad Spirit to congratulate your safe Arrival on the happy Shore."[33] Reprints of selections of Rowe's texts, especially of the poetry, can be found in surprising places, such as the *Critical Review* (1796) and the Cincinnati, Ohio, *Star in the West* (1838).[34] Like Rowe, these writers find poetry a way to elevate the emotion, and they bring together the polish and virtue of the now-normative discourse of gentility.

An important descendent of Rowe's *Letters* is Sarah Fielding's *Familiar Letters between the Principal Characters in David Simple* (1747). Composed of forty-five letters (the last five by Henry Fielding), two dialogues (by James Harris), and "an exceptionally powerful and haunting concluding chapter," "A Vision,"[35] the two-volume text has confused critics primarily, I believe, because it has not been related to Rowe's. It is not correct, for instance, as this book has demonstrated, to say that "it is not a novel in any sense in which the term would have been understood in the 18th century."[36] The first letter actually signals the genre. Cynthia has arrived in Bath on a trip for her health and writes Camilla, who answers her letters from London. She has entered Rowe's world of harmony with Valentine, as she describes him as "lover," "husband," and "companion" and compares them to "*Adam* and *Eve* in Paradise" as they "indulge" in a morning walk.[37] She writes that "little Expence" is necessary for the real, "substantial" happiness she feels, and then her mind "wanders" to the ways humankind makes itself miserable. Her letters compare her state of mind to the follies and amusements she sees at Bath and provide a means to discuss interesting topics, as does her encounter with Elmira, who thinks women should not write poetry because it is "too masculine" (1:93). In her first letter she begins a series of anecdotes and mini-tales, many with moral reflections that set the expectation for the text as a whole. She writes, "I am so well acquainted with your way of thinking, that I flatter myself, that, was you present, you would generally speak the Words I in fancy say for you" (2:94–95). The expectation is clearly that the same could be said of the reader.

In his preface, Henry Fielding pointed out that the various adventures all tended "to one great End," ironically a description applied to Rowe's *Letters* to their detriment. He continued, "I know not of any essential Difference between this, and any other way of writing Novels, save only, that by making use of Letters, the Writer is freed from the regular Beginnings and Conclusions of Stories, with some other Formalities, in which the Reader of Taste finds no less Ease and Advantage, than the Author himself" (1:xi–xii). Fielding does not need these formalities, beginnings, and endings because the tales are lively and familiar in form. Some are like moral folk tales, as is the story of the "deformed" Lydia, whose mother sees her as a "monster of nature." This excellent story describes her encounters with various people, and while some, like the school boys, act in stereotypical ways (they taunt and beat her), others, like Lydia, prove that people cannot be judged by their looks. Others are in the amatory tradition. Lindamira abandons a man of sense for a fool whom she marries for a coach and six; Isabinda's story, which includes her mother's and other anecdotes, begins in the second letter and stretches into several subsequent letters. She is the prototype of the witty, willful, naive heiress that became so popular in the 1750s and 1760s. Like them, she does not "think it any great Crime, to let these Monkeys [who are courting her—or her fortune] play over a few of their Tricks, for my Diversion" (1:72), but this, of course, gets her in trouble. Mixed in Fielding's text are also philosophical essays, quotations and examples from classical authors, fables, poetry (original and quoted), and other kinds of discourses. Some of the characters, like the admirable Philocles, have the same names as Rowe's characters of the same type. Not all of the letters are by characters from *David Simple*, and they are written in different styles. Delia in the country tells Lydia's story to Leonora in London; Lyimachus describes people he meets on a trip to Cambridge as examples of those incapable of polite conversation; Sophronia describes her contented retirement where she reads and imagines the company of philosophers. Henry locates Sarah's text with the "*Persian* Letters, many of which are written on the most important Subjects in Ethics, Politics, and Philosophy" and include "two or three Novels" (1:xi), but he could have more appropriately cited Rowe's *Letters*.

Beauty and Politeness

Rowe's fictions were powerful, concentrated carriers of the politeness movement especially because virtue was becoming the point at which politeness and beauty intersected in the movement, and the results can be discerned in strikingly different domains. In this part of the chapter, I will look at some important ways that she integrated politeness ideology and sensibility into the fabric of her fictions. First, she made the countryside a special setting, one that the genteel needed to appreciate and use in new ways. Some of Rowe's settings slide almost imperceptibly from the artifice of the fairy tales and the French romances into what was becoming a distinctively English countryside, one tinged with timelessness that would resist industrial and agrarian modernity. As Ann Bermingham says of a slightly later time, "The English saw their landscape as a cultural and aesthetic *object*" (emphasis mine).[38] By blending recognizable symbolic settings, all with moral tints, lifestyle and literary appreciation were intermingled at the levels of apprehension and practice. In many ways, they are very much creations of their time. One of the most popular structures in every genre was country versus city. In the line of epistolary fiction that followed Rowe, one correspondent is almost invariably in the country and one in the city, thereby symbolizing the private and the public. The distinction between the solitude, and therefore the interiority and autonomy of the country, and the surveillance and discipline of city life is especially sharp in Rowe's fictions, and it is replicated and expanded upon in many novels that follow hers.

Rowe's work shares and propagates the structures of feeling relating nature and the self long recognized in Addison's and Thomson's best work. Thomson, the poet Rowe and Hertford so admired, drew from *The Moralists* "a loosely coherent pattern of philosophical ideas and attitudes with which he felt an immediate sympathy":

> Already in the first edition of *Winter* Shaftesbury's influence is apparent in the consciously 'sublime' celebration of personified 'Nature' as a direct manifestation of divine power, and the treatment of the powerful quasi-religious feelings that 'Nature' arouses in the receptive, contemplative mind, feelings that are accompanied by a renewal and refinement of the moral and 'social' passions. The first edition of *Spring* and the 1730 text of the concluding *Hymn* could without exaggeration be described as Shaftesburian poems.[39]

Shaftesbury, a student of Locke's, carried into his work Locke's conception of the self as existing in the aware and remembering mind, "a thinking intelligent being, that has reason and reflection, and can consider itself as itself, the same thinking thing in different times and places." At one point in her life, Rowe considered moving "unless I can have this house entirely to myself" (*Misc. Works*, 2:102). This letter and the next few hint at intrusions that are affecting her lifestyle. Similarly, her characters will change their situations when necessary to protect the person they think they are and to live in the manner they believe necessary for their well-being. Hertford offers her "a pretty peaceful apartment," something many noble women did for their less wealthy women friends, and Rowe refuses by drawing upon the words of Thomson and Addison. She quotes Thomson's *Sophonisba*: "I want to be alone, to find some shade, / . . . / And there to listen to the gentle voice, / The sigh of peace.—" (*Misc. Works*, 2:111).

The permeation of Shaftesbury's thought about selfhood in the circle that read, corresponded, and cultivated it is pervasive. In Shaftesbury's dialogue, Philocles stands in for the author, and his description of the most pleasing natural setting has been described as "mediating between art and nature rather than pitching one against the other, it is about the idea of being free in a very differently envisioned best possible world" and allowing oneself to accent "an intensely felt affinity or kinship of humanity with nature." "Nature was free, and being free, it helped the human spectator to feel free as well."[40] In one of Rowe's stories, a physician named Leander writes to his friend that he has met a woman, the picture of "virtue or harmony" (*Letters*, 1:67). He is carrying Thomson's *Summer* on his evening walk and quotes,

> These are the haunts of meditation, these
> The scenes, where ancient bards th' inspiring breath,

Extatic, felt; and from the world retir'd,
Convers'd with angels. (*Letters*, 1:66)

Robert Inglesfield calls this section of *Summer* and lines 1371–89, which he quotes, "a remarkable passage, entirely characteristic of Thomson in its idealizing preoccupation with the conscious cultivation of refined feeling and the pursuit of morally elevating philosophical truth in emotionally congenial natural surroundings."[41] Rowe consistently dramatizes and narrates refined feeling and a steady moral, philosophical truth. The woman Leander meets fits his "visionary" mood in her composure, complexion "clear as the light," and "a mind within conscious of its own dignity, and heavenly original" (*Letters*, 1:67). The allusive words pile up and work almost subliminally to elevate the experience and fiction itself. The woman dies, and Rowe here and in other letters creates an aesthetic of dying and mourning, one that will become increasingly appealing in the eighteenth century.[42]

Male and female characters in *Letters* write their most reflective and self-reflexive letters in such spaces. Sometimes Rowe's women succeed by dropping down the social scale, either by retiring to the country or by disguising themselves as upper servants. Sometimes, as later heroines do, with great effort they scale down their desires and, in consequence, their image of happiness, as Frances Burney's Cecilia does. Rosalinda, one of Rowe's fairy-tale heroines, describes the ideal:

> Just at the bounds of this luxuriant retreat stands an antient oak; the extended boughs are a shelter from the mid-day sun, which perhaps your Ladyship would endure, rather than screen your beauty in such a rustick shade: *Elysian* groves and myrtle bowers are better suited to the delicacy of your imagination; but I am now reconciled to nature in its greatest negligence, and seated in this venerable recess, find virtue and liberty the principal springs of human happiness. My hours are here at my own disposal, nor am I obliged to devote them to ceremony or vain amusements. I find myself under no necessity . . . to do a thousand unreasonable things for fear of being singular and out of the mode. (*Letters*, 3:129)

"Liberty," "virtue," and a beautiful natural setting make perfect happiness—as does "I am now reconciled . . . ."

The feeling of harmony led to a feeling of liberty, a constitutive term in the movement and the one that has led contemporary critics to identify it as Whig.[43] Rowe's fictional and actual letters depict contact with nature as renewing and inspiring and a source and sign of "dear liberty." Stuart Curran has argued that for women writers the garden was beginning to "exist for its own sake, for its capacity to refine the vision of the actual."[44] That "actual" expanded the mind's comprehension to include the metaphysical. Certainly true of Rowe's gardens in which understanding of the immediate situation, worldly value-laden contexts, and God's world are all refined, they became the kind of place in which characters like Haywood's Betsy Thoughtless attained freedom and an integrated identity. Located on a river with pleasant gardens, walks, and inviting places to sit, this retreat becomes a place of contemplation and, after the death of her husband, the stage for the exhibition of her virtue and prudence, both coming from a new, firm sense of self. Here and in Rowe's stories, that originality and freedom of expression are celebrated is part of the location where gender is not a primary consideration. Again Rowe's place in a structure of feeling that quickly became comprehensive is evident. Yu Liu describes Addison's "Pleasures of the Imagination" series as containing "peculiar outburst[s] against claustrophobia,"[45] and women's novels often move between suffocatingly claustrophobic scenes and brief library ones that are often set outdoors. For instance, Cecilia in Frances Burney's novel flees the house in which Delville has told her he is going abroad to avoid her since he can never consent to the clause in the will that would necessitate his taking her family name. Avoiding her favorite walks in the park part of the estate, she runs into the "thick and unfrequented wood." "When she thought herself sufficiently distant and private to be safe, she sat down under a tree" and weeps "without caution or restraint." "Happy at least to be alone," she stays in "this private spot" from breakfast until dinner time.[46]

Although a utopian state dependent upon and in harmony with nature is attained by some later novel heroines, Rowe is in step with the poetry by English women that was already holding up this state as ideal and gave much more specific detail than the French fairy tales. Mary Chudleigh wrote in the central verse of *To Clorissa* (1703),

> When all alone in some belov'd Retreat,
>
> . . . .
>
> 'Tis then I tast the most delicious Feast of Life:
> There, uncontroul'd I can my self survey,
>   And from Observers free,
>   My intellectual Pow'rs display,
> And all th' opening Scenes of beauteous Nature see.[47]

This is the scene, both exterior and interior, that Rowe creates. Chudleigh's "worldview is strongly inflected by individual concerns."[48] Octavia Walsh follows her in a poem published in the year Rowe's fictions appeared in the collected edition: "In this Retreat permit me now to seek / For my own self, from whom I long have stray'd." Walsh notes, "For 'tis almost, ye Pow'rs, a tedious Week, / Since here we parted in this sacred Shade." The words for her week's experience, as well as "tedious," are "noisy," "buisy," and "strife."[49] Like novelistic characters, she took for granted that she had a unique personal interior space to which she could go to renew her sense of self and commitments to action and belief. Women seem to have embraced Locke's still controversial claim that self-identity was in the mind and safe in the continuity of memory and consciousness.[50] Certainly they can be described as Foucault in "The Subject and Power" conceives identity, as tied to self-knowledge and conscience.

Influentially, Rowe created fictional correspondents that were the same ones Klein describes as propagating the movement: "the learned, the literate, and the godly."[51] In "polite" correspondence, it was more important to imagine the stance and perspective of the addressee, and a register adjusted for the audience emerged. Unlike the *Spectator* that deliberately incorporated a variety of styles and registers, Rowe carefully maintained one that did not vary and became the model of polite discourse. Content and ideology were inseparable from the register, and analysis of the components of context—field, tenor, and mode—that constitute register develops understanding of the contrasts between them and why hers are more consistent carriers of the politeness movement. While Addison uses all three to represent conflicts, Rowe's presentation is largely unvaried. Especially with tenor, the social roles, relationships, and statuses of the participants, and mode, the rhetorical modes and channels of communication, her consistent elevation and polish are contrasts to his. The contrasts highlight how interactive Addison's anecdotes are with sex, gender, age, and ethnicity on display, and his considerable dependence on satire, a mode Rowe seldom uses, emerges. A comparison of field, the nature of the social interaction taking place, highlights how interior the action is in Rowe's fictions. Although some of the same encounters and conflicts are staged in both, Rowe's move quickly to the character's mind and how he or she copes with the experience.

The characters that Rowe created in her fairy tales were carefully posed in deliberately aestheticized settings and postured in highly ideological ways. The bodies of these characters did indeed convey aesthetic and ideological principles even as they appeared to be "natural," to come from within the character. When, for instance, Melinda leaves her brother's raucous house, she seems to be acting from her conceptual self. These characters are literate, even literary, and Rowe made them godly, thereby replicating Klein's triad. As Pierre Bourdieu points out, "The unconscious repeated perception of works of a certain style encourages the interiorization of the rules which govern the production of these works." Readers mastered "the generic and specific code of the work," which was especially strong and persistent in Rowe's fictions.[52] Not only did they read and appreciate the texts for their aesthetic and moral qualities, but they interiorized the assumptions and ideology behind the code. They accepted that "godly" is a key term. It brings Rowe's near mysticism into a domesticated, everyday social practice that brought "aesthetic concerns into close contiguity with ethical ones."[53] In this model and in Rowe's life there was an "elision" of moral and aesthetic response: "no sooner are actions viewed . . . than straight an inward eye distinguishes, and sees the fair and shapely, the amiable and admirable, apart from the deformed, the foul, the odious, or the despicable."[54] Rowe banished the latter category thereby creating something like Heaven where pure happiness and beauty do not require the sight of "the despicable" for comprehension and appreciation. Francis Hutcheson offered a comprehensive vision. For him, "the beauty of regularity, order, and harmony in the arts and sciences is essentially the same in character as the 'moral sense of beauty' that men find and naturally delight in when confronted with virtue in affections, characters, actions and manners, because such virtue itself tends to regularity, order and harmony."[55] Rowe described the ideal effect of reading as "a sort of divine contentment spreads on the mind; I seem to want nothing but to be wiser and better" (*Misc. Works*, 2:112).

This intersection also opens up a line of inquiry as yet unpursued. The most numerous kind of printed letter in the long eighteenth century was religious. We are familiar with the letter of theological controversy, but thousands of letters were written by "ordinary Christians" sharing their religious comforts, doubts, experiences, and advice. These letters created communities and cultures of theological consensus remarkably isolated from the doctrinal controversies raging in London, Oxford, and among country parsons.[56] Like Defoe's books of practical divinity, they modeled devotional practices and spread them, thereby reinforcing both individual faith and a sense of religious community. Evident in the culture is the issue of how much religion and piety could be brought into polite conversation. The results of too much ranged from appearing to be a prude to provoking political controversy. An important part of the polish that some of Rowe's characters attain is religion, and in some cases religion is necessary for their peace of mind and, therefore, their exemplary lifestyles. Joining the project of other women writers in trying to reform aristocratic males, most of her examples are of male characters. Sometimes the morality and religion of her characters are as low-key as Addison's secular humanism, and sometimes it is the otherworldly devotion of, for instance, James Janeway's *Invisibles, Realities, Demonstrated in the Holy Life . . . of Mr. John Janeway* (1673). Sometimes it is unattainable, as with the guilt-ridden Aurelia who still loves her seducer. Rather than the strong emotionality of many fictional protagonists of the first third of the century, Aurelia can describe her situation rationally and even analytically (*Letters*, 3:206–7). Rowe clearly worked at maintaining the middle register, as her letters to Hertford very occasionally reveal anxieties about falling into language beyond this sociable center.

Finally, Rowe influenced the literary uses of female bodies. A very different consequence of virtue becoming the intersection of politeness and beauty was the increasing attention to women's bodies. Because so many of Rowe's fictional and actual correspondents were notable people, she understood the fact that familiar letters at that time necessarily illustrated the interpenetration of the private and public—the space women's bodies dramatically occupied. She knew this truth for herself. Her correspondence with John Dunton had resulted in his publishing a description of her body. Visitors already had access to some of her letters and Hertford's, and she mentions that her *History of Joseph* "has been so often transcrib'd, and is got into so many hands" that she is going to publish it (*Misc. Works*, 2:176). The letters and the portrayals of the virtuous men's and women's bodies are equally symbols and ways to read their interiority. As Elizabeth Heckendorn Cook has explained,

> Against the swarm of public print forms that proliferated in the early decades of the century, the letter became an emblem of the private; while keeping its actual function as an agent of the public exchange of knowledge, it took on the general connotations it still holds for us today, intimately identified with the body, especially a female body, and the somatic terrain of the emotions, as well as with the thematic material of love, marriage, and the family.[57]

"Somatic terrain" is an apt phrase, for Rowe is a sensual writer alive to her emotions and also to the physical sensations of weather and the outdoors. Before Richardson she associated women's letters with their bodies, thereby finding the means to write about the private-public existence and the implications. Cook continues, "The letter-narrative exposes the private body to publication . . . it puts into play the tension between the private individual, identified with a specifically gendered, classed body that necessarily commits it to specific forms of self-interest, and the public person, divested of self-interest, discursively constituted, and functionally disembodied" (8). In writing to Hertford and occasionally in letters to others, Rowe's classed body emerges in relationship to another classed body. As strangers read her fictional and personal letters, she may not have been disembodied, but she was certainly differently embodied.

Taught to read bodies in letters from Richardson's novels, critics are blind to an important, even central way Rowe writes the body. Clare Brant makes the association between letter and woman's body even more explicit and reveals a critical oversight. As she points out, "Entranced by fiction that fetished letters as substitutes for and extensions of women's bodies, . . . critics see only erotic relations between letters and women's bodies." She notes that "it was still common practice in the eighteenth century for doctors to diagnose by correspondence" and that the most common excuse for delayed correspondence was illness, an obvious reference to a different kind of body.[58] Rowe's letters to friends and family frequently refer to their indispositions and her concerns for their health. She especially expresses fears about smallpox, a disease that she had had and that distorts the body as it runs its course and can permanently mark it. In *Letters*, characters are ill and indisposed, and the state of their minds affects their bodies and vice versa. Some are dangerously ill, and a few die. Just as her contemporaries did, Rowe wrote frequently about her physical health, sometimes related to her mental state, and about concerns for that of her friends, in her case, for Hertford, who seems to have often suffered from colds. Health was the major reason given for delayed correspondence, and it associated the letter with the body in vivid, personal, even mortal ways that affected both correspondents.

Another of her fictional strategies was to make virtue and beauty synonymous as the true body, and this association has also not been traced in her texts or in later fiction. Her women characters, and indeed Rowe herself, who was by all accounts a notably attractive woman, are most attractive when they are in simple, natural settings. *Pamela*, of course, is the archetype of many of these characteristics. Before that novel, however, Rowe had associated the letter with the beautiful and virtuous body, giving the letter symbolic, "speaking" power. Rowe writes to Hertford, "Mrs.— has pleas'd me, by letting me know, that you made one of the best figures, for person and dress, at the coronation" (*Misc. Works*, 2:77). Over and over Richardson reveals how private conduct and a tolerance of transgressions within the private, domestic walls are actually matters with profound public implications, and Rowe does the same with virtuous actions. After *Pamela*, the identification of letter with body, especially a woman's body, was indelibly fixed. Stealing or misreading a woman's letter became a violation. Moreover, *Pamela* emphasized the classed body communicated in epistles, and it was especially effective during the time when accomplishments and politeness trumped rank. The identification of beauty, graces, and polish with virtue is essential to Richardson's making Clarissa's letters and her body interchangeable.

Another revisionary tactic was that in important ways the narratives within letters move from one pose to another. Rowe could thus create aesthetic models that harmonized beauty, politeness, and virtue. In each the woman is still, and she is writing about her reflections or describing a pose with setting, thereby doubling the stillness and its virtuous beauty. This image persists. John Skinner summarizes:

Far from the energetic movement of *Humphry Clinker*, [Virginia Woolf] envisaged the archetypal correspondence as involving two individuals, isolated and immobile, surmounting obstacles in order to communicate; by the very terms of the definition, such individuals were normally women, and it is in the context of such social conditioning, finally, that classic letter fiction may be regarded as a potentially female genre.[59]

Missing from critical exploration of body imagery in letters is engagement with contemporary Christian expressions. Referring back to Crashaw and the seventeenth-century poets is not really adequate for a time in which a man could write upon being moved by a sermon, "How did my heart throb? How did every bowel within me roll" and a woman wrote, "I find I need not drop the body to enjoy the presence of my God . . . yet my desires are insatiable: I long to plunge deeper into God."[60] Rowe has carefully excluded such statements from her *Letters*, but they animate her poetry and her devotional exercises throughout her life.

Technologies of the Self

Klein explains, "The kernel of 'politeness' could be conveyed in the simple expression, 'the art of pleasing in company,' or, in a contemporary definition, 'a dextrous management of our Words and Actions, whereby we make other People have better Opinions of us and themselves.'"[61] Somewhat contradictorily, freedom of various kinds was a constituent element of politeness, and yet as Klein's eighteenth-century definition indicates, it was inseparable from the disciplined body and from virtue. Social expectations and pressures were somewhat different for men and for women, and to a great extent women lived in a highly gendered world, and, therefore, they were developing a parallel as well as a shared code of the practices of politeness. That this complex dynamic came to seem natural, to be normalized and institutionalized as the character of an English citizen, is one of the most fascinating movements in history, and Rowe is so important because she depicted it so fully as natural and as resulting in a satisfying conceptual self. In this section, I want to look at two practices that Rowe propagated and that became important parts of the women's gentility movement. The first is self-discipline, and the second is the creation of an elsewhere, what might be considered a daring alternate polite society.

A poem by Anna Laetitia Barbauld concisely captures the epitome of the polite woman, the woman who has learned internal and external control:

Her even lines her steady temper show;
Neat as her dress, and polish'd as her brow;

Strong as her judgment, easy as her air;
Correct though free, and regular though fair:
And the same graces o'er her pen preside
That form her manners and her footsteps guide.[62]

In many ways this poem describes the Rowe that Barbauld believed in and reflected upon in a tribute to her—an important example as a poet, an intellect, and a virtuous, happy human being. "Free," "easy," and "strong" celebrate the individual, and "steady," "polish'd," and "regular" capture an important aspect of the lifestyle. Of Rowe specifically Barbauld wrote, "Smooth like her verse her passions learn'd to move, / And her whole soul was harmony and love."

Close reading of literature and social history suggests that self-mastery was increasingly an almost consumingly important endeavor for women[63] and that the novel made visible the technologies of self-mastery. Rowe's fictions pioneer some of the techniques of resistance, of the ways human beings create a conceptual self. For example, the resolutions of her contemporaries' fictions tend to be the establishment of the heroine in a socially recognized and sanctioned situation, such as marriage. Rowe advances the creation of psychologically rich characters by establishing the conclusion in which the woman has attained personal contentment, whether it be by living singly, in harmony with another woman or small family, or by marrying. In other words, the goal is a state of mind as much as a situation. Because the interior life is where the most important action is, there is less physical movement and wandering in her stories, a useful convention as women were accorded less freedom in the society.

Rowe reinforced the concept that politeness was the outward sign of virtue and accomplishments, both requiring self-mastery. The conversations of her most exemplary characters with their references to literature and their easy assumption of benevolence and right moral judgments contrast to passages in which she satirizes, for example, the dying Amanda who orders clothes from France "as if she designed to expire genteely, and appear polite, even in the languishments of death" (2:35–36). Even "languishments" suggests a fashionable feminine pose. Rowe creates the beautiful life and depicts the virtuous life. Breaking with most of the didactic prose of her time, the virtuous life is not the sole requirement for happiness. Moreover, her heroines differ widely in their propensities, temperaments, and preferences and are self-aware about these characteristics. Lavinia in part, 2, letter 4 is one of the women who retires to the country to avoid the temptation of an improper passion. The style of the letter indicates her lively temper, her ability to laugh at herself, and, most of all, her delight in the city and its fashionable abundance. As noted, her element is the world of the duke's shapely legs with clocks on his stockings and his gilded wainscots, not her "Gothick heap" of a home. She writes self-consciously about not being happy but hoping to acclimate herself and find her "delicacy" worn off. Reading the religious musings of characters as ideological, while correct, is incomplete. Amintor's coming to terms with the death of his wife is nuanced and more an appropriate subject for ecocriticism than identification with a flattened ideology. In the final six-letter sequence, Laura, Charlotte, and Philocles are all somewhat developed and change over the course of their encounters. Charlotte, for example, comes to take initiative and display agency.

An important technology of self-mastery is the establishment of a routine, one that gives order. Foucault locates the roots of discipline in armies and monasteries, and both emphasize regimens and self-control. Parts of Rowe's day were inviolable. Besides the time for prayer and devotions, there were the times for the practice of her charity and for walks. Her reading is for enjoyment as well as educational improvement and devotion, and late in life she enjoys painting, coloring prints, and making an elaborate screen. The balance and the routines include places identified with activities; for example, she says she takes possession of a field hedged with hawthorn "when I would indulge in serious thought" (*Misc. Works*, 2:137). David Hill Radcliffe describes the Countess of Hertford's lifestyle as "quasi-monastic" and a "regimen" that involved two hours of serious reading at dawn and "twice daily contemplative walks" around a two-mile circuit. Her park at Percy Lodge becomes "a cloister."[64] Bowerbank describes these practices as self-directional and also as an "appropriation and transformation of the self-perfecting techniques of monasticism to serve an expansive modern order."[65] Rowe's letters and writings about her show that many people suggested she think and live in more ordinary ways, but she portrays how the technology of social production can be resisted and even turned into a technology of the self. For her, a regular routine, one that nurtures the soul, also comes to have an untouchable quality that protects the conceptual self. Later Elizabeth Montagu described Lady Barbara Montagu's and Sarah Scott's routine at Bath Easton as a convent, "for by its regularity it resembles one."[66] Many later women describe routines they developed. Some refer to using outdoor spaces and ritual retreats as places to domesticate "*savage* feelings" in order to attain "the outward countenance that produces the proper state of mind in others."[67] In these accounts, the woman "retires" and enjoys solitude, but, when company comes or it is family time, she invariably metamorphosizes into a generous, lively, social being able to make others comfortable with her hospitality and ability to converse "charmingly." It is notable that her demeanor and conversation are means of control, of producing the "proper," polite state of mind in others.

It is possible to interpret these women as maintaining their social charms because of the virtuous contemplation, but it is also possible to be a bit cynical and see both as mastered performances. If the contemplation nurtures the soul, it also protects solitude, for who can demand an end to apparent devotions? Thus, privacy and a private space are fortified. The inherent possibilities of sincerity or self-conscious manipulation perhaps produce fictions such as Sheridan's *Memoirs of Miss Sidney Bidulph*, whose ambiguities of tone and meaning continue to frustrate critics. The novels by and for women after Rowe are about nothing so much as self-mastery and the hope of achieving a conceptual self that brings peace of mind. Clare Brant explains how important the idea of establishing a character in letters and life was and in a highly pertinent example shows how "the familiar letter of friendship deals in character as it conjoins the character of friend to the subjectivities of 'I' and 'you.'"[68] All of these possibilities are evident in Rowe's fictions, and Joseph Roach has pointed out that the eighteenth century offers "the widest range of materials pertaining to the study of performance styles of any period." He notes that this concentration on speaking bodies extended beyond the theatre, the opera, and choreography to everyday life.[69] Following Foucault, he argues that bodies and especially posturing and posed bodies not only express the more familiar body disciplined by both ideological state apparatuses and social forces but reveal technologies of self-mastery that seem to come from within, to appear natural.

Exemplary women characters come to symbolize moral and, perhaps less familiarly argued, aesthetic figures. Roach points out that the bodies of the actors "stand in for the aesthetic and ideological significance of the character."[70] Interestingly, beautiful settings and the decorum of the characters create the impression that they are beautiful when, in fact, Rowe seldom elaborates on the physical appearance of the women. Roach and other theorists argue that the actor/author stands in for the character and the character for the members of the audience who "project their desires" on the character. Although this certainly does not happen in the majority of fiction, this tripartite movement occurs with Rowe's fiction. It is especially effective because of her well-known reputation, one enhanced by her late-life publications that created a particular type of woman author. This constructed character of a woman author was used to construct the female characters. Specific values, desires, and even actions became predictable and could be used by readers to construct themselves. Cheryl Nixon argues that such texts encourage self- and gender-theorization, both obvious drives in Rowe's texts.[71] Her life and her fictions thus become useful models of virtue, beauty, and the harmonious life.

A reason that these fictions are so often set in the country is that a routine could be established there more easily than in the city where the schedules of plays, parties, and even auctions and visits imposed an irregularity. Rowe's women often mention the Mall, and as a destination for a walk or a carriage ride it was more similar to times for fixed country walks. That very fact highlighted the need for a routine with at least semiprivate time for reflection and particular kinds of conversation. Self-mastery and especially the art of making oneself happy (or at least tranquil and content) in difficult circumstances became increasingly important in women's fiction. Some, of course, accepted it with better grace and true contentment than others, but it was the subtle explorations and coming-to-terms that provide absorbing interest in Burney's *Cecilia*, Sheridan's *Sidney Bidulph*, and Griffith's *History of Lady Barton* (1771). Haywood's *Betsy Thoughtless* is an early, dilated example of Rowe's strategy when she writes in Betsy's self-imposed year of country withdrawal. The influence of nature and the poses of Betsy in that year replicate Rowe's strategies. Shown an arbor within a garden upon her introduction to her country refuge, Betsy returns the next morning:

> She threw herself upon the mossy seat, where scenting the fragrancy of the sweets around her, made more delicious by the freshness of the morning's gale, —"How delightful, —how heavenly," said she to herself, "is this solitude, how truly preferable to all the noisy giddy pleasures of the tumultuous town, yet how have I despised and ridiculed the soft serenity of a country life."[72]

She takes the miniature of Trueworth that she always carries and reflects on the times that she has owed him gratitude and not paid it. After her husband's death, she returns to a country retreat and, as her letters to Trueworth show, "Her even lines her steady temper show."

Rowe was known to take almost daily walks, as was Hertford. So well was this practice and its benefits known that James Thomson included this sentence acknowledging inspiration in his dedication of the 1728 *Spring* to Hertford: "Happy! if I have hit any of those Images and correspondent Sentiments, your calm Evening Walks in the most delightful Retirement have oft inspired."[73] The women in Hertford's circle cultivated this relationship to nature, often sacrificing sleep for the sustenance they found in it. One of Rowe's coterie poems, *To Mrs. Arabella Marrow, in the Country*, wishes her every delight nature can bring—verdant fields, flowers, gentle breezes as she enjoys her "soft recess." The letters of a correspondent whom Helen Sard Hughes calls "obscure" record the lifestyle Rowe describes in her fairy tales and, as Hughes says, include many emergent practices, such as seeking out picturesque prospects and "speaking" symbols of mortality, such as cemeteries and Windsor Castle. This lady, Grace Cole, "rises at five . . . and 'rambles' in the dewy 'Wilderness.'"[74] Many of the women took solitary walks before breakfast, and, in addition to composing the mind for the day, the walks were described as exercise. Carter, for instance, attributed her headaches to lack of exercise. Rowe seems to have walked most regularly in the evening, and occasionally her poems include a line like this: "Among the trees with God himself to walk."[75] Rowe has her characters take evening walks. Leonora in *Friendship in Death* takes her "accustom'd Walk" (36), and Marcella habitually "took an Evening walk" (*Letters*, 1:11).

The record of Catherine Talbot's struggle to organize and manage her use of time in the hope of what Bowerbank describes as an attempt to "produce a better nature" reveals how control of time seemed to define "one's very being." In *Reflections on the Seven Days of the Week*, Talbot writes,

> To be continually attentive to our Conduct in every minute Instance, to set a Watch before our Mouth, and to keep the Door of our Lips, to set Scourges over our Thoughts, and the Discipline of Wisdom over our Hearts, requires a Soberness of Mind, Diligence, a resolute Adherence to Duty, that may undoubtedly deserve the Name of Self-Denial, and Mortification: Though in Effect, nothing so certainly ensures our Happiness, both here and hereafter.[76]

Shaftesbury had written, "The admiration and love of order, harmony, and proportion, in whatever kind, is naturally improving to the temper, advantageous to social affection, and highly assistant to virtue, which is itself no other than the love of order and beauty in society."[77] As William Dowling observes in quoting Shaftesbury, the next step was to create a way of life: "To philosophise . . . is but to carry good-breeding a step higher. For the accomplishment of breeding is, to learn whatever is decent in company or beautiful in arts; and the sum of philosophy is, to learn what is just in society and beautiful in nature and the order of the world."[78]

Whether influenced by Shaftesbury, Rowe's lifestyle, personal discovery, or, most likely, by all three, most of the Bluestockings write about such routines of reading and walking, and, in the midst of chaotic, fraught lives, characters in novels regroup in such spaces and practices. Catherine Talbot recommended that people "accommodate ourselves with Joy and Thankfulness to the present Scene, whatever it is, and to make the most of that Good, which every Thing has in it. To a free Mind all is agreeable."[79] A description of Carter captures an increasingly frequent portrayal of happy women: "she was famous for the power of her will—understood as the power of disciplined self-regulation."[80] Although other characters in novels would not have diagnosed "power of her will" and later generations might say "Christian forebearance," careful reading shows that in most cases an iron exertion of the will undergirded both self-control in trying, even infuriating circumstances and also a studied, determined happiness. Bowerbank allies this philosophy with women's self-monitoring and concludes that Talbot represents "the great many women who created a range of self-technologies—diaries, devotions, letter writing, and other daily practices—to codify and to cultivate a correspondence, a homology, of good nature in the self, society, and cosmos."[81] These are, of course, the terms that made the politeness movement so attractive.

In contrast to but serving some of the same purposes as the regimens such as walking was creating an elsewhere, a realm of freedom *and* politeness that allowed an alternate domestic economy. This elsewhere of imagination, inner life, fantasy, or private, natural spaces could be real, remembered, or imagined. It was an important kind of freedom, often a resisting technology of the self. In a letter to Hertford in 1719, Rowe happily says she has "some imaginary regions of my own framing, some poetical dominions, *Where fancy in her airy triumph reigns*." She describes herself living in the "enjoyment of these visionary worlds" (*Misc. Works*, 2:39). In a later letter, she creates an entire pastoral home similar to those in her fiction for Hertford. She imagines everything as "elegant as the abode of some sylvan Goddess . . . and nature pours out all her blessings for you. . . . I had a thousand times rather enjoy your conversation in my own private retreat . . ." (*Misc. Works*, 2:105).

Many of the scenes in her fictions and private letters are pastoral. As Michael McKeon points out, it is as much about temporality and time as it is of location and geography. "Pastoral's temporal dimension can be felt as a subtly emotional inflection of spatial detachment, the evocation of an immediacy that is nonetheless elusive, perhaps irreversibly unavailable."[82] Rowe's strategic juxtaposition of the actual world, often with a specific place in mind, the pastoral rural setting, and an allusion to the eternal creates an "elsewhere" that fits this description. About the Hertford estate Rowe writes to Arabella Marrow, their mutual friend, "'Tis a great delight to me to find every body in as visionary a disposition as myself. Whether we are got into fairy land, or . . . lull'd us all into a golden dream, is very uncertain" (2:223). Other women shared the creation of an elsewhere. Elizabeth Carter, for instance, wrote to Elizabeth Montagu,

> My imagination without wing or broomstick oft mounts aloft, rises into the Regions of pure space, & without lett or impediment bears me to your fireside, where you set me in your easy chair, & we talk & reason, as Angel Host and guest Aetherial should do. . . . We shall say what has not been said before, or if the substance be old, the mode & figure shall be new.[83]

This elsewhere is imagined, but created out of the lived experience of conversations and letters. During the time Rowe was considering moving closer to Hertford, she writes, "I have form'd many a visionary plan of coming nearer to —, and appearing, and retiring, just as your Ladyship commands, or my own caprice should direct" (*Misc. Works*, 2:116).

Rowe created landscapes that, like her characters' thoughts, flowed from the immediate situation to a widening sense of continuities and transitions. James Grantham Turner, whose groundbreaking *The Politics of Landscape* stands behind much writing on the ideological and aesthetic uses of landscape, offers a quotation from Emerson as "the central ideological fact of rural literature" as his conclusion. It points to the kind of liberty that Rowe describes that expands from what the eye can see to the boundless realm of Heaven that she imagines and stretches toward. As Ralph Waldo Emerson wrote,

> The charming landscape which I saw this morning is indubitably made up of some twenty or thirty farms. Miller owns this field, . . . and Manning the woodland beyond. But none of them owns the landscape. There is a property in the horizon which no man has but he whose eye can integrate all the parts, that is, the poet.[84]

Ann Bermingham points out that the English garden was being transformed "from a small-scale, formal structure to an extensive, natural-looking landscape garden," and Rowe was ahead of her time in depicting and explicating its beneficial possibilities. According to Bermingham, it came to be laid out as a series of multiple views and invited walking through them; it was a space "free to ramble" and to be rambled in.[85] Providing multiple kinds of views as in figure 21 and, in Rowe's creations, multiple uses (gardens, agricultural fields, and forests), any sense of confinement evaporated.

The seamlessness and harmony brought together God, nature, all kinds of beauty, virtue, and the individual's interior life, and Rowe's landscapes drew upon Addison's earlier writings and pointed toward later designs. Addison consistently advocated for mixing gardens with different kinds of cultivated fields and enumerated the benefits: "the Eye would always be discovering new Objects and be lost in that inexpressible somewhat to be found in the Beauty of Nature."[86] That Addison and the *Spectator* drew together imagination and freedom and the aesthetic enjoyment of prospects, especially varieties of "unbounded Views," is another reason they are so important to the movement. He wrote,

> A spacious Horison is an Image of Liberty, where the Eye has Room to range abroad, to expatiate at large on the Immensity of its Views, and to lose it self amidst the Variety of Objects that offer themselves to its Observation. Such wide and undetermined Prospects are as pleasing to the Fancy, as the Speculations of Eternity or Infinitude are to the Understanding.[87]

Fig. 21. Jennings Park by Michael Angelo Rooker. Engravings as well as descriptions in poetry and fiction portrayed the ideally pleasing landscape that invited the stroller through varied scenes, one opening after another to the eye. From *A Collection of Landscapes drawn by D. Sandby; Esq. R.A. and engraved by Mr. Rooker* (London, 1777).

This conception had, of course, enormous resonance throughout the century and stands behind many major aesthetic and philosophical theories.

Brant argues that letters seem to "dematerialise bodies," but Cook asserts that "the letter constructs the writing subject as corporeal," "subjectivity as embedded in and inseparable from a discrete body." Brant describes a process by which writers who "describe their letters as conversational often follow it with an evocation of the recipient's presence."[88] In fact, Rowe's and the Bluestockings' letters first dematerialize the body, making it a spirit, and then imagine the presence of the friend with startling physicality. Just as the public/private are collapsed by letters, so the presence/absence of writer and recipient collapse barriers of time and space analogously to the trope of letters from the dead to the living. They are speaking from minds that conceive the seamlessness of the material and the supernatural, often eternal, worlds. Cancelling time and space, this passage refers to many kinds of elsewhere and smoothly transitions from one to another. Like so much of Rowe's writing, the concrete materialism of fireside and easy chair is easily juxtaposed with wings, pure space, and "guest Aetherial." Probably to Elizabeth Vesey, Carter wrote, "What a delightful tete a tete might we have, my dear friend, if you were not stunned by the buzz of an assembly room . . . while I am silently drinking my solitary dish of tea in Clarges-street. Yet, after all, what impediments are seas and mountains to the flight of thought, and the magic of affection? In spite of interposing kingdoms here you are with me for the whole evening. . . ."[89]

Certainly the women's letters record closeness unaffected by distance and remarkable license to speak freely on a variety of subjects not usually encouraged fully in women's discourse. Hidden within the discipline of their routines are means of resistance and liberation, and the same technologies of the self are even more apparent in the creation of kinds of elsewhere. Critics find a variety of kinds of evidence. Deborah Heller, for instance, suggests that Vesey's identity as "The Sylph" "emblematized for [the Bluestockings] the possibility of a female self soaring beyond the limitations of conventional female identity and conduct. Montagu and Carter often imagine the aerial mobility of the Sylph as their own and connect it with their sense of doing something new."[90] Surely using the trope of friendship after death, Carter wrote her friend Catherine Talbot that were she to die on a trip to Goodwin Sands, she would some day "accost you in the most agreeable manner possible, in the dress and attitude of Mrs. Rowe's etherial beings."[91] Carter replicates the care with which Rowe described how her spirits attempted to avoid frightening those they visited and also how their permission to visit their surviving friends came at random times. This letter, like so many of Rowe's to Hertford, gives readers access to a special friendship and to their community, one unrestricted by time or space. The correspondence brings writer, recipients, *and* readers closer to God and to a distinctive lifestyle.

Notably Carter asserts that they will say "what has not been said before." This elsewhere is a place of freedom unlike any other, as women have the freedom to think and speak from the conceptual self. Carter in her translation of Epictetus writes, "So that when you have Shut your Doors, . . . remember, never to say that you are alone, for you are not: but God is within, and your Genius is within."[92] For women like Carter, this was also an elsewhere that affirmed the conceptual self. So many of these women find God *and* themselves in this elsewhere. Bowerbank describes Catherine Talbot, who often found an elsewhere in her letters to Carter: "If only for the moment of writing the letters to Carter, Talbot is able to escape time—that is, normal time—so convincingly naturalized as real or the only time, determined by the . . . changing of the seasons, the aging of the body; validated by the regularity of the clock, calendar, and cycle of workdays." Talbot also wrote about finding her self: "Were but the calm retreat secured in one's own mind, had one a fortress built there with walls of solid philosophy, and a comfortable easy chair, quilted pure and soft with ease of temper, one should enjoy perfect quiet in the midst of a hurricane."[93] Rowe often places herself in just such a place.

Rowe and the Midcentury Novel

Novels that should be classified with Rowe's fiction have all of the elements of the politeness movement and dramatize the technologies of the self that she consistently illustrated. Many of these novels conclude as Rowe's stories of Rosalinda and others do with invented societies that include family, carefully selected friends, and compatible neighbors. One of the first of the texts in the line that Rowe established is Mary Collyer's *Felicia to Charlotte: Being Letters from a Young Lady in the Country, to Her Friend in Town. Containing A Series of the most interesting Events, interspersed with Moral Reflections; chiefly tending to prove, that the Seeds of Virtue are implanted in the Mind of Every Reasonable Being* (1744), an epistolary novel of 310 pages with an obvious link to Shaftesbury's moral sense. Collyer, like Rowe, quotes poetry by Milton, Spenser, Thomson, Young, and others, and the later novels in this vein routinely include poetry that raises the literary and aesthetic level. The novel is like a drawing out of Rowe's fairy tales.

Like the princess in *The Isle of Happiness* and Rowe's stories, the man who has passed every test of temperament and like-mindedness assures the couple's happiness. "My soul itself was all harmony! and inspired by his presence, every vein was harmony too," Felicia exclaims, and this harmony extends to her human circle, to nature, and to Heaven (1:170). Alessa Johns has identified such constructs as one of the kinds of utopias women created in the century. Members of the community live close together or visit frequently, making extended stays, and long letters reinforce the common sensibilities and contrasts to outsiders. Johns identifies them as "the most comprehensive women's utopian type,"[94] and many of the best novels of the period by women conclude this way. As the potential is developed, they become effectively ideological, as Frances Brooke's *History of Emily Montague* and *The Excursion* (1777) and Mary Hamilton's *Munster Village* (1778) do. Within many of these novels are remarks on the most important philosophical issues of the day, as was true with Rowe's *Letters*.

Felicia to Charlotte was so lastingly popular that it was selected for serialization in James Harrison's *Novelists Magazine*.[95] An unusually learned woman, in addition to the poetry, Collyer has Felicia's aunt educate her children with, among other things, "an English Seneca," and she refers easily to major Enlightenment writers. Characters read the *Spectators* for pleasure and improvement. Collyer was the successful translator of Pierre Carlet de Chamblain de Marivaux's *La Vie de Marianne*, which she titled *The Virtuous Orphan* (1743). Some of the Bluestockings knew Collyer; Montagu described her to Carter as "a very good woman who has seven children" and said that she hoped her translation of Salomon Gessner's *The Death of Abel* (1761) "may turn out to her praise and profit, especially the latter which to an anxious mother must be most welcome."[96] Susan Staves calls *Felicia to Charlotte* "one of the most interesting of the epistolary novels of the 1740s or 1750s" and judges that Collyer "succeeded in using the epistolary form to show how conflicts between parents and children might be resolved and to portray an ideal husband and wife living a model domestic life."[97] All of the letters are by Felicia, and the novel begins with Felicia having arrived at her aunt's home in the country where, she says, "to pass away some of my hours, which I foresee will lie pretty heavy upon my hands, I will send you an account of all that happens worth your notice."[98] Her description is remarkably similar to that of Rowe's Laura:

> I am now I don't know how many miles distant from dear London, the seat of your joys; and must not expect for a long time to see again the Mall, the playhouse, or the drawing-room; but I begin to fancy, that in a month or two I shall be reconciled to gloomy shades, tall trees, and murmuring brooks, and all the sylvan scenes which surround me; and even cease to regret my distance from the genteel diversions of the gay and polite world. (1:3)

Laura had written, "I should think [my brother's country estate] more finely situated in the *Mall*, or even in *Cheapside* than here. Indeed I hardly know where we are, only that it is at a dreadful distance from the theatre royal in *Drury-Lane*, from the opera, from the masquerade, and every thing in this world that is worth living for" (*Letters*, 3:224).

The story is simple, and essays and didactic "discoveries" take up most of the text. Felicia is courted by the aristocratic Mellifont and fears that her father will insist she marry him. From the second letter, she has been enamoured with Lucius, whose name is, of course, the same as Rosalinda's husband, and he has many similarities to Laura's beautiful hermit in Rowe's stories. There are notable physical resemblances, too, as both have "elegant" shapes, wear their hair in unfashionable long, luxurious curls, and their thoughts center on "truth and virtue."[99] Staves calls Collyer's Lucius "a new kind of masculine hero, an early example of the man who is desirable because of his virtue and his sensibility," but, of course, Rowe had created several of them earlier. Staves continues with a useful explication of Lucius's Shaftesburian moral sense.[100] Felicia and her cousin Amelia see him for the first time as he stands by a beautiful river and says, "O Nature! how beautiful, how lovely are all thy works!"

(1:10). Her father comes to love Lucius, Mellifont and Belinda become engaged, and there is one final threat to Felicia's happiness. Before this, complications are slight, such as Felicia inheriting £10,000 from an East Indian uncle and thereby becoming even richer than Lucius. Much more than Rowe's fiction, *Felicia to Charlotte* is a novel of sensibility and, therefore, a gauge of how rapidly this structure of feeling became dominant.[101] As in many eighteenth-century novels, the serious threat arises very suddenly, is intense, and is quickly resolved. Lucius's father, who has been depicted at the beginning of the novel as a dissolute gambler, is finally arrested for his debts. There are dramatic descriptions of the misery of prison. Lucius, who already has a smaller fortune than Felicia, gives up two-fifths of it to save his father and then honorably breaks his engagement to Felicia. Her father, however, gives Lucius a large estate so he will not have to "depend on my daughter, for the enjoyment of any of the elegancies of life" (2:16).

Lucius's generous act in saving his father has brought pages of an outpouring of sensibility and the reform of his own father, who is rapidly folded into the bosom of the extended family. Everyone, most notably Lucius's father, is proved to have this basic goodness and, as the ending underscores, universal sociability, benevolence, and humanity. Not only are philosophical discussions drawn out, but situations are milked for their sentimental and didactic emphasis.[102] Lucius's father, for instance, voices his fear of prison and then asks pathetically, "Will you not come to see me?" (1:302). Lucius recounts how tempted he was to preserve his fortune: "ten thousand pleasing, distracting ideas crowded upon my mind, and overwhelmed my senses in a mazy whirl of bitter giddiness" (301). He describes the conflict as between love and *nature*, thus the Shaftesburian concept of human nature and relationships "rightly" overcomes the passions.

Collyer allies her novel with the kind of satisfying fairy tales that Rowe created. In Letter 3, Felicia writes, "no wonder you think these humbler scenes, these . . . simple charms which please me, are almost wholly fictitious, and little else but the invention of a luxuriant fancy,—a sort of fairy-land that exists no where but in my own imagination" (1:17). Later she says there "are no fiery dragons to conquer, or inchanted castle to storm," but by denying them she brings them to mind (1:123). Linking her story to this genre allows her more freedom than the realism of Haywood. She invites her readers into an imagined world where their fears and thoughts can be expressed and a happy ending assured. In this transitional moment in the history of the novel, the courtship novel could become a fairy tale, an aesthetic and happy story. Collyer has Felicia speak of genre: "And indeed whatever name is given to my story, whether of rural adventures, novel, or romance, I should be very well satisfied, though all the world thought it fictitious, might I at last . . . have it concluded, like the most celebrated pieces of imaginary scenes of love and gallantry, in a happy catastrophe" (123). Then she and her little cousin Polly enter into a scene in which she makes garlands and wreaths for the child, who is compared to a sylvan deity. In an episode much like Rosalinda's settling into her new life, Felicia finds her new home like a fairyland, evaluates it, and expresses a preference for a Hertford-style estate:

> I fancied myself in fairy land.... 'Tis true, there is something disagreably [sic] formal, in the studied regularity that reigns here: statues, obeliks [sic], and triumphal arches, are but aukwardly mimicked in box and yeugh [sic] ... Lucius may possibly continue them ..., with only a few alterations, in order to render the whole more easy, free, and natural. Besides, as the house and gardens are in the midst of a wood, this spot, even in the summer season, will agreably set off the wildness of the prospect, and, by a pleasing contrast, heighten the variegated scene (2:40–41).

Collyer includes an interesting comparison of estate styles, an unexpected bonus in the book. Felicia and Lucius go with a group of friends to visit Lord M***'s estate. This depiction of the actual estate of Lord Middleton with Woolaton Hall, its impressive Elizabethan mansion, precedes such descriptions, real and fictional, in novels written in the picturesque and tourist era. They leave the coaches and walk through the park, enjoying the varied landscapes. At her home after her marriage, she enjoys the variety of parks, groves, and gardens and imagines them varying in attractiveness at different seasons. This detail and sense of contrasts and seasons are typical of Rowe's fiction, and, as Rowe did with the two sides of Rosalinda's home, Collyer constructs Felicia's with "the triumph of nature" on one side and "the boast of art on the other" (*Felicia*, 2:38). In fact, the language is strikingly similar. Rowe writes, "The opposite side of the structure discloses a quite different view; as that seems the triumph of nature, this appears the insult of art; the gardens and groves are so exquisitely fine and regular, that I fancy myself in Fairy-land" (*Letters*, 3:134). It was Middleton's garden that reminded Felicia of fairyland: "I could think of nothing but castles and embowering shades, arising spontaneously to the charms of music; of the work of fairies." (1:92). Her own garden replicates the harmony and double pleasure of Rowe's. On one side is a wilderness, an area artfully planted with diverse trees and cultivated to appear wild and left natural, on the other "the boast of art," an English formal garden. As Felicia describes the area, she repeats how the gardens open and stretch forward: "A vista, which carries the eye from the center of the building to a considerable distance" and "In the midst of each walk, ... on either hand, the eye is carried through a number of triumphal arches, composed of the same leafy materials" (2:38–39).

As in so many other aspects, Rowe was writing at a pivotal moment, one that turned the words and spaces for British land use into sites of contestation and negotiation, and she and Collyer both reflect this time and portray new uses and relationships. "Forest," for example, was shifting from a site of class conflict to one pitting military and economic significance against what John Evelyn called its ornamental aspects and others increasingly saw as "a desirable space of freedom, belonging, and well-being in resistance to the rise of utilitarianism."[103] In *The Invention of the Countryside*, Donna Landry has demonstrated that "'the countryside', an imaginary, generalized space" that became a defining characteristic of the nation, came into being between 1671 and 1831. Her book describes a preference for "fine open country" giving way to "pictorial criteria."[104] As indicative of liberty, most of the prospects described in Rowe's *Letters* are fine open country, and gardens seem to flow seamlessly into the "ocean-like" open prospects. Panoramic rather than "framed," her scenes open out when thematically appropriate and contrast to the sheltered, often dark garden spaces where intimate conversations occur. She has the art, however, to use a kind of freeze-frame pictorial moment as the scene unfolds. For instance, appropriately for his story in mood and result, Bellamour rides through fine open country to unanticipated fulfillment, and the prospects in those letters fit Landry's description of what had become "old-fashioned" by 1770. He describes scenery as he rides, then dismounts and contemplates a spring watering a valley, then rides again following the stream, then stops again and portrays the scene of the "low house, behind which there was a plat of trees" (*Letters*, 1:132). The views of spacious, open country are enriched, thus, by pictorial interludes.

Felicia describes their married life as "peaceful retirement," "repose," and harmony with religion "an inexhaustible spring of rational and sublime delight" for them (2:41). Significantly, for many of these characters, the way they live in relation to nature and one another is not an essential attribute but one we see developing. In fact, as Rowe did and Collyer does here, an amatory pastoral is constructed that transforms Heaven into a kind of pastoral idyll.[105] Lucius and Felicia discover a thick grove where they "presented our evening orisons" (2:61), thus bringing to mind the elsewhere that brings together images of different kinds of utopias and of harmony. Collyer models the novel in which the Christian couple is the central interest while the old-style aristocratic couple and the more modern secular ones are contrasted or even ridiculed. In *Felicia to Charlotte*, for example, scenes between Mellifont and Felicia are a comic interlude ridiculing this older literary couple. As with Fineer in *Betsy Thoughtless*, such men always fail the test of discourse.

Collyer follows Rowe in constructing the identification of authorial sensibility, characters, and readers. Like Rowe's fiction, contemporary domestic issues and novelistic episodes animate Collyer's novel. If we forget that it was written six years before *Clarissa*, it seems like an anti-*Clarissa*. Felicia's fear of the power of her father and the likelihood of his commands about her marriage ignoring her feelings is extreme. She writes to Charlotte that it is fanciful to think "that however offended he may be at first, affection will soon take place of resentment, and at last swallow up all thought of displeasure" (1:173). The conflict flares briefly as at one point he accuses her of being a disgrace to the family and says, "It is still in my power to punish you" (1:207). His suspicions and charges are unfair for, unlike Clarissa, she is entirely ready to sacrifice herself to his order regardless of the resulting lifelong unhappiness. She never wavers from the lengthy letter she writes pledging her total obedience to his will (1:172–74). This father, however, unlike Clarissa's, never surrenders his authority and respects her. Trial scenes are constructed in this novel, too. At one point, her aunt assembles the family and says that they are there to "enquire after" whether she has affection for "an unworthy object; whether she has violated her regard for virtue; behaved, in any instance, inconsistent with a decent modesty; or had any thought of disposing of herself without your consent" (1:223). Her next statement underscores what is at stake (and not readily apparent to the modern reader): "In short, it is your Felicia's honour and duty we are to vindicate" (1:223).

In order to help vindicate her and perhaps win her father over to Lucius's character, Charlotte mails all of Felicia's letters to her father. In the scene in which Felicia's father and aunt are reading her letters, Charlotte's reaction to them is cleverly revealed by the "scheme" to vindicate Felicia and make Lucius's case with them. Charlotte has been persuaded of Lucius's merit, of the sincerity of their love, of the promise of happiness in marriage, and, of course, of Felicia's virtue and loyalty to her father. The reactions of her aunt and father are additional signs of how the letters are to be taken and that Felicia models desirable behavior and even thoughts. "What a strange scheme! could any thing be more extravagant!" Felicia exclaims, but she, unlike Pamela and later Clarissa, has no concerns at all about the content of her letters. She finally goes to her aunt's closet and observes her father and aunt reading all the letters. "We were reading your soul, it was talking to us," her aunt says.

Collyer, however, adds a satiric edge that Rowe rarely includes. Prudilla, for instance, is a good addition to the time's satiric portrayals of moral hypocrites but is given additional interest and significance as the vehicle for characterizations and discussions of forms of faith and the moral philosophies of Locke, Shaftesbury, Hutcheson, and Hume.[106] Felicia attacks fashionable conduct by describing Lucius as not having "the least notion of the art of handling a snuff-box with grace" or of "how to murder the reputation of those who are absent" (1:23). Mellifont, speaking in ridiculous romantic discourse and dressed "with an old rusty helmet [*sic*] on his head" and carrying a pike, offers her "the ravagers of the mountains and the vallies," that is, the stuffed skins of "several" badgers.[107]

In describing Lucius's reaction to her decorous confession of an inclination toward him, she continues, "You are now ready to imagine that I shall describe him throwing himself at my feet, while with a flow of rapture, he admires my superlative goodness, blending his praises with two or three hundred adorables, transcendent excellencies . . . and that to conclude his panegyric, he tells me how astonished he is, that a goddess so heavenly fair . . . —But if these were your thoughts, you were extremely mistaken; for I did not hear him utter the least syllable of this sublime nonsense." Like Rowe's heroes, Lucius and Felicia have their feet firmly on the ground and she is even anti-sentimental. For all the aesthetic romance of the setting and overall story, the characters are realistic.[108] Collyer here parodies the more extravagant romantic tales of the decades immediately before her novel and inserts the same kind of rational ideology that Rowe exhibits, as Felicia continues, "He is too good a christian to deify his mistress, and has too good an opinion of me to think I should be pleased with such senseless homages . . . his love was incapable of blinding him so far as to make him forget that I was . . . the same species with himself" (1:69). She can refer to "Amaranthine bowers," "flowry lawns," and "silent solemn scenes of peaceful innocence" while emphasizing that her own story is one of the complications of economic difference and parental conduct (1:122). In fact, Lucius becomes more the sensibility character as the novel progresses, and his tears and even the occasional throwing himself at someone's feet testify to the spontaneity of his best feelings (cf. 1:273).

Part of Rowe's legacy was the skeleton of an alternate politeness movement for women. As Philip Carter demonstrates, the politeness movement was committed to "constructing and establishing, rather than simply confirming, ideas of *male* gender" and new standards of masculinity (emphasis mine);[109] thus, a parallel movement was imperative for women. Linguists teach us that "*polite* and *politeness* are lexemes in the English language whose meanings are open to negotiation by those interacting in English" and are constantly in flux. Richard Watts points out, "*Polite* can only be used in reference to a person's behavior (or an aspect of his/her behaviour, and in particular to his/her use of language) and, by extension, to that person's character."[110] By Rowe's time, consensus emphasis was on politeness as a cultivated attribute. "Accomplishments" became so important for women because that meant abilities that entertained—playing an instrument, singing, and having read the right plays and poetry including some in French. Interestingly, accomplishments for men depended far less on actual learning than on conduct that carried legacies from rakish abilities—speaking so well that one held the stage, moving in drawing rooms and gardens as actors did to draw attention and command. Men needed to have "parts," a term suggesting physical attractiveness as well as abilities and talent for overt performance, while women who displayed wit and commanded center stage set themselves up as targets for rapists as Betsy Thoughtless and Harriot Stuart experienced.

To compare the country-house novels and episodes by men and by women writers illuminates an important aspect of the women's alternate politeness movement and a contrasting literary line. For men, the estate is not the place to develop or critique community. Sometimes it is a place of confinement as in Richardson's *Pamela*, but more often a vision of a past, sometimes satirized and sometimes nostalgically regretted as in Swift's book 3 of *Gulliver's Travels* and Smollett's *Humphrey Clinker*. Thornhill in *The Vicar of Wakefield* also uses his estate to confine women on whom he is preying, and it seems an almost gothic relic of the past. For women, it is the space in which community develops and can survive. When the core has formed, the society can expand and spread its benefits. In many ways, this process is the movement in *David Simple* as the individual characters come together, identify worthy recipients of charity, and spread David's money and their ideology. Through benevolence they identify additional group members.[111] Women, especially Brooke in *The History of Lady Julia Mandeville*, recognize the importance of market towns, and how tenants, tradesmen, and clergy are treated becomes a major theme and source of powerful judgments of patriarchy and even nation. Betty Schellenberg has pointed out the importance of novels in which the protagonist is *not* in sustained tension with his or her social environment but part of "an intimate and exclusive conversational circle [that is] both a paradigm for and a means toward social consensus."[112] In Rowe, self-mastery and the construction of a lifestyle in the wake of a life-changing event provide the energy of the narrative. It is faith, however, in this model that allows the later novels to concentrate on creating a community, and often a secular one.

Lady Julia Mandeville brings to the fore Rowe's restraint, her moderate, more "realistic" claims, and the admirable conciseness of her communication of ideas. The relationship between humankind and nature and the importance of retreats into beautiful natural settings are the same. Moreover, piety, beauty, and other emphases in Rowe's work are present. These fictions create virtuous, beautiful, even aesthetic marriages. As critics of Rowe's poetry have demonstrated, Rowe's definition of love included all of the kinds of love, including sexual, companionate, and divine. She expresses a unity and flow among kinds of love that is hard for the twenty-first-century reader to conceptualize. God and the divine's relationship to humankind is the supreme model, and her sexually explicit expressions of it, perhaps best expressed in her Canticles based on the Song of Songs, must be recognized and factored in. As Clarke says, "it was sensuously, physically experienced." "Her poetic sensibility, vividly aroused by the sensuous pleasures of earthly life, fed by visionary impulses of a self-gratifying kind,"[113] is in her fiction as well and is the foundation of her seamless idea of love. Out of the radicalism of the model of divine romance came, in Achinstein's words, an "assault upon patriarchal marriage."[114] In fact, Rowe forges a link between amatory fiction, which does this routinely, and her religious poetry and the kinds of "beautiful" marriages she constructs for women.

Another group of novels that carry Rowe's influence create another kind of society, have quite different tones, and model two themes of major importance for the times. First, Rowe, like many of the later novelists, including Frances Sheridan and Elizabeth Griffith, shows characters struggling to attain peace of mind and managing to carve out an autonomous existence within repressive conditions, especially marriages. This quest is a persistent theme in women's writing, and, again, Rowe has revised the trajectory and reward. "The Almighty has been gracious in giving thee a Mind submissive and resign'd," the Lady observes regarding Galesia in Jane Barker's *Patch-Work Screen*, and many characters and texts endorse this conclusion.[115] In contrast, Rowe produces and dramatizes steadfastness rather than stoicism. "Enduring," "resolute," "steady," "persevering," "stable," "unwavering"—the synonyms for "steadfast" describe the characters, as those for "stoicism" ("imperturbable," "unemotional," "resigned") do not. Rowe's work is different from the novel of resignation and submission in that the individualism of the protagonist is strongly protected and the "social consensus" of the group is radical rather than conservative. In fact, comparisons reveal how conservative some later women were, as Brooke is with the ending of *Emily Montague*, in which all of the women are tamed and even silenced and a picturesque, conservative England triumphs over the sublime scenes and rethinking of institutions characteristic of Canada. Rather than protest that they will never disobey a father as Collyer's Felicia does, Rowe's defy, run away, and refuse untested reconciliations.

Second, over and over, faith in regimens of self-mastery produces stories of liberation and calls attention to the fact that Rowe introduces "liberty" into fiction, the term that was already a site of hegemonic struggle depicted in plays and poetry. Especially in the turn-of-the-century marriage plays, women demand "dear liberty," and what that means is negotiated with husbands and public opinion. Poets Sarah Fyge Egerton, Anne Finch, Mary Jones, and Sarah Dixon, among others, used the same terms and styled the condition "liberty." As critics note, Sarah Fyge Egerton's "'The Liberty,' one of her best-known poems, breathes that same air of personal and political freedom celebrated in Whig rhetoric of the Williamite period."[116] Johns rightly identifies novels like *Millenium Hall* as carrying a liberal perspective defined as proceeding from the belief that "aspects of Enlightenment universalism derived from natural law offered women emancipatory possibilities," including "economic notions of the autonomous commercial individual" and "of certain types of equality and self-direction." Societies in this model in novels became in her words "a reproductive utopian model."[117] The novel became a major space for modeling her theory and Nancy Fraser's regarding the possibilities for the formation of contestatory, or at least alternative, subaltern counterpublics. Both see a movement from private or limited issues to those "of concern to everyone."[118]

Rowe herself was notably independent, and she, like these characters and the Bluestockings, was an example of a counterpublic sphere that went beyond opinion formation but, of course, could exercise authoritative decision-making. She wrote to Hertford that "something of mechanism in my reasoning faculty" depended on the space, physical and mental, that she occupied. "Here my hours are absolutely at my own disposal," she wrote, and in various ways "reason" is valorized.[119] As Norma Clarke observes of Rowe, "We . . . see a quietly determined individual leading a life based on the demands of her art. She insists on solitude and praises its efficacy for *clear thinking*."[120] Her family and friends, admiring of her writing, usually respected her lifestyle and began to present her as a writer of the type we associate with Romanticism: "The love of solitude, which seems almost inseparable from a poetic genius, discovered itself very early in Mrs. Rowe."[121] Her independence included a freedom from the need to please others with her writing, and it was picked up by other writers. Rowe once wrote to Cleora, "Without any apology, I am going to talk to myself" (*Letters*, 1:91). Felicia writes to Charlotte, "You must not be offended if I tell you, I write as much to amuse myself as to please you" (1:2).

This life was glorified in novels such as Sarah Scott's *Millenium Hall*, and domestic scenes came to feature accomplished women forming female-only families in aesthetic settings like Rowe's little societies. In the midcentury novel for women, the cultivation of the mind and spirit became a viable choice; at least briefly in fiction, marriage was not the only way to be normal and happy. *Millenium Hall* extended the depiction of the prosperous, well-run, harmonious farm or estate in which human beings and the land were cultivated with love and care into the polite novel about women's abilities. An interesting precursor is Rowe's portrayal of the sea captain's wife's domestic economy. Although her husband drops in periodically to replenish and distribute money, she is the administrator of the home, and her autonomy is taken for granted. *Millenium Hall* is truly an "elsewhere." Judith Bloome describes it as "a small island of freedom that is encapsulated. It is an illusory, harmonious space that does not engage its surrounding world, whatever implications it may have for an idealized world, or future utopia."[122] Rowe's texts *refer* to the "surrounding world" as Scott's does, and in looking at their texts together we are aware that for all its appearance of modernity and utopian socioeconomic unit building, Scott's novel is as much a fairy tale as Rowe's.

Astutely, Harriet Guest recognizes that the ladies' "estate management is strongly reminiscent of the representations of virtuous public men in retirement in James Thomson's *Seasons*," and they "taste / The Joy of God to see a happy World!"[123] The conceptions of Thomson and Shaftesbury are fully integrated into this text and Rowe's, and the characters produce the polite, harmonious world. The duty of these authors' characters is to themselves, to the self. Julie tells Hypolite that she will always prioritize duty over love, and duty appears to figure large at Millenium Hall. Yet, rather than assumed responsibility as in Rowe's work, it comes easily as a technology of the self. It is part of the daily routine and quickly gives way to cultivating the self in conversation, reading, and other self-directed activities. Given its name by Sir George, the wandering male traveler, in a letter to a male friend, the novel employs descriptions of settings recalling Rowe's: picturesque dwellings, gardens, landscapes, and set arrangements of characters. Although critics relate the name to the one-thousand-year reign of peace foretold in Revelations, Sir George's tone often conjures up an image of columns in today's popular magazines called "signs of the apocalypse." Nevertheless, like Bellamour, who tells the stories of Melissa and Rosella in *Letters*, and David Simple, who elicits and judges women's stories, he adds significance and narrative authority to the women's stories.[124] In all of these fictions, however, the times of passivity of the listening male contrast to the speaking women who are telling stories of either steadfastness or unusual actions or both.

Sarah Fielding's *Adventures of David Simple* (1744) required a second edition only ten weeks after its publication and was rapidly translated into other languages. In 1775, the publisher R. Snaggs named it "one of the twelve best-selling novels to be issued in cheap abridgements as 'little Books of Entertainment.'"[125] Its interpretation has been complicated by a persistent desire to associate it with Richardson or her brother Henry, in spite of the fact that it "does not quite fall into either the more satiric tradition of her brother Henry or the written-to-the moment epistolary style of her friend Samuel Richardson."[126] In fact, it should be related to Rowe's *Letters* and the kinds of fiction that are its immediate contexts and seen as an important transition text, as Rowe's are. Fielding called it a "moral romance," and it is a fascinating combination of two fictional economies. David's story is a philosophical quest "to seek out one capable of being a real Friend," a quest for which he is willing to "travel through the whole World."[127] David, like Collyer's Lucius, is a sensibility character, but his benevolence is eccentric and occasionally satirized. Harriet Guest, for instance, points out that in one passage he "is compared to a spoiled child growing into the fashionable woman who cares only to be the center of admiration."[128] Like almost all sensibility heroes, he challenges readers to test their responses and, therefore, their sensibility against his. As Patricia Meyer Spacks says, "only those who share David's natural goodness will understand what he felt," and she quotes, "The Raptures *David* felt at that Moment . . . are not to be expressed; and can only be imagined by those People who are capable of the same actions."[129] In contrast, the stories of Cynthia and Camilla are stories of struggle, suffering, and, finally, fairy-tale romance endings.

Another similarity to Rowe's strategies is the fact that Fielding is drawing a community of readers together, recreating the shared sensibilities and ideology of author, Camilla, Cynthia, and women readers. Emily Friedman notes that readers are "bound together by the experience of reading the same novel,"[130] but the complexity of Fielding's text dictates that different groups of readers are bound together by the way they are reading and for what they are reading, or, perhaps more accurately, that Fielding was participating in the reading revolution described in chapter three based on rising numbers of readers' "newfound capacity to read in a variety of ways."[131] Friedman notes that Fielding's fictions include essays, fables, allegory, and literary criticism, an indication of her faith in her reader's ability to read and enjoy diverse discourses and modes.[132] As Friedman says, Fielding is addressing a rational reader, again an important assumption of Rowe's.

Stark, arresting realism marks the women's experiences, and Fielding draws upon Rowe's themes and narrative strategies. Readers are invited to apprehend Cynthia's and Camilla's situations and then admire their courage, steadfast selfhood, and canny resistance to familial and social pressures. Rather than testing their sensibilities, they respond to the model offered by Fielding and her female characters, partly through their understanding of the situation of women. Cynthia, for instance, refuses a marriage that she describes as being an upper servant but is forced into the situation of a humble companion. Camilla describes the plight of a middle-class woman who needs to work with passion: tradespeople "think we were endeavouring to take their Bread out of their mouths," "Men think our Circumstances gives them a Liberty to shock our Ears with Proposals ever so dishonorable. . . ." And, of course, there is the lack of experience seeking work and a lack of skills.[133] David, like Harley in *The Man of Feeling*, however, focuses on the suffering and his own pleasurable feelings when he can comfort or help. Joseph Bartolomeo explains, "one may also view David as unconsciously seeking, as a reward or even as advance payment for his generosity, the same pleasures available to the sentimental reader of the novel itself," and he finds "some degree of self-interest and self-indulgence behind the hero's displays of beneficence." "Within this sentimental economy David can essentially purchase pleasure by giving money to others," he concludes. This reading highlights the different economies to which he and the women characters belong.[134] To some extent *Volume the Last* continues this division. For instance, when David and Camilla's children die, he is as "on every tender Occasion, motionless with Grief; and *Camilla* . . . was at once a Picture of the highest Sorrow and the highest Resignation" (326).

Sensibility requires victims, and as the stories of victims multiply, Fielding narrows the blame and focuses sharply on two topics. One is the situation of poor women.[135] As the narrative continues, the incidents become more varied and, therefore, reinforce the incremental case being made. Some are shorter, as are the encounter with the drudge-wife whose husband is a jolly companion (41–43) and the woman married to the ill-natured man (197–98). Others are presented in wildly different genres from the central narrative or from the story of Cynthia, as is Isabelle's sensational, Behn-like narrative. Vulnerable to coercion, false accusations, and homelessness, the women are the objects of the sensibility gaze. The second topic is the overwhelming importance of money; David has many of the characteristics of victims, including some that critics have identified as feminine, but as long as he has money he avoids most experiences of victimhood and can rescue himself and others. Thus, the bifurcation of the text is developed as the women's experiences and David's diverge, and, as with the collections of letters, readers are called upon to read in different ways and relate to the text, its characters, and stories in different ways.

When Cynthia or Camilla tells her story, the narrator mentions David's reactions, but for long stretches only the woman narrates, thereby turning the text into the kinds of episodes and stories written by Behn, Haywood, Davys, and Rowe. Cynthia has been forced into the dreaded position of the humble companion, while Rowe's women often become servants. Camilla's father has been victimized by his second wife and suspects Camilla and Valentine of incest. In Fielding's text humankind is presented as desiring to dominate, specifically with Cynthia trapped and Camilla accused of incest by her stepmother. David's Shaftesburian benevolence comes crashing against the realism of poverty, the evil in human nature, and women's lack of options beyond the leap of faith that is escape into the unknown. Revealingly, Cynthia is enslaved because of her virtue, her moral beauty that makes her feel gratitude to the woman who has given her a home. Thus, David and Cynthia can recognize a shared ideology even as David is on a fable-like quest and she is enmeshed in the actual situation of numerous, impoverished women.

The conclusion brings the two stories together, apparently reconciling the genres. Like the "pastoral adventures" and utopian endings of Rowe's and Collyer's novels, *David Simple* ends with the marriages of Cynthia and Valentine, Camilla's brother, and of David and Camilla and with their forming a "little Society" with Valentine and Camilla's reformed father. In many ways, Fielding is replicating the utopian, fairy-tale endings in Rowe's fictions, but there is a major difference. Fielding's critique is of human nature, especially its capitalistic drives for power and advancement; Rowe recreates a harmony she sees between earth and Heaven and in all kinds of love. Fielding attempts a similar resolution in David's summary of the end of his search, as he styles Valentine his brother, Cynthia his friend, and Camilla and himself in a "Union of two Hearts." As Bartolomeo says, however, *Volume the Last* (1753) demonstrates that the ending merely "obscures the tensions engendered by the sensibility of the hero."[136] David's sensibility has been possible because of his money, and the same realistic forces, including natural causes and human greed, faulty institutions, envy, and unequal power, that made Camilla, Cynthia, and many other characters victims have not been reconciled as they are in Rowe's overarching vision of a spiritual utopia. Cynthia, who has occasionally given a clear-sighted, cold analysis of the commercial world and human nature and served as something of a bridge or translator between the utopian and worldly discourses, is dangerously subsumed into the other characters' retreat.[137] When the characters pool their money, they make themselves vulnerable, and the text becomes a serious exposé of sensibility. Many of these narrative issues are solved in "The Vision," the allegory that concludes her *Familiar Letters between the Principal Characters*. In it, the narrator finds a winding lane that leads to a small utopian community of people ruled by the Goddess of Benevolence, or Real Love. The difference between this place and all the others that the narrator has visited is signaled at once because the people are cheerful and extend a hand to help her along her way. Mutual support, compassion, respect, and duty reign, and "the Rule of their Lives was the Gospel."[138] The harmony and easy unity with eternity created in Rowe's fictions are replicated here: "Here every Seed of real unaffected Virtue was cultivated and improved; and, consequently, all the real Happiness Human Nature is capable of, was here enjoyed, and doubled by the Hopes of yet greater" (2:392). As in *Pilgrim's Progress*, however, the narrator awakens to realize it has all been a dream.

Along with all of the positive aspects of the legacy, Rowe's example probably contributed to the stereotype that such a lifestyle results in being somewhat out of touch with reality, or, at least, everyday life, and also that writers cultivate retirement, even aggressive solitude. Johns describes the major characters in Sarah Fielding's *David Simple* as "the sentimental creation of a club of tenderhearted, childlike adults who scorn brutality and insensitivity" and points out that "worthy readers are encouraged to join the club of initiates as they experience tender sensations."[139] Both in the creation of like-minded individuals and in the generation of the tripartite union of author, character, and reader, Fielding draws upon Rowe's strategies, but these characters are fundamentally not like hers, nor are the outcomes. Rowe's autonomous characters who are determined to save body *and* soul are less benevolent and far less sentimental. In fact, it could be argued that about this time novels by women divide into those emphasizing the union of reason and religion as an integral part of a character and those still concentrating on women's trials and even victimization in courtship and marriage. In the first group, suffering is overshadowed by action, and, in the second, it is sentimentalized and drawn out.

Fielding never wrote utopian fiction again; instead she rejected the possibility of what Schellenberg calls "the achievement of full stability and a self-perpetuating rhythm of life," an ending to fictions that her contemporaries found satisfying through the end of the century. Both types, however, modeled technologies of the self, and, whether the tests of the major characters came before or after the little societies were formed, the ideals of conversation, virtue, beauty, and harmony pulled readers into value-centered conversations. Rowe, Collyer, and Scott portrayed how self-selecting, harmonious communities could reinforce the conceptual self and narrate its maintenance in social institutions such as marriage. In dramatic contrast, Fielding explored the problems with creating a society that obliterated self in community and failed to leave room for technologies of the self. Schellenberg points out the frequency with which David's "timidity" leads him to act against Cynthia's advice and even his own prudence;[140] protagonists in Rowe's fairy tales, in *Felicia to Charlotte*, and in *Millenium Hall* cannot be described this way.

An 1803 poem in *Poetical Magazine* called "*Retirement*" includes the lines "Not plac'd in others is my joy / My bliss is centred in myself." It describes a withdrawal from "vain" desires and longings and implies a lack of dependence on others for her happiness. "*Centred*," a term we use in the same way, signals this independence and also a sturdy philosophy, almost invariably Christian orthodoxy. As the jurisprudential tradition with its emphasis on natural law and civic humanism increased in influence, the writers who followed Rowe continued to create ideal communities based on the concept of Christian conscience, charity, and love. They continued to articulate that rational religion was a means of resistance. Sarah Scott, for instance, wrote, "I admire a Woman who chuses to avoid Injuries rather than indolently to grieve under them . . . when People practise that Excess of Christian Meekness, which is now thought only a female Virtue, of turning the other Cheek to him who has smote the one . . . only from a want of Courage to resist, she may be a greater Coward than others, and perhaps a better Wife in the Opinion of some Men, *but not a better Christian*" (emphasis mine).[141] In both of these kinds of novels, happy women are "centered" and have attained an identity, recognizing that they are the "same thinking thing in different times and places" and have the right, even duty, to act from that sense of self. The quest in Rowe's and these novels is the creation of a steadfast, self-conscious, contented person, and it seems inevitable that, as this type of text proliferated, narratives that tested, critiqued, and replicated the conclusions would multiply.

Again, Rowe is recognized as the model of the centered individual, as Joanna Lipking's observation demonstrates: "In page after page [of the 'Life'] Mrs. Rowe appears in a state of fine interior balance."[142] This was a goal and, as Bowerbank argues, sometimes was achieved: "Talbot's idea of Carter—an independent, inviolable, unified subject, splendid in her steadfast integrity—was essential to her sense of what a woman has the potential to be."[143] As generations read Rowe's fiction and learned of the first generation of Blues,[144] characters noted for their hard-won integrity and steadfast selfhood proliferated. Susan Staves writes that Rowe's heroines anticipate Elinor Dashwood in Jane Austen's *Sense and Sensibility*, as they do not succumb "to the temptations of passion, retire into the country, think about what they ought to do, meditate, and successfully resist."[145] Such recognition of Rowe's influence on countless fictional characters is rare.

CONCLUSION

Lifestyle as Legacy

As important as Rowe's influence on the English novel is, the legacy of her lifestyle may be equally so. What woman before her led such a well-publicized life that was invariably recognized as modest, domestic, social, contented, and philanthropic?[1] Because she was "perhaps the most popular woman writer of the eighteenth century,"[2] interest in her life was high. It is remarkable how novels after 1739 replicate the portrayal of the way Rowe actually lived the life that critics have reconstructed. "She lives a regular life built around books, community, prayer and thought." She takes quiet walks in "two or three flowery fields hedg'd round with hawthorn."[3] Even such small details become essential to the ambiance and meaning of novels. Collyer's Felicia becomes a great walker; not only does she come to prefer it to coach rides because she can experience both details and prospects more fully, but she becomes stronger and healthier. She and Amelia leave the coach in which they are taking "an airing" to walk and enjoy both beds of violets and views of "spacious meadows and fields, which . . . extended to an inconceivable distance, where our sight was only bounded by a clear sky. . . . Our eyes at one view took in abundance of little villages, which arising from amidst the trees at a great distance, agreeably diversified this delightful landscape" (1:8–10). Amelia and Felicia come to walk regularly, seeking companionship and the enjoyment of nature; on one they give a rare fictional description of the beauty of an agricultural crop: "a gentle breeze . . . waved the yellow corn; . . . while the bearded ears hung their heavy heads surcharged with myriads of glittering pearls, the fruits of a hasty shower" (1:192). When Charlotte comes to visit, she describes Felicia as "such a walker," while her own gait is "mincing," suggesting lack of muscle, fitness, and freedom of movement (2:302). Strikingly, Charlotte writes to Lady Harriot, "It is now, Madam, that I begin to live, to know myself, and to know the human mind. . . . I sometimes venture to walk out alone" (2:310). This echoes Rowe's description of retirement as the place where she experiences "most exact and impartial notions" and where "you fortify yourself against the tyranny of custom, and the impositions of persons" (*Misc. Works*, 2:27–28).

The notoriety of Rowe's lifestyle is a thing of wonder, yet as Norma Clarke observes, "The apparent paradox that a writer, whose public identity was built on her desire to live in retirement from the world in a state most nearly approximating to the retirement afforded by heaven, should be 'too well known' to need to be described passed without comment."⁴ How well details of her life were known is clear from Anna Laetitia Barbauld's tribute to her:

> She lov'd the work, and only shun'd the praise.
> Her pious hand the poor, the mourner blest;
> Her image liv'd in every kindred breast.
> THYNN, CARTERET, BLACKMORE, ORRERY approv'd,
> And PRIOR prais'd, and noble HERTFORD lov'd;
> Seraphic KENN, and tuneful WATTS were thine.⁵

Here the long-lived memory of Hertford's and Rowe's friendship and Hertford as uniting "the Peeress, Poetess, and Christian" is kept alive and reinforces Rowe's aesthetic identity.⁶ Rather than distinguishing themselves in social performances, Rowe and Hertford demonstrated that liberty comes from protecting interior distinctiveness and performing obscurity. Significantly, some fictional characters such as Betsy Thoughtless and Harriot Stuart can be happy and maintain their active mental lives only when they become nearly invisible, blending into a social position with conventional outward conduct that makes them seem homogeneous and, therefore, unremarkable.

Rowe's legacy was created and disseminated by her published writings, including her fictional and personal letters, and by publicity about her, including knowledge of her friendships with prominent men and women and the much-reprinted "Life" prefaced to *Miscellaneous Works*. During her lifetime, she made her life a text to be written and guarded. After her death, her life as represented in all of these ways became a text for others to interpret, abridge, and use in various ways. As a conclusion, I develop my illustration of the significance of Rowe's influence by relating her to the Bluestockings. Tellingly, to do so recalls major themes from earlier chapters, such as their special relationship to nature, their willingness to claim and display personhood, and the importance of rational religion. My argument is not that Rowe was a Bluestocking, and the extent to which she was a direct influence cannot be determined. After all, she differed dramatically in religion, rank, and education from the privileged, Anglican women who formed the Bluestockings. Regardless, she was a major empowering example and modeled a lifestyle that was ahead of its time. The much-reprinted and excerpted "Life" in Rowe's *Miscellaneous Works* had reported that "she was ignorant of every . . . fashionable game. Play, she believed, at best, was but an art of losing time, and forgetting to think" (*Misc. Works*, 1:lxv), and, of course, the Bluestockings banned cards, gaming, and other distracting pastimes. "The bluestocking ideal," Norma Clarke points out, "was of self-realisation through intellectual cultivation,"⁷ and that included stimulating, nearly continuous, and nurturing conversations of all kinds. The Bluestockings recast the terms and perceptions that had defined, marginalized, and circumscribed intellectual women and their work, and Rowe did the same for women writers.[8] Her lifestyle flowed into the Bluestockings in whom private and public circulated and penetrated each other.

The Bluestockings

The Bluestockings are now attracting new study, but they have never been linked in any depth to Rowe.[9] Susan Staves, for instance, writes that "Rowe was a particularly important figure to the later bluestockings, who refer to her works in their letters" but then, given the breadth of her project, can only make a few comments about Rowe's significance to the construction of a new history of women's writing.[10] I would say that Rowe was a more important figure to the first wave of Blues than to the later ones. Anni Sairo appropriately, I believe, dates "the Bluestocking corpus" from the late 1730s,[11] the time of Rowe's final publications. Although Rowe's influence can be traced into the second generation of Blues and beyond, I shall largely limit my discussion to the 1740s and 1750s. It was then that the Bluestockings came to prominence as a group of men and women drawn together for good conversation by the hostesses Elizabeth Montagu, Elizabeth Vesey, and Frances Boscawen, and they became an influential, widely discussed milestone in women's history. According to a much-repeated story, Benjamin Stillingfleet responded to an invitation with an apology that he had no suitably elegant clothes. He was told to come in his everyday coarse blue stockings, and Admiral Boscawen with wry but symbolic humor began calling the group the Bluestockings. There was never fixed membership, and Montagu once summarized the goals as the same as for "polite letters": "to inspire candour, a social spirit, and gentle manners; to teach a disdain of frivolous amusements, injurious censoriousness, and foolish animosities."[12] Vesey created a blue room for the meetings, and Montagu's new house was designed to allow "her to make an exhibition of her 'Virtue, Prudence and Temperance.'"[13]

Rather than following the well-known example of the French salons, Samuel Richardson's North End Circle, and Samuel Johnson's Club, the hostesses modeled their gatherings on the comparatively informal style of country-house and Tunbridge Wells spa parties—gatherings like those of the Countess of Hertford. Hertford's *Letter to the Honorable Mrs. Knight* (1731), *To the Countess of Pomfret: Life at Richkings* (1740), and a letter to Mary Rich give a detailed picture of the legacy. In each, she describes the same daily routine with reading and a variety of activities. In the better known *Life at Richkings*, she writes,

> We sometimes ride, and sometimes walk;
> We play at chess, or laugh, or talk:
> Sometimes, beside the crystal stream,
> We meditate some serious theme;
> Or in the grot, beside the spring,
> We hear the feather'd warblers sing,
> Shakespeare (perhaps) an hour diverts,
> Or Scot directs to mend our hearts.
> With Clark, God's attributes we explore;
> . . . .
> Gay's Pastorals sometimes delight us,
> Or Tasso's grisly spectres fright us:
> Sometimes we trace Armida's bowers,
> And view Rinaldo chain'd with flowers.

That Rowe had paraphrased these parts of *Jerusalem Delivered* is probably coincidental, but it shows a shared sensibility and the quality and variety of their reading. Hertford's activities end with shared vespers, then cards, often ombre ["(tho' I confess the change / From pray'r to cards is somewhat strange)"], supper of food produced on their estate, and "talk of hist'ry, Spain, or wit," but none of "Scandal."[14] The style of address is similar to Rowe's epistolary triad. She assumes she knows how Pomfret will react (line 20). In the poem to Knight, she adds details about the routine. After breakfast and "roving" "around the terraces and grove," they gather for prayers at nine. She gives more details about the time when they read or sew together (she depicts herself with embroidery), and the same practices and values are described:

> Again at two to dine we meet,
> Our fare is plain, our dinner neat;
> No seasoned dish allures our taste.

Then they walk again, separate for individual activities such as reading or writing letters, meet for vespers, supper, "and with a cheerful heart / Converse an hour and so we part."[15]

The description could be of any of the Bluestockings' visits to each other. For example, Elizabeth Robinson Montagu, one of the leading Bluestockings, spent a great deal of time before her marriage with Lady Margaret, Duchess of Portland, at her country house and enjoyed reading, the gatherings of accomplished women and men, and walks around Bulstrode. Sylvia Myers has described this formative influence on Montagu, calling Bulstrode "the catalyst for Elizabeth Robinson's aspirations." Mary Delany, then Pendarves, wrote, "A fairy spot of ground to be enjoyed with a friend is preferable to the whole world without that happiness." "Significantly, she speaks of female friendship as ideally taking place in a landscape—a 'fairy spot of ground.' Much of her work on Delville and Bulstrode aimed to create such 'fairy spots' for her friends and friendships."[16] In the Bluestockings' hands, the association of fairies with domesticity, beauty, and femininity increased,[17] and it became a kind of code for a special elsewhere that they shared. Delany and Lady Margaret collaborated to create the elaborate gardens at Bulstrode. They built a "Paradise Garden," "an enclosed pleasure garden adapted from the Moorish gardens of Spain" with fashionable touches such as a "Chinese House" and a pond of "Chinese fish."[18] A contemporary of Hertford's and like her, she not only worked on the designs but also worked manually in the gardens.

Later scholars have filled out our knowledge of how time was spent. Portland, for instance, did ornamental sewing, knotting, drawing, writing, and made objects in jet and amber, a precursor to the Bluestocking's enjoyment of handicrafts. She amassed one of the greatest collections of natural history, fine art, and antiquities ever made in England; the sale took thirty-eight days and "netted over eleven thousand pounds (almost a million U.S. dollars in today's terms)."[19] Reading was a major occupation, and, as with Hertford and Rowe and the later Bluestockings, noteworthy books were read almost immediately upon publication as were interesting and improving texts from earlier periods.[20] As in Hertford's home, devotional activities were woven seamlessly into the routine. For instance, Myers recounts that Portland and Robinson read Samuel Clark's sermons together, Eve Bannet describes Sarah Scott reading Clarke and writing to her circle about it, and he was an author mentioned along with John Scott in Hertford's Richkings poem.[21] Although often overlooked except with Montagu and rather spectacular acts such as the dinners for chimney sweeps, the women had unusual alertness to the condition of the poor, talked about it with each other, and expressed it in print in low-key ways. In *To the Countess of Pomfret*, for instance, Hertford provides an extensive view of Richkings that begins with the lawn and portico but quickly moves to the hay, corn, and flocks suffering from a drought. "While Wiltshire swains a harder fate sustain: / The downs burnt up, for want of genial rain" (lines 11–12).

Admittedly, Mary Astell and their own intellectual lives, publications, and patronage are the most important foundation for the Blues' present identity. And, of course, as Elizabeth Eger notes, "The bluestockings inevitably invite comparison with their French counterparts, the *salonnières*";[22] however, they and their gatherings differ in significant ways, and they are not really "counterparts." Among the differences are the importance of the countryside and nature, the sustained commitments to philanthropy and education, the acceptance and enjoyment of a wide range of activities, and the shared assumption of the central importance of religion. Moreover, the influence of the country-house and spa gatherings has been underestimated. Montagu, Vesey, and Boscawen all held such parties at Tunbridge Wells before they did in London. Notably Lady Barbara Montagu held such gatherings at her home in Bath-Easton.[23] Later, Anne Miller's Bath-Easton gatherings nurtured poets including Mary Savage and Anna Seward and produced volumes of artistically and culturally important poems.

Perhaps as much a gracious gesture to the less affluent members of the group as a sign of their commitment to ease and familiarity, dress at the gatherings has been described as unpretentious, even informal. However, because of Stillingfleet's blue worsted stocking, "informal" has been exaggerated, and I would describe their dress as varied, tolerant, and even eclectic. These gatherings were fashionable and *aesthetic*, and setting mattered, although the manner of country-house "informality" had a strong influence. The rooms in which they met were elegantly and originally decorated. Montagu's feather screens, which were viewed as they were built at her country estate in Berkshire and then moved to her Portman Square mansion, were spectacular and have been described as exuberant and "joyful ostentation."[24] Food was carefully chosen to enhance the artistic setting, and the women expressed location and personal style rather than dressing down. Montagu, who was fabulously wealthy and wanted to dominate, was described as "brilliant in diamonds."[25] They did not always meet in London, and country-house or spa socializing required dress suitable for changes in activity, such as moving out of the drawing room to take a walk over varying terrain. Hertford mentions that she can't "endure a hoop that would overturn all the chairs and tables in my closet" when she is in her own home.[26] Rowe's and their negative comments on fashionable dress arise from a sense of mobility and comfort rather than morality. Even Rowe wrote that she enjoyed "glitter."

As Moyra Haslett observes, "Their most deeply felt association was as a kind of virtual community, meeting and conversing through exchanged letters."[27] Certainly that was true of Rowe as well as Hertford, as she was constricted by her official position and Rowe disliked travel. As we have seen, she frequently and vividly imagined Hertford as similar to a character in a book she was reading or as actually with her, often walking in gardens. In a lovely letter to Vesey Carter writes, "I kept my appointment most faithfully of meeting you on the sea shore the last moonlight nights. It did me inexpressible good, I hope you shared it?"[28] This kind of communion was obviously not dependent on physical presence and cancelled the limitations of time and space. In another letter, Carter wrote that she kept her friends "always within sight: and my imagination has such telescopic eyes, that they will easily reach you even in 'La divisa dal mondo ultima Irlanda.'"[29] The frequency, density, range, and detail of their letters are astonishing. As Judith Hawley observes, the inner circle "often worked as a kind of reading group; their letters exchange recommendations for further reading and test and revise literary judgements." For instance, Talbot and Carter wrote about Richardson's novels.[30] Carter says in a letter to Talbot, "I imagine you have seen the Life of Savage and Letters from Felicia to Charlotte. I am told, but I have not seen it, that Mr. Warburton has wrote something against the Pleasures of Imagination."[31] Lady Barbara (Bab) Montagu read the *Memoirs and Letters of Mme de Maintenon* to Scott at Clifton, and Scott and Montagu carried on a vigorous correspondence about them.[32] By then they would have read Rowe's letters filled with references to her reading and recommendations to Hertford. Especially with plays Rowe kept up, and references are to the older ones by playwrights like Dryden but also to Thomson's *Sophronisba* (1730) and Fielding's rather shocking *Modern Husband* (1732).

Sairio has called attention to the women's geographical mobility, how they met in spa towns, "in the countryside," and in London, which "required the friendships to be maintained . . . in extensive correspondence." These intimacies were also nurtured by involvement and respect for individual endeavors. Rowe painted landscapes and received a screen from Hertford that she enjoyed immensely. She colored so many prints for it that she had enough to give to a friend. At one point she mentioned that she was "as proud of adjusting a tulip or a butterfly in a right position on the screen, as of writing heroics," and she bragged that all the "women and children about town, who have any thing of a nice and elegant taste," enjoy it.[33] Friends also sent her art, and she copied and painted some, including "The Pastoral Muse" and Watteau's "The Seasons." Hertford painted and had a turning lathe and made snuffboxes, toothpick cases, and butterprints, which she gave to her friends.[34] The Bluestockings are better known for their material projects, such as private collecting like the Duchess of Portland's "friendship box" of miniatures,[35] collections like Montagu's feathers, and crafts such as Mary Delany's cut-paper flower collages, and for others' groundbreaking, strikingly learned publications such as Montagu's *Essay on the Writings and Genius of Shakespeare, with some Remarks on the Misrepresentations of Msr Voltaire* (1769) and Carter's translation of Epictetus. Carter, for instance, was an important source and even collaborator as Montagu researched her *Essay on Shakespeare*; Talbot and Montagu corresponded about classical drama and ancient and modern history and philosophy, and Montagu encouraged Hester Chapone to publish *Letters on the Improvement of the Mind*, written for her fifteen-year-old niece (Chapone dedicated the third edition to Montagu).[36] Rowe's and Hertford's friendship was certainly maintained through correspondence as theirs was, but the unusual amount of time spent together around the time Rowe was writing *Letters* and the nature of their surviving writings suggest that Hertford collaborated and played an important part in encouraging Rowe to publish and continue *Letters*.

Bannet quotes Montagu's encouragement to Scott regarding the usefulness of novels: "A novel written so as to excite to good actions, is a very usefull and consequently a very respectable work. . . . If people will not read sermons let them receive doctrine in the form of a novel, it all answers the same purpose." Bannet sees Scott's *Millenium Hall* and *Sir George Ellison* as extensions and further explorations of Montagu's concerns about how best to use her power, wealth, lands, and influence.[37] Sylvia Myers refers to how the women "wove a fabric of connectedness which supported their *autonomous* interests" (emphasis mine).[38] Linguists often use four measures to assess strength of ties: longevity of relationship, geographical proximity, formal social relationships in terms of comparative rank, and type of relationship (as "intimates/equals/acquaintance").[39] Montagu, for example, spent her summers at her estate at Sandleford in Berkshire, spring and fall at Denton near Newcastle where she managed her collieries, winter at her London home, and also frequently visited Tunbridge Wells, Bath, and the stately homes of friends.[40] Given the frequent, lengthy separations of the women, the significance of letters is heightened. The women in the group were impressive intellects and elegant letter writers, and the letters are essential to understanding the Blues. Wilkes, the Gordon riots, the war with France, and other political debates as well as literature, philosophical questions, and travel are subjects of lively discussion.

That Hertford was an important conduit is crucial for understanding the Rowe legacy. Dependent on conversation and especially on letters, the women took care of each other emotionally and financially. When Hertford lost her son and later her husband, it was Rowe whom she summoned and who stayed with her. What Sairio found in her analysis of the 1760 correspondence of Bluestockings is true in the Rowe-Hertford circle. It was "primarily of friendship in emotional sense, but there were also elements of collaboration [as evident in Rowe's *Letters*] and patronage in their interactions."[41] About the time Rowe was writing some of her heroic epistles, Hertford wrote *An Epistle from Yarrico to Inkle* as a companion poem to her verse version of the *Spectator*'s story of Inkle and Yarico. Very much in the tradition of the Ovidian heroides, it is an early, important antislavery poem that gives startling details, such as that Inkle was able to raise his price for her because she was pregnant.[42]

Patronage became important not only because it encouraged women's intellectual work and publication but because it allowed women to remain in the group. Several women provided annual support to Elizabeth Carter and Sarah Fielding, and Fielding's *Lives of Cleopatra and Octavia* is dedicated in gratitude to Henrietta Louisa Fermor, Countess of Pomfret, a close friend and important correspondent of Hertford. The Duchess of Portland kept Elizabeth Elstob, the groundbreaking Old English scholar, in her home for eighteen years. Rowe did not need financial support, but she received patronage-type benefits. She was, for instance, taught languages in the Thynne family, and her translations added to the cultural capital of her work and her reputation as an accomplished woman. At a difficult time in her life, Hertford offered her an apartment in one of her homes. While the miniatures painted of Rowe signal deep, personal friendship, the engraving by George Vertue is an important form of patronage because it provided the kind of prestigious portrait that adorned the best literary efforts of men and women.

Catherine Talbot and others read Rowe's manuscripts when they visited Hertford, by then Duchess of Somerset. Talbot described Rowe from the circle's personal experience as "our favourite."[43] Carter called Hertford's collection "that most excellent green book which I so sincerely wish to have the world better for" and recommended it to friends who might have the opportunity to see it. Carter strongly urged Talbot to edit and publish Rowe's letters and other papers that were in "the possession of the Duchess of Somerset at whose country home Talbot made lengthy visits." Carter did not shy away from reminding Talbot to get to work on the project in "a few of your leisure hours."[44] On one extended visit Talbot wrote her "Fairy Tale."[45] Hertford wrote about Carter's translation of Algarotti to the Countess of Pomfret in 1739 and shortly afterward (24 December 1739) sent her Carter's *Ode to Melancholy*, which Pomfret called a "sublime and agreeable entertainment." In February 1742, Hertford was writing that Carter gave her *A Dialogue between Body and Mind*. Pomfret wrote that she was "sorry she takes a pedantic turn, for her way of thinking deserves to wear polite language."[46] The letters between these two women are like those of the Bluestockings, and in extended discussions of, for instance, Lady Mary Wortley Montagu's texts they are a critical reading group, guiding, sharing, and discussing the most notable publications of their day.

The Bluestockings' benevolence extended as the years passed to what Gary Kelly calls "the rescue and reclamation of women, especially lower-class women,"[47] which can be related to the plots of novels like *Millenium Hall*. Because they were wealthier, of higher rank, and worked in more visible settings, the commitments to education and to particular kinds of educational and uplifting philanthropy that they shared with Rowe are much more visible than hers. For instance, we know far more about the school of industry for poor women run by Sarah Scott and Lady Barbara

Montagu and Sarah Trimmer's development of Sunday schools than we do about Rowe's work with the Frome schools. As in Rowe's fictions and life, the goal was to empower women to be morally and intellectually autonomous and, whenever possible, economically self-sufficient.[48] Betty Schellenberg points out that in their work "conflict, which most commonly supplies the energy of narrative, is replaced by an impulse towards alignment, consensus, and mutual reinforcement, while the normativeness and commonality of human experience are emphasized more than its complexity and uniqueness."[49]

Betty Rizzo's fascinating meditation on saved letters is highly pertinent. By birth, Hertford certainly had the characteristics of savers: "They must . . . have interesting lives; space and time for writing, preserving, and organizing; and, I think, a strong sense of the significance of their own existence." "The letters saved . . . are from certain loved or respected correspondents." She goes on to point out that collecting is a means of "managing and editing the lives of both recipient and correspondent,"[50] and that is certainly true of the book with Rowe's letters. She, Rowe, and their society are preserved as models of friendship, sociability, and personal conduct. When augmented by the letters in *Miscellaneous Works*, readers have an amalgamated version of the friendship and lifestyle of these exemplary women, one that cast a very long shadow and acted as a kind of conduct book.

Rowe's *Letters* became a public variant of the private practice of ideal, polite correspondence, and the circulation of the early Bluestockings' letters was similar. Critics note that "works naming the Bluestockings . . . attest to a public awareness and an impact which are being furthered and celebrated, yet not initiated, by print."[51] Stuart Curran has collected women writers' encomiastic tributes to other women writers and points out that it was both reality and convention that women looked "to a predecessor or contemporary for example and support." Moreover, the eighteenth century benefitted from "the multiplication of female muses into an enveloping and empowering network of like-minded creative and creating women."[52] He finds that Rowe "played a crucial role in the second generation of the eighteenth century in transforming the image of woman writer from scandalous resident of the demimonde . . . to respectable nurturer of civilization—which is to say, a bluestocking." The key is "like-minded"—women whose writing resembled Rowe's in style and content but also continued to propagate elements of her lifestyle. In analyzing the tributes of Elizabeth Carter and Anna Aikin [Barbauld], Curran points out that Carter "accurately, even candidly, represents Rowe's position in this important cultural shift." He rightly finds "the bluestocking program" in their poems, and in another essay he argues that this generation developed "an independent and shared woman's poetic."[53]

At this point, I want to concentrate on three congruences between Rowe's and the Bluestockings' commitments and lifestyles. Each also offers contrasts to the masculine politeness movement. First, more than for men, direct experience with nature was central to the politeness movement. As we have seen, both exercise and finding bowers and "recesses," private room-like spaces, were important for their mental and physical health. Rowe, for instance, took almost daily quiet walks in "two or three flowery fields hedg'd round with hawthorn,"[54] including during the winter as she writes to Hertford on one occasion that she "sometimes have dar'd the inclemency of the sky by walking in the fields this frosty weather: The prospect exactly answer'd your comparison of a landscape cut in white paper" (*Misc. Works*, 2:142). Hertford frequently described her long walks of more than a mile, which she took in the early morning and the evening. "Between six and seven the beauty of the evenings, the sweetness of the air, the flowers, the verdure, the music of the birds, all contribute to invite us to the Park," she writes.[55] It was important that they developed a refined taste regarding nature, and Hertford's letters consistently depict it. She gives detailed descriptions of prospects and specific kinds of birds and blooming flowers that she has enjoyed on a day's walk. Critics refer to "aesthetic walking," walking "done to explore the hidden beauties of nature, to develop the picturesque gaze, and to stimulate the imagination and play." The sensuality of the experience is often mentioned. Mary Delany, for instance, wrote that the Duchess of Portland "invited me to take a tour in her chaise to smell her sweet hay in her farm-fields; all our senses were regaled."[56] Publicized as fostering connections with nature and the divine and often associated with Rousseau, it encouraged both aesthetic and spiritual sensibilities.[57] These private practices were publicized through such means as Thomson's Dedication to *Spring*, in which he refers to Hertford's "calm evening walks," and lines in *The Seasons*. Another dimension of the discriminating mind that produced the proper valuing of the material world, they went beyond appreciation to investing places with memories, attachments, and cultural values and to working out new ways to express humankind's relationship to nature.[58] The country homes and walks, spas, and coastal prospects were all invested with aiding the development of identity and lifestyle.

Perhaps as important as the Bluestocking gatherings to the women was walking. It was universally accepted that moderate exercise was good for women, and the influential *Medicina Gymnastica* by Francis Fuller listed benefits "to the circulation, to the muscles, and to the respiratory system." Hertford writes happily that she seems "to have got a new supply of strength and spirits, and am both able and willing to walk as far as when I first served the Queen. Twice round the Park seems much less to me now [that would have been nearly 4 miles]. . . . The weather at present is so mild that it would tempt anything that has limbs to use them; and I feel myself too happy in being freed from my complaints not to take advantage of it by travelling my little domains, where every object I see affords me an amusement in my own quiet way." Fuller also discussed a "sense of physical well-being, that psycho-physical glow" that many of the women noted in happy descriptions of walks.[59] Considerable stress was put on "moderate" in some publications, and only walking and riding were highly recommended. John Locke was typical, however, in writing that he wanted "in my wife a healthy constitution," a woman who could "endure upon occasion both wind and sun," and in recommending daily, long walks.[60] John Gregory's influential *A Father's Legacy to his Daughters* recommended "those exercises that oblige you to be much abroad in the open air, such as walking, and riding on horseback. This will give vigour to your constitutions, and a bloom to your complexions. . . . An attention to your health is a duty you owe to yourselves and to your friends."[61] As Betty Rizzo has demonstrated, the higher the class, the more restricted physical exercise and even the body.[62] Of course, recreational walking in gardens and on purpose-built paths on estates was popular by both sexes, but walking was central to the happiness of the women. To some extent the insistence upon almost daily, long, and even vigorous walks is a sign of their independence and protection of their lifestyles. It was one of the most enjoyable and significant parts of their lives. Walking seems to have had quite different meanings for men and women until the time of pedestrian tourism. Walking on footpaths was especially *de classé* for men. "It was supposed that no man of substance would ever walk, except with a gun over his shoulder," and to do otherwise led to suspicions of being the laboring poor, "beggars, fleeing serfs, unscrupulous pedlars, or thieves."[63] The recreational, social, and aesthetic walks described by women featured groves, occasional seats (benches and natural features such as banks and large rocks), lanes, and private places sheltered and created by hedgerows.

Rowe's and the Bluestocking women's letters refer to walking in a variety of ways. Over and over Carter remembers and describes scenes and experiences from walks, in this case with Bethia D'Aeth, who was the daughter of Sir Thomas D'Aeth of Knowlton, Kent, and then wife to Herbert Palmer. She moved from Deal to Wingham in 1761. Her home was "the termination of Carter's long country walks," and Carter writes, "Each fav'rite Brook and Tree, / Where gayly past the happy Hours, / Those Hours I past with thee." In another poem, she refers to their "lov'd Retreat of K[nowlto]n Grove" and describes it as "Groves that wave o'er Contemplation's Dream." In this poem, she makes a move similar to some of Elizabeth Rowe's.[64] She tells Bethia,

> While *K[nowlto]n*'s flow'ry Prospects fade away,
> And all my lov'd *Bethia* loses here,
> The blooming Walks of *Eden* shall repair.[65]

In several of her poems a specific shady walk or grove dissolves into Eden, the garden of Eternity. In a quite different mood, Carter responds to an incident on a walk with Vesey: "There was not the least danger of my losing you in my walk from Canterbury, or any other walk. I may lose my watch or my purse, but the last treasure I am ever likely to lose by any carelessness of my own is my friends."[66]

Alone or with a favorite companion, walks could take restricted time before breakfast or, when recreational or social, at least half of the morning or afternoon. Women's walking practices were shaped by advice such as Locke's:

> The more they exercise and the more they are in the air the better health they will have . . . : but yet 'tis fit their tender skins should be fenced against the busy sunbeams . . . : to avoid this and yet to give them exercise in the air, some little shady grove near the house would be convenient for them to play in . . . : and if all the year you make them rise as soon as it is light and walk a mile or two and play abroad before sun-rising, you will by that custom obtain more good effects than one; and it will make them not only fresh and healthy, but good housewives too.[67]

Walking in the late afternoon or early evening, as Rowe did, was equally acceptable, as domestic chores were done and the sun was no longer "hot and piercing." Critics of later literature have reinforced the theme of walks as a symptom of women's autonomy. For instance, Sally Palmer writes, "By taking a walk, choosing a direction and destination as well as a pace, a companion, and a time, a woman restless and dissatisfied with her constricted role could advance toward several enabling social goals," including "feminine solidarity."[68] In their letters and in the literature they and later women produced, a sense of balance and of connecting with a deeper, more profound, even transcending reality, with each other, and with themselves is a persistent theme. These accounts anticipate the way walking for Wordsworth became an emblem of "the wholeness of the person walking with the land he walks on" and an action that "makes us think better, allows us to transcend ourselves . . . [and] be more fully ourselves."[69]

Women often mentioned that their walks were more than individual indulgences. In 1738, Portland mentioned that she picked "Herbs to put into an Herbal" on her walks at Bulstrode,[70] and some literary historians believe walking for pleasure and exercise gave way to more purposeful endeavors, such as this, botanical study, and tourism, which might include "collecting" landscapes through sketching or describing. As Landry says, "Between the 1770s and the 1830s, walking often became what hunting and shooting had been, an absorption in the natural world with scientific requirements and outcomes, accompanied by a descriptive discourse that sought to advertise and justify the pleasures that would be found therein."[71] Ideological and aesthetic uses of landscape became more self-conscious and more polarized. In contrast, in Rowe's generation of women there is occasional justification for solitariness but not for walking, which needed none, and they celebrate the healthful benefits, physical, emotional, and devotional. In Rowe's fictions and the country-house visits and descriptions, the routine of walking becomes both idealized and normalized.

Rowe and other women were ahead of their time in finding walking to restore "the natural proportions of our perceptions, reconnecting us with both the physical world and the moral order inherent in it," attitudes associated with Romanticism.[72] These women reproduce striking contemporary contradictions. For example, Priestley's experiments with mice yielded important information, including another reason trees are useful, but Barbauld used them to write about an innate longing for liberty. Both Jonathan Bate and Sylvia Bowerbank raise the question of "what sort of efficacy did . . . the taste for nature's beauties have in contesting greed, convenience, consumption and other (ugly) trends of early capitalism?"[73] The estates that Rowe's characters establish are caring human and ecological systems where production is providing healthy work and sustenance remarkably free from profit priorities, and Montagu worked tirelessly to improve the lives of the miners and their families on her property.

Second, these women were ahead of their time in taking their own subjectivity for granted and being willing to display it. By subjectivity, I am relying on Foucault's conception that the person is tied to his/her own identity by conscience and self-knowledge, and, as he does in his late work, I have concentrated in my book on the ways human beings turn themselves into subjects, specifically recognizing their own interiority as constituting their identity.[74] I can do so easily because "liberation into self-hood" was a heritage and "felt fact" for Nonconformists like Rowe. As Keeble demonstrates, to "secure assurance of a title to the 'paradise within' was . . . a literary endeavour"; people were the authors of their own lives, their historians and interpreters.[75] As Gary Kelly asserts, by this time subjectivity was seen as "true personal merit" separate from rank and was equated with moral and intellectual discipline represented by virtue and reason. Like Foucault, he finds it easiest to identify in resistances to the social and public.[76] Through David Porter's work, Eger argues that the Bluestockings' tastes and collections could be read as deliberate expressions of their subjectivity and suggests that Montagu's choice of chinoiserie over the contemporary preference for the classical style was a resistance to the masculine and is representative of her subjectivity.[77] They also reinforced the individuality of friendships, as her early mentor Lady Margaret had included chinoiserie in her Paradise Garden.[78] Deborah Heller posits that "the Sylph—as constructed by Montagu, Carter and Vesey herself—was based on, and expressed, a notion of the self that viewed it as an indeterminate, undefinable and, hence, unbounded origin of action." She goes on to use "the notion of autonomous subjectivity . . . as a way of speaking of the 'active' component of the modern subject, one that could resist the passive, discursively constituted subject." Like Foucault, she sees an "intensification of the notion of subjective interiority" in the eighteenth century and, like myself, finds it expressed in a variety of ways in Bluestocking culture and, I would add, in Rowe's life.[79]

The lives of Margaret Cavendish, Aphra Behn, Delarivière Manley, and other earlier women showed the effectiveness of singularity in protecting freedom but also the resulting marginalizing of their writing, which handicapped their influence. In spite of its dangers, one way Rowe and the early Bluestockings established and maintained their freedom was through a different kind of singularity. In contrast to the earlier women, their active lives, country retreats, and piety appeared exemplary and desirable. Rowe, the early Bluestockings, and Barbauld made the reality of their autonomy and interiority visible. In the face of very strong discursive construction of women's subjectivity, they demonstrated resistance and the ability to construct themselves. Like Rowe, they simply accepted their "genius," whatever this interior core was that was the origin of action and the crafting of their lifestyles.[80] Carter in her translation of Epictetus writes that they are never alone for "your Genius is within."[81] Genius here, of course, is like *genius loci*, the guardian deity of a locality or the special character of a place. For women like Carter, the inner life was one of rational thought and creative activities such as translating and writing fiction or poetry. This experienced space was also an elsewhere that affirmed the conceptual self and the fountain of feminist writing that Nancy K. Miller identified with an insistence on singularity and the imagining of "other styles of identity."[82]

Expressions of subjectivity found in devotional literature and in poetry are both highly developed in Rowe's work, and, as her fiction illustrates, moral and specifically religious experiences and reactions allowed expression of the range of strong human emotions extrapolated upon in sentimental literature.[83] In an important essay, George Starr explains that "sentimentalism seems clearly if indirectly indebted to the English religious tradition in another of its functions: namely, as a technique for reviving the role of emotion in human conduct" and an adjustment to a time when religious energies "could be a liability rather than an asset."[84] By omitting Rowe and the line of novels most indebted to her work from the history of the novel, a hiatus between this religious tradition and Laurence Sterne, Starr's chief example, appears puzzling. An important common denominator that Starr brings out is the importance of the "earlier religious habits of self-scrutiny," one that leads Rowe's characters and the Blues toward self-knowledge and subjecthood and characters like Yorick into "absorption in his own emotional life" (185). Another contrast is between the changes in characters in Rowe's fictions and reforms of characters such as Lucius's father in *Felicia to Charlotte* versus the change that Starr describes in sentimental fiction as "reminiscent of the Protestant (and ultimately Pauline) pattern of dramatic conversion," a "sudden, total transformation that comes about not through reflection, resolution, and deliberate action but rather through something like an infusion of grace" (189–90). Rather than sudden, the women's religious identity was gradually developing, rational, and reflected upon. One of the most important achievements of Rowe and the women was to portray their own and their characters' subjectivity as the foundation of their acceptance, autonomy, and authority in the world and also as the means to their hopes for eternal life.

Barbauld's tribute to Rowe both acknowledges Rowe's symbolism and recognizes the exercise of a quality women needed to protect: "Smooth like her verse her passions learn'd to move." Eighteenth-century people knew Rowe had passions—religious, of course, which were sometimes deemed bordering on Enthusiasm, and political ones that led to ejaculations such as "*William!* A Name my Lines grow proud to bear!"[85] She was part of a small group of women who talked about desire and sexuality openly.[86] As the revisions and exclusions in her collections show, as, for instance, patriotic or strong partisan fervor faded, some expressions such as these from *William passing the Boyne* became more problematic: "The Inspiration comes, my Bosom glows, / I strive with strong Enthusiastic Throws. / Oh! I am all in Rapture . . ." "ease the Pangs" (lines 571–79). At some level they, like twentieth- and twenty-first-century critics, also recognized her sexual passions—one of the qualities that probably led Pope to publish *On the Death of Mr. Thomas Rowe* with his *Abelard to Eloisa*.

In contrast to later women writers, the sheer physicality of Rowe's work is striking; her heart pounds, her nerves surge and tremble, she holds her breath or breathes rapidly. She can express exhilaration, outrage, joy, celebration of vengeance, and the recollection of intense sexual enjoyment. Occasionally such emotions are expressed in fiction by later women writers, but, as in Lennox's *Harriot Stuart*, when the heroine does so, the consequences are unpleasant. Guilt, embarrassment, and remorse invariably arise, and occasionally men are incited to cross the line of propriety, including threatening rape. Interestingly, Harriot expresses these feelings in poetry more often than prose.

Barbauld, a masterful poet, certainly understood the effort it took for "Smooth like her verse," and she was a passionate woman. William McCarthy tellingly juxtaposes Frances Burney describing "an almost set smile, which had an air of determined complacence . . . which never risked being off guard" with evidence of "her natural impatience."[87] He describes a youthful incident when she explicitly resisted her father's injunctions against emotion and especially intense emotion. In terms that strongly recall Rowe's poetry and even the title of her *Devout Exercises of the Heart* and some descriptions of nature, she wrote, "The devout heart . . . bursts into loud and vocal expressions of praise and adoration. . . . The mind is forcibly carried out of itself; and, embracing the whole circle of animated existence, calls on all above, around, below, to help to bear the burden of its gratitude." Indeed, his biography foregrounds her passionate yet reasoned commitment to causes, and he points out that her indignation over persecution of Dissenters led to reviewers chastising her "Puritanic rage."[88] Thus, Rowe represented the tensions in the technology of self-mastery of disciplining the passions.

In fact, many of the women who most admired and referred to Rowe were passionate—given to anger and strong commitments. Norma Clarke, a superb critic of Rowe, argues that "it was above all the strength of passion, and the autonomy conferred by passion" that Carter "drew from her enthusiasm" for Rowe.[89] Clarke portrays Carter as having "designs" on the professional place Rowe held ("Soft Passions," 356), and I agree that women's sense of professionalism and desire for it have been drastically underestimated. Unlike Rowe, however, women writers after her are far less able to integrate passion into their writings and lifestyles. Carter is typical in celebrating the suppressing of passion. Although she was "extremely charmed with" *Friendship in Death*, Hester Chapone objected to most of Rowe's writing on this ground, and her own writing is carefully moderated.[90]

Harriet Guest points out that "there is an important sense, in the decades I am most concerned with, that religion is also what makes a kind of publicity available to and even an obligation for women."[91] She is speaking of Carter and the 1750s and after, but it was Rowe who set the example. For a large percentage of the people of Rowe's time, religion was a major component of personality and of their apprehension of reality. Where we may think scientifically or probabilistically, they reasoned and felt from religious understanding. Silvia's extended musing on "Arcadian" versus health-related death is but one example in *Letters*. Therefore, Rowe's association of some of her stories with the intention to "impress the Notion of the Soul's Immortality" was in the mainstream of other genres, and it was influential that she adapted the theme and movement into fiction.

Thus, third, there was the centrality of "rational" religion. After all, the child in Letter 3 of *Friendship in Death* had told his mother, "As soon as my Spirit was releas'd from its uneasy Confinement, I found myself an active and reasonable Being" (9). By that time reason was no longer a body of knowledge but identified with experience as a kind of energy, "comprehensible only in its agency and effects."[92] Again, this is a stream of thinking that unites a line of women writers. Lady Mary Chudleigh, for instance, recommended and illustrated rational Christian devotion and, like Rowe, suggests that God can only be appreciated by rational thought. She describes the same harmony between the beauty of the earth and of God. As Rebecca Mills says, the wonders of God's creation "can only be fully appreciated by those ruled by Reason." She quotes generously from Chudleigh's poetry, including *The Offering* and *The Resolve*.[93] Chudleigh advised, "The way to be truly easie, to be always serene, [is] to have our Passions under a due Government."[94] Her beautifully structured poem *The Resolve* reads,

> If Reason rules within, and keeps the throne,
>   While the inferior faculties obey,
> And all her laws without reluctance own,
>   Accounting none more fit, more just than they;
> . . . .
> Then am I happy in my humble state,
>   Although not crowned with glory nor with bays:
> A mind, that triumphs over vice and fate.[95]

Typically, she characterizes a union of reason and religion as the foundation and bulwark for intellectual and spiritual freedom. Privileged in all discourses and a tension-inducing barrier and threshold for women, it was a powerful sorting term, one that as the Methodist movement gained prominence became more powerful. The kind of reasoning together that distinguished the best and most productive dialogues existed in conversations, correspondence, and shared devotional compositions among the women.

Texts such as Carter's *Answers to Objections Concerning the Christian Religion* (originally letters rather than a set of personal essays) exemplify the inseparability of reason and religion for them, the significance of religion, and also their care for each other.[96] Chudleigh's earlier devotional essays, Rowe's *Devout Exercises*, Talbot's *Reflections on the Seven Days of the Week*, and the dialogues from the dead written by Montagu, Barbauld, and Piozzi are only a few examples, and many more are found in the letters as the women relate experiences with nature, reading, and friends to their religious life. The practice of integrating reading, praying, and meditating in their daily lives also united them. Although Rowe was a dedicated Nonconformist and the Bluestockings staunchly Church of England, they avoided partisan and doctrinal disputes.[97] What was said of Rowe could have been said of most of them: "Her love of piety was not confined to those of her own party in religion; and it ought to be related as an exemplary instance of Christian moderation that she continued all the latter part of her life in constant communion with some who differed from her in articles which she thought of great importance" (*Misc. Works*, 1:xcvi). In their time as in ours, religion was often a subject that aroused more resistance than encouragement. As Gary Kelly argues, "These values and practices of the Bluestockings were validated for them by their particular religious orientation. . . . Religion had a historic role in female intellectual culture and social practice, seen in the devotional and other-worldly orientation of the female conduct-book tradition and in the injunction to 'good works,' or practical philanthropy, as a manifestation of true faith and as a licence to social and economic activism and reform by women otherwise barred from the public political sphere."

Political and theological strife, the rise of Evangelicalism, and even the vast quantity of published sermons and moral essays made Rowe's matter-of-fact treatment of piety an example that broke barriers. Just how needed her example was is evident in the fact that the theme of embattled Protestantism did not fade. Charlotte Lennox's *Harriot Stuart* (1750), for instance, features threats to and tests of Dumont's and Harriot's faiths. At one point Harriot is confined in a French convent, and a high point in the book is when she receives the news that Dumont has become a Protestant ("how shall I describe the extacy which in a moment took possession of my whole soul").[98] Gaining momentum from Rowe's time forward was the general opinion that "it was tasteless . . . to *insist* on its differences from the 'liberal' Anglican culture of politeness" and also Nonconformists' fears that they might be identified with the "disputatious spirit" of the seventeenth-century Presbyterians."[99] Kelly goes on to note that this style was adopted by writers such as the Nonconformist Barbauld and the Evangelical Sarah Trimmer.[100] In fact, this register remained common in conduct books, which always functioned as books of practical divinity, as Defoe's illustrate. Scott referred to "rather practical than speculative divinity," and the phrase describes their interest.[101] Although they read some controversial and doctrinal religious literature, their appreciation was in applications.

Rowe's occasional otherworldliness and even mysticism in her poetry and devotional writing gave way in her fiction to consistent expressions of the kind of secular moral humanism equated with reason and social virtue. In very different ways, both the *Spectator* and *Letters* entered the market and established themselves "as a kind of fashion," thereby appropriating the forces of fashion for didactic purposes.[102] Both maintained their influence; Montagu, for instance, copied the entire *Spectator* before she was nine years old.[103] The use of the epistolary form for women's didactic fiction increased, and the best and still-readable examples, such as Frances Burney's *Evelina*, Mary Hays's *Emma Courtney* (with memoir and philosophy), and Frances Sheridan's *Sidney Bidulph* (a diary-letter), belong in the line that followed *Felicia to Charlotte, Familiar Letters between the Principal Characters in David Simple*, and *Millenium Hall*. Mary Hays's *Letters and Essays, Moral and Miscellaneous* (1793) was but one collection following her form. Soon after the publication of Rowe's fiction, "moral and entertaining" became a part of book titles, as it was in *Conversations Moral and Entertaining, between an English Gentleman and a Knight of Malta* (1740) and *Leonora: or, characters drawn from real life . . . with reflections moral and entertaining* (1745). Books like Rowe's continued to be published, although they now seem peculiar and not within the category of "novel," as does Elizabeth Harrison's *Miscellanies on Moral and Religious Subjects, in Prose and Verse* (1756). In its day, it was popular and compared favorably to Rowe's texts with their "brightness of imagery."[104]

Alessa Johns cautions readers against the tendency to choose civic humanism or conduct-book domesticity thereby giving "too little weight to the social meanings of religion and charity."[105] Kathryn King raises the possibility that Rowe's "decision in the last decade of her life to re-enter the commercial world of print, even at some risk to her carefully groomed status as a genteel amateur, is a measure of her determination to advance her religious views."[106] This is speculation, but Rowe's letters in *Miscellaneous Works* do show continued concern for the souls of others. Toward the end of his life, Defoe had written that his writing was "a Testimony of my good Will to my Fellow Creatures,"[107] and his and Rowe's sense of social duty and rational, non-sectarian religion authorized many of the women's publications, as Montagu's encouragement of Scott regarding novel writing shows. Although Chapone needed money and also expressed a desire to escape feelings of helplessness and insignificance, she saw publishing and even selling the copyright to her *Letters on the Improvement of the Mind* as largely a moral and religious act. Harriet Guest illustrates the extent to which Carter saw publishing her translation of Epictetus as "a socially useful act" and how her introduction and commentary drew out its benefits.[108]

Joanna Lipking identifies Rowe with Steele's paragon, Emilia, a woman with "rational piety, modest hope, and cheerful resignation."[109] The importance of Rowe's public practice of reason-based faith is, perhaps, highlighted by the fact that it seems an oxymoron to many people today. Critics, however, are beginning to identify it in unexpected places. Barbara Taylor opens her introduction of a section of *Women, Gender, and Enlightenment* with a description of Wollstonecraft's "piety," a piety strongly informed by reason in the terms in which Rowe wrote.[110] The transformation of religious belief that Taylor describes fits the easy assumption of the importance and rationality of religion found in the first generation of Bluestockings. Some of their friendships have been described as having "an emotional relationship of rare intensity, a sort of rational or platonic love . . . grounded in their shared Christian principles."[111] Elizabeth Eger argues that Wollstonecraft "rarely exercised a strict distinction between the categories of platonic and sexual love, and expressions of both can be found in her passionate rhetorical commitment to reason."[112] In a leap that Eger does not take, it should be asked "Where but in Rowe's work did women find a similar conflation of kinds of love, including for God, with *reason* as a constituent component and a taking for granted that passionate love of all kinds is a rational virtue?" In fact, Sharon Achinstein argues correctly, I believe, that Rowe's religious ardor "participated in the restructuring of female sexuality through religious license." She credits her with finding a way to write "emancipatory sexual desire in socially subversive ways."[113] Many of her writings, including her poems about her husband and the Canticles, celebrate heterosexual pleasure and confer a divine blessing on it. Many of her contemporaries who were familiar with Thomas Rowe's poems in *Miscellaneous Works* would have thought, along with Claudia Kairoff, that some of her poems, including Canticle 2.8.9, seemed "perilously close to an evocation of her lost husband."[114]

Over time, women learned to make new arguments to illustrate rational piety and, simultaneously, admit passion. Just as Rowe and the early Bluestockings learned to establish and maintain their freedom partly through their singularity, Barbauld crafted a devastatingly effective argument on this point. Defending her own and Rowe's religious language, she asserted that "Love borrows the language of Devotion" and insists that they were not inappropriately transposing the language of passionate, sexual love onto expressions of religion.[115] Among women, the sentiment survives. Wallace cites a 1988 article in *Ms.* to bolster her argument that walking for women can be "a possible form of psychotherapy because it can 'help give you a better perception of reality, shore up your courage, and awaken your senses.'" Kate Braestrup writes in "Until We Meet Again" in *Goodhousekeeping Magazine*, "Prayers are not . . . formulas; they are love poems."[116] Rowe and Barbauld were in a strong Nonconformist tradition that included Isaac Watts, Philip Doddridge, and Joseph Priestley and insisted upon "a view of religion not simply as a matter of reason, but as 'an elevated passion, or affection.'"[117] In the 1770s, Carter wrote increasingly freely about "a religious sublime that discloses its 'real delight.'"[118] Such expressions had become common in women's writing, as a poem in Charlotte Lennox's *Life of Harriot Stuart* illustrates:

> 'Tis now deep contemplation's hour;
> The soul on Reason's wings may rise,
> All nature's boundless vast explore,
> And, soaring, pierce beyond the skies.[119]

The movement from the familiar outdoor, evening setting to reason and then to the sublime is a dignified expression of the combination of passion and reason. Rowe was permitted both reason and passion because she, like Carter, managed to maintain an image of humility about her very public reputation for piety, and they modeled both discourse and conduct for later women like Lennox.

Because they were so well known, they modeled a self-conscious drive toward moral and intellectual autonomy. In London, Carter always rented a place for herself, and she bought her home in Deal with money from the subscriptions to *Epictetus*; she charged her father rent for the rooms he occupied.[120] Partly because so many of them were widowed (Rowe, Montagu, Chapone) or single (Carter, Talbot), they could display duty to self above duty to others. In a famous letter, Montagu remarked that she could not see why women needed husbands "unless she were to defend her Lands & Tenements by sword or gun." Their religion validated a dedication to saving body and soul. What is especially interesting is that several of the women, notably Rowe, Carter, and Scott, thought of themselves as Norma Clarke characterizes Rowe and as Guest describes Carter as inhabiting "a thoroughly private space, in her own eyes as well as in her reputation"[121] even though they were among the best-known women in England. As Guest continues, Carter "did not live in a hole in the ground." By appearing to take their private status for granted, they actually exercised considerable freedom, but, as Guest says, the private sphere she "inhabited" was a "private sphere within which her secure possession of the freehold estate of her religion gave her social and national significance."[122] This statement is equally descriptive of Rowe, and it was true throughout the century. Guest's phrase, "freehold estate of religion," is brilliantly insightful and not just because conscience and saving the soul authorized autonomy. Among the many phrases uniting the women's vision of the ideal lifestyle might be "freehold estate," the exclusive right to possess and use a piece of land or other asset for an indefinite period. Montagu, for instance, wrote that Carter had purchased herself "an estate on Parnassus which yr Heirs cannot sell or mortgage."[123] These are, of course, the phrases used in Nonconformist claims to Heaven and the effort to "secure assurance of a title to the 'paradise within.'"

Fig. 22. Oast or "vinegar bottle" houses such as Elizabeth Carter owned survive in parts of southeast England. Lav and Steve's Travel Blog, www.travelblog.org/Europe/United-Kingdom/England/Kent/blog-254457.html.

In the long term, the Blues' promotion and support of women and the lasting image of their intense friendships with each other, their wide learning, and interest in public affairs created the possibilities of such lifestyles and careers. Their sense of themselves in terms of a collective gender identity and as representatives of women devoted to the life of the mind cast a long, enabling shadow, one that women of the generation after the first group of Blues recognized, as Amelia Opie said, as allowing an intelligent woman to be herself. Like Rowe, they created a satisfying way of life for themselves and "brought into public notice the idea that respectable women could study, write, and publish."[124] In fact, the terms used by modern feminists bring Rowe to mind and make the case for her influence. Sylvia Myers speculates that Carter's admiration for and reflection on Rowe helped lead her to choose to "retreat to Deal" in the belief that she could "function better as a virtuous woman poet" there than in London. Both Montagu and Vesey visited her there and saw a bit of magic in her small house built in the shape and style of the oast houses common in southeast England (fig. 22). They all referred to it as her vinegar bottle. Oast houses like hers had at least one kiln for drying hops, and the idiomatic "vinegar bottle" is an allusion to the shape of the thick stone bottles with yellow necks in which vinegar was sold but perhaps also to the classic British fairy tale believed to have originated in the west country. In the tale, a fairy grants the woman who lived in the vinegar bottle increasingly beautiful and larger homes, but they never satisfy. At the end, she is back in the vinegar bottle, but with a beautiful globe so that she could rule over the world.[125] Revisions to her *On the Death of Mrs. Rowe* and her second published poem (*Ode to Melancholy*) suggest Carter's deep engagement with the poet and her poetry,[126] one that, at various times in their lives, the first Bluestockings shared.

Throughout her life, Rowe read and actively engaged the literature she inherited and continued to read new publications voraciously. Imitating, adapting, and moving beyond fictional kinds such as amatory, patchwork, apparition, epistolary, and French fairy tales, drawing upon her experiences as an experimental, poetic artist, and domesticating discourse styles, she created new kinds of fictions with new focii and revisionary models. As an early student of the politeness movement and the poetry inspired by it, she created a modern, novelistic discourse and characters and plots suffused in it. This style was sturdy and distinctive enough to hold texts, even epistolary ones, together. From her own beliefs and experiences, she modeled in life and fiction characters whose chief responsibility was to themselves and who took for granted that they had a self and a soul. Sometimes this assumption appears in unusual statements in the novels. For example, Felicia writes to Charlotte, "You must not be offended if I tell you, I write as much to amuse myself as to please you" (1:2), which is similar to Rowe's fictional Letter 1 to Cleora (Hertford): "Without any apology, I am going to talk to myself" (*Letters*, 1:91).

Because we have never included Rowe in the history of the English novel, we have not recognized the extent to which she revolutionized prose fiction, especially amatory romances and the female bildungsroman. We did not hear the novelists who followed her and coined names for the new genres she pioneered. Collyer's "pastoral adventure" and Fielding's "moral romance" (for *David Simple*) were insightful then and would be useful today. Sabine Augustin has noted the limitations of novels that "explored [women's] role and status largely through courtship novels in the tradition of Richardson and Fielding,"[127] and Rowe was not, of course, in either tradition because she was earlier, nor did she limit her studies of women to courtship and the marriage plot. Her major focus was on achieving a harmonious life without yielding to social pressures, a theme other writers first struggled with and then made central subjects of the novel. How revolutionary she was in creating women characters who, like d'Aulnoy's women, reflected on their emotions, hopes, and fears at every stage of the plot has gone unrecognized.

Filling a gap between the fiction of the 1720s and the Richardson era, she set a course that hundreds of novels followed and others were inflected by. Permutations that imitated, critiqued, and tested followed, and the plot of the woman in difficult situations attempting to attain peace of mind and a steadfast philosophy of conduct became, perhaps, the most common kind of English fiction. The way she conducted her life, the values from reading to walking to conversing that she described and lived, and the independence that was early recognized as the mark of a writer were passed along through the Bluestockings and other women and are not lost today. She demonstrated in life and fiction an "ability to be different . . . to transcend the bounds of convention."[128] The fact that the quoted phrases are Heller's description of the Bluestockings is arresting. In a time when women were often depicted as competitive, jealous, and even vicious toward other women, she presented herself and Hertford and many women characters in harmonious friendships that were a "feast of reason and the flow of soul."[129]

By 1740, the flowering of a parallel politeness movement for women is clear, and Rowe was an important developer and disseminator of it. Moreover, her work accelerated the establishment of the novel as elite reading and actualizes the way "genre is both a set of conventions and mode of social understanding."[130] Rather than depending on gatherings, this alternative practice was defined by participation in domestic life and local friendships, reading, and private activities such as collecting, walking, reflections in favorite places, and writing long letters that open the heart and mind. Personal activities, literary criticism, descriptions of natural scenes, commentary on philosophical publications and controversies, and political commentary filled pages and pages of their letters and texts. Just as Shaftesbury's and Addison's politeness was defined by behaviors, so was the women's. The praise for the pleasing social skills of women like Rowe and Hertford silently carries evidence that they were often quiet, never aggressive participants in conversations although they could express intelligent, even strong opinions and engage with different opinions. Among themselves in life and in fiction, and this is critically important, women created friendships that moved beyond the model of platonic souls inherited from Katharine Philips; they became a modern pattern of enjoyment and of alliances among women that still serves women well. Reinforcing their right to an intellectual life and even to being a deliberative body, to hobbies and occupations, and, because of their long influence over the next generation of women writers who were more political and outspoken, as Barbauld, Seward, and More were, they qualify as a subaltern counterpublic.

In many ways, the politeness movement was a patriarchal act of determining women's place and function. Women were often described as having an especially valuable civilizing influence, and gatherings in country houses and London drawing rooms (as opposed to in coffeehouses and clubs) became work and measures of their organizational and social abilities.[131] However, just as with any technology of social production, the subordinate group needed to find ways to resist and adapt. As Nancy Fraser demonstrates, subordinated groups have the power to constitute quite influential alternate publics. As noted, she argues that they "invent and circulate counterdiscourses to formulate oppositional interpretations of their identities, interests and needs."[132] This is what Rowe pioneered. Transmitting these interpretations through quite public lifestyles represented as retired and occasionally through novels that gave extended portrayals of how women might become influential counterpublics, they most frequently used what might be called the apparatuses that accompanied their nonfictional publications. Introductions were especially important, as Carter's to *Epictetus* illustrates. Fraser points out that subaltern counterpublics "function as spaces of withdrawal and regroupment," and Rowe's fictions illustrate that repeatedly and are replicated in the fictions in the lines of novels she influenced. The protection of their private spaces outside of London by Carter and Scott clearly shows their awareness of the need for withdrawal and regroupment.

Fraser goes on to point out that these spaces "function as bases and training grounds for agitational activities directed toward wider publics."[133] While the women would certainly recoil from "agitational," they were bases and training grounds for activities and publications that stretch into our own time. Their charitable activities and often invisible support for other women—both publications and lifestyles—were revolutionary and contributed to the establishment of women's importance in education and social work. Often overlooked is their powerful recognition and practice that success as "a self-governed subject was determined by her reckoning and control of time."[134] Rowe practiced it, and the Bluestockings wrote endlessly about it and shared strategies for it. Women's midcentury poetry and beyond values the possession of time above almost everything else. The right to selfhood, the valuing of spaces in which personal reflection and autonomy flourish, and women's active patronage and encouragement of other women were subversive activities and are not always appreciated today. Looking at the women who immediately followed Rowe and comparing them to the next generation through the lens of Fraser's theory reveals how, if the first were a "weak" public, the second generation through their work with education, abolition, and other very public causes qualifies as a "strong public." In other words, their deliberative practices went beyond opinion formation to decision-making and serious influence on the "masculine" authentic public sphere.[135]

Richard Watts points out that politeness especially when connected to conversation, letters, and other kinds of language use "was manipulated in a socially selective way" to become "a hegemonic discourse in which the ability to control a specific language variety was interpreted as providing access to high social status from which power could be exercised."[136] He repeatedly points out the relationship between those desiring upward mobility and the politeness movement, and, of course, women wanted upward mobility, although of a different kind. Both their initial success in gaining respect and access to public discussions and to the means to publication and the ridicule and the resistance that followed, an inevitable response to those who manage some upward mobility, are well-known stories. The politeness movement brought classes, especially the gentry and professional ones, into a new contact zone, and the Bluestockings unsettled the rising public-private divide. Rowe's and their parallel politeness practices created what Gary Kelly calls a "dialectic" between the spheres.[137] Rowe's writings and lifestyle became better known after her death, and the rank, prestige, religion, London base, and a wide variety of prestigious publications made the Bluestockings even more prominent. This statement is particularly interesting because women could hope to exercise only very limited kinds and amounts of power. Kelly, however, points out that the ways the Bluestockings were described in addition to "circle" underscore their public influence: "Club," "which alluded to the gentlemen's clubs that were increasingly important in the formation of civil society"; "Lodge," "referring to the 'lodges' of exclusively male secret societies," which promoted mutual interests and causes; and "Colledge," "referring to institutes of higher education . . . and in recognition of the circle's interest in intellectual life and the promotion of scholarship, literature, and culture." He concludes that "the Bluestocking programme may seem piecemeal, but it has an underlying coherence and rationale, which can be summarised."[138]

Watts refers to the "gentrification of politeness," but there was a feminization of politeness that was, first, a movement toward the identification of politeness with character and an insistence on the inseparability of the innate and cultivated. There was much at stake here because the union strengthened the argument for women's education, but it also covertly contributed to the argument that women were not as limited by "nature" as they were sometimes depicted. Rather than emotional, mental, and physical weaklings, they were stronger in every way. Commitments to virtue, to exercise, and to cultivating their minds and talents were stronger than in the masculine movement and also more aimed at individual improvement. Even more distinctive was a commitment to friendship, one often described and carefully nurtured. Taking the legacy of the English friendship poem begun by Katherine Philips, they refined a concept of friendship that conformed to the ideals of the politeness movement and developed a model that satisfied their needs and aspirations within gender conceptions and expectations. Fiction by women following Rowe dramatized the need for this alternate politeness culture. Fielding's *Familiar*

Letters between the Principal Characters in David Simple, for instance, begins with the princess insisting to the old woman "that their Conversation and Behaviour that Evening should be upon an equality and without reserve" (2:227). The woman explains her desires for society in the terms of the Bluestockings—she hopes for equality and respect in conversation with men, and she deplores "that Part of the human Species who are eternally busy, though they have nothing to do; and eternally talking, though they have nothing to say" (2:260). Like the Bluestockings, her sincere friend is a single woman, and the program they followed is recommended; for instance, exercise is important as the woman's mother rode her horse two or three hours a day to regain her health.

Today the reputation of the Bluestockings is rising while Rowe and her writing remain confined to a single file folder labeled "Pious Writer" or even "Pious Writer with a Macabre Fascination with Death." Reputations and commonplaces are hard to change, and, as we have seen, after her death she was increasingly treated more as a saint and a religious and educational writer than a dedicated, creative, experimental author. *Devout Exercises* and the predominance of religious poetry in *Miscellaneous Works* began to distract many eighteenth-century people from her fiction, and her religious poetry certainly does today. Even most specialists have a shaky grasp of the progress of Rowe's writing career from the daring, often secular poet of her youth to the flowering as fiction writer in the final decade of her life. That fiction writer produced new poems, often in the most respected forms of poetry. That there were eleven editions of the collected *Letters* in the 1770s, four in the 1790s, and seven in the first decade of the nineteenth century is powerful evidence of their sustained popularity and influence. In 1796, *Miscellaneous Works* was expanded to *The Works of Mrs. Elizabeth Rowe*. But, in a sign of the writer she was to become, in the 1790s, while Rivington published only one edition of *Devout Exercises*, it was published in Boston, Philadelphia, New Haven, New York, Hartford, and Dotham, Massachusetts.

Laetitia Barbauld wrote in her *Life of Richardson* that his "fictitious adventures" "have been moulded upon the manners of the age, and, in return, have influenced not a little the manners of the next generation, by the principles they have insinuated, and the sensibilities they have exercised" (vii–viii). This statement is true about Rowe's writing, too. Stuart Curran challenged literary historians: "What, then, would it take to conceive a new model of literary history that does not merely assimilate women to a paradigm drawn up and enacted by men? . . . I would suggest the value of beginning with unfamiliar names that obviate conditioned, even newly conditioned, reflexes; the value of asking in fundamental ways how a woman writing at any historical point . . . would distinguish herself from a contemporary man; the value of starting from the point of view of normative female experience and expectations; the value of looking to the field of genres associated with female writing."[139] Rowe has not been assimilated, and the "empty 30s," the decade when almost no original fiction was published, contribute to our passing over her. The ways in which she can be "distinguished" from her contemporaries and those immediately before her, male and female, have played out in my book. I hope it will encourage others to integrate her accurately and fairly into literary history.

NOTES

Introduction • Locating Elizabeth Singer Rowe

1. Achinstein, "Romance of the Spirit," 423.
2. Clarke, "Soft Passions and Darling Themes," 354.
3. Figures from the ESTC.
4. Although dated 1733, the first collected edition includes the third edition of *Friendship in Death* and the second edition of part 1 of *Letters Moral and Entertaining*, both dated 1733, and the second editions of parts 2 and 3, dated 1734. Each section begins numbering anew except part 3 and includes the original title pages. The 1736 fourth edition is numbered sequentially (481 pages) without title pages. By the 1780s, the four volumes were available in tidy, compact editions averaging 156 pages. Although I did recounts, on editions of *Robinson Crusoe*, see Novak and Fisher, "Publishing History and Modern Editions," 3–4; and Hutchins, *Robinson Crusoe and Its Printing*.
5. Rowe as a personality and a writer has attracted significant, discriminating attention in recent years. Sarah Prescott's work is especially notable. See her "Elizabeth Singer Rowe (1674–1737): Politics, Passion, and Piety," 71–78; and *Women, Authorship and Literary Culture*, esp. chaps. 5 and 6. See also Hansen, "Pious Mrs. Rowe," 34–51; Clarke, "Soft Passions and Darling Themes," 353–71; Messenger, *Pastoral Tradition and the Female Talent*, chap. 7; and my *Eighteenth-Century Women Poets*, 113–74 et passim.
6. Prescott, "Elizabeth Singer Rowe: Gender, Dissent, and Whig Poetics," 195. She argues that Rowe and Isaac Watts are examples of Nonconformist intervention in the construction of Whig ideology.
7. Alison Conway has brought the term "backward looking forms" to prominence and makes a persuasive case for our turning our attention to such forms in *Protestant Whore*, 11–12. She does not discuss some of the kinds of literature that I do, nor does she mention Rowe. See L. Marschalk and P. Backscheider, "Empty Decade: Fiction in the 1730s," unpublished manuscript.
8. Moretti, *Graphs, Maps, Trees*, fig. 1, p. 6. In a more detailed graph, fig. 2, he shows another dip in the late 1770s, which can be identified as 1776–1784, Raven and Forster, *English Novel 1770–1829*, 1:46, table 6.
9. Davys, *Works of Mrs. Davys*, 1:iii.
10. Rowe's will is printed in Stevens-Cox, *Elizabeth Rowe (1674–1737)*, 248–49.
11. *General Evening Post* no. 534 (26 February 1737), 3; identical or similar announcements of her death appeared in many papers, including *Universal Spectator and Weekly Journal*, no. 439 (5 March 1737), 3; *Common Sense or the Englishman's Journal*, no. 5 (5 March 1737), 3;

Weekly Miscellany 218 (4 March 1737), 5; and *London Evening Post*, no. 1449 (26 February 1737), 1. I am grateful to Elizabeth Kent for collecting these.

12. M. Marshall, "Teaching the Uncanonized," 2.
13. *Gentleman's Magazine* 9 (May 1739): 261–62, 282–86; and 10 (February 1740): 70–72.
14. Lavoie, *Collecting Women*, 36.
15. Duncombe, *Feminiad*, 16n4. In the poem, he notes that "polish'd Orrery delighted hears" her poetry, 16.
16. On the publication history of her poems, see the *ODNB*; Stecher, *Elizabeth Singer Rowe, the Poetess of Frome*, 230–38; and Backscheider, *Eighteenth-Century Women Poets*, 114–15. Tonson was praised for promoting and supporting Whig literary culture, see A. Williams, "Patronage and Whig Literary Culture," 160–65. Williams does note that "it is hard to see how the close relationship between public life and poetry . . . could accommodate female authorship" but cites the example of Octavia Walsh, whose poetry was probably collected by her family and a few examples of it published ten years after her death in *Poems upon Divine and Moral Subjects* (1716), 167, 172n76.
17. Later editions led the list of authors with the Earl of Roscommon and sometimes styled her "Mrs. Singer" (1707, 1719) and sometimes "Philomela" (1709).
18. Wright, "Matthew Prior and Elizabeth Singer," 72.
19. Finch, *Poems of Anne Countess of Winchilsea*, 192. Finch was contributing to the myth that the Stuarts, in contrast to King William and Queen Anne, were important supporters of the arts; for an account of the actual patronage situation, see A. Williams, "Patronage and Whig Literary Culture," 149–72.
20. Masters, *Written in a blank Leaf of Mrs. Row's Works*, in *Familiar Letters*, 244.
21. E. Carter, *On the Death of Mrs. Rowe*, in *Poems on Several Occasions*, 10–11. This poem is slightly revised from its first publication in *Miscellaneous Works*, cx–cxii.
22. Little, *On Reading Lady Mary Montague and Mrs. Rowe's Letters*, in *Poetical Works of Janet Little*, 154.
23. Barbauld, *Verses on Mrs. Rowe*, in *Poems*, 101.
24. The edition is E. Rowe, *Poetry of Elizabeth Singer Rowe (1674–1737)*, ed. M. Marshall.
25. Prescott, "Elizabeth Singer Rowe (1674–1737): Politics, Passion and Piety," 71.
26. Clarke, "Soft Passions and Darling Themes," 353–71; quotations from 353.
27. Ibid., 362; see also Prescott, "Debt to Pleasure," 438–39; Spencer, "Imagining the Woman Poet," 112; and Achinstein, "Romance of the Spirit," 413–38.
28. See Prescott, "Elizabeth Singer Rowe: Gender, Dissent, and Whig Poetics," 175–79, 191; K. King, "Political Verse and Satire," 203–22; and Achinstein, "'Pleasure by Description,'" 64–87.
29. Staves, *Literary History*, 105–7, 217–27.
30. For an overview of this problem, see Eardley, "Recreating the Canon," 270–89.
31. See, for example, Prescott, "Elizabeth Singer Rowe: Gender, Dissent, and Whig Poetics," 173.
32. On the subjects and publication of her poetry and a more detailed biography, see Backscheider, "Elizabeth Singer Rowe: Lifestyle as Legacy," 41–65.
33. A number of literary historians, including Margaret Doody and Kathryn King, have argued correctly that religious experience and religious literature were central experiences for the vast majority of people in the eighteenth century, see Doody, *Daring Muse*, 139–43.

34. E. Rowe, *A Description of Hell, in Imitation of Milton*, in *Divine Hymns and Poems*, 100–103 and *Miscellaneous Works*, 1:52.

35. Patricia Crawford describes the importance of Nonconformist women to the survival of their denominations and argues that the tradition of women's participation in church "continues to the present day," "Challenges to Patriarchalism," 123–24. The unbroken stream through the early nineteenth century of Nonconformist women whose published fiction and poetry have marked traces of Dissenting history and ideology also testifies to their importance.

36. Jonathan Pritchard in the *ODNB* entry notes that she "busied herself in diverse temporal concerns, offering financial support for the school in Frome, participating in the affairs of the town's meeting-house and its congregation, maintaining a great many friendships through a voluminous correspondence, and even interesting herself in the colonial settlement of Georgia."

37. Respectively, Prescott, *Women, Authorship and Literary Culture*, 141–66; and Achinstein, "'Pleasure by Description,'" 85.

38. This is evident from quotations and references in her writing, and see Hughes, "Elizabeth Rowe and the Countess of Hertford," 731.

39. Bigold, "Elizabeth Rowe's Fictional and Familiar Letters," 9. See also Staves, *Literary History*, 105–6, 223–24.

40. E. Rowe, *Poetical Beauties*, 6–7.

41. Walmsley points out what a contrast Nicole's view of the afterlife is to hers in "Whigs in Heaven," 320–21.

42. For a description of the courtship of Rowe, see my "Elizabeth Singer Rowe: Lifestyle as Legacy," 48–51. The least known suitor is Colman, see Chapman, "Benjamin Colman and Philomela," 214–31. Rowe remained an attractive and apparently flirtatious woman; a 1722 letter written by Grace Thynne describes both a Strode relative and the widowed Heneage Finch "in love with her," Hughes, *Gentle Hertford*, 69.

43. Wright, "Matthew Prior and Elizabeth Singer," 71–82.

44. This manuscript letter is preserved in the Keeper's Office, British Museum, Anderdon, *Collectanea Biographica*, n.p.

45. Prior, *Poems on Several Occasions*, 31.

46. The poems are conveniently grouped by year in the standard edition, *Literary Works of Matthew Prior*, 1:196–214. Compare, for instance, *To a Lady: She refusing to continue a Dispute with me, and leaving me in the Argument* (1:200–202) with surviving correspondence, Wright, "Matthew Prior and Elizabeth Singer," 71–82. See my "Elizabeth Singer Rowe: Lifestyle as Legacy" for a more detailed discussion, 49–50.

47. Information from *ODNB*, s.v. "Seymour [née Thynne], Frances," Hughes, *Gentle Hertford*; and "Elizabeth Rowe and the Countess of Hertford," 726–46; Prescott, *Women, Authorship and Literary Culture*, 174–85; and "Provincial Networks, Dissenting Connections, and Noble Friends," 29–42. Hertford's best-known poem is *To the Countess of Pomfret*, B&I, 45–47.

48. Finch, *A Letter to Mrs. Arrabella Marow*, in *Anne Finch Wellesley Manuscript Poems*, 47–48.

49. Hughes, *Gentle Hertford*, 44; *Miscellaneous Works*, 1:xxxiii.

50. Duncombe, *Feminiad*, 17.

51. See Hughes, *Gentle Hertford*, 103; and *Letters*, 1:98–99, 114–15. Hughes has collated the letters in the fiction, Hertford's Green Book, and *Miscellaneous Works* and points out that the latter two include another letter Rowe wrote on his death. She also notes that Letter 2 to Cleora has only "slight verbal variations" from a copy in the Green Book, Hughes, "Elizabeth Rowe and the Countess of Hertford," 734–36; and Bigold, "Elizabeth Rowe's Fictional and Familiar Letters," 1–14.

52. Young was part of a social whirl in London and at country houses such as the Earl of Dorset's and at Pope's Twickenham. Contemporaneous with Rowe's dedication was the publication of his collection of satires, *Love of Fame, the Universal Passion* (1728). Rowe's friends, and probably Rowe, had sent around a copy of his tragedy *Busiris*, Hughes, *Gentle Hertford*, 41, 47, 103.

53. Young, *Correspondence of Edward Young, 1683–1765*, 72. He gave some of his letters to be kept at Longleat. Kathryn King says Rowe's approaching him was "shrewd," K. King, "Elizabeth Singer Rowe's Tactical Use," 170.

54. The 1746 edition of *The Seasons* does not include the lines quoted by Rowe. Sambrook includes them from the first edition of *Winter. A Poem* in Appendix A, Thomson, *Seasons*, 261.

55. Hughes, "Thomson and the Countess of Hertford," 462.

56. Bingley, "Introduction," *Correspondence*, 1:iv-vi. This account seems to be based on Samuel Johnson's *Life of Savage*, see also the *ODNB*, s.v. "Richard Savage."

57. Cockburn, *Works of Mrs. Catharine Cockburn*, 1:xl. Birch, her editor, says that the letter, which was to Alexander Pope, was never sent.

58. The Sacheverell trials are but one example of the religious dimension to the party turmoil in Anne's reign. George I arrived in England in September 1714, and in 1715 the Riot Act was passed, habeas corpus was suspended, and the Jacobite Rebellion began.

59. The printed poem carries the date of 19 July 1706, but it was not published until after their courtship was over, I. Watts, *Horae Lyricae*, 293–94.

60. Swift, *Correspondence of Jonathan Swift*, 2:437–38 and 468, respectively. Swift to Robert Harley, Lord Oxford, 11 October 1722 and 6 November 1723.

61. See also Pointon, "'Surrounded with Brilliants,'" 52–53; Pointon gives numerous similar examples of real and fictional characters' valuing and holding miniatures, 48–71.

62. Ibid., 48–54, 63; Backscheider, *Eighteenth-Century Women Poets*, 300–301; Lanser, "Befriending the Body," 183. See also Foskett, *Miniatures*; and Eger, "Paper Trails and Eloquent Objects," 115.

63. This set and others, including one of the Duchess of Portsmouth, are in the Victoria and Albert Museum. Rosse was the daughter of miniature painters, Richard and Anne Gibson, and intimate friends with Samuel Cooper, Peter Cross, and George Vertue; I am grateful to Katherine Coombs, one of the curators there, and to Catharine MacLeod of the National Portrait Gallery for their advice.

64. The Beale portrait was offered for sale but not sold by Christie's, London, in May 1993; the Rosse copy was sold at Bonham's, London, in March 1997. I am grateful to Jennifer Tonkin and Jo Lanston of these auction houses for their research on them and to Christie's and Bonham's for permission to reproduce them. I have not been able to locate either miniature.

65. Talley, *Portrait Painting in England*, 298; and Walsh and Jeffree, *Excellent Mrs. Mary Beale*, 65, respectively.

66. Vigué, *Great Women Masters of Art*, 116.

67. See Coombs, *Portrait Miniature in England*, 74.

68. *ODNB*; Arthur Grimwade, "Master of George Vertue," 83–89; and Walpole, "Life of Mr. George Vertue," 5:2. I am grateful to my research assistant Benjamin Arnberg for his work on Vertue.

69. These miniatures are in the Scottish National Portrait Gallery. I am grateful to Kim Macpherson, curatorial assistant, for her assistance.

70. Myrone, "Society of Antiquaries and the Graphic Arts," 3:104; see also *ODNB*.

71. Hughes, *Gentle Hertford*, 69.

72. The portrait of Seymour is dated 1724 and the engraving of Finch 1728, after his death in 1726, by the National Portrait Gallery. If done from the life, the date cannot be right. Quotation from Clayton, *English Print, 1688–1802*, 19–20.

73. Walpole, "List of Vertue's Works," in *Catalogue of Engravers*, 5:295, 296. The list also includes "Mrs. Elizabeth Rowe," 293.

74. Salaman, *Old Engravers of England*, 178.

75. Vertue, *Description of Four Ancient Paintings*, 4; Barber, *Portrait of a Seventeenth-Century Painter*, catalogue for the Geffrye Museum, 1999–2000.

76. Edwards, "Lady Jane Grey Revealed." Information on the Syon Portrait is drawn from this source.

77. Ribeiro, *Fashion and Fiction*, 340, 346, 272.

78. Joanna Lipking provides an interesting comparison of commendatory verse written about Rowe and Thomas, Lipking, "Fair Originals," 64–69.

79. I am not the first critic to explore the construction of Rowe's pious image, but I am the only one to use her portraits; cf. Hansen, "Pious Mrs. Rowe," 34–51; and Prescott, *Women, Authorship and Literary Culture*, chap. 6. My project, however, is to contextualize her reputation in different ways, to trace its evolution through attention to smaller time periods, and to look at aspects other than piety.

80. "A Concise Account of Mrs. Elizabeth Rowe," *London Magazine*, February 1754, 56.

81. *Gentleman's Magazine* 10 (February 1740), 70.

82. Information from *ODNB*. The portrait is from Gibbons, *Memoirs of Eminently Pious Women*, between pp. 446 and 447. This rare edition is in the Guildhall Library, Corporation of the City of London.

83. Lacey, *From Sacred to Secular*, 35, image from 36.

84. This image seems to be "Rowe" only in the artist's creation; it departs significantly from the images done in her lifetime.

85. Spencer, "Imagining the Woman Poet," 109–11; on nightingale legends, see B&I, 857–59.

86. National Portrait Gallery, Egerton.

87. Clarke, "Soft Passions and Darling Themes," 355.

88. Reeves, *Pursuing the Muses*, 34, 142. She notes that at about the same time Mary also received *The Dialogues of Eumenes* (1763), which she finds highly similar in characters, plots, and "lush description of nature, the same triumphant moral conclusions," 35.

89. Burney, *Early Diary of Frances Burney*, 1:8–9.

90. E. Rowe, *Miscellaneous Works*, 2:214; Rogers, *Monuments and Monumental Inscriptions in Scotland*, 2:269. The tombstone substitutes "day" for "steep" at the end of the first line.

91. British Library, RB 23 A.15 954.

92. Lavoie also notes the revisions of the life and gives telling examples, noting the fre-

quent addition of *On the Death of Mr. Thomas Rowe*, *Collecting Women*, 44–48. She analyzes Gibbons's *Memoirs* in some depth, 46–47.

93. An example is *Friendship in Death in Twenty Letters to which Letters . . .* , which was printed for a Who's Who of London booksellers in 1793, T. Longman, R. Law, G. G. and J. Robinson, T. Cadell, J. Johnson, J. Nichols, F. & C. Rivington, W. Otridge, W. Goldsmith, W. Lowndes, and Ogilvy and Speake, quotation from xl–xli in the 1739 edition.

94. Richetti, *Popular Fiction before Richardson*, 242. On Rowe's "huge readership," see also K. King, "Elizabeth Singer Rowe's Tactical Use," 160; and Prescott, *Women, Authorship and Literary Culture*, 182–83, 185.

95. Richetti, *Popular Fiction before Richardson*, 243, 245.

96. K. King, "Elizabeth Singer Rowe's Tactical Use," 170; and Clarke, *Rise and Fall*, 83.

97. C. Turner, *Living by the Pen*, 48–50. In the ten pages on which Turner mentions Rowe, she devotes more space to Rowe as a poet than as a writer of fiction.

98. Spencer, *Rise of the Woman Novelist*, 81; Ballaster, *Seductive Forms*, 32–33; and Richetti, *English Novel in History, 1700–1780*, 196. Ballaster says that Richetti's suggestion that there was a market for moral fiction is "premature" (33).

99. Staves, *Literary History*, quotation from 218 (emphasis mine); on Rowe and the questions of her time, see 105–6, 223–24.

100. Hansen, "Pious Mrs. Rowe," 51.

101. Quotation from Prescott, *Women, Authorship and Literary Culture*, 185.

102. Staves, *Literary History*, 169.

103. Marilyn Williamson suggests that Harriet Beecher Stowe can be fruitfully related to Rowe, *Raising Their Voices*, 257–58.

104. Cf. K. Rowe, "Feminism and Fairy Tales," 237–57.

105. D'Aulnoy, *Hypolitus*, 181.

106. N. Miller, *Subject to Change*, 8.

107. In applied linguistics, the field of activity can be situation or place and contrasts to the mental/physiological field that includes emotion, cognition, and physiological states. A mode is not "tied exclusively to a particular form or genre" but can be deployed within them, *Oxford Dictionary of Literary Terms*.

108. Rothstein, *Gleaning Modernity*, 121–23, 125.

109. Hitchcock and Cohen, "Introduction" to *English Masculinities, 1660–1800*, 20; and P. Carter, *Men and the Emergence of Polite Society*, 45, 66–76, respectively.

110. Fraser, "Rethinking the Public Sphere," 527.

111. Beasley, *Novels of the 1740s*, 165, 166, respectively.

112. K. King, "Elizabeth Singer Rowe's Tactical Use," 174.

Chapter One • Positioning Rowe's Fiction

1. David, "'Story of Semiramis,'" 91–101, and Backscheider, *Eighteenth-Century Women Poets*, 152–56.

2. Bigold, "Elizabeth Rowe's Fictional and Familiar Letters," 1.

3. K. King, "Novel before Novels," 36–37.

4. Among the novelists who include periodical-style essays are Oliver Goldsmith in *The Vicar of Wakefield* and Frances Brooke in *The History of Emily Montague*. As the novel became more polemical toward the end of the century, these intrusions became more common.

5. Cook, *Epistolary Bodies*, 17.

6. Brant, *Eighteenth-Century Letters*, 1, 47–48. Whyman has also demonstrated that the lower classes, even in rural and provincial areas where literacy was believed to be low, were active letter writers and found creative ways to send and receive letters, *Pen and the People*.

7. See Robert Adams Day's list of "English Letter Fiction 1660–1740" in *Told in Letters*, 237–58, and of "Epistolary Miscellanies," 259–66; although incomplete, these are highly useful.

8. R. Day, *Told in Letters*, 49–50. See also Brant's chapter on manuals, *Eighteenth-Century Letters*, 33–59. She points out that *The Ladies Complete Letter-Writer* (1763) claimed to be the first manual for women and helped establish the conventions that constructed "the man of letters."

9. See Zeeuw, "Letter-Writing Manual," 163–92, esp. 166–68, 172.

10. Brant, *Eighteenth-Century Letters*, 39.

11. *Ladies Complete Letter-Writer*, 160–61, 227–28. There is also a letter from "Cleora" to Rowe, "To Mrs. Rowe, on the Vanity of all sublunary Enjoyments," 162–63, which is taken from *Letters*, 1:112–13. These are in the section "Letters on various Subjects of IMPORTANCE and AMUSEMENT."

12. MacArthur, *Extravagant Narratives*, 61.

13. Mackie, *Market à la Mode*, 224–25.

14. Kathryn King has made us aware of the often subtle political undercurrents in early women's fiction, see *Jane Barker, Exile*, esp. 147–79; and "Novel before Novels," 36–57. I have been influenced by her work. Toni Bowers does the same with a larger number of texts in *Force or Fraud*.

15. Mackie, *Market à la Mode*, 27–28, and see also 16; she does not discuss Rowe.

16. Addison, *Spectator*, 1:108–11 for 30 March 1711, and E. Rowe, *Letters*, 3:178.

17. Cf. "On a Church-Yard" in *Choice of the best poetical pieces*, 1:24–25.

18. The quoted phrases are Brant's, but my point is quite different, *Eighteenth-Century Letters*, 281.

19. Anni Sairio gives an example from Catherine Macaulay's *Letters on Education*, "Bluestocking Letters," 143.

20. Quoted in Richetti, *Popular Fiction*, 244.

21. Ibid., 247 and 251, respectively.

22. The phrase is in ibid., 251.

23. Clarke, *Rise and Fall*, 193–98. Prescott gives a similar list of common amatory plots and incidents such as shipwrecks and "Turkish cruelty," "Debt to Pleasure," 437.

24. Staves, *Literary History*, 224–25; Marilyn Williamson summarizes twentieth-century opinion: "Rowe used amatory fiction for sacred purposes," *Raising Their Voices*, 254; Prescott, "Debt to Pleasure," 427–45.

25. Haywood, *Love in Excess*, 63. Sarah Prescott also discusses this similarity between Haywood and Rowe, although she interprets some scenes differently, "Debt to Pleasure," 429, 438–42.

26. Richardson printed it for Henry Lintot and also printed at least part of volume 2 of the 1739 *Miscellaneous Works in Prose and Verse of Mrs. Elizabeth Rowe*, Sale, *Samuel Richardson*, 199–200; and Maslen, *Samuel Richardson of London*, 133. Richardson printed vol. 2 in 1738–1739, and it is possible that he did only *Original Poems and Translations by Thomas Rowe* himself. It has a separate title page dated 1738. Maslen, misleadingly, does not give the full title of the 1740 publication.

27. Richardson, *Clarissa*, 3:52 and 5:283. All quotations are from this 1751 3rd edition.

28. Ibid., 8:249.

29. Rowe has a number of poems, especially dialogues, in which she wrote from the masculine point of view. Examples are some of the Canticles and poems in the popular epistolary response form such as *Lord Guilford Dudley to Lady Jane Gray* in *Letters*.

30. Behn, *Love Letters*, 99. I discuss Rowe's poetic paraphrases of the Canticles at length in chapter three.

31. Clarke, *Rise and Fall*, 192–93.

32. Behn, *Love Letters*, 52. All quotations are from this edition.

33. Cf. Nussbaum, "Women Novelists," 745–67; Bowers, *Force or Fraud*, esp. 295–309; Batchelor, "'Latent seeds of coquetry,'" 158–61.

34. Ballaster, *Seductive Forms*, 31.

35. Nussbaum, "Women Novelists," 754. Batchelor points out that satires of these scenes as in *Joseph Andrews* may suggest "a power so great it must be disabled through satire," "'Latent seeds of coquetry,'" 159.

36. Roulston, "Having It Both Ways?" 285; this essay classifies four categories of threesome narratives, 278–79.

37. See, for example, K. King, "Unaccountable Wife and Other Tales," 155–72; Andreadis, *Sappho in Early Modern England*, 142–43; Roulston, "Having It Both Ways?" 290–93; and Donoghue, *Passions between Women*, 177–81.

38. Scott, *Description of Millenium Hall*, 157–58.

39. This is a point that John Richetti also makes in "Mrs. Elizabeth Rowe," 526.

40. See Backscheider, "Story of Eliza Haywood's Novels," 31–37, quotation from 31.

41. Manley, *The Happy Fugitives* in *Power of Love*, 291.

42. Prescott, "Debt to Pleasure," 439.

43. Preface to Aubin, *Life and Amorous Adventures of the Lady Lucy*, x.

44. Prescott writes, "The role that death plays in Rowe's text could also be seen in terms of the alternative endings available for the feminocentric plot of seduction or resistance," "Debt to Pleasure," 440.

45. Elizabeth R. Napier, s.v. Elizabeth Singer Rowe, *DLB* 39:411. Brown's *Letters* were in a 5th edition by 1708.

46. Keener, *English Dialogues of the Dead*, 277–95.

47. See Sutherland, *Defoe*, 263–65. Rodney Baine has given the subject in-depth treatment, *Daniel Defoe and the Supernatural*. In the few pages they devote to the book, along with Sutherland, both Maximillian Novak and John Richetti bring the commercial possibilities of the publication to the fore, Novak, *Daniel Defoe: Master of Fictions*, 653, 664–68; and Richetti, *Life of Daniel Defoe*, 169–72. Richetti correctly notes that the books by Defoe in this category are "extended reprisals of Defoe's complicated attitudes to the spiritual world and include a good deal of satire of credulity and superstition" and that the possibility of the presence of the supernatural in daily life might be called an "obsessive theme" in Defoe's work, 169, 173. See also my contextualizing of it in *Daniel Defoe: His Life*, 520–26.

48. The count is Kincade's, Headnote to *Essay on the History and Reality of Apparitions*, xxxvi; all citations are to this edition. Novak summarizes evidence of widespread belief in spirits and Defoe's numerous writings on the subject in an essay centered on *A True Relation of the Apparition of Mrs. Veal* (London, 1706), which he believes Defoe wrote, "Defoe's Spirits, Apparitions and the Occult," 9–20.

49. Frangos, "Ghosts in the Machine," 321–24, quotation from 321.

50. [Defoe], *True Relation*, 3. There were numerous other accounts of this appearance. See Starr, "Why Defoe Probably Did Not Write *The Apparition of Mrs. Veal*," 427–50. I am inclined to agree with him, but this does not diminish the account's importance as evidence of the time's interest in spirits.

51. Close analysis of the texts I am discussing suggests either that the time when spirits and ghostly visits were real or even sent by the Devil had passed or that these writers did not believe or include this idea, which figures prominently in Keith Thomas's *Religion and the Decline of Magic*, 589–90. Rowe, Defoe, and Aubin also ignore the clerical opinion that it was an "offense for a dying person to promise to return to the land of the living" that Thomas cites, 588, 593. Starr's Introduction to *Serious Reflections* is an accurate and sensible introduction to Defoe's writings about the possibility of a spirit world and threats to sound religious belief in Introduction to *Serious Reflections*, 3:1–2, 41–47.

52. Starr, Introduction to *Serious Reflections*, 44.

53. Defoe, *Essay on the History and Reality of Apparitions*, 31.

54. Kincade, Headnote, xxx. Her list of notables, including Richard Baxter, John Aubrey, Cotton Mather, and Francis Hutcheson, is impressive, xxxii–xxxiv. See also Shaw, *Miracles in Enlightenment England*, esp. 3–15. Shaw notes that miracles and "wonders" were being asserted and investigated in everyday life as well as in philosophical and religious discussions.

55. Neuber, "Poltergeist the Prequel," 1–17.

56. See Thomas, *Religion and the Decline of Magic*, 91, 225–26, 592–600, 645–56, and 665–68; Valenze, "Prophecy and Popular Literature," 79–88 and 91–92.

57. Among the most important doctrinal documents were the Book of Common Prayer, Articles and Ordinals, the creeds, and the catechisms. These opinions were disputed for decades, and the Bangorian and Salters' Hall controversies were fierce examples of the way they played out among believers. See my explication of the relationship between these controversies and Defoe's *Robinson Crusoe*, *Daniel Defoe: His Life*, 418–20, 446.

58. Lacey, *From Sacred to Secular*, 63; although the study is of American publications, most of the books and images were originally British.

59. Frangos, "Ghosts in the Machine," 315.

60. Defoe, *Essay on the History and Reality of Apparitions*, 155.

61. Quotation from Walmsley, "Whigs in Heaven," 121. He finds many similar beliefs and expressions in Addison, Watts, and Rowe. The *Spectator* essay he quotes also takes up the issue of superstition, but, as Addison consistently does, he summons the authority of Christian (here Milton) and classical thought (Hesiod), 1:54–55, then concludes with his opinion.

62. Christine Göttler, "Preface: Vapours and Veils," xxiii–xxiv.

63. Wesley, *Journal*, 5:103; Shaw, *Miracles in Enlightenment England*, 178–79; Rack, *Reasonable Enthusiast*, 432.

64. Bannerman, *The Genii* in *Poems by Anne Bannerman*, 11–12, lines 151–52, 173–76.

65. Defoe, *Essay on the History and Reality of Apparitions*, 76.

66. Ibid., 99–114, quotation from 113. Harper argues that some apparition literature used female ghosts to warn or even punish cruel men and to extract justice, "'Matchless Sufferings,'" 425–44.

67. Kincade, Headnote, lxxxiv.

68. See Thomas on this "Protestant" shift in emphasis in ghost stories, *Religion and the Decline of Magic*, 587–97; and Frangos, "Ghosts in the Machine," 315, 316. Norma Clarke

reminds readers that Anne Killigrew is already in Heaven at the beginning of Dryden's poem "To the Pious Memory of the Accomplisht Young Lady Mrs. Anne Killigrew" (1686), and Dryden was one of Rowe's favorite poets, *Rise and Fall*, 175–76.

69. Burnet, *Some Passages*, 18; Johnson, *Profane Wit*, 71–74; Lamb, *So Idle a Rogue*, 56–61. There were eight editions of Burnet's *Some Passages* before 1728.

70. E. Rowe, *Friendship in Death*, 1. Frangos remarks that this text "contains striking allusions to rules and laws governing the spirits, which suggests that the invisible world is as orderly and logical a place as the natural world," "Ghosts in the Machine," 325.

71. Quoted from Ken's *The Practice of Divine Love* in Walmsley, "Whigs in Heaven," 324. Walmsley discusses the prevalence of this belief, 324–26.

72. [Newbery], *History of Little Goody Two-Shoes*, 38.

73. Janeway, "To all Parents, School-masters and School-Mistresses, or any that have any hand in the Education of Children," in *Token for Children*, A4.

74. Andrew Baughen, quoted in C. Miller, "Where Some Earn Loyalty," B1.

75. Thomas, *Ends of Life*, 230.

76. Richardson, *Clarissa*, 8:17; Rowe left seven letters, four of which are printed in *Miscellaneous Works*, the one to Watts in his edition of her *Devout Exercises of the Heart*, and the letter to Theophilus Rowe, which was considered by him to be "of too private a nature," *Miscellaneous Works*, 1:xli. This letter with its enclosure, preserved in Hertford's papers, is printed in Hughes, "Elizabeth Rowe and the Countess of Hertford," 739–40. I do not know if Arabella Marrow's was ever published.

77. Richardson, *Clarissa*, 8:123–25, quotations from 123, 125.

78. Bayle's *General Dictionary*, 8:794nM. and in *Miscellaneous Works*, 1:xl.

79. Ronald Paulson's "Aesthetics of Mourning" can be read to trace the path this took later in the century, *Breaking and Remaking*, 227–45.

80. Grieder, Introduction to *Rash Resolve*, 6.

81. Clarke, *Rise and Fall*, 196.

82. See Barker's "To the Reader" in *Patch-Work Screen* in the *Galesia Trilogy*, 51–54; Aubin's "Preface to the Reader" for *Strange Adventures*, 114–15; Defoe, *Moll Flanders*, 1; Davys, Preface, *Works of Mrs. Davys*, iii; and E. Rowe's "Dedication to Dr. Young," *Friendship in Death*, n.p.; see also Downie, "Mary Davys's 'Probable Feign'd Stories,'" 309–26, in which he works with most of these texts (not with Rowe).

83. R. Day, *Told in Letters*, 190.

84. Gildon, *Post-Boy Robb'd of his Mail*, 3. All references to this text are to this edition.

85. See Donovan, "Women and the Framed-Novelle," 947–80. She identifies a tradition, describes the importance of the form for women, and argues that it enabled the articulation of a feminist standpoint, as Lukács used the term "standpoint."

86. C. Wilson, *Galesia Trilogy*, 74.

87. I have excluded from the count the three letters composed of Rowe's poems, the eight to Cleora, and the ten "by another hand" at the end of the volume.

88. Hinnant, "*Moll Flanders*, *Roxana*, and First-Person Female Narratives," 50.

89. Anderson, "Tactile Places," 343.

90. K. King, *Jane Barker, Exile*, 194; and "Galesia, Jane Barker, and a Coming to Authorship," 99.

91. Casanova, "'Hell in epitomy,'" 77.

92. See K. King, *Jane Barker, Exile*, 29–67, 181–93.

93. Manley, *Power of Love*, xv.

94. See R. Day, *Told in Letters*, 40–41. Day's discussion of Gildon's texts are still the best, 67–68, 100–103, 151.

95. Swenson, "Representing Modernity," 55, 65–73, and see the entire essay, 55–80.

96. Anderson makes this point also and quotes the same passage, "Tactile Places," 344. Barker, "To the Reader," *Patch-Work Screen* in *Galesia Trilogy*, 52; recipe, 141. There is also a recipe for "French Soup," featuring several kinds of meat, necks, and broken bones, 151.

97. K. King, "Novel before Novels," 37.

98. Swenson, "Representing Modernity," 72.

99. See Clarke's summary, *Rise and Fall*, 242–43.

100. Printed in C. Wilson, *Galesia Trilogy*, 326–29, quotation from 329, and see 329n92. Kathryn King's groundbreaking study of Barker as a Jacobite poet and novelist has led to application of her methodology to other women writers and to extension into studies of Barker, *Jane Barker, Exile*, see esp. chap. 4, "A Jacobite Novelist." This poem is in the Magdalen Manuscript, "the greatest part of which were writ since the author was in France," and thus probably dates late in Barker's life, a sign she did not forget, C. Wilson, *Galesia Trilogy*, 291; Casanova, "'Hell in epitomy,'" 78–79.

101. Aubin, married to a French Huguenot, has been described as expressing "genuine cultural anxiety over the weakening moral structure of a perplexingly changing society" and producing "a comprehensive picture of global amorality, corruption, and disorder," Beasley, "Politics and Moral Idealism," 216–36, quotations from 218, 230. On Aubin and pirates, see Baer, "Penelope Aubin and the Pirates of Madagascar," 49–62.

102. K. King, "Novel before Novels," 42.

103. Davys, "Familiar Letters," 272–73. All quotations from this text are from this edition.

104. Critics disagree about whether Davys is suggesting they will marry. Alice Wakely finds that "hints are dropped in favor of a marital ending" and interprets the couple as "arguably" reaching resolution "in a Whiggish fashion, through mutual agreement between them," "Mary Davys and the Politics of Epistolary Form," respectively 265 and 263. Clarke concludes that they "move inexorably towards [marriage]," *Rise and Fall*, 258; while Lindy Riley rejects the possibility of marriage, "Mary Davys's Satiric Novel *Familiar Letters*," 216–20. Susan Glover argues that "the answers are unimagined, the uncertainty left unresolved," *Engendering Legitimacy*, 85.

105. See Martha Bowden's account of Davys's life and political and religious loyalties, especially as they pertain to *Familiar Letters*, *Reform'd Coquet*, ix–xiii, xviii–xx, xxxv–xxxviii. Bowden argues that the marriage of the couple is far from certain.

106. These are not, of course, confined to the patchwork books. Chris Mounsey argues that Aubin's novels "make space for queerness in a variety of forms of antiheteronormative sexual practice" and discusses episodes in *Count Vinevil*, *The Noble Slaves*, and *The Life and Amorous Adventures of Lucinda*, "Conversion Panic, Circumcision, and Sexual Anxiety," 247–50, 252–53, and 257–58.

107. I made this point in a footnote to *Fantomina* in Backscheider and Richetti, *Popular Fiction by Women, 1660–1730*, 248n19. Tonya McArthur, "Jane Barker," 595–618, quotation from 597.

108. Riley, "Mary Davys's Satiric Novel *Familiar Letters*," 215.

109. Tiffany Potter says this of a character in Davys's *Accomplish'd Rake*, "'Decorous Disruption,'" 91.

110. On the history and conventions of secret histories in the period, see Rabb, *Satire and Secrecy*, 95–128 et passim, and Conway, *Protestant Whore*. See also Malcolm Bosse's introduction to *The Post-Man Robb'd of his Mail*, 7.

111. Whether she was the king's mistress or not, his half-sister or not, is disputed, see Hatton, *George I*, 48–55, 99–100, 134; Beattie, *English Court*, 240–42, 240n4; Joyce Marlow, *Life and Times of George I*, 33–34. Hatton writes, "There is of course no reason why a half-sister should not be a mistress" and mentions that some historians "assume" that the relationship made incest "fashionable," 134–35.

112. Hatton, *George I*, 63.

113. Mac Cuarta, Introduction to *Ulster 1641*, 3.

114. Siochrú, "Atrocity," 57–58; Perceval-Maxwell, *Outbreak of the Irish Rebellion*, xi. I am grateful to my research assistant, Elizabeth Kent, for her work on this topic.

115. The two groups controlled about two-thirds of the land in Ireland. The Old English included Protestants but were predominantly Catholic, and their land, significant parts of it possessed since medieval times and therefore without proper titles—or any titles at all—was especially vulnerable to appropriation, Perceval-Maxwell, *Outbreak of the Irish Rebellion*, 9–12, 221–22.

116. Siochrú, "Atrocity," 62. Perceval-Maxwell, *Outbreak of the Irish Rebellion*, 232–33. Davys would have inherited accounts that were largely accurate eyewitness accounts, hysterical descriptions, pure fabrications, and outright propaganda. Ethan Howard Shagan offers examples like Davys's, "Constructing Discord," 7, 9, 12–15; see also Cope, "Experience of Survival," 295–96, 312–14. Cope summarizes the most recent work by historians on victims' testimony, 296–99.

117. After a few days confinement, Irish Protestants were carted to Portadown and forced off the Bann River bridge; the number who died is probably around 100, see Simms, "Violence in County Armagh, 1641," 124–27; and on the burning, ibid., 127–28. Simms provides evidence for other massacres and notes at least one other woman who led a massacre, 131–32.

118. Quoted, with other similar statements, in Perceval-Maxwell, *Outbreak of the Irish Rebellion*, 231–32.

119. Quotation from Bernard Capp, "George Wharton," 671. In fact, the evidence is that few died in the early weeks, but as many as 10,000 (Catholic and Protestant) died during the first winter, Siochrú, "Atrocity," 59–60. All recent historians note the exaggerations but also the impossibility of arriving at accurate figures. Most cite Simms's study of Armagh, which leads to the conclusion that one-fifth of the Protestant population in that area was killed in 1641–1642, Mac Cuarta, Introduction, 4–5. Historians note, however, that depositions such as the ones she and others use "provide evidence of what people believed and said in the early months of the rising rather than a record of objective reality," Gillespie, "Destabilizing Ulster, 1641–2," 109.

120. Grell, "Godly Charity or Political Aid?" 743. See also Siochrú, "Atrocity," 67–71, 85–86.

121. David A. O'Hara, *English Newsbooks*, 36–42.

122. Grell argues that it was widely seen in England and on the continent "as yet another part of the greater catholic plan for the destruction of the Reformed religion in Europe," "Godly Charity or Political Aid?," 746.

123. Black, *Hanoverians*, 77.

124. Kvande, "Jane Barker and Delarivière Manley," 174. See my "Hanging On and Hanging In," 30–66.
125. John Dryden, "Discourse," 4:60; Wilputte's "Harridans and Heroes" guided me to this passage, 35.
126. Roulston is speaking of Sarah Scott's *Millenium Hall*, "Having it Both Ways?" 287. I am carrying the argument further and in, perhaps, a different direction.
127. Donoghue, *Passions between Women*, 178.
128. There were times when Barker probably was economically desperate.
129. K. King, *Jane Barker, Exile*, 147.
130. Cheryl Nixon, "'Stop a Moment at This Preface,'" 123–53. Quotation from 123, where Nixon is extrapolating from Sarah Fielding's preface to *The Governess*.
131. R. Day, *Told in Letters*, 188. See also his continued discussion of this novel, 189–91, 194–95.
132. Joule, "Mary Davys's Novel Contribution," 40–45, quotation from 43.
133. Richetti, *Popular Fiction*, 247.
134. Review of *Miscellanies on Moral and Religious Subjects, in Prose and Verse* by Elizabeth Harrison, *Literary Magazine, or Universal Review* 1 (15 September–15 October 1756): 282. Richetti identifies the reviewer as Johnson, *Popular Fiction*, 244.

Chapter Two • Isles of Happiness

1. Rowe, "Dedication to Dr. Young," *Friendship in Death*, n.p. Until Alexander Pope published his 1735 *Works*, Young was considered the best of the English satiric poets; *Love of Fame*, a series of polished, poetic satires, had been published in 1725. Rowe mentions *A Paraphrase on the Book of Job* (1719) and *A Poem on the Last Day* (1713), which she calls "The Last Judgment."
2. This translation was actually part of a fashionable, aristocratic collection and was considerably racier than d'Aulnoy's tale. For that reason, I have used the translation embedded in the first translated edition of the novel *Hypolitus, Earl of Douglas* (1708). On the differences in the translation, see M. Palmer, "*History of Adolphus* (1691)," 565–67. D'Aulnoy's texts seem to have been included in many collections, excerpted, abridged, and translated with varying degrees of authenticity. Her *Memoirs of the Court of England* and *History of the Earl of Warwick*, for instance, were published with Delarivière Manley's *Letters*, see R. Day, *Told in Letters*, 220n32. See also Buczkowski, "First Precise English Translation," 59–78. I am grateful to my research assistant Benjamin Arnberg for his work on this edition.
3. N. Palmer and M. Palmer, "French *Conte de Fée* in England," 38. Anne Duggan says Perrault admires lower-class characters, especially women, *Salonières, Furies, and Fairies*, 209.
4. Perrault and his booksellers included the already-existing sobriquet in editions in France and England from 1697.
5. Elizabeth Harries points out that the voice is often that of a worldly wise, educated woman making "wry and sometimes sardonic" comments on narrative conventions or the world around them, *Twice upon a Time*, 15–16, 24–25.
6. The classification system is Harries, *Twice upon a Time*, 17, and used in other studies such as Beale, "Framing the Fairy Tale," 73–90. D'Aulnoy's influence is great in all of the genres in which she wrote; cf. Ballaster, *Seductive Forms*, for discussion of her *Memoirs of the Court of England* and *Travels into Spain*, 59–62, 123–31.

7. That hers was the first and had this effect is generally accepted, see Harries, *Twice upon a Time*, 23–24; Warner, *From the Beast to the Blonde*, 161; Hannon, "Politics of Disguise," 73. Other French women published collections of fairy tales. Among the best known were Henriette-Julie de Castelnau, Comtesse de Murat, author of *Contes de fées* (Paris, 1698) and *Les Nouveaux Contes de fées* (Paris, 1710), and Charlotte-Rose Caumont de La Force, author of *Les Contes des Contes* (Paris, 1698) and *Les fées: Contes des Contes* (Paris, 1725). These women saw themselves as working in a shared movement; Murat's hero in "Anguillette" is a descendent of d'Aulnoy's story of Princess Carpillon, one of the interpolated tales in *The History of the New Gentleman-Citizen*.

8. Duggan, *Salonnières, Furies, and Fairies*, 244–45n5. On d'Aulnoy's and Perrault's participation in the same salon games and knowledge of each other's work, see 202–6.

9. This edition is assumed lost, but bibliographic evidence indicates that it included *Graciosa and Percinet*, *The Fair One with the Golden Locks*, *The Blew Bird and Florina*, and *The Hobgoblin Prince*, N. Palmer and M. Palmer, "English Editions of French *Contes de fées*," 228. For the sake of consistency and clarity, I have used the most common names of the tales in the first English translations, including those in *The History of the New Gentleman-Citizen*.

10. The authoritative account of the publication of d'Aulnoy's tales in English is still N. Palmer and M. Palmer, "English Editions of French *Contes de fées*," 227–32; and M. Palmer, "Madame d'Aulnoy in England," 237–53. Building on Melvin Palmer's work, David Blamires gives a good account of permutations in editions of d'Aulnoy's tales in English translation, "From Madame d'Aulnoy to Mother Bunch," 69–86. I am grateful to my research assistant, Lacy Marschalk, for her work on d'Aulnoy's publication history.

11. Hunter, *Before Novels*, 142–43, 372n6. Keith Thomas mentions this widely held opinion and summons evidence to contradict it, *Religion and the Decline of Magic*, 608–14, 608n2.

12. N. Palmer and M. Palmer, "French *Conte de Fée* in England," 44.

13. DeJean, "Transnationalism and the Origins of the (French?) Novel," 45.

14. Duggan, *Salonnières, Furies, and Fairies*, 14. She does not elaborate on her statement about Radcliffe.

15. Holt, *Fairy Tale Inscrib'd*, 1.

16. In the past, the first vogue is usually dated 1690–1715 and the second 1730–1758, see esp. Raymonde Robert, *Le conte de fées littéraire*, 300–320. As Lewis Seifert notes, the early group is "a much more cohesive corpus" and, in contrast to the later group, "arose within and as a response to a specific cultural climate," *Fairy Tales, Sexuality*, 5–12, quotation from 5. It is now more common to date the first as 1690–1705, the second as 1705–1730 and described as "*L'élargissement oriental*" and "marked by Galland's translation-adaptation of the *Arabian Nights*," and the third as 1730–1756, a time of considerable diversification, Sermain, *Le Conte de Fées*, 18–29; and Citton, "Fairy Poetics," 550. Robert's table of the publication of French fairy tales actually makes the three vogues clear, with the influence of the Orient obvious in the middle period, 22–30. The first group is by far the most studied.

17. DeJean, "Transnationalism and the Origins of the (French?) Novel," 45; Watson, "Jane Johnson," 37–40. Christine A. Jones assesses the case Melvin Palmer made in 1969 that "Madame d'Aulnoy may have done more than any other writer in France (or in England for that matter) to influence the forms and popularity of the modern English novel," "Madame d'Aulnoy Charms the British," 239.

18. S. Day, *Search for Lyonnesse*, 314. On characteristics of the genre, see Harries, *Twice upon a Time*, 6–7, 15–17, and 22–32.

19. Quoted in N. Palmer and M. Palmer, "French *Conte de Fée* in England," 43. They cite other French examples, 43–44.

20. Addison, *Spectator* 419 (1 July 1712), ed. Donald Bond (Oxford: Clarendon, 1987), 3:570–71. Subsequent quotations are from this source.

21. Harries, "Fairy Tales about Fairy Tales," 159; Hannon, *Fabulous Identities*, 185.

22. Cited in Leavis, *Fiction and the Reading Public*, 146–47. Richetti's *Popular Fiction* led me to this citation.

23. Reproduced in Harries, *Twice upon a Time*, 75. She finds the frontispiece an example of nostalgia, 75–78.

24. *Adventurer* 4 (18 November 1752): 22–23. English writers spelled d'Aulnoy's name in various ways, and this rather phonetic one is common.

25. *Adventurer* 4 (18 November 1752): 19–24.

26. By the eighteenth century, sorcery, witchcraft, and magicians bringing into play some occult controlling principle were relegated to superstition or obviously imaginative stories. The *OED* offers a quotation from Thomas Fuller: "When they cannot flie up to heaven to make it a Miracle, they fetch it from hell to make it Magick" (1642).

27. This is the "restoration" plot, the most common kind in the sixteenth to eighteenth centuries; the "rise" plot is largely irrelevant for my study. These terms are widely used by specialists; on defining the fairy tale, see Bottigheimer, *Fairy Tales*, 8–17, quotation from 10.

28. On genres of fairy tales, see Harries, *Twice upon a Time*, 16–17, 22–32, 58–72 et passim, and on erroneous claims that Perrault was first, 27–32, 72. Seifert points out that Perrault was one of sixteen writers in the first wave, *Fairy Tales, Sexuality*, 6–7, 15. See Farrell, "Celebration and Repression of Feminine Desire," 56–58, for a comparison of d'Aulnoy and Perrault; and see Zipes, *Trials and Tribulations*, 1–8, for a discussion of some of the errors resulting from confusing the kinds of fairy tales. This is not to deny commonalities, including sources such as the fairy tales of Giovanni Francesco Straparola, who also embedded them in texts such as *Piacevoli notti* (1551), or Giambattista Basile, cf. Bottigheimer, "France's First Fairy Tales," 17–31; and *Fairy Tales*, 58–101. The essay helpfully distinguishes literary fairy narratives from folk and alleged nursery tales.

29. Respectively, Seifert, "On Fairy Tales, Subversion, and Ambiguity," 54; and Warner, *From the Beast to the Blonde*, xvi. An entire volume of *Le Cabinet des fées* (1785–1789) was made up of d'Aulnoy's tales. Seifert does not mention the 1717 *Le Cabinet* published in Amsterdam and containing "d'Aulnoy's entire oeuvre," C. Jones, "Madame d'Aulnoy Charms the British," 247.

30. Warner speculates that readers came to prefer "Perrault's dryer worldliness," while d'Aulnoy's irony, satire, and "grotesque, even cruel undercurrent of brutality, ugliness, and murder beneath the frothy, rococo atmosphere" made readers and publishers uncomfortable, *From the Beast to the Blonde*, 166. On the transformations of d'Aulnoy's persona in England, see C. Jones, "Madame d'Aulnoy Charms the British," 239–57.

31. Quoted from Cowley's *Albina* in Backscheider, *Spectacular Politics*, 183; and see the description of what nursery tales were like, 182–86. "The Blew Bird and Florina," one of the tales in D'Aulnoy's *Les Contes des fées*, translated as *The History of the Tales of the Fairies* (1716), includes many violent scenes, such as the one in which a queen's brains are "bashed out." As in *The Island of Happiness*, a moral is reinforced through the narrative and repeated, explicit statements. The dedication to the translation of Perrault reminds the reader that Plato banished Homer but honored Aesop and promises that the tales instruct readers on

virtue and "the most material and important Truths," Samber, "Dedication to the Countess of Granville," in Perrault, *Histories, or Tales of Past Times*.

32. Harries, "Fairy Tales about Fairy Tales," 152, 157, 170, respectively. Her essay implies that the embedded exposés of the patriarchal system in women's fairy tales reflect society's desire that fairy tales produce properly gendered women, 152–75.

33. Zipes, "Of Cats and Men: Framing the Civilizing Discourse of the Fairy Tale," 189.

34. D'Aulnoy wrote folk-tale, Perrault-type fairy tales, as well as the literary tales. The best classification is probably still that by Kurt Krüger. He divides the tales into six *Volksmarchen* and nineteen art tales (*Kunstmarchen*), which he puts in five categories, summarized by Mitchell, *Thematic Analysis*, 33. Allison Stedman argues that d'Aulnoy intended them to be "a powerful new literary enterprise" and a new contribution to the salon-inspired literary innovations, "D'Aulnoy's *Histoire*," 32–53. Recent studies develop this line of thought and classify them as a distinctly modern genre, Jean-Paul Sermain, *Le Conte de Fées*; Jomand-Baudry and Perrin, *Le Conte merveilleux au XVIIIe siècle*.

35. Seifert, *Fairy Tales, Sexuality*, 31. He works extensively with the marvelous in this book, see esp. 32–34 on some of the textual features of the marvelous.

36. Kind, *Edward Young in Germany*, 60. Kind goes on to note that "the same conditions" made works by Rowe popular, 61.

37. "The Story of Finetta the Cinder-Girl" is in the frame novel *The History of Don Gabriel* in *A Collection of Novels and Tales of the Fairies*. Harries, "Fairy Tales about Fairy Tales," 161–65. See also Hannon, *Fabulous Identities*, 125–56; and Duggan, "Nature and Culture," 149–67. On their relationship to their political and social milieux, see Robert, *Le conte de fées littéraire*, 327–430.

38. E. Marshall, "Stripping for the Wolf," 263.

39. Rowe read and published in coterie, thematic miscellanies like this one. See my "Elizabeth Singer Rowe: Lifestyle as Legacy," 51–52.

40. Janet Todd lists the two poems as "attributed to" and notes that *History of Adolphus* is the only source, Behn, *Works of Aphra Behn*, 1:455–56. Behn left several literary works, the best known being *The Younger Brother*, which Charles Gildon, who had been left the manuscript, edited and brought to the Drury Lane stage in 1696. *The Lover's Watch* (1686) is Behn's translation of *Le Montre* by Balthazar de Bonnecorse.

41. I am grateful to my research assistant Benjamin Arnberg for locating this edition. See Bottigheimer, *Fairy Tales*, 14–15.

42. D'Aulnoy, *Hypolitus, Earl of Douglas*, 192. In this edition, the tale is on pp. 177–96. Shirley Day has an extensive discussion of the text in *Search for Lyonnesse*, 169–201. Critiques of ambition such as Adolphus's pervade d'Aulnoy's fiction; in many ways Warwick in *Le Comte de Warwick* resembles Adolphus. Warwick's daughter Julie is left defenseless because of his quest for personal glory, see Duggan, *Salonnières, Furies, and Fairies*, 174–76.

43. Hertford, *Story of Inkle and Yarrico*, 9.

44. Quoted in Heller, "Subjectivity Unbound," 221.

45. Brooke, *History of Emily Montague*, 299.

46. Byatt, "Fairy Stories."

47. *Robin Goodfellow*, 1–2, 4, respectively.

48. On the frame for this tale, see Stedman, "D'Aulnoy's *Histoire*," 41–48, and on the frames and d'Aulnoy's "vibrant oral economy," see Harries, *Twice upon a Time*, 69–72. Stedman points out that the majority of fairy tales published in France between 1690 and 1715

were interpolated or framed tales; of thirty-five works containing fairy tales, only eight were collections of fairy tales, 51n22.

49. R. Day, *Told in Letters*, 152.

50. Seifert, *Fairy Tales, Sexuality*, 227n13; Robert, *Le Conte de fées littéraire*, 291–320.

51. Sarah Prescott says that letters between them "formed the basis for Rowe's popular epistolary fictions," *Women, Authorship and Literary Culture*, 174, 180–81. Melanie Bigold demonstrates that the eight letters addressed to Cleora (Hertford) "are all culled directly from the letter-book," "Elizabeth Rowe's Fictional and Familiar Letters," 7. On Thynne's anger at Rowe misleading her about the authorship of *Friendship in Death*, see K. King, "Elizabeth Singer Rowe's Tactical Use," 169–72. King says that the *Letters* were "collaborative" between the two women. Authorship in the traditional sense of the letters not signed "Cleora" is not certain; in her discussion of the composition, Helen Sard Hughes quotes a letter in which acquaintances say they were told Thynne wrote "*some* [of] the last ten in the book" (emphasis mine), "Elizabeth Rowe and the Countess of Hertford," 736 and see 734–37. The authorship of Letter 10 is not certain; neither Sarah Prescott nor Kathryn King attributes it definitively to Hertford, and Sarah Prescott writes that she believes Letters 6–10 "are trickier" and assumes they are fictional and by Rowe (e-mail correspondence, 11 September 2006).

52. This strange book asserts, "These pretended Fairies were [no]thing but *Sylphids* and *Nymphs*" and that studying the histories of fairies "would have given you some Idea of the Condition to which the Sages are resolv'd one Day to reduce the World," Villars, *Diverting History of the Count de Gabalis*, 86–87. The Sages were the group the Count is invited to join.

53. Bigold, e-mail correspondence, 23 July 2008; Defoe, another Nonconformist, has a Dialog in *Religious Courtship* that could have served as warning to Rosalinda. The device of the threat of a "Papist" suitor persisted, as in Charlotte Lennox's *The Life of Harriot Stuart* (1750).

54. Bowerbank, *Speaking for Nature*, 17–18.

55. Walmsley, "Whigs in Heaven," 322–23; he also analyzes this letter from *Friendship in Death*.

56. Brewer, *Pleasures of the Imagination*, 618–19.

57. More, *Sensibility*, 282.

58. The phrase is Donna Landry's, *Invention of the Countryside*, 17.

59. Mitchell, *Thematic Analysis*, 94–95.

60. Doody, "Sensuousness in the Poetry," 28–30, quotation from 30.

61. McKeon, "Pastoral Revolution," 289. I have drastically revised his oppositional term.

62. Ibid., 271, 279. Rowe's contrasts to the pastorals written in the eighteenth century are also made clear in Broome, *Fictive Domains*, 103–35. Neither writer mentions her.

63. Quoted in Hughes, "Elizabeth Rowe and the Countess of Hertford," 730.

64. Duggan, "Women and Absolutism," 302–15.

65. Blamires, "From Madame d'Aulnoy to Mother Bunch," 83–86, quotations from 83 and 86.

66. An opera of *Psyche and Cupid* with dances is arranged by Percinet to entertain Graciosa, *Diverting Works*, 380. Mitchell names four of these scenes and discusses the motifs drawn from La Fontaine's *Amours de Psyché et de Cupidon*, *Thematic Analysis*, 84–94.

67. Although there are many songs in d'Aulnoy's tales and much poetry in, for instance, *The Golden Bough*, this seems the most likely and appropriate song for Rowe to have been remembering.

68. On the practice and significance of paraphrasing Psalms in Great Britain and on Rowe's writing of them, see Backscheider, *Eighteenth-Century Women Poets*, 126–37. Allison Stedman notes that d'Aulnoy's published paraphrases, when printed together with a few pages of meditations, went through at least eighteen editions between 1697 and 1763, thereby "rivaling the demand for new editions" of the novels and fairy tales, "Sacred Writings, Secular Identities," 347. See also Seifert, "Marie-Catherine le Jumel de Barneville," 12.

69. R. Day, *Told in Letters*, 150, 152–53, 156–57.

70. Backscheider and Richetti, *Popular Fiction by Women, 1660–1730: An Anthology*, 325.

71. Thomas describes the seventeenth century as the time when "fairy mythology settled down into something approximating its modern form," and Rowe's stories are of this type. The fact that servants mention the fairies, however, links them to the less educated classes and perhaps to the lingering belief that fairies pinched and punished servants who were not clean and neat personally and not scrupulously performing their cleaning duties, *Religion and the Decline of Magic*, 611–13. Hannon notes that d'Aulnoy's "narratives are remarkable for their demystifying of the fictional illusion," *Fabulous Identities*, 189.

72. Cf. Lieberman, "'Some Day My Prince Will Come,'" 332–43. A wide-ranging, well-known feminist critique of the fairy tales is Karen Rowe's "Feminism and Fairy Tales," 237–57. She concludes that fairy tales "perpetuate cultural ideals which subordinate women," 253.

73. Warner, *From the Beast to the Blonde*, 25.

74. Birberick, "Changing Places," 290. The tale is *The Story of Fortunio*, "Belle-Belle ou le Chevalier Fortuné."

75. About *Histoire*, see S. Day, *Search for Lyonnesse*, 188.

76. Hannon, *Fabulous Identities*, 78–79.

77. Farrell, "Celebration and Repression of Feminine Desire," 57–58, 63n16, respectively.

78. D'Aulnoy, *Diverting Works*, 369.

79. Ibid., 385, 376, respectively.

80. Heidegger, "Building Dwelling Thinking," 327; and see Naess on ecosophy, *Ecology, Community and Lifestyle*.

81. Hannon, *Fabulous Identities*, 81.

82. Cited in ibid., 84.

83. Zipes, *Beauties, Beasts, and Enchantment*, 349; first translation by Warner, *From the Beast to the Blonde*; as she says, the English version is "mealy-mouthed," 167. Surely such revisions suggest how threatening d'Aulnoy's attacks on arranged marriages were in 1700.

84. Bottigheimer, *Fairy Tales*; she does not discuss Rowe, both quotations from 13.

85. Hannon, "Politics of Disguise," 73–74.

86. Sermain, *Le Conte de Fées Du Classicisme aux Lumières*, 184. Translation: "It is through an analysis of the literary choices specific to the classical *conte* that we attempt to characterize and understand its imaginary, which offers an original worldview that the other fictional genres cannot express."

87. Hunter, *Before Novels*, 154.

88. Ibid., 155–56.

89. Doody, "Sensuousness in the Poetry," 26.

90. Schellenberg notes that Polly Suckling is "entranced by the finery of the great house" the girls visit, *Conversational Circle*, 150, and see her discussion of *The Governess*, 150–56. The great house represents an alternate, aesthetic world, an imagining of a fairy-tale existence for Polly and her friends.

91. Fielding, *Governess*, 130. Subsequent citations are to this edition.
92. Harries, *Twice upon a Time*, 85.
93. Fielding, *Familiar Letters*, 2:237, reworded but repeated 2:272. All references to this text are to this edition.
94. See, for example, Donovan, "Women and the Framed-Novelle," 973.
95. S. King, *Dreams of Youth*, 39.
96. Sherwood, *Governess*, 45–89. I am grateful to my research assistant Lacy Marschalk for her research on this text. A few pages of the 1822 edition, including "Mrs. Teachum on Fairy Tales," are included in Candace Ward's Broadview edition of Fielding's *The Governess*, 234–39.
97. Bottigheimer, "Fairy Tales and Fables."
98. Grenby, "Tame Fairies Make Good Teachers," 1, 4–5. Lane alone produced six collections of fairy tales, mostly d'Aulnoy's.
99. See Backscheider, "Literary Culture as Immediate Reality," 518–23.
100. Beaumont's *Magazin des enfans* was translated into English as *The Young Misses Magazine* (1757), Harries, *Twice upon a Time*, 87–90, 182nn42–45.
101. Bigold, "Elizabeth Rowe's Fictional and Familiar Letters," 3 and 13n11. Bigold describes the contents and documents the letter book as a showpiece in this essay, 1–14. The account of the fairy tale that follows draws information from Hughes, *Gentle Hertford*; and Rhoda Zuk, "'A Fairy Tale' Introductory Note," 3:123. The fairy tale is printed in this volume, 125–36.
102. It was posthumously published and frequently reprinted, see Grenby, "Tame Fairies Make Good Teachers," 12.
103. Ibid., 11–12, 20n10.
104. Unlike other fairies who could be viciously malevolent or appear as monsters, the trooping fairies were devoted to feasting and dancing, Briggs, *Anatomy of Puck*, 13–16.
105. B&I, 384.
106. Quoted in Hunter, *Before Novels*, 150.
107. The manuscript from Greville's notebook of poems is reprinted in B&I, 602–4. The publication history is complicated, see Rizzo, "Frances Greville Letters," 313–62. See the discussion of this poem and responses to it in B&I, 589–91.
108. Doody, "Sensuousness in the Poetry," 27. She discusses other fairy poems, 26–31.
109. The most complete list of responses was given to me by the late Betty Rizzo and includes a list of seventeen poems.
110. Tuite, *Poems by Lady Tuite*, 32–57, 91–107, esp. *On Reading These Last Lines of My Answer to Mrs. Greville*, 111–15.
111. Cowper, *Addressed to Miss [Macartney, Afterwards Mrs. Greville] On Reading the Prayer for Indifference, Poems of William Cowper*, 1:74.
112. Plays exhibit this freedom as well. Examples are Thomas Hull's *The Fairy Favour: A Masque* (1767), George Colman's *The Fairy Prince: A Masque* (1771), and Hester Thrale Piozzi's *The Two Fountains* (1789). See Gwin J. Kolb, "Mrs. (Thrale) Piozzi," 68–81.
113. Cited in R. Day, *Told in Letters*, 224n4.
114. Hemlow, *History of Fanny Burney*, 18–19.
115. S. Wilson, *Myths and Fairy Tales*, 1.
116. Zipes, *Beauties, Beasts, and Enchantment*, 4.
117. Gilbert and Gubar, *Madwoman in the Attic*, 37–41, 259, 263–64, 351, and 430.

118. Byatt, "Fairy Stories."

119. Haase, "Feminist Fairy-Tale Scholarship," 19. He gives numerous examples, 20–25.

120. Byatt, "Great Green Worm," see esp. 193 and 203–4. Byatt's story departs freely from d'Aulnoy's.

121. Quoted in Harries, *Twice upon a Time*, 154, and see her discussion of derivative and original modern fairy tales, 153–54.

122. S. Wilson, *Myths and Fairy Tales*, 5.

123. See Grenby, "Tame Fairies Make Good Teachers," 3. This essay provides an overview of some of the transformations of the fairy tale, 1–24.

124. K. Rowe, "Feminism and Fairy Tales," 237–40.

Chapter Three • *Toward Novelistic Discourse*

1. *Madagascar: or, Robert Drury's Journal*, long attributed to Daniel Defoe, was also published that year; Furbank and Owens in *Defoe De-Attributions* call the attribution "supererogatory" and assign it to Robert Drury, 148.

2. Tollet, *Written in a Book of Novels*, *Poems on Several Occasions*, 23.

3. Alison Conway has brought this term to prominence and makes a persuasive case for our turning our attention to such forms, *Protestant Whore*, 11–12.

4. Cook, *Epistolary Bodies*, 6. Ulric Neisser in the widely used "Five Kinds of Self-Knowledge" describes the interpersonal self as the self in interaction with another person, and the conceptual self as the self-concept that "draws its meaning from the network of assumptions and theories in which it is embedded," and he lists as among theories social roles, internal entities (the soul, the unconscious mind), and socially significant dimensions of difference, 35–59, quotation from 36.

5. Richetti, *Popular Fiction before Richardson*, xxvi ("Introduction: Twenty Years On") and 201.

6. Riley, "Mary Davys's Satiric Novel *Familiar Letters*," 207–8.

7. Gevirtz, "Ladies Reading and Writing," 64.

8. F. N. W., "To Madam Aphra Behn," 29, 32.

9. L. Davis, *Factual Fictions*, 117.

10. Ibid., 212–13.

11. Lindy Riley does an excellent job of explicating the ambiguity of this conclusion with Artander's sudden use of obsolete romantic heroes: "Will Berina prove just as dishonest as he . . . ?" "Will Artander finally be jolted into an awareness that Berina is truly different from others of her sex in that she has rejected the pose of the romantic heroine . . . ?" "Mary Davys's Satiric Novel *Familiar Letters*," 218–19.

12. Richetti, *Popular Fiction before Richardson*, 262. This style did not disappear, as texts by Mary Wollstonecraft or Mary Hays demonstrate; I am grateful to the anonymous reader for the Johns Hopkins University Press for this reminder.

13. Jajdelska, *Silent Reading*, 110.

14. Defoe, *Roxana*, 253–55.

15. See Weinbrot, *Augustus Caesar in 'Augustan' England* and *Britannia's Issue;* and Sowerby, *Augustan Art of Poetry*. Margaret Doody argues that these values can be found in novels as well as poetry, *Daring Muse*.

16. The first volume of Rowe's collected poems came out in the year that Nahum Tate dedicated his *Miscellanea Sacra* to Princess Anne and gave as its timely purpose: "The Ref-

ormation of Poetry, and Restoring the *Muses* to the Service of the Temple, is a Glorious Work."

17. Most of these texts are usefully collected in Womersley, *Augustan Critical Writing*. Sowerby quotes Dryden's "Postscript" as the impetus for the book: "our Poets, even in those who being endu'd with Genius, yet have not Cultivated their Mother-Tongue with sufficient Care; or . . . have judg'd the Ornament of Words and Sweetness of Sound unnecessary," *Augustan Art*, 1. This section has been influenced by this book. The best discussion of Rowe's place in this movement is Prescott, "Elizabeth Singer Rowe: Gender, Dissent, and Whig Poetics," 173–99.

18. E. Rowe, *Poems on Several Occasions*, 2:46–47.

19. K. King, "Political Verse and Satire," 215.

20. This was a frequently repeated narrative and experience in her work, and it came to have a variant in her life after Thomas Rowe's death. In a letter to Sarah Rowe, she wrote, "The charming form appears for ever in my sight, and I half deceive myself with imaginary joys; but when I recover from the soft delusion, I grow perfectly wild and savage, and fly humankind, because I can see nothing that resembles him," *Miscellaneous Works*, 2:199. She enclosed a poem commemorating the anniversary of her husband's death in the letter.

21. This book is artificially divided into two volumes; after *The Fable of Phaeron* concludes on p. 72, the numbering begins again with 1 and *The Wish*, *Poems on Several Occasions*, 1:47–48.

22. Another interesting point of comparison is which imagery from the Old Testament she uses in each version. See also the similar revision of Canticles, chap. 1, in the 1696 and the *Miscellaneous Works* versions, respectively, 1:36–39, and 1:247–48.

23. Anne Bannerman's *Genii* may have been partly inspired by this and similar tours in Rowe's work.

24. Lanser, *Fictions of Authority*, 26.

25. Haywood, *Invisible Spy*, 261.

26. Margaret Ezell discusses the uses of poetry in women's fiction and argues that Barker "presents" readers "with both Barker the novelist and Barker the poet in one printed package"; in effect, this is what later volumes of Rowe's fictions do for her, "From Manuscript to Print," 146–50, quotation from 148. I have drawn from her categories.

27. The *New Arcadia*, Sidney's revision of what is now called the *Old Arcadia*, was published first in 1590; in 1593, books 3–5 of the *Old Arcadia* were published with the *New* to make a book experienced by readers as complete.

28. Ezell, "From Manuscript to Print," 140–60, quotations from, respectively, 147, 148.

29. *Athenian Mercury*, 18 June 1695; the poem was published in *Philomela* as *To a Friend who Persuades me to leave the Muses*.

30. I. Watts, *Horae Lyricae*, 71; Milton, *Paradise Lost*, 4:846–48: "abasht the Devil stood,/ And felt how awful goodness is, and saw/ Vertue in her shape how lovely, saw, and pin'd"; Rowe, *Letters*, 3:240.

31. Ezell notes that women writers came to include poetry "to animate spiritual expression" and lists texts published from the 1650s through the eighteenth century, "From Manuscript to Print," 148–49.

32. There were multiple editions of *England's Heroicall Epistles* in the seventeenth century, two in 1737, the year of Rowe's death, and it appeared in various collections of his works throughout the century (1748, 1753, 1788, 1793).

33. Drayton, *Works of Michael Drayton*, 3:133, lines 11–12, 14. All quotations from the *Heroicall Epistles* are from this edition.

34. *Poetical Miscellanies*, 75; and E. Rowe, *Letters*, 3:214. I am grateful to Lacy Marschalk for her contributions to the publication history of the poem.

35. *Ovid's Epistles*, 121.

36. Ezell, "From Manuscript to Print," 148.

37. Significantly, this criterion comes from Laetitia Barbauld's introduction to *Correspondence of Samuel Richardson*, xxiii.

38. Laidronette abandons her family in favor of scholarly pursuits; Patricia Hannon says that she qualifies as a *femme savante* and "undertakes an intellectual apprenticeship that might be perceived as a challenge to the increasing conformity demanded by absolutism," *Fabulous Identities*, 111–12.

39. This section has benefited from the theory in Stedman, "D'Aulnoy's *Histoire d'Hypolite*," 32–53; and Nixon, "'Stop a Moment at This Preface,'" 123–53.

40. Bowerbank, *Speaking for Nature*, 47. In the chapter on Wroth, she notes that her groves "expose the grim realities of rape, abuse, violence, and alienation that, in every grove, threaten woman's safety and well-being," 50. *Urania* was in libraries such as the Hertfords', and book catalogues from the eighteenth century indicate that *Urania* was available.

41. Congreve, Preface to *Incognita*, 5.

42. Bourdieu, *Distinction*, 3.

43. Harries, *Twice upon a Time*, 40–43, quotations from 41.

44. Later editions of Dryden's *Ovid* included Oenone and Paris epistles by John Cooper and a "Mr. Salusbury." All of these editions would have been available to Rowe; I am grateful to my research assistant Lacy Marschalk for her contributions to this note. John Cooper's *Oenone to Paris* was in the same book. The *ODNB* notes that "circumstantial evidence supports" a connection between Carey and George Savile, marquess of Halifax, who was an urbane, witty writer and patron to other writers, s.v. Henry Carey.

45. Prescott, *Women, Authorship and Literary Culture*, 183–85.

46. Kirschbaum, "Thoughts 'All Easy and Sociable,'" 48.

47. *Weekly Miscellany* 308 (11 November 1738): 1–2.

48. *General Evening Post* obituary, 534 (26 February 1737): 3. This obituary is printed in many periodicals, including *Common Sense, or the Englishman's Journal*, no. 5 (5 March 1737), 3; *Weekly Miscellany* 218 (4 March 1737): 5; and *Gentleman's Magazine* 8 (March 1737): 188.

49. *Weekly Miscellany* 220 (11 March 1737): 3.

50. Prescott, *Women, Authorship and Literary Culture*, 174; on the literary acquaintances made, see 175–80.

51. Radcliffe, "Genre and Social Order," 448.

52. *Gentleman's Magazine* 6 (December 1736): 741.

53. Helen Sard Hughes quotes the apostrophe from *Spring*, the complimentary lines from several versions of *Hymn on Solitude*, and some manuscript poems in the Alnwick manuscript in "Thomson and the Countess of Hertford," 439–68.

54. Quoted in Prescott, *Women, Authorship and Literary Culture*, 179.

55. C. Jones, "Madame d'Aulnoy Charms the British," 242.

56. Wall, *Prose of Things*, 123–24, 133, 135.

57. Duggan, *Salonnières, Furies, and Fairies*, 217–18.

58. The authority on altered personal letters in Rowe's fiction is Melanie Bigold, some of whose work on this subject is forthcoming.

59. Cook, *Epistolary Bodies*, 5.

60. Hannon in *Fabulous Identities* describes the *conteuses*' writing in these terms, 160.

61. K. King, "Elizabeth Singer Rowe's Tactical Use," 169–72, quotations from 171.

62. Nixon, "'Stop a Moment at This Preface,'" 123.

63. Cook, *Epistolary Bodies*, 30. On the letters and relationship to readers, see also Staves, *Literary History*, 223–25.

64. Quoted in Prescott, *Women, Authorship and Literary Culture*, 185.

65. The full title was *A Vindication of Providence: or, a True Estimate of Human Life. In which the Passions are consider'd in a New Light* (London, 1728); it was a sermon preached at St. George's Church "soon after the late King's death" (George I in 1727). The sermon suggests Rowe's timely reading and engagement with current events. This sermon was advertised with her *Friendship in Death* in the *London Evening Post* on 27 February and 2 March 1728, and *Vindication*, *Friendship in Death*, and *Letters* were advertised together in the *Craftsman*, 379 (6 October 1733): 2; 380 (13 October 1733): 3; and 381 (20 October 1733): 3, among other dates.

66. Radcliffe, "Genre and Social Order," 463n10.

67. Chartier, *Inscription and Erasure*, 111.

68. Benveniste, "La Nature des Pronoms," 34–37.

69. See Stedman on this aesthetic, "D'Aulnoy's *Histoire d'Hypolite*," 33. Shirley Jones Day describes "the aesthetic of the *conte de fées*," which includes the exotic, *Search for Lyonnesse*, 236.

70. Benveniste, "La Nature des Pronoms," 35–36.

71. Although still contested by some literary historians, that a "reading revolution" occurred in the eighteenth century is generally accepted. Attention has turned to what kind of revolution there was, and the contention that "studious" or "intensive" reading, in which texts were read "respectfully" and reread, transmitted to the next generation, and even memorized, was supplanted by "consumerist" or "extensive" reading, during which the reader was detached and read many texts rapidly and allegedly superficially or, at best, for specific kinds of information or experiences, has given way to two trends. One is that these two sharply contrasting reading styles (and perhaps others) existed at the same time. The other is the active seeking of explanations and methodologies that will better define the "reading revolution." For examples and summaries of controversies, see Chartier, *Inscription and Erasure*, 113–15.

72. Ibid., 123.

73. Prescott, *Women, Authorship and Literary Culture*, 183.

74. Chartier, *Inscription and Erasure*, 125.

75. Radcliffe, "Genre and Social Order," 447, 449.

76. Chartier, *Inscription and Erasure*, 108–9.

77. She left these for Isaac Watts to edit and publish, and he included Rowe's letter to him in the preface, *Devout Exercises of the Heart*, xxvii–xxviii.

78. Napier, s.v. "Elizabeth Singer Rowe" in *Dictionary of Literary Biography*, 39:412.

79. Rothstein, *Gleaning Modernity*, 224.

80. Chartier, *Inscription and Erasure*, 114.

81. Ibid., 111.

82. Jajdelska, *Silent Reading*, quotations from 3 and 7.

83. This idea is adapted from Nixon, "'Stop a Moment at This Preface,'" 133.

84. George A. Starr introduced the importance of casuistical thinking in the early novel in his *Defoe and Casuistry*, and Eric Rothstein applies the method to an expanded list of texts in *Gleaning Modernity*, 123–44.

85. Hannon, *Fabulous Identities*, 215.

86. Rothstein, *Gleaning Modernity*, 125.

87. N. Miller, *Subject to Change*, 8.

88. Donoghue, *Passions between Women*, 180.

89. Wilputte, "Harridans and Heroes," 48.

90. Davys, *Cousins: A Novel*, 2:205.

91. This is a purchasing power conversion, see Webb, "Inflation."

92. Althusser, *For Marx*, 252, 231, 233, respectively.

93. By *naturalized* I mean what is accepted in a society as self-evidently true, as "the way the world is." It is historically constructed from hegemonic processes; thus, to move ways of thinking and living into the category of naturalized is of major significance.

94. Rothstein, *Gleaning Modernity*, 123.

95. Bourdieu, *Distinction*, 5

96. Hunter, *Before Novels*, 141.

97. Riley, "Mary Davys's Satiric Novel *Familiar Letters*," 206. Riley is writing of Davys alone.

98. K. King, "Novel before Novels," 50.

99. This paragraph has been influenced by Lewis Seifert's discussion of the style of the *conteuses* in *Fairy Tales, Sexuality*, 8–12.

100. Since Shaftesbury "a characteristic feature of eighteenth-century culture," the politeness movement with its emphasis that "*civic* liberty is *discursive* and *cultural* liberty" has been defined "as a partisan achievement," Klein, *Shaftesbury and the Culture of Politeness*, 198. A proliferation of books with titles like *The Culture of Whiggism* and *Defoe and Whiggism* indicate that this tendency has become more pronounced for the past few years. I do not intend to deny that Rowe could also draw upon readers who already identified some kinds of novels as refined, see K. King, "Novel before Novels," 36–57.

101. Again, this is an adaptation of Cheryl Nixon's theory about paratexts, which I am extending to Rowe as author function, "'Stop a Moment at This Preface,'" 133–34. Cook argues in *Epistolary Bodies* that epistolary fiction demands reconsideration of Foucault's claim that letters lack the author function; it seems clear to me that Rowe's have it.

102. Roulston, "Eighteenth-Century Ménage-à-Trois," 287.

103. Critics agree that Richardson's revisions in *Pamela* were designed to polish the characters' and novels' discourse, see, for example, Gaskell, *From Writer to Reader*, 63–74. He notes that the "chief aim . . . was to elevate and dignify the tone of the novel" and gives examples of, for instance, Richardson correcting Pamela's grammar and refining her phraseology, making her more of what he describes as a lady, quotation from 65. The most detailed study is still Eaves and Kimpel, "Richardson's Revisions of *Pamela*," 61–88. They demonstrate that his changes were "to elevate or correct the language," 64.

104. Nurmi and Palander-Collin, "Letters as a Text Type," 38–40. They explain that modal verbs negotiate possibilities, obligations, and predictions.

105. Hannon, *Fabulous Identities*, 18.

106. Lanser, *Fictions of Authority*, 8.

Chapter Four • The Beautiful Life

1. *Misc. Works*, 2:41, n.d. The reference is to "The Moralists, A Philosophical Rhapsody. Being a Recital of Certain Conversations upon Natural and Moral Subjects," which was published in 1709, two years before *Characteristics of Men, Manners, Opinions, Times* (1711).

2. Foucault, "Technologies of the Self," 16–18, and *History of Sexuality. Vol. 1*, 92–102, 127, respectively. See also Fraser, "Rethinking the Public Sphere."

3. The term is Raymond Williams's; in *Marxism and Literature* he explains that he chose "feeling" "to emphasize a distinction from more formal concepts of 'world-view' or 'ideology,'" with change, what is always a formative process rather than "a past tense" or a "fixed form." He explains that he is "concerned with meanings and values as they are actively lived and felt, and the relations between these and formal or systematic beliefs are in practice variable (including historically variable), over a range from formal assent with private dissent to the more nuanced interaction between selected and interpreted beliefs and acted and justified experiences," 132.

4. Klein, *Shaftesbury and the Culture of Politeness*, 7; Klein, "Third Earl of Shaftesbury," 186. Discussions of this movement are numerous, see also Langford, *Polite and Commercial People*; Bryson, *From Courtesy to Civility*; P. Carter, *Men and the Emergence of Polite Society*; Klein, "Politeness for Plebes," 363–82; and Brewer, "'Most Polite Age and the Most Vicious,'" 341–45.

5. Quoted in Klein, "Third Earl of Shaftesbury," 201.

6. Respectively, *Misc. Works* (London, 1739), 1:xxxv; James Granger, continued by the Rev. Mark Noble, *Biographical History of England*, 3:310; excerpted life in *Misc. Works*, 2nd ed. (London, 1749), 1.i, and *Misc. Works* (London, 1739), 1:lxii.

7. Bayle's *General Dictionary, Historical and Critical*, 8:790.

8. Dated 1763 and quoted in Hammond, *Professional Imaginative Writing in England*, 148. This definition conforms to Philip Carter's analysis leading him to conclude that it was less moral than "personal presentation" associated with pleasing, with refinement, and, later, with sensibility, *Men and the Emergence of Polite Society*, 39–40, 43–74.

9. Helen Sard Hughes reports that Rowe enjoyed Shaftesbury's *Characteristics* and Berkeley's *Minute Philosopher*, "Thomson and the Countess of Hertford," 445. At least ten editions of *Characteristicks* were published between 1711 and 1800.

10. Klein, "Politeness for Plebes," 364.

11. Mackie, *Market à la Mode*, 2. Mackie is speaking of the *Tatler* and *Spectator* only.

12. On the increase and popularity of the familiar letter and its blend with fiction, see R. Day, *Told in Letters*, 48–68. The opinion is persistent; P. D. James quotes Jane Austen's *Northanger Abbey* approvingly: "Everybody allows that the talent of writing agreeable letters is peculiarly female," "Foreword" to *Eight Hundred Years of Women's Letters*, vii.

13. *Letters*, 1:22–25. In a letter that can be dated to 1726 because of its reference to the publication of Thomson's *Winter*, Rowe writes Hertford, "Mr. — continues his design of writing a poem on the inscription of the *Athenian* altar, *To the unknown God*." She continues to say that Pascal "has made a very just reflection" on "whether the Deity is known or unknown" and that she does not know "what class" Mr. — belongs to, *Misc. Works*, 2:54. Thus, the fictional letter seems based on actual events.

14. As Arja Nurmi demonstrates, Nurmi and Palander-Collin, "Letters as a Text Type," 26–27. In music, the register is the range of a voice or instrument.

15. Klein, *Shaftesbury and the Culture of Politeness*, 4.

16. Keeble, *Literary Culture of Nonconformity*, 232–33.

17. Cf. Jajdelska, *Silent Reading*, 118–29. She analyzes salutations, while Anni Sairio is more interested in identifying elements within the letters that reveal strength of network ties and individual intimacy, see "Methodological and Practical Aspects," 107–35.

18. Keeble, *Literary Culture of Nonconformity*, 247, and see 245–62.

19. Ibid., 249; *Misc. Works*, 2:196, beginning of Letter 13.

20. Among the debates about letters were whether they are true utterances from the heart or "calm and deliberate performance." Cook summarizes major eighteenth-century statements on this topic in *Epistolary Bodies*, 86–88, quotation from 85.

21. Collyer, *Felicia to Charlotte*, 1:20.

22. See Macleod's fascinating "'Thinking Minds of Both Sexes,'" 247–64.

23. MacArthur, *Extravagant Narratives*, 43.

24. Brant, *Eighteenth-Century Letters*, 1, 47–48.

25. The publication seems to have been something of a saga; Lady Mary expressed anxiety about their publication on her deathbed, and he received £200 for them, Grundy, *Lady Mary Wortley Montagu*, 612, 612n61, and 625–26.

26. I am grateful to my research assistant Lacy Marschalk for her research on collections of letters and discovering this advertisement.

27. R. Day, *Told in Letters*, 152.

28. Cook, *Epistolary Bodies*, 66.

29. Ibid., 67 and 196n45.

30. See the overview by Fitzmaurice, "Commerce of Language," esp. 313, 310, respectively.

31. Ibid., 309–28, quotations from 315 and 316, respectively.

32. Bannet, *Empire of Letters*, 152. This manual was published with several different titles and in England, Scotland, and America.

33. The part quoted is from *Misc. Works*, 1:xlii; and *Friendship in Death*, 24–25. Brett, *Brett's Miscellany*, 25–26. Several times the part of the letter selected alludes to the certainty of their meeting in Heaven.

34. *Critical Review* (London, 1796), 15:344 (this is the collected annual; originally published in November 1795); and *Star in the West* (3 November 1838), 228. I am grateful to my research assistant Lacy Marschalk for these references.

35. Sabor, Introduction to *The Adventures of David Simple*, xi; he summarizes opinion about its authorship, concluding as I do that it is largely by Sarah, xxxii, n. 11.

36. Bree, *Sarah Fielding*, 47. Correctly, she contrasts it to Richardson's *Familiar Letters*. April London in the *Dictionary of Literary Biography* calls it unproblematically a novel, s.v., "Sarah Fielding," 39:198.

37. Fielding, *Familiar Letters*, 1:50. All quotations are from this edition.

38. Bermingham, *Landscape and Ideology*, 9.

39. Inglesfield, "Thomson and Shaftesbury," 68–69. Rowe thanked Hertford for arranging a subscription to Thomson's poems, *Misc. Works*, 2:94.

40. Liu, *Seeds of a Different Eden*, 133–34.

41. Inglesfield identifies this passage as "obviously deeply influenced by Shaftesbury," "Thomson and Shaftesbury," 89.

42. Paulson, *Breaking and Remaking*, 203–45.

43. Increasingly changes in landscape aesthetics and use-value have been associated with Whig or Tory sensibility and ideology, and this would include Rowe's depiction of natural

settings, cf. Everett, *Tory View of Landscape*; Sharon Achinstein, "'Pleasure by Description,'" 84–85; Klein, *Shaftesbury and the Culture of Politeness*, 143 et passim; Sarah Prescott's chapter "Gender, Authorship and Whig Poetics," in *Women, Authorship and Literary Culture* (also printed in Womersley, ed., *Cultures of Whiggism*, and see his Introduction: 9–26). Klein and others remind readers that Shaftesbury "was defining what we take as a characteristic feature of eighteenth-century culture as a partisan achievement," *Shaftesbury and the Culture of Politeness*, 198. This labeling works as long as Whiggism refers to today's use of the term for general characteristics and modern identification of the methods of Whig historians and propagators of a broad ideology. Allegedly, Whig writing turned from "the oppositionalist tradition in English politics" to a discourse that focused on virtue and liberty, Klein, *Shaftesbury and the Culture of Politeness*, 143. Anyone who has worked closely with political parties and alliances in the first third of the eighteenth century, however, knows how complex, divided, and evolving Whigs were.

44. Curran, "Romantic Poetry," 190.

45. Liu, *Seeds of a Different Eden*, 92.

46. Burney, *Cecilia, Or Memoirs of an Heiress*, 520–21. I am grateful to Jamie Kinsley for reminding me of this incident.

47. Lady Mary Chudleigh, *To Clorissa* in *Poems and Prose of Mary, Lady Chudleigh*, 68.

48. Rumbold, "Rank, Community and Audience," 127.

49. Walsh, *On Solitude*, 339–40, quotation from 339.

50. Locke, *Essay concerning Human Understanding*, 328–48; and on the controversy see Dacome, "Noting the Mind," 605 and 605n8.

51. Klein, *Shaftesbury and the Culture of Politeness*, 3, and see his Introduction, 1–14.

52. Bourdieu, "Artistic Taste and Cultural Capital," 207, 210.

53. Klein, *Shaftesbury and the Culture of Politeness*, 4.

54. Quoted in Dowling, *Epistolary Moment*, 104.

55. Everett, *Tory View of Landscape*, 19.

56. Brant, *Eighteenth-Century Letters*, 13, 27, 32, 281–82, and 311–30. Her chief examples for this kind of letter are from Methodists who were encouraged to write about religion every day. Philip Carter in *Men and the Emergence of Polite Society* takes up the Church of England briefly and traces its changing linkage of religion and the politeness movement, cf. 41–44.

57. Cook, *Epistolary Bodies*, 6.

58. Brant, *Eighteenth-Century Letters*, 19–20.

59. Skinner, *Introduction to Eighteenth-Century Fiction*, 63.

60. Quoted in Brant, *Eighteenth-Century Letters*, 328.

61. Klein, *Shaftesbury and the Culture of Politeness*, 3–4.

62. Barbauld, *On a Lady's Writing*, 786.

63. Lucia Dacome points out the "new standards of mental control" in the century, "Noting the Mind," 620–25.

64. Radcliffe, "Genre and Social Order," 448–49.

65. Bowerbank, *Speaking for Nature*, 84.

66. Quoted in Bannet, "Bluestocking Sisters," 27.

67. Bowerbank, *Speaking for Nature*, 84, 94–97, quotation from 95.

68. Brant, *Eighteenth-Century Letters*, 27.

69. Roach, "Power's Body," 99–118, quotation from 100.

70. Ibid., 101.

71. For an applied discussion of this theory see Nixon, "'Stop a Moment at This Preface,'" 123–53.
72. Haywood, *History of Miss Betsy Thoughtless*, 606.
73. Thomson, *Spring. A Poem*, Dedication to the Countess of Hertford, n.p.
74. Hughes, "Romantic Correspondence of the Year 1729," 187–200, quotation from 188.
75. E. Rowe, *Soliloquy XX, Misc. Works*, 1:190. One of the tributary poems "By a Friend" prefaced to *Misc. Works* mentions joining Rowe on "her ev'ning walk," 1:cix. See also the poem in *Letters* which combines an evening walk with devotional reflections, 1:63–64.
76. Bowerbank, *Speaking for Nature*, 98, and she quotes Talbot on 100.
77. Shaftesbury, *Characteristics of Men*, 1:279.
78. Dowling, *Epistolary Moment*, 104.
79. Quoted from Talbot's *Essays on Various Subjects* (1771) in Bowerbank, *Speaking for Nature*, 83–84.
80. Clarke, "Soft Passions and Darling Themes," 367.
81. Bowerbank, *Speaking for Nature*, 83–84.
82. McKeon, "Pastoral Revolution," 272.
83. Quoted in Eger, "'Noblest commerce of mankind,'" 292. She is exploring space and the impact of gender, among other things, in this essay.
84. Quoted in J. Turner, *Politics of Landscape*, 195.
85. Bermingham, *Landscape and Ideology*, 10, 12.
86. On Addison's influence see Liu, *Seeds of a Different Eden*, 97–98, 101–12, quotation from 98.
87. *Spectator* 412 (23 June 1712), Bond, 3:540, 541. This section has been influenced by Liu, chap. 4, "Landscape and Freedom: Joseph Addison's Affinity with Nature," in his *Seeds of a Different Eden*. As Liu does, Stephen Bending credits Addison with a major part in the "actual reformation" of garden aesthetics; he, like many recent theorists, associates this with "Whiggish" historical methods and claims, "Natural Revolution?" 243.
88. Brant, *Eighteenth-Century Letters*, 22; and Cook, *Epistolary Bodies*, 32. Brant argues that this "is tied to a fantasy that the addressee will surmount absence."
89. E. Carter, *Answers to Objections*. As Hawley notes, this was a letter her editor turned into a personal essay, *Bluestocking Feminism*, 2:424 and 464nn19, 20.
90. Heller, "Subjectivity Unbound," 221.
91. E. Carter, *Series of Letters*, 1:4–5.
92. Quoted in Clarke, "Soft Passions and Darling Themes," 367.
93. Quoted in Bowerbank, *Speaking for Nature*, 104.
94. Johns, *Women's Utopias*, 10. Johns does not discuss Rowe or Collyer.
95. C. Turner, *Living by the Pen*, 149.
96. Quoted in Bannet, "Bluestocking Sisters," 47; E. Carter began to recommend it actively.
97. Staves, *Literary History*, respectively 236 and 230.
98. Collyer, *Felicia to Charlotte*, 1:2. The second volume was published in 1749; it was sold with the first (both are in the Garland edition), and there were later editions, including one in 1755. All quotations are from the Garland edition.
99. E. Rowe, *Letters*, 3:235–36; and Collyer, *Felicia to Charlotte*, 1:22–23.
100. Staves, *Literary History*, 237–39. For some Shaftesburian passages in the novel, see 1:35, 170, 261, 272.

101. Jerry Beasley calls Lucius "one of the earliest 'men of feeling' as well as one of the first avowed and practicing lovers of nature in eighteenth-century English fiction," *Novels of the 1740s,* 171.

102. Critics have consistently noted that a purpose of the novel is to illustrate Shaftesbury's philosophy. The novel is considerably more didactic and representative of sensibility fiction, cf. Collyer, *Felicia to Charlotte,* 1:142–46, 156, 298–99, 306; many of these passages are about marriage, see 1:143–44, 284–85.

103. Bowerbank calls the forest "a political structure that pitted the people against the king," *Speaking for Nature,* 15, and see her history, 14–18; see also Landry, *Invention of the Countryside,* 2–6.

104. Landry, *Invention of the Countryside,* quotations from 1 and 66, and see her discussion of changing tastes in landscapes, 65–68.

105. McKeon emphasizes that pastoral presupposes people, and this is as important as setting, see "Pastoral Revolution," 275–76. Prescott identifies this as an example of the "mingling of amatory concerns and didactic purposes . . . characteristic of women's fiction of the 1720s in particular," "Debt to Pleasure," 438.

106. The best discussion of this focus in the novel is Hughes, "Early Romantic Novel," 574–78; see also Staves, *Literary History,* 238–39.

107. Collyer, *Felicia to Charlotte,* 1:165; Schofield, *Masking and Unmasking the Female Mind,* treats this episode at length, 95–96.

108. Collyer, *Felicia to Charlotte,* 1:69. Schofield sees the novel as "unmasking" the romance genre and credits Collyer with revitalizing the romance "topos." She also points out realistic elements in the plot, *Masking and Unmasking the Female Mind,* 91–97.

109. P. Carter, *Men and the Emergence of Polite Society,* 45.

110. R. Watts, *Politeness,* 13, 36.

111. For a stimulating account of benevolence, see Landry, "Picturing Benevolence," 150–71.

112. Schellenberg, *Conversational Circle,* quotation from 3. See also, for example, Staves, *Literary History,* 238–41.

113. Clarke, "Soft Passions and Darling Themes," 360, 361.

114. Achinstein, "Romance of the Spirit," 422 (and see this article section, esp. 426).

115. Barker, *Patch-Work Screen* in *Galesia Trilogy,* 140.

116. K. King, "Political Verse and Satire," 213.

117. Johns, *Women's Utopias,* 18–19.

118. Johns calls them "universal," *Women's Utopias,* 19; but Fraser has broader concerns, "Rethinking the Public Sphere," 531.

119. Alnwick MS> 11, Letter 124 and Letter 3, respectively; for statements of independence and protection of her lifestyle, see her letters, *Misc. Works,* 2:111–12, 163–64, 176–77 et passim.

120. Emphasis mine; Clarke, "Soft Passions and Darling Themes," 355.

121. Quoted in Clarke, "Soft Passions and Darling Themes," 355, from *Misc. Works,* 1:lvi.

122. Broome, *Fictive Domains,* 150.

123. Guest, "'These Neuter Somethings,'" 190 and see 191, 193.

124. Although views of these narrators/listeners are debated by critics, I agree with Susan Lanser's suggestion that there is a "subtle rejection of the traveling gentleman's entire narrative enterprise," and I would also call it an "enterprise," *Fictions of Authority,* 227 and 225–30; see also Schellenberg's analysis of *Millenium Hall, Conversational Circle,* 89.

125. Landry, "Picturing Benevolence," 152–53.

126. For a summary of the problems in critical treatment of Fielding's opus because of an inability to go beyond this binary, see Friedman, "Remarks on Richardson," 308–26.

127. Fielding, *Adventures of David Simple*, 21. All quotations are from this edition. I am not considering *The Adventures of David Simple, Volume the Last* (1753) because of its later date of publication. Staves also sees David's story as a philosophical tale, and she gives a useful reading of the theme of oppression, *Literary History*, 253–56. Patricia Meyer Spacks associates David with the naïf, "a stock figure in classic satire," and offers a sophisticated reading of the sentimental novel through *David Simple, Novel Beginnings*, 128, and see 128–45.

128. Guest, "'These Neuter Somethings,'" 180–81.

129. Spacks, *Novel Beginnings*, 133; Johns also quotes this passage in her discussion of creating a community of feeling readers, *Women's Utopias*, 68–70.

130. Friedman, "'To such as are willing to understand,'" 183. Her essay helpfully focuses on the "unity of *purpose*" in Fielding's novels, 182–200.

131. Chartier, *Inscription and Erasure*, 114. Schellenberg notes that in *Volume the Last* Fielding divides the "implied audience" and invites the reader to become part of a community with the author and her characters, *Conversational Circle*, 127–28. I would argue that the talent for taking advantage of readers' ability to read in several ways is one of the distinguishing marks of Fielding's fiction.

132. Friedman, "Remarks on Richardson," 311.

133. Fielding, *Adventures of David Simple*, 132. In her authoritative study of the ladies' companion, Betty Rizzo notes that Fielding consistently presents in her texts this occupation and marriage as "the only two options open to a lone young woman of no fortune" and that she conflates the two "as very similar in their degrading demands," *Companions without Vows*, 43, and see 41–60.

134. Bartolomeo, "Fragile Utopia of Sensibility," 44–45.

135. A number of critics have explicated the anti-patriarchal drive in *David Simple*, cf. Woodward, "Sarah Fielding's Self-Destructing Utopia," 65–81. In contrast, Fielding satirizes and condemns women of fashion and those wealthy enough to ignore or tyrannize the less fortunate.

136. Bartolomeo, "Fragile Utopia of Sensibility," 48. Schellenberg also sees "stress fractures" "visible just beneath the surface" of *David Simple, Conversational Circle*, 23; and Johns describes *Volume the Last* as "exploding" the concept of a utopian community, *Women's Utopias*, 89.

137. Johns, *Women's Utopias*, 75, 85–86.

138. Fielding, *Familiar Letters*, 2:390.

139. Johns, *Women's Utopias*, 68.

140. Schellenberg, *Conversational Circle*, 125–26; her analysis of the failure of the circle is highly pertinent, 125–30.

141. Quoted from *A Journey through Every Stage of Life* by Alessa Johns, *Women's Utopias*, 61; this section has benefitted from her discussion of these three ideologies, 50–63.

142. Lipking, "Fair Originals," 69.

143. Bowerbank, *Speaking for Nature*, 97.

144. On the first Blues' fame, see Eger, *Bluestockings*, esp. 63, 73–74, 79.

145. Staves, *Literary History*, 225. Bannet also notes that Austen inherited women writers'

attempts to "develop models of gentility," but she goes no farther back than Charlotte Lennox, "Theater of Politeness," 89–90.

Conclusion • Lifestyle as Legacy

1. Although Katherine Philips, Anne Finch, Catherine Trotter Cockburn, and a few others were in the virtuous-woman-writer category, none were known for the lifestyle that Rowe developed.
2. Lavoie, *Collecting Women*, 36.
3. Clarke, "Soft Passions and Darling Themes," 356; *Misc. Works*, 2:137.
4. Norma Clarke is analyzing John Duncombe's *The Feminiad, Rise and Fall*, 87.
5. Barbauld, *Verses on Mrs. Rowe, Poems*, 103.
6. Clarke, *Rise and Fall*, 89. The phrase is from John Duncombe's *Feminiad: A Poem* (London, 1754), 17.
7. Clarke, "Bluestocking Fictions," 463.
8. This is not to say, of course, that the example of women like Mary Astell was not critically important.
9. Some excellent studies of the mature characteristics of the Blues are Myers, *Bluestocking Circle*; Eger, "'The noblest commerce of mankind,'" 288–305; Kelly, "General Introduction," ix–liv. An excellent bibliography compiled by Janice Blathwayt is in *Reconsidering the Bluestockings*, 39–57. The notes to this chapter make clear the renewed interest in the Blues.
10. Staves, *Literary History*, 227.
11. Sairio, "Methodological and Practical Aspects," 110.
12. Quoted in Guest, "Bluestocking Feminism," 72–73.
13. Eger, *Bluestockings*, 74; on their fame, see esp. 63, 73–74, 79.
14. Hertford, *To the Countess of Pomfret*, 45–47. The letter to Mary Rich is in Hughes, *Gentle Hertford*, 149–50.
15. This poem is printed in Hughes, *Gentle Hertford*, 131–33.
16. Moore, "Queer Gardens," quotation from 18 June 1728, 52, and see her *Sister Arts*, 29–38.
17. See T. Davis, "What Are Fairies For?" 46–50. She is speaking of nineteenth-century developments and does not mention "beauty"; I am pushing this movement earlier.
18. Moore, *Sister Arts*, 65.
19. Ibid., 45, 65, and see her theorizing of women's collections, 60–65.
20. Myers, *Bluestocking Circle*, 21–44. A list of readings is given on p. 23.
21. Ibid., 37; and Bannet, "Bluestocking Sisters," 34.
22. Eger, "'The noblest commerce of mankind,'" 290. Among those who see an English identity and origin are Heller, "Bluestocking Salons," 61–62.
23. On Lady Miller's gatherings see Backscheider, *Eighteenth-Century Women Poets*, 31–32, 207, 272–73; on Lady Barbara's, see Bannet, "Bluestocking Sisters," 25–55.
24. Eger, "Paper Trails and Eloquent Objects," 129.
25. This quotation continues, "solid in judgement, critical in talk," quoted from Frances Burney in Heller, "Bluestocking Salons," 64.
26. Hughes, *Gentle Hertford*, 148.
27. Haslett, *Pope to Burney, 1714–1779*, 147.
28. E. Carter, *Series of Letters* (21 November 1771), 4:41.

29. E. Carter, *Series of Letters* (29 April 1763), 3:214.
30. Hawley, Introduction to *Elizabeth Carter*, 2:xvii.
31. E. Carter, *Series of Letters* (9 October 1744), 1:75.
32. For their correspondence and differing opinions, see Bannet, "Bluestocking Sisters," 40–42.
33. *Misc. Works*, 2:142, 174–77, 159, respectively. She also expressed some anxiety that Hertford would want the screen, and she even argues that it is a benefit to the town, *Misc. Works*, 2:163.
34. Hughes, *Gentle Hertford*, 149.
35. Included were the duchess, Elizabeth Montagu, Mary Pendarves [Delany], and Mary Howard (Lady Andover), Moore, "Mary Delany and Her Circle," 102; Pointon, "'Surrounded with Brilliants,'" 63–64; and Eger, "Bluestocking Circle," 37.
36. The women's correspondence is filled with progress reports and statements of interest and encouragement; for one example, see Elizabeth Eger's description of the Montagu-Carter correspondence, Introduction to *Elizabeth Montagu*, lix–lxxxii. See Schellenberg on their encouragement of publication, "Bluestocking Women and the Negotiation," 75–80.
37. Bannet, "Bluestocking Sisters," 35–39, quotation from 43. And on the women encouraging each other, see 45–46.
38. Myers, *Bluestocking Circle*, 19–20.
39. Sairio, "Methodological and Practical Aspects," 110, 120. She lists the primary places they lived and visited, 112.
40. Eger, *Bluestockings*, 67.
41. Sairio, "Methodological and Practical Aspects," 117.
42. First published around 1726, it appeared as *The Story of Inkle and Yarrico. A most moving Tale from the Spectator. Attempted in veres by The Right Hon. The countess of* *** (London, 1738), 13–16. In spite of the errors on the title page, it is a generously printed publication.
43. E. Carter, *Series of Letters* (2 August 1748), 1:290.
44. Clarke, "Bluestocking Fictions," 466–67. In this important essay, Clarke speculates on the reasons that Talbot did not do so.
45. Respectively, Clarke, "Bluestocking Fictions," 467; and Myers, *Bluestocking Circle*, 153, 215.
46. Hertford, *Correspondence*, 1:96–97, 179–81, 183, and 3:6–10, 32. The quotation is from 3:32, dated O.S. 19 February 1741 in the text. I am grateful to my research assistant Lacy Marschalk for her research on this correspondence.
47. Kelly, "General Introduction," 1:xlvii.
48. On the Bluestockings, see ibid., 1:xlvii–xlviii.
49. Schellenberg, *Conversational Circle*, 5.
50. Rizzo, "Two Versions of Community," 193.
51. Bigold, "Elizabeth Rowe's Fictional and Familiar Letters," 1–14; K. King, "Elizabeth Singer Rowe's Tactical Use," 171–72; Betty Schellenberg makes the point that manuscript circulation remained an important means of production and dissemination for the Bluestockings, "Bluestocking Women and the Negotiation," 63–83, quotation from 67, and see Montagu calling her letters "public," 69; Schellenberg notes that they were "influenced by Rowe's authorial model," 64.
52. Curran, "Romantic Women Poets," 161, 163.

53. Curran, respectively, "Romantic Women Poets," 161; and "Romantic Poetry," 185–207, quotation from 197.
54. Clarke, "Soft Passions and Darling Themes," 356.
55. Hughes, *Gentle Hertford*, 149.
56. Quoted in Moore, *Sister Arts*, 68.
57. S. Palmer, "'I Prefer Walking,'" 161.
58. Bowerbank, *Speaking for Nature*, 22.
59. Hughes, *Gentle Hertford*, 282; Fuller, *Medicina Gymnastica* quoted in Brailsford, *Sport and Society*, 173. Brailsford gives a brief history of the opinions about the relationship between exercise and health, 161–79. See Fuller, *Medicina Gymnastica*, 1–2, 12–13. I am grateful to my research assistant Benjamin Arnberg for his contributions to this research.
60. Locke, *Correspondence of John Locke*, 2:686–87.
61. Gregory, *Father's Legacy to his Daughters*, 48–49.
62. Rizzo, "Equivocations of Gender and Rank," 70–72; she points out that "a differentiated physical appearance was sought in polite women from girlhood," 71. For typical stress on moderate exercise and even tied to women's menstrual cycles, see Whytt, *Observations on the Nature*, 516–17; this is in the section on headaches.
63. Wallace, *Walking, Literature, and English Culture*, 29. I am grateful to my research assistant Benjamin Arnberg for his research on walking.
64. Norma Clarke argues that the 1740s was a more important decade for Carter than the 1730s, which was the time of her early celebrity. Clarke says, "Her independent spirit gave her the confidence to make up an independent life, one which took courage from the example of Elizabeth Rowe." She points out words that "evoke Rowe's poetry," *Dr. Johnson's Women*, 50, 64.
65. Respectively, *Translated* and *To [Miss D'Aeth]* in Carter, *Poems on Several Occasions* (2nd ed., London, 1766), 53 and 22–25; both of these poems first appeared in the 1762 edition of *Poems on Several Occasions*. Clarke, *Dr. Johnson's Women*, 64–65. I am grateful to my research assistant Elizabeth Kent for her work on this note.
66. E. Carter, *Series of Letters* (29 April 1763), 3:213–14.
67. Locke, *Correspondence of John Locke*, 2:686–87.
68. S. Palmer, "'I Prefer Walking,'" 157. Wallace has a chapter titled "The Results of Destination," *Walking, Literature, and English Culture*.
69. Wallace, *Walking, Literature, and English Culture*, 6–7.
70. Quoted in Myers, *Bluestocking Circle*, 35. The Chelsea Physic Garden began giving herbalizing instruction, and making botanical collections with some scientific underpinnings became increasingly popular.
71. Landry, *Invention of the Countryside*, 208, and see 205–19.
72. Wallace, *Walking, Literature, and English Culture*, 13.
73. Bowerbank, *Speaking for Nature*, 22.
74. Foucault, "Afterword," 208–9, 212.
75. Keeble, *Literary Culture of Nonconformity*, 204, 208.
76. Kelly, "General Introduction," 1:xx–xxi.
77. Eger, *Bluestockings*, 69.
78. Moore, *Sister Arts*, 65.
79. Heller, "Subjectivity Unbound," 217, 219–20; Foucault, "Afterword," 214.

80. Deborah Heller makes a similar argument about Elizabeth Vesey as the Sylph, "Subjectivity Unbound," 217–20. She points out that Vesey was viewed by some as odd and eccentric.
81. Quoted in Clarke, "Soft Passions and Darling Themes," 367.
82. N. Miller, *Subject to Change*, 8.
83. Johns describes this well in her chapter on Sarah Fielding, *Women's Utopias*, 68–73.
84. Starr, "Sentimental Novels," 184. I see more contrasts than similarities between Rowe's work and liftestyle and the Blues. I am closer to Hughes's position on this point, "Early Romantic Novel," 578–79.
85. Quoted in K. King, "Political Verse and Satire," 212. In this essay, King refers to Rowe as the "icon" of the generation of "forward-looking" women who "attached themselves to the new Whig order and advanced a cultural and political agenda," 212.
86. Keeble notes that this is a long-standing characteristic in nonconformist fiction, *Literary Culture of Nonconformity*, 237–39.
87. McCarthy, *Anna Letitia Barbauld*, 131.
88. See McCarthy's account of the early 1790s with Barbauld's responses to new debates over the Test Act, the Birmingham riots, and the death of John Howard, ibid., 302–22, quotations from 33 and 109. Barbauld was a Bluestocking, and the earlier generation's thought marked her own; elements of her character, for instance, followed Epictetus, *ibid.*, 57–58.
89. Clarke, "Soft Passions and Darling Themes," 353. The quotation is from her abstract.
90. Clarke, "Bluestocking Fictions," 468.
91. Guest, *Small Change*, 136.
92. Quotation from Ernst Cassirer in Heller, "Bluestocking Salons," 60.
93. Mills, "Mary, Lady Chudleigh (1656–1710)," 54–55, quotation from 55.
94. Chudleigh, *Poems and Prose*, 45.
95. Chudleigh, *Resolve*, 4.
96. Judith Hawley prints two of them in *Bluestocking Feminism*; she identifies Letter 6 as to Vesey and notes that Vesey seems to have shared the letter with friends who, like herself, felt religious doubt, 2:421–25 and 464n19.
97. Jon Mee discusses the way religion was treated at Bluestocking gatherings and contrasts it to the tradition in Johnson's and Dissenting circles that encouraged "sparks of friction" and "collision of mind with mind." He also notes the differing degrees of tolerance and suspicion of Nonconformists among the leading Bluestockings, "'Severe contentions of friendship,'" 21–39.
98. Lennox, *Life of Harriot Stuart*, 180.
99. Mee, "'Severe contentions of friendship,'" 25.
100. Kelly, "Bluestocking Feminism," 169. See also Bannet, "Bluestocking Sisters," 27–35.
101. Quoted in Bannet, "Bluestocking Sisters," 28.
102. See Mackie, *Market à la Mode*, xv.
103. Keener, *English Dialogues of the Dead*, 97.
104. Review in *Literary Magazine* 6 (15 September–15 October, 1756): 282 (the review prints selections from it that sound much like Rowe's).
105. Johns, *Women's Utopias*, 92. She is speaking specifically of Sarah Scott's writing.
106. K. King, "Elizabeth Singer Rowe's Tactical Use," 174.
107. Defoe, *Augusta Triumphans*, 4.
108. Guest, *Small Change*, 114–15, and see 141–42 on Carter's advice on Montagu regard-

ing what to publish. The translation is printed in Hawley's volume of *Bluestocking Feminism* (vol. 2).

109. Lipking, "Fair Originals," 69. Fielding names an important character "Emilia" in *Familiar Letters*.

110. Taylor, Introduction to "Section 7," 410.

111. Eger, Introduction to *Elizabeth Montagu*, 1:lxi; she is speaking specifically of Montagu and Carter.

112. Eger, "Paper Trails and Eloquent Objects," 110.

113. Achinstein, "Romance of the Spirit," 426, 421; she discusses Song of Songs and heterosexual pleasure in this essay.

114. Kairoff, "Eighteenth-Century Women Poets and Readers," 161.

115. McCarthy, *Anna Letitia Barbauld*, 157.

116. Wallace, *Walking, Literature, and English Culture*, 6; and Braestrup, "Until We Meet Again," 188.

117. Mee, "'Severe contentions of friendship,'" 27; see also Keeble, *Literary Culture of Nonconformity*, 260–62.

118. Guest, *Small Change*, 142–51, quotation from 142.

119. Lennox, *To Death* in *Life of Harriot Stuart*, 179.

120. Guest, *Small Change*, 128.

121. Ibid., 116.

122. Ibid., 121.

123. Quoted in ibid., 125.

124. The quotation is Myers's description of their achievement, *Bluestocking Circle*, 11.

125. MacDonald, *Old Woman Who Lived in a Vinegar Bottle*; Guest, *Small Change*, 128 and 128n62; Gaussen, *Woman of Wit and Wisdom*, 30–38. Gaussen describes the landscape and gardens around Carter's home in Deal.

126. The importance of the elegy for Rowe to understanding Carter has been consistently interpreted as Myers does, *Bluestocking Circle*, 56–57, 59.

127. Augustin, *Eighteenth-Century Female Voices*, 201.

128. Heller, "Subjectivity Unbound," 221.

129. Myers, *Bluestocking Circle*, 44.

130. I have borrowed this insight from O'Brien, "Imperial Georgic," 161.

131. A telling contrast is between these social events and the chaos of Sir Joshua Reynolds's dinner parties, where there were never enough chairs or forks, Wendorf, *Sir Joshua Reynolds*, 49–52.

132. Fraser, "Rethinking the Public Sphere," 527.

133. Ibid., 527–28, and see also 534–35.

134. Bowerbank, *Speaking for Nature*, 97. Bowerbank illustrates this insight with Talbot, 97–105.

135. Jürgen Habermas formulated the concept of the authentic public sphere as the space where private people come together as a public; perhaps because we are a democracy, the distinction between it and the public "sphere" of state and court is seldom invoked, nor do critics usually remember that "private" encompassed not only the "conjugal family's internal space" but also "civil society . . . of commodity exchange and social labor," *Structural Transformation of the Public Sphere*, 27, 30.

136. R. Watts, *Politeness*, 39–40. Bannet argues that "politeness was not essential in high

rank" and demonstrates its relationship to cultural capital in transatlantic fiction, "Theater of Politeness," 73–92, quotation from 77.

137. Kelly, "Bluestocking Feminism," 163.
138. Kelly, "General Introduction," 1:x, xlvii.
139. Curran, "Romantic Women Poets," 147.

Primary Sources

Addison, Joseph. See *Spectator*.
Anderdon, James Hughes. *Collectanea Biographica being an Historical and Pictorial Biography of Illustrious, Celebrated and Remarkable Persons*. Vol. 89. 105 vols. London, 1853.
Aubin, Penelope. *The Life and Adventures of the Lady Lucy*. 1726; New York: Garland, 1973.
———. *The Life and Amorous Adventures of Lucinda*. London, 1722.
———. *The Life of Charlotta Du Pont, An English Lady*. London, 1723.
———. *The Noble Slaves: or, The Lives and Adventures of Two Lords and Two Ladies*. London, 1722.
———. *The Strange Adventure of the Count de Vinevil and His Family*. In *Popular Fiction by Women, 1660–1730: An Anthology*, edited by Paula R. Backscheider and John J. Richetti. Oxford: Clarendon, 1996.
Bannerman, Anne. *Poems by Anne Bannerman*. Edinburgh, 1800.
Barbauld, Anna Laetitia. *Correspondence of Samuel Richardson*. London, 1804.
———. *On a Lady's Writing*. London, 1773. In *British Women Poets of the Long Eighteenth Century: An Anthology*, edited by Paula R. Backscheider and Catherine E. Ingrassia, 786–88. Baltimore: Johns Hopkins Univ. Press, 2009.
———. *Poems*. London, 1773.
———. *The Poems of Anna Letitia Barbauld*. Edited by William McCarthy and Elizabeth Kraft. Athens: Univ. of Georgia Press, 1994.
Barker, Jane. *Galesia Trilogy and Selected Manuscript Poems of Jane Barker*. Edited by Carol Shiner Wilson. New York: Oxford Univ. Press, 1997.
———. *Love Intrigues*. In *Popular Fiction by Women, 1660–1730: An Anthology*, edited by Paula R. Backscheider and John J. Richetti. Oxford: Clarendon, 1996.
Bayle, Pierre. *A General Dictionary, Historical and Critical*. Vol. 8. 10 vols. London, 1734.
Beaumont, Jeanne-Marie Le Prince de. *Magazin des Enfans, or The Young Misses Magazine*. London, 1757.
Behn, Aphra. *Love Letters between a Nobleman and His Sister*. New York: Viking-Virago, 1987.
———. *The Lover's Watch; or, The Art of Making Love*. London, 1686.
———. *Poems on Several Occasions, with A Voyage to the Island of Love*. London, 1684.
———. *The Works of Aphra Behn*. Edited by Janet Todd. 7 vols. Columbus: Ohio State Univ. Press, 1992.
———. *The Younger Brother, or The Amorous Jilt*. Edited by Charles Gildon. London, 1696.

Brett, Peter. *Brett's Miscellany*. Dublin, 1748.
Brooke, Frances. *The History of Emily Montague*. Edited by Lorraine McMullen. Toronto: McClelland & Stewart, 1995.
Brown, Tom. *Letters from the Dead to the Living*. 5th ed. London, 1708.
Burnet, Gilbert. *Some Passages of the Life and Death of the Right Honourable John Earl of Rochester*. 1680; Hildesheim, Germany: Georg Olms Verlagbuchhandlung, 1968.
Burney, Frances. *Cecilia, or Memoirs of an Heiress*. 1988; Oxford: Oxford Univ. Press, 1992.
———. *Early Diary of Frances Burney, 1768–1778: with a Selection from her correspondence, and from the Journals of her Sisters Susan and Charlotte Burney*. 2 vols. London, 1889.
Carter, Elizabeth. *Answers to Objections Concerning the Christian Religion*. In *Bluestocking Feminism: Writings of the Bluestocking Circle, 1738–1785*, edited by Gary Kelly. Vol. 2, *Elizabeth Carter*, edited by Judith Hawley, 421–25. London: Pickering & Chatto, 1999.
———. *Poems on Several Occasions*. 2nd ed. London, 1766.
———. *A Series of Letters between Mrs Elizabeth Carter and Miss Catherine Talbot from the Year 1741 to 1770*. Edited by Montagu Pennington. 4 vols. London, 1809.
Caumont de La Force, Charlotte-Rose. *Les Contes des Contes*. Paris, 1698.
———. *Les fées: Contes des Contes*. Paris, 1725.
Choice of the best poetical pieces of the most eminent English poets. 6 vols. Vienna, 1783.
Chudleigh, Lady Mary. *The Poems and Prose of Mary, Lady Chudleigh*. Edited by Margaret J. M. Ezell. New York: Oxford Univ. Press, 1993.
———. *The Resolve*. In *Eighteenth-Century Women Poets*, edited by Roger Lonsdale. Oxford: Oxford Univ. Press, 1989.
Cockburn, Catharine Trotter. *The Works of Mrs. Catharine Cockburn*. Edited by Thomas Birch. 2 vols. London, 1751.
Collyer, Mary. *Felicia to Charlotte*. 1744; New York: Garland, 1974.
Colman, George. *The Fairy Prince: A Masque*. London, 1771.
Congreve, William. Preface to *Incognita: or Love and Duty Reconciled: A Novel*. Edited by H. F. B. Brett-Smith. New York: Houghton Mifflin, 1922.
Cooper, Sir Anthony Ashley, 3rd Earl of Shaftesbury. *Characteristics of Men, Manners, Opinions, Times*. Edited by John M. Robertson. 2 vols. London: Grant Richards, 1900.
———. *The Moralists, A Philosophical Rhapsody. Being a Recital of Certain Conversations upon Natural and Moral Subjects*. London, 1709.
Cowper, William. *The Poems of William Cowper*. Edited by John D. Baird and Charles Ryskamp. 3 vols. Oxford: Clarendon, 1980.
d'Aulnoy, Marie-Catherine. *A Collection of Novels and Tales of the Fairies, Written by that Celebrated Wit of France, the Countess d'Anois*. 2 vols. London, 1721.
———. *A Collection of Novels and Tales of the Fairies, Written by that Celebrated Wit of France, the Countess d'Anois*. 3 vols. London, 1728.
———. *The Diverting Works of the Countess d'Anois*. London, 1715.
———. *The History of Adolphus, Prince of Russia; and the Princess of Happiness With a Collection of Songs and Love-Verses. By Several Hands. To which is added, Two Letters in Verse from Sir. G.E. to the E. Of M. With Mr. D. [sic] Answer to them*. London, 1691.
———. *History of the Earl of Warwick*. London, 1708.
———. *Hypolitus, Earl of Douglas*. 1708; New York: Garland, 1973.
———. *Le Cabinet des fées*. Vol. 2. 41 vols. Geneva, 1785.

———. *Les Contes des fées*. 4 vols. 1697. Translated as *The History of the Tales of the Fairies*. London, 1716.

———. *Les Contes nouveaux ou les des fées à la mode*. 4 vols. Paris, 1698.

———. *Memoirs of the Court of England*. London, 1707.

———. *Tales of the Fairies*. London, 1699.

Davys, Mary. *The Cousins: A Novel*. In *The Works of Mary Davys*. 2 vols. London, 1725.

———. *Familiar Letters betwixt a Gentleman and a Lady*. In *The Works of Mrs. Davys*. 2 vols. London, 1725.

———. *The Reform'd Coquet, Familiar Letters Betwixt a Gentleman and a Lady, and The Accomplished Rake*. Edited by Martha F. Bowden. Lexington: Univ. Press of Kentucky, 1999.

———. *The Works of Mrs. Davys*. London, 1725.

De Castelnau, Henriette-Julie, Comtesse de Murat. *Contes de fées*. Paris, 1698.

———. *Les Nouveaux Contes des fées*. Paris, 1710.

Defoe, Daniel. *Augusta Triumphans*. London, 1728.

———. *An Essay on the History and Reality of Apparitions*. Edited by Kit Kincade. New York: AMS Press, 2007.

———. *Moll Flanders*. Edited by G. A. Starr. Oxford: Oxford Univ. Press, 1971.

———. *Religious Courtship*. London, 1722.

———. *Robinson Crusoe*. Edited by Michael Shinagel. 2nd ed. New York: W. W. Norton, 1994.

———. *Roxana*. Edited by Jane Jack. London: Oxford Univ. Press, 1964.

[Defoe, Daniel]. *Madagascar: or, Robert Drury's Journal*. London, 1729.

[Defoe, Daniel]. *A True Relation of the Apparition of Mrs. Veal*. London, 1706.

De La Force, Charlotte-Rose Caumont. *Les Contes des Contes*. Paris, 1698.

———. *Les feés: Contes des Contes*. Paris, 1725.

Drayton, Michael. *The Works of Michael Drayton*. Edited by J. William Hebel. 5 vols. Oxford: Shakespeare Head, 1932.

Dryden, John. "Discourse concerning the Original and Progress of Satire." In *The Works of John Dryden*, edited by H. T. Swedenberg Jr. Vol. 4, *Poems, 1693–1696*, edited by A. B. Chambers and William Frost, 3–90. 20 vols. Berkeley: Univ. of California Press, 1974.

Duncombe, John. *The Feminiad. A Poem*. London, 1754.

Fielding, Sarah. *The Adventures of David Simple*. Edited by Peter Sabor. 1744; Lexington: Univ. Press of Kentucky, 1998.

———. *The Adventures of David Simple. Volume the Last*. Edited by Peter Sabor. 1753; Lexington: Univ. Press of Kentucky, 1998.

———. *Familiar Letters between the Principal Characters in David Simple*. 2 vols. London, 1747.

———. *The Governess*. Edited by Candace Ward. 1749; Peterborough: Broadview, 2005.

Finch, Anne. *The Anne Finch Wellesley Manuscript Poems*. Edited by Barbara McGovern and Charles H. Hinnant. Athens: Univ. of Georgia Press, 1998.

———. *The Poems of Anne Countess of Winchilsea*. Edited by Myra Reynolds. Chicago: Univ. of Chicago Press, 1903.

Fuller, Francis. *Medicina Gymnastica*. London, 1705.

Gibbons, Thomas. *Memoirs of Eminently Pious Women*. Vol. 2. 2 vols. London, 1777.

Gildon, Charles. *The Post-Boy Robb'd of his Mail*. 2nd ed. London, 1706.

———. *The Post-Man Robb'd of his Mail*. Edited by Malcolm Bosse. 1719; New York: Garland, 1972.
Goldsmith, Oliver. *The Vicar of Wakefield*. In *The Collected Works of Oliver Goldsmith*. Vol. 4. Edited by Arthur Friedman. 5 vols. Oxford: Clarendon, 1966.
Granger, James. Continued by Mark Noble, *A Biographical History of England*. 3 vols. Extra Illustrated. London, 1806.
Gregory, John. *A Father's Legacy to his Daughters*. 2nd ed. London, 1774.
Haywood, Eliza. *The History of Miss Betsy Thoughtless*. Edited by Christine Blouch. Peterborough: Broadview, 1998.
———. *The Invisible Spy*. In *Fiction and Drama of Eliza Haywood*, edited by Paula R. Backscheider. Oxford: Oxford Univ. Press, 1999.
———. *Love in Excess*. Edited by David Oakleaf. Peterborough: Broadview, 1994.
Hertford. *See* Seymour, Frances.
Holt, Jane Wiseman. *A Fairy Tale Inscrib'd, to the Honourable Mrs. W——, with Other Poems*. London, 1717.
Hull, Thomas. *The Fairy Favour. A Masque*. London, 1767.
Janeway, James. *A Token for Children*. London, 1676.
Jones, Mary. *Miscellanies in Prose and Verse*. Oxford, 1750.
King, Sophia. *The Dreams of Youth*. In *Trifles of Helicon. By Charlotte and Sophia King*. London, 1798.
The Ladies Complete Letter-Writer; teaching the art of inditing letters. London, 1763.
Lennox, Charlotte. *The Life of Harriot Stuart, Written by Herself*. Edited by Susan K. Howard. 1750; Madison: Fairleigh Dickinson Univ. Press, 1995.
Little, Janet. *The Poetical Works of Janet Little*. Air, 1792.
Locke, John. *The Correspondence of John Locke*. Edited by E. S. de Beer. 8 vols. Oxford: Clarendon, 1976.
———. *An Essay concerning Human Understanding*. Oxford: Oxford Univ. Press, 1975.
Lonsdale, Roger, ed. *Eighteenth-Century Women Poets*. Oxford: Oxford Univ. Press, 1989.
MacDonald, Margaret Read. *The Old Woman Who Lived in a Vinegar Bottle: A British Fairy Tale*. Little Rock, AR: August House LittleFolk, 1995.
Manley, Delarivière. *The Power of Love: In Seven Novels*. London, 1720.
Masters, Mary. *Familiar Letters and Poems on Several Occasions*. London, 1755.
Milton, John. *Paradise Lost*. In *John Milton: Complete Poems and Major Prose*, edited by Merritt Y. Hughes. New York: Odyssey Press, 1957.
More, Hannah. *Sensibility: A Poem*. In *Sacred Dramas: Chiefly Intended for Young Persons; The Subjects Taken from the Bible*. London, 1782.
Murat, Henriette-Julie de Castelnau, comtesse de. *Contes de fées*. Paris, 1698.
———. *Les Nouveaux Contes des fées*. Paris, 1710.
[Newbery, John.] *The History of Little Goody Two-Shoes*. London, 1762.
Ovid's Epistles: with his Amours. London, 1729.
Perrault, Charles. *Histories, or Tales of Past Times*. London, 1729.
Piozzi, Hester Thrale. *The Two Fountains. A Faery Tale in Three Acts*. Edited by Stuart Sherman and Margaret Anne Doody. Philadelphia: Johnsonians, 1994.
Poetical Miscellanies; consisting of original poems and translations. By the best hands. Publish'd by Mr. Steele. London [1714].

Pope, Alexander. *The Twickenham Edition of the Poems of Alexander Pope*. Edited by John Butt. London: Methuen, 1961.
Prior, Matthew. *The Literary Works of Matthew Prior*. Edited by H. Bunker Wright and Monroe K. Spears. 2 vols. Oxford: Clarendon, 1959.
———. *Poems on Several Occasions*. London, 1718.
Richardson, Samuel. *Clarissa*. 8 vols. 3rd ed. 1751; New York: AMS, 1990.
Robin Goodfellow: a fairy tale. Written by a Fairy. London, 1770.
Rogers, Charles. *Monuments and Monumental Inscriptions in Scotland*. 2 vols. London, 1871.
Rowe, Elizabeth Singer. *Devout Exercises of the Heart*. 2nd ed. Edited by Isaac Watts. London, 1738.
———. *Divine Hymns and Poems on Several Occasions . . . By Philomela, and Several Other Ingenious Persons*. London, 1704.
———. *Friendship in Death*. New York: Garland, 1972.
———. *Letters Moral and Entertaining*. In *Friendship in Death*. New York: Garland, 1972.
———. *Miscellaneous Works in Prose and Verse of Mrs. Elizabeth Rowe*. Edited by Henry Grove and Theophilus Rowe. 2 vols. London, 1739.
———. *Philomela; or, Poems by Mrs. Elizabeth Singer, now Rowe*. London, 1737.
———. *Poems on Several Occasions*. 2 vols., bound as one. London, 1696.
———. *The Poetical Beauties of the Pious and Ingenious Mrs. Elizabeth Rowe*. London, 1770.
———. *The Poetry of Elizabeth Singer Rowe (1674–1737)*. Edited by Madeleine Forell Marshall. Lewiston: Edwin Mellen Press, 1987.
Samber, Robert. "Dedication to the Countess of Granville." In Charles Perrault, *Histories, or tales of past times*. London, 1729.
Scott, Sarah. *A Description of Millenium Hall*. Edited by Gary Kelly. Peterborough, ON: Broadview, 1995.
Seymour, Frances, Countess of Hertford. *Correspondence between Frances, Countess of Hertford (Afterwards Duchess of Somerset), and Henrietta Louisa, Countess of Pomfret, between the Years 1738 and 1741*. Edited by William Bingley. 3 vols. London: Richard Philips, 1805.
———. *Letter to the Honorable Mrs. Knight*. In *The Gentle Hertford: Her Life and Letters* by Helen Sard Hughes, 131–33. New York: Macmillan, 1940.
———. *The Story of Inkle and Yarrico. A most moving tale from the* Spectator. London, 1738.
———. *To the Countess of Pomfret: Life at Richkings*. In *British Women Poets of the Long Eighteenth Century: An Anthology*, edited by Paula R. Backscheider and Catherine E. Ingrassia. 45–47. Baltimore: Johns Hopkins Univ. Press, 2009.
Shaftesbury. *See* Cooper, Anthony Ashley.
Sherwood, Mary Martha. *The Governess; or, The Little Female Academy*. Wellington, Salop, 1820.
Spectator. Edited by Donald Bond. 5 vols. 1965. Reprint, Oxford: Clarendon, 1987.
Steele, Richard. *See Poetical Miscellanies*.
Swift, Jonathan. *The Correspondence of Jonathan Swift*. Vol. 2, *1714–1723*. Edited by Harold Williams. 5 vols. Oxford: Oxford Univ. Press, 1963.
Talbot, Catherine. *Essays on Various Subjects*. London, 1772.
———. *A Series of Letters between Mrs Elizabeth Carter and Miss Catherine Talbot from the Year 1741 to 1770*. Edited by Montagu Pennington. 4 vols. London, 1809.
Tate, Nahum. *Miscellanea Sacra: Or, Poems on Divine and Moral Subjects*. London, 1696.

Thomson, James. *The Seasons.* Edited by James Sambrook. Oxford: Oxford Univ. Press, 1981.

———. *Spring. A Poem.* London, 1728.

Tollet, Elizabeth. *Poems on Several Occasions.* London, 1724.

Tuite, Eliza. *Poems by Lady Tuite.* London, 1796.

Vertue, George. *A Description of Four Ancient Paintings, Being Historical Portraitures of Royal Branches of the Crown of England.* [London, 1740].

Villars, Abbé Nicolas-Pierre-Henri de Montfaucon de. *The Diverting History of the Count de Gabalis.* 2nd ed. London, 1714.

W., F. N. "To Madam Aphra Behn on the Publication of Her Poems." In *Poems on Several Occasions, With a Voyage to the Island of Love* by Aphra Behn, n.p. London, 1684.

Walpole, Horace. *A Catalogue of Engravers, Who Have Been Born or Resided in England.* 2nd ed. Vol. 5. 5 vols. London, 1765.

Walsh, Octavia. *On Solitude.* In *British Women Poets of the Long Eighteenth Century,* edited by Paula R. Backscheider and Catherine E. Ingrassia, 339–40. Baltimore: Johns Hopkins Univ. Press, 2009.

———. *Poems upon Divine and Moral Subjects.* London, 1716.

Watts, Isaac, ed. *Devout Exercises of the Heart.* 2nd ed. London, 1738.

———. *Horae Lyricae.* London, 1709.

Wharton, Anne. *Penelope to Ulysses.* In *Ovid's Epistles: with his Amours.* London, 1729.

Wesley, John. *The Journal of the Rev. John Wesley, A. M.* Edited by Nehemiah Curnock. 8 vols. London: Epworth Press, 1938.

Whytt, Robert. *Observations on the Nature, Causes, and Cure of those Disorders which have been commonly called Nervous Hypochondriac or Hysteric.* Edinburgh, 1765.

Young, Edward. *The Correspondence of Edward Young, 1683–1765.* Edited by Henry Pettit. Oxford: Clarendon, 1971.

———. *Love of Fame, the Universal Passion.* 2nd ed. London, 1728.

———. *A Paraphrase on Part of the Book of Job.* London, 1719.

———. *A Poem on the Last Day.* Oxford, 1713.

———. *A Vindication of Providence: or a True Estimate of Human Life, In which the Passions are considered in a New Light.* London, 1728.

EIGHTEENTH-CENTURY PERIODICALS ARE CITED IN THE NOTES.

Secondary Sources

Achinstein, Sharon. "'Pleasure by Description': Elizabeth Singer Rowe's Enlightened Milton." In *Milton and the Grounds of Contention,* edited by Mark Kelly, Michael Lieb, and John Shawcross, 64–87. Pittsburgh: Duquesne Univ. Press, 2003.

———. "Romance of the Spirit: Female Sexuality and Religious Desire in Early Modern England." *English Literary History* 69, no. 2 (2002): 413–38.

Althusser, Louis. *For Marx.* London: Allen Lane, 1969.

Anderson, Misty G. "Tactile Places: Materializing Desire in Margaret Cavendish and Jane Barker." *Textual Practice* 13, no. 2 (1999): 329–52.

Andreadis, Harriette. *Sappho in Early Modern England: Female Same-Sex Literary Erotics, 1550–1714.* Chicago: Univ. of Chicago Press, 2001.

Armstrong, Nancy. *How Novels Think: The Limits of Individualism from 1719–1900.* New York: Columbia Univ. Press, 2005.

Augustin, Sabine. *Eighteenth-Century Female Voices: Education and the Novel.* Frankfurt: Peter Lang, 2005.

Backscheider, Paula R. *Daniel Defoe: His Life.* Baltimore: Johns Hopkins Univ. Press, 1989.

———. *Eighteenth-Century Women Poets and Their Poetry.* Baltimore: Johns Hopkins Univ. Press, 2005.

———. "Elizabeth Singer Rowe: Lifestyle as Legacy." In *New Contexts for Eighteenth-Century British Fiction,* edited by Christopher D. Johnson, 41–65. Newark: Univ. of Delaware Press, 2011.

———. "Fashioning Novels, Novelizing Fashions." In *Eighteenth-Century Genre and Culture: Serious Reflections on Occasional Forms,* edited by Dennis Todd and Cynthia Wall, 190–217. Newark: Univ. of Delaware Press, 2001.

———. "Hanging On and Hanging In: Women's Struggle to Participate in Public Sphere Debate." In *Everyday Revolutions: Eighteenth-Century Women Transforming the Public and Private,* edited by Diane Boyd and Marta Kvande, 30–66. Newark: Univ. of Delaware Press, 2008.

———. "Literary Culture as Immediate Reality." In *A Companion to The Eighteenth-Century English Novel and Culture,* edited by Paula R. Backscheider and Catherine E. Ingrassia, 504–38. Oxford: Blackwell, 2005.

———. *Spectacular Politics: Theatrical Power and Mass Culture in Early Modern England.* Baltimore: Johns Hopkins Univ. Press, 1993.

———. "The Story of Eliza Haywood's Novels: Caveats and Questions." In *The Passionate Fictions of Eliza Haywood,* edited by Kirsten Saxton and Rebecca Bocchicchio. Lexington: Univ. Press of Kentucky, 2000.

Backscheider, Paula R., and Catherine E. Ingrassia, eds. *British Women Poets of the Long Eighteenth Century.* Baltimore: Johns Hopkins Univ. Press, 2009.

Backscheider, Paula R., and John J. Richetti, eds. *Popular Fiction by Women, 1660–1730: An Anthology.* Oxford: Clarendon, 1996.

Baer, Joel H. "Penelope Aubin and the Pirates of Madagascar: Biographical Notes and Documents." *Eighteenth-Century Women* 1 (2001): 49–62.

Baine, Rodney. *Daniel Defoe and the Supernatural.* Athens: Univ. of Georgia Press, 1968.

Ballaster, Ros. *Seductive Forms: Women's Amatory Fiction from 1684 to 1740.* Oxford: Clarendon, 1992.

Bannet, Eve Tavor. "The Bluestocking Sisters: Women's Patronage, Millenium Hall, and 'The Visible Providence of a Country.'" *Eighteenth-Century Life* 30, no. 1 (2006): 25–55.

———. *Empire of Letters; Letter Manuals and Transatlantic Correspondence, 1688–1820.* Cambridge: Cambridge Univ. Press, 2005.

———. "The Theater of Politeness in Charlotte Lennox's British-American Novels." *Novel* 33, no. 1 (1999): 73–92.

Barber, Tabitha. *Portrait of a Seventeenth-Century Painter, Her Family, and Her Studio.* In Catalogue for the Geffrye Museum, 1999–2000.

Bartolomeo, Joseph F. "A Fragile Utopia of Sensibility: *David Simple.*" In *Gender and Utopia in the Eighteenth Century,* edited by Nicole Pohl and Brenda Tooley, 39–52. Hampshire, UK: Ashgate, 2007.

Batchelor, Jennie. "The 'latent seeds of coquetry': Amatory Fiction and the 1750s Novel." In *Masters of the Marketplace: British Women Novelists of the 1750s,* edited by Susan Carlile, 145–64. Bethleham: Lehigh Univ. Press, 2011.

Beale, Hazel. "Framing the Fairy Tale: French Fairy Tales and Frame Narratives 1690–1700." In *Framed! Essays in French Studies*, edited by Lucy Bolton et al., 73–90. Oxford: Peter Lang, 2007.

Beasley, Jerry. *Novels of the 1740s*. Athens: Univ. of Georgia Press, 1982.

———. "Politics and Moral Idealism: The Achievement of Some Early Women Novelists." In *Fetter'd or Free? British Women Novelists, 1670–1815*, edited by Mary Anne Schofield and Cecilia Macheski, 216–36. Athens: Ohio Univ. Press, 1986.

Beattie, John M. *The English Court in the Reign of George I*. Cambridge: Cambridge Univ. Press, 1967.

Bending, Stephen. "A Natural Revolution? Garden Politics in Eighteenth-Century England." In *Refiguring Revolutions: Aesthetics and Politics from the English Revolution to the Romantic Revolution*, edited by Kevin Sharpe and Steven N. Zwicker, 241–66. Berkeley: Univ. of California Press, 1998.

Benveniste, Émile. "La nature des pronoms." In *For Roman Jakobson: Essays on the Occasion of His Sixtieth Birthday; 11 October 1956*, compiled by Morris Halle, Horace G. Lunt, Hugh Mclean, and Cornelis H. Van Schooneveld, 34–37. The Hague: Mouton, 1956.

Bermingham, Ann. *Landscape and Ideology: The English Rustic Tradition, 1740–1860*. Berkeley: Univ. of California Press, 1986.

Bigold, Melanie. "Elizabeth Rowe's Fictional and Familiar Letters: Exemplarity, Enthusiasm, and the Production of Posthumous Meaning." *British Journal for Eighteenth-Century Studies* 29, no. 1 (2006): 1–14. (The name of the journal is now *Journal for Eighteenth Century Studies*).

Bingley, William. Introduction to *Correspondence between Frances, Countess of Hertford (Afterwards Duchess of Somerset), and Henrietta Louisa, Countess of Pomfret, between the Years 1738 and 1741*. Edited by William Bingley. 3 vols. London: Richard Philips, 1805.

Birberick, Anne. "Changing Places: d'Aulnoy's *Le Nouveau gentilhomme bourgeois*." In *Intersections. Actes du 35e congrès annuel de la North American Society for Seventeenth Century French Literature, Dartmouth College, 8–10 mai 2003*, edited by Faith E. Beasley and Kathleen Wine, 285–94. Tübingen: Narr, 2005.

Black, Jeremy. *The Hanoverians: The History of a Dynasty*. London: Palgrave Macmillan, 2004.

Blamires, David. "From Madame d'Aulnoy to Mother Bunch: Popularity and the Fairy Tale." In *Popular Children's Literature in Britain*, edited by Julia Briggs, Dennis Butts, and M. O. Grenby, 69–86. Aldershot, UK: Ashgate, 2008.

Blathwayt, Janice. "A Bluestocking Bibliography." In *Reconsidering the Bluestockings*, edited by Nicole Pohl and Betty Schellenberg, 39–57. San Marino, CA: Huntington Library Press, 2003.

Bosse, Malcolm. Introduction to *The Post-Man robb'd of his Mail*. New York: Garland, 1972.

Bottigheimer, Ruth. "Fairy Tales and Fables." Encyclopedia of Children and Childhood in History and Society. www.faqs.org/childhood.

———. *Fairy Tales: A New History*. Albany: State Univ. of New York Press, 2009.

———. "France's First Fairy Tales: The Restoration and Rise Narratives of *Les facetieuses nuictz du Seigneur Francois Straparole*." *Marvels and Tales* 19, no. 1 (2005): 17–31.

Bourdieu, Pierre. "Artistic Taste and Cultural Capital." In *Culture and Society: Contemporary Debates*, edited by Jeffrey C. Alexander and Steven Seidman, 205–15. Cambridge: Cambridge Univ. Press, 1990.

———. *Distinction: A Social Critique of the Judgement of Taste.* Translated by Richard Nice. Cambridge, MA: Harvard Univ. Press, 1984.

Bowden, Martha. "Mary Davys: Self-Presentation and the Woman Writer's Reputation in the Early Eighteenth Century." *Women's Writing* 3, no. 1 (1996): 17–33.

———, ed. *The Reformed Coquet.* Lexington: Univ. Press of Kentucky, 1999.

Bowerbank, Sylvia. *Speaking for Nature: Women and Ecologies in Early Modern England.* Baltimore: Johns Hopkins Univ. Press, 2004.

Bowers, Toni. *Force or Fraud: British Seduction Stories and the Problem of Resistance, 1660–1760.* Oxford: Oxford Univ. Press, 2011.

Boyd, Diane, and Marta Kvande, eds. *Everyday Revolutions: Eighteenth-Century Women Transforming Public and Private.* Newark: Univ. of Delaware Press, 2008.

Braestrup, Kate. "Until We Meet Again." *Good Housekeeping* 251, no. 5 (November 2010): 187–95.

Brailsford, Dennis. *Sport and Society: Elizabeth to Anne.* London: Routledge & K. Paul, 1969.

Brant, Clare. *Eighteenth-Century Letters and British Culture.* Houndmills, UK: Palgrave Macmillan, 2006.

Bree, Linda. *Sarah Fielding.* New York: Twayne Publishers, 1996.

Brewer, John. "'The Most Polite Age and the Most Vicious': Attitudes towards Culture as a Commodity, 1660–1800." In *The Consumption of Culture, 1600–1800: Image, Object Text,* edited by Ann Bermingham and John Brewer, 341–61. New York: Routledge, 1995.

———. *The Pleasures of the Imagination: English Culture in the Eighteenth Century.* Chicago: Univ. Chicago Press, 1997.

Briggs, Katharine M. *The Anatomy of Puck: An Examination of Fairy Beliefs among Shakespeare's Contemporaries and Successors.* London: Routledge & Kegan Paul, 1959.

Broome, Judith. *Fictive Domains: Body, Landscape, and Nostalgia, 1717–1770.* Lewisburg, PA: Bucknell Univ. Press, 2007.

Bryson, Anna. *From Courtesy to Civility. Changing Codes of Conduct in Early Modern England.* Oxford: Oxford Univ. Press, 1998.

Buczkowski, Paul. "The First Precise English Translation of Madame d'Aulnoy's Fairy Tales." *Marvels and Tales* 23, no. 1 (2009): 59–78.

Byatt, A. S. "Fairy Stories, The Djinn in the Nightingale's Eye." www.asbyatt.com/Onherself.aspx.

———. "The Great Green Worm." In *Wonder Tales,* edited by Marina Warner. London: Chatto & Windus, 1994.

Capp, Bernard. "George Wharton, *Bellum Hybernicale,* and the Cause of Irish Freedom." *English Historical Review* 112, no. 447 (1997): 671–77.

Carter, Philip. *Men and the Emergence of Polite Society, Britain 1660–1800.* London: Longman, 2001.

Casanova, Jorge. "'Hell in epitomy': Jane Barker's Visions and Recreations." In *Re-Shaping the Genres: Restoration Women Writers,* edited by Zenon Luis-Martinez and Jorge Figueroa-Dorrego, 67–96. Bern: Peter Lang, 2003.

Chapman, Clayton. "Benjamin Colman and Philomela." *New England Quarterly* 42, no. 2 (1969): 214–31.

Chartier, Roger. *Inscription and Erasure: Literature and Written Culture from the Eleventh to the Eighteenth Century*. Translated by Arthur Goldhammer. Philadelphia: Univ. of Pennsylvania Press, 2007.

Citton, Yves. "Fairy Poetics: Revisiting French Fairy Tales as (Post)Modern Literary Machines." *Eighteenth-Century Studies* 39, no. 4 (2006): 549–55.

Clarke, Norma. "Bluestocking Fictions: Devotional Writings, Didactic Literature and the Imperative of Female Improvement." In *Women, Gender, and Enlightenment*, edited by Sarah Knott and Barbara Taylor, 460–73. Houndmills, UK: Palgrave Macmillan, 2005.

———. *Dr. Johnson's Women*. London: Hambledon & London, 2000.

———. *The Rise and Fall of the Woman of Letters*. London: Pimlico, 2004.

———. "Soft Passions and Darling Themes: From Elizabeth Singer Rowe (1674–1737) to Elizabeth Carter (1717–1806)." *Women's Writing* 7, no. 3 (2000): 353–71.

Clayton, Timothy. *The English Print, 1688–1802*. New Haven, CT: Yale Univ. Press, 1997.

Conway, Alison. *The Protestant Whore: Courtesan Narrative and Religious Controversy in England, 1680–1750*. Toronto: Univ. of Toronto Press, 2010.

Cook, Elizabeth Heckendorn. *Epistolary Bodies: Gender and Genre in the Eighteenth-Century Republic of Letters*. Stanford: Stanford Univ. Press, 1996.

Coombs, Katherine. *The Portrait Miniature in England*. London: Victoria and Albert Publications, 1998.

Cope, Joseph. "The Experience of Survival during the 1641 Irish Rebellion." *Historical Journal* 46, no. 2 (2003): 295–316.

Crawford, Patricia. "The Challenges to Patriarchalism: How Did the Revolution Affect Women?" In *Revolution and Restoration: England in the 1650s*, edited by J. S. Morrill, 112–28. London: Collins & Brown, 1992.

Curran, Stuart. "Romantic Poetry: The I Altered." In *Romanticism and Feminism*, edited by Anne K. Mellor, 185–207. Bloomington: Indiana Univ. Press, 1988.

———. "Romantic Women Poets: Inscribing the Self." In *Women's Poetry in the Enlightenment: The Making of a Canon, 1730–1820*, edited by Isobel Armstrong and Virginia Blain, 145–66. Houndmills, UK: Macmillan, 1999.

Dacome, Lucia. "Noting the Mind: Commonplace Books and the Pursuit of the Self in Eighteenth-Century Britain." *Journal of the History of Ideas* 65, no. 4 (2004): 603–25.

David, Alun. " 'The Story of Semiramis': An Oriental Tale in Elizabeth Rowe's *The History of Joseph*." *Women's Writing* 4, no. 1 (1997): 91–101.

Davidson, Jenny. *Hypocrisy and the Politics of Politeness: Manners and Morals from Locke to Austen*. Cambridge: Cambridge Univ. Press, 2004.

Davis, Lennard J. *Factual Fictions: The Origins of the English Novel*. Philadelphia: Univ. of Pennsylvania Press, 1996.

Davis, Tracy C. "What Are Fairies For?" In *The Performing Century: Nineteenth-Century Theatre's History*, edited by Tracy C. Davis and Peter Holland, 32–59. Houndmills, UK: Palgrave Macmillan, 2007.

Day, Robert Adams. *Told in Letters: Epistolary Fiction before Richardson*. Ann Arbor: Univ. of Michigan Press, 1966.

Day, Shirley Jones. *The Search for Lyonnesse: Women's Fiction in France, 1670–1703*. Bern: Peter Lang, 1999.

DeJean, Joan. "Transnationalism and the Origins of the (French?) Novel." In *The Literary Channel: The Inter-National Invention of the Novel*, edited by Margaret Cohen and Carolyn Dever, 37–72. Princeton, NJ: Princeton Univ. Press, 2002.

Donoghue, Emma. *Passions between Women: British Lesbian Culture, 1668–1801*. New York: HarperCollins, 1993.

Donovan, Josephine. "Women and the Framed-Novelle: A Tradition of Their Own." *Signs: Journal of Women in Culture and Society* 22, no. 4 (1997): 947–80.

Doody, Margaret. *The Daring Muse: Augustan Poetry Reconsidered*. Cambridge: Cambridge Univ. Press, 1985.

———. "Sensuousness in the Poetry of Eighteenth-Century Women Poets." In *Women's Poetry in the Enlightenment: The Making of a Canon, 1730–1820*, edited by Isobel Armstrong and Virginia Blain, 3–32. Houndmills, UK: Macmillan, 1999.

Dowling, William C. *The Epistolary Moment: The Poetics of the Eighteenth-Century Verse Epistle*. Princeton, NJ: Princeton Univ. Press, 1991.

Downie, J. A. "Mary Davys's 'Probable Feign'd Stories' and Critical Shibboleths about 'The Rise of the Novel.'" *Eighteenth-Century Fiction* 12, no. 2 (2000): 309–26.

Duggan, Anne E. "Nature and Culture in the Fairy Tale of Marie-Catherine d'Aulnoy." *Marvels and Tales: Journal of Fairy-Tale Studies* 15, no. 2 (2001): 149–67.

———. *Salonnières, Furies, and Fairies: The Politics of Gender and Cultural Change in Absolutist France*. Newark: Univ. of Delaware Press, 2005.

———. "Women and Absolutism in French Opera and Fairy Tale." *French Review* 78, no. 2 (2004): 302–15.

Eardley, Alice. "Recreating the Canon: Women Writers and Anthologies of Early Modern Verse." *Women's Writing* 14, no. 2 (2007): 270–89.

Eaves, T. C. Duncan, and Ben Kimpel. "Richardson's Revisions of *Pamela*." *Studies in Bibliography: Papers of the Bibliographical Society of the University of Virginia* 20 (1967): 61–88.

Edwards, J. Stephan. "Lady Jane Grey Revealed. The Syon Portrait." http://somegreymatter.com/syonportrait.htm.

Eger, Elizabeth. "The Bluestocking Circle." In *Brilliant Women: Eighteenth-Century Bluestockings*, edited by Elizabeth Eger and Lucy Peltz. New Haven, CT: Yale Univ. Press, 2008.

———. *Bluestockings: Women of Reason from Enlightenment to Romanticism*. Houndmills, UK: Palgrave Macmillan, 2010.

———. Introduction to *Elizabeth Montagu*. Edited by Elizabeth Eger. Vol. 1 of *Bluestocking Feminism: Writings of the Bluestocking Circle, 1738–1785*, edited by Gary Kelly, lv–lxxxii. London: Pickering & Chatto, 1999.

———. "'The noblest commerce of mankind': Conversation and Community in the Bluestocking Circle." In *Women, Gender and Enlightenment: A Comparative History*, edited by Sarah Knott and Barbara Taylor, 288–305. Houndmills, UK: Palgrave Macmillan, 2005.

———. "Paper Trails and Eloquent Objects: Bluestocking Friendship and Material Culture." *Parergon* 26, no. 2 (2009): 109–38.

Eger, Elizabeth, and Lucy Peltz. *Brilliant Women. Eighteenth-Century Bluestockings*. New Haven, CT: Yale Univ. Press, 2008.

Everett, Nigel. *The Tory View of Landscape*. New Haven, CT: Yale Univ. Press, 1994.

The Excellent Mrs. Mary Beale. Edited by Elizabeth Walsh and Richard Jeffree. London: Inner London Education Authority, 1975. Published in conjunction with the exhibition "The Excellent Mrs. Mary Beale" shown at the Geffrye Museum, London, and Towner Art Gallery, Eastbourne.

Ezell, Margaret. "From Manuscript to Print: A Volume of Their Own?," In *Women and Poetry,*

1660–1750, edited by Sarah Prescott and David E. Shuttleton, 140–60. Houndmills, UK: Palgrave Macmillan, 2003.

Farrell, Michèle. "Celebration and Repression of Feminine Desire in Mme d'Aulnoy's Fairy Tale: *La Chatte blanche*." *L'Esprit créateur* 29, no. 3 (1989): 52–64.

Fitzmaurice, Susan M. "The Commerce of Language in the Pursuit of Politeness in Eighteenth-Century England." *English Studies* 79, no. 4 (1998): 309–28.

Foskett, Daphne. *Miniatures: Dictionary and Guide*. Woodbridge, Suffolk: Antique Collectors' Club, 1987.

Foucault, Michel. "Afterword: The Subject and Power." In *Michel Foucault: Beyond Structuralism and Hermeneutics*, edited by Hubert Dreyfus and Paul Rainbow, 208–26. Chicago: Univ. of Chicago Press, 1982.

———. *The History of Sexuality. Vol. 1: An Introduction*. New York: Vintage, 1990.

———. "Technologies of the Self." In *Technologies of the Self: A Seminar with Michel Foucault*, edited by L. H. Martin et al., 16–49. London: Tavistock, 1988.

Frangos, Jennifer. "Ghosts in the Machine: The Apparition of Mrs. Veal, Rowe's *Friendship in Death* and the Early Eighteenth-Century Invisible World." In *Spirits Unseen: The Representation of Subtle Bodies in Early Modern European Culture*, edited by Christine Göttler and Wolfgang Neuber, 313–28. Leiden: Brill, 2008.

Fraser, Nancy. "Rethinking the Public Sphere: A Contribution to the Critique of Actually Existing Democracy." In *The Cultural Studies Reader*, edited by Simon During, 518–36. London: Routledge, 1999.

Friedman, Emily. "Remarks on Richardson: Sarah Fielding and the Rational Reader." *Eighteenth-Century Fiction* 22, no. 2 (2009–2010): 308–26.

———. "'To such as are willing to understand': Considering Fielding's Community of Imagined Readers." In *Masters of the Marketplace: British Women Novelists of the 1750s*, edited by Susan Carlile, 182–200. Bethlehem: Lehigh Univ. Press, 2011.

Fulford, Tim. "'Nature' Poetry." In *The Cambridge Companion to Eighteenth Century Poetry*. Edited by John Sitter, 109–31. Cambridge: Cambridge Univ. Press, 2001.

Furbank, P. N., and W. R. Owens. *Defoe De-Attributions: A Critique of J. R. Moore's "Checklist."* London: Hambledon Press, 1994.

Gaskell, Philip. *From Writer to Reader: Studies in Editorial Method*. Oxford: Clarendon, 1978.

Gaussen, Alice C. *A Woman of Wit and Wisdom*. London: Smith, Elder, 1906.

Gevirtz, Karen B. "Ladies Reading and Writing: Eighteenth-Century Women Writers and the Gendering of Critical Discourse." *Modern Language Studies* 33, no. 1/2 (2003): 60–72.

Gilbert, Sandra, and Susan Gubar. 1979. *The Madwoman in the Attic: The Woman Writer and the Nineteenth-Century Literary Imagination*. New Haven, CT: Yale Univ. Press, 1984.

Gillespie, Raymond. "Destabilizing Ulster, 1641–2." In *Ulster 1641: Aspects of the Rising*, edited by Brian Mac Cuarta, 107–21. Belfast: Institute of Irish Studies, 1993.

Glover, Susan Paterson. *Engendering Legitimacy: Law, Property, and Early Eighteenth-Century Fiction*. Lewisburg, PA: Bucknell Univ. Press, 2006.

Göttler, Christine. "Preface: Vapours and Veils: The Edge of the Unseen." In *Spirits Unseen: The Representation of Subtle Bodies in Early Modern European Culture*, edited by Christine Göttler and Wolfgang Neuber, xv–xxvii. Leiden: Brill, 2008.

Grell, Ole Peter. "Godly Charity or Political Aid? Irish Protestants and International Calvinism, 1641–1645." *Historical Journal* 39, no. 3 (1996): 743–53.

Grenby, Matthew O. "Tame Fairies Make Good Teachers: The Popularity of Early British Fairy Tales." *The Lion and the Unicorn* 30, no. 1 (2006): 1–24.

Grieder, Josephine. Introduction to *The Rash Resolve*. New York: Garland, 1973.

Grimwade, Arthur. "The Master of George Vertue: His Identity and Oeuvre," *Apollo* 127, no. 312 (1988): 83–89.

Grundy, Isobel. *Lady Mary Wortley Montagu: Comet of the Enlightenment*. Oxford: Oxford Univ. Press, 1999.

Guest, Harriet. "Bluestocking Feminism." In *Reconsidering the Bluestockings*, edited by Nicole Pohl and Betty A. Schellenberg, 59–80. San Marino, CA: Huntington Library, 2003.

———. *Small Change: Women, Learning, Patriotism, 1750–1810*. Chicago: Univ. of Chicago Press, 2000.

———. "'These Neuter Somethings': Gender Difference and Commercial Culture in Mid-Eighteenth-Century England." In *Refiguring Revolutions: Aesthetics and Politics from the English Revolution to the Romantic Revolution*, edited by Kevin Sharpe and Steven Zwicker, 173–94. Berkeley: Univ. of California Press, 1998.

Haase, Donald. "Feminist Fairy-Tale Scholarship." In *Fairy Tales and Feminism: New Approaches*, edited by Donald Haase, 1–36. Detroit: Wayne State Univ. Press, 2004.

Habermas, Jürgen. *The Structural Transformation of the Public Sphere: An Inquiry into a Category of Bourgeois Society*. Translated by Thomas Burger with the assistance of Frederick Lawrence. Cambridge, MA: MIT Press, 1991.

Hammond, Brean S. *Professional Imaginative Writing in England, 1670–1740*. Oxford: Clarendon, 1997.

Hannon, Patricia. *Fabulous Identities: Women's Fairy Tales in Seventeenth-Century France*. Amsterdam: Rodopi, 1994.

———. "A Politics of Disguise: Marie-Catherine d'Aulnoy's 'Belle-Etoile' and the Narrative Structure of Ambivalence." In *Anxious Power: Reading, Writing, and Ambivalence in Narrative by Women*, edited by Carol J. Singley and Susan Elizabeth Sweeney, 73–89. Albany: SUNY Univ. Press, 1993.

Hansen, Marlene. "The Pious Mrs. Rowe." *English Studies* 76, no. 1 (1995): 34–51.

Harper, Heather. "'Matchless Sufferings': Intimate Violence in the Early Modern Apparition Narratives of Daniel Defoe and Elizabeth Boyd." *Women's Writing* 16, no. 3 (2009): 425–44.

Harries, Elizabeth. "Fairy Tales about Fairy Tales: Notes on Canon Formation." In *Out of the Woods: The Origins of the Literary Fairy Tale in Italy and France*, edited by Nancy L. Canepa, 152–75. Detroit: Wayne State Univ. Press, 1997.

———. *Twice upon a Time: Women Writers and the History of the Fairy Tale*. Princeton, NJ: Princeton Univ. Press, 2001.

Haslett, Moyra. *Pope to Burney, 1714–1779: Scriblerians to Bluestockings*. Houndmills, UK: Palgrave Macmillan, 2003.

Hatton, Ragnhild Marie. *George I: Elector and King*. Cambridge, MA: Harvard Univ. Press, 1978.

Hawley, Judith. Introduction to *Elizabeth Carter*. Edited by Judith Hawley. Vol. 2 of *Bluestocking Feminism: Writings of the Bluestocking Circle, 1738–1785*, edited by Gary Kelly, ix–xix. London: Pickering & Chatto, 1999.

Heidegger, Martin. "Building Dwelling Thinking." In *Martin Heidegger. Basic Writings from*

Being in Time (1927) to The Task of Thinking (1964), edited by David Krell, 323–39. New York: Harper & Row, 1977.

Heller, Deborah. "Bluestocking Salons and the Public Sphere." *Eighteenth-Century Life* 22, no. 2 (1998): 59–82.

———. "Subjectivity Unbound: Elizabeth Vesey as the Sylph in Bluestocking Correspondence." In *Reconsidering the Bluestockings*, edited by Nicole Pohl and Betty Schellenberg, 215–34. San Marino, CA: Huntington Library, 2003.

Hemlow, Joyce. *The History of Fanny Burney*. Oxford: Clarendon, 1958.

Hinnant, Charles Haskell. "*Moll Flanders*, *Roxana*, and First-Person Female Narratives: Models and Prototypes." *Eighteenth-Century Novel* 4 (2004): 39–72.

Hitchcock, Tim, and Michèle Cohen, eds. *English Masculinities, 1660–1800*. New York: Longman, 1999.

Hughes, Helen Sard. "An Early Romantic Novel." *Journal of English and German Philology* 15, no. 4 (1916): 564–98.

———. "Elizabeth Rowe and the Countess of Hertford." *PMLA* 59, no. 3 (1944): 726–46.

———. *The Gentle Hertford: Her Life and Letters*. New York: Macmillan, 1940.

———. "A Romantic Correspondence of the Year 1729." *Modern Philology* 37, no. 2 (1939): 187–200.

———. "Thomson and the Countess of Hertford." *Modern Philology* 25, no. 4 (1928): 439–68.

Hunter, J. Paul. *Before Novels: The Cultural Contexts of Eighteenth-Century English Fiction*. New York: Norton, 1990.

Hutchins, Henry. *Robinson Crusoe and Its Printing, 1719–1731: A Bibliographical Study*. New York: Columbia Univ. Press, 1925.

Imbert-Terry, Henry M. *A Constitutional King: George the First*. London: John Murray, 1927.

Inglesfield, Robert. "Thomson and Shaftesbury." In *James Thomson: Essays for the Tercentenary*, edited by Richard Terry, 67–92. Liverpool: Liverpool Univ. Press, 2000.

Jajdelska, Elspeth. *Silent Reading and the Birth of the Narrator*. Toronto: Univ. of Toronto Press, 2007.

James, P. D. Foreword to *Eight Hundred Years of Women's Letters*, edited by Olga Kenyon, vii–viii. Boston: Faber & Faber, 1993.

Johns, Alessa. *Women's Utopias of the Eighteenth Century*. Urbana: Univ. of Illinois Press, 2003.

Johnson, James William. *A Profane Wit: The Life of John Wilmot, Earl of Rochester*. Rochester: Univ. of Rochester Press, 2004.

Jomand-Baudry, Régine, and Jean-François Perrin, eds. *Le Conte merveilleux au XVIIIe siècle: une poétique expérimentale*. Paris: Kimé, 2002.

Jones, Christine A. "Madame d'Aulnoy Charms the British." *Romantic Review* 99, no. 3–4 (2008): 239–56.

Jones, Robert W. *Gender and the Formation of Taste in Eighteenth-Century Britain: The Analysis of Beauty*. Cambridge: Cambridge Univ. Press, 1998.

Joule, Victoria. "Mary Davys's Novel Contribution to Women and Realism." *Women's Writing* 17, no. 1 (2010): 30–48.

Kairoff, Claudia Thomas. "Eighteenth-century Women Poets and Readers." In *The Cambridge Companion to Eighteenth Century Poetry*, edited by John Sitter, 157–76. Cambridge: Cambridge Univ. Press, 2001.

Keeble, N. H. *The Literary Culture of Nonconformity in Later Seventeenth-Century England*. Athens: Univ. of Georgia Press, 1987.

Keener, Frederick M. *English Dialogues of the Dead: A Critical History, an Anthology, and a Check List*. New York: Columbia, 1973.

Kelly, Gary. "Bluestocking Feminism." In *Women, Writing and the Public Sphere, 1700–1830*, edited by Elizabeth Eger et al., 163–80. Cambridge: Cambridge Univ. Press, 2001.

———. "General Introduction: Bluestocking Feminism and Writing in Context." In *Elizabeth Montagu*, edited by Elizabeth Eger. Vol. 1 of *Bluestocking Feminism: Writings of the Bluestocking Circle*, edited by Gary Kelly, ix–liv. London: Pickering & Chatto, 1999.

Kincade, Kit. Headnote to *An Essay on the History and Reality of Apparitions*, by Daniel Defoe, edited by Kit Kincade, xviii–lxxxvi. New York: AMS Press, 2007.

Kind, John Louis. *Edward Young in Germany*. New York: AMS Press, 1966.

King, Kathryn R. "Elizabeth Singer Rowe's Tactical Use of Print and Manuscript." In *Women's Writing and the Circulation of Ideas: Manuscript Publication in England, 1550–1800*, edited by George Justice and Nathan Tinker, 158–80. Cambridge: Cambridge Univ. Press, 2002.

———. "Galesia, Jane Barker, and a Coming to Authorship." In *Anxious Power: Reading, Writing and Ambivalence in Narrative by Women*, edited by Carol J. Singley and Susan Elizabeth Sweeney, 91–104. Albany: SUNY Univ. Press, 1993.

———. *Jane Barker, Exile: A Literary Career 1675–1725*. Oxford: Clarendon, 2000.

———. "The Novel before Novels (with a Glance at Mary Hearne's Fables of Desertion)." In *Eighteenth-Century Genre and Culture: Serious Reflections on Occasional Forms, Essays in Honor of J. Paul Hunter*, edited by Dennis Todd and Cynthia Wall, 36–57. Newark: Univ. of Delaware Press, 2001.

———. "Political Verse and Satire: Monarchy, Party and Female Political Agency." In *Women and Poetry, 1660–1750*, edited by Sarah Prescott and David E. Shuttleton, 203–22. Houndmills, UK: Palgrave Macmillan, 2003.

———. "The Unaccountable Wife and Other Tales of Female Desire in Jane Barker's *A Patch-Work Screen for the Ladies*." *Eighteenth Century: Theory and Interpretation* 35, no. 2 (1994): 155–72.

King, Kathryn, and Jeslyn Medoff. "Jane Barker and Her Life (1652–1732): The Documentary Record." *Eighteenth-Century Life* 21, no. 3 (1997): 16–38.

Kirschbaum, Robin. "Thoughts 'All Easy and Sociable': Elizabeth Singer Rowe and Coterie Exchange." In *Readers, Audiences and Coteries in Early Modern England*, edited by Geoff Baker and Ann McGruer, 47–60. Newcastle-upon-Tyne: Cambridge Scholars Press, 2006.

Klein, Lawrence E. "Politeness for Plebes: Consumption and Social Identity in Early Eighteenth-Century England." In *The Consumption of Culture 1600–1800: Image, Object, Text*, edited by Ann Bermingham and John Brewer, 362–82. London: Routledge, 1995.

———. *Shaftesbury and the Culture of Politeness: Moral Discourse and Cultural Politics in Early Eighteenth-Century England*. Cambridge: Cambridge Univ. Press, 1994.

———. "The Third Earl of Shaftesbury and the Progress of Politeness." *Eighteenth-Century Studies* 18, no. 2 (1984–1985): 186–214.

Kolb, Gwin J. "Mrs. (Thrale) Piozzi and Dr. Johnson's *The Fountains: A Fairy Tale*." *Novel* 13, no. 1 (1979): 68–81.

Kvande, Marta. "Frances Burney and Frances Sheridan: Epistolary Fiction and the Public Sphere." In *Everyday Revolutions: Eighteenth-Century Women Transforming Public and Private*, edited by Diane E. Boyd and Marta Kvande, 159–87. Newark: Univ. of Delaware Press, 2008.

———. "Jane Barker and Delarivière Manley: Public Women against the Public Sphere." *Eighteenth-Century Novel* 5 (2006): 143–74.

Lacey, Barbara E. *From Sacred to Secular: Visual Images in Early American Publications*. Newark: Univ. of Delaware Press, 2007.

Lamb, Jeremy. *So Idle a Rogue: The Life and Death of Lord Rochester*. London: Allison & Busby, 1993.

Landry, Donna. *The Invention of the Countryside: Hunting, Walking and Ecology in English Literature, 1671–1831*. Houndmills, UK: Palgrave Macmillan, 2001.

———. "Picturing Benevolence against the Commercial Cry, 1750–98: Or, Sarah Fielding and the Secret Causes of Romanticism." In *1750–1830*, edited by Jacqueline M. Labbe. Vol. 5 of *The History of British Women's Writing*, edited by Jennie Batchelor and Cora Kaplan, 150–71. Houndmills, UK: Palgrave Macmillan, 2010.

Langford, Paul. *A Polite and Commercial People. England, 1727–1783*. Oxford: Oxford Univ. Press, 1987.

Lanser, Susan S. "Befriending the Body: Female Intimacies as Class Acts." *Eighteenth-Century Studies* 32, no. 2 (1998–1999): 179–98.

———. *Fictions of Authority: Women Writers and Narrative Voice*. Ithaca: Cornell Univ. Press, 1992.

Lavoie, Chantel M. *Collecting Women: Poetry and Lives, 1700–1780*. Lewisburg, PA: Bucknell Univ. Press, 2009.

Leavis, Queenie D. *Fiction and the Reading Public*. 1932. Reprint, London: Chatto & Windus, 1965.

Levy, Michelle. "Women and Print Culture, 1750–1830." In *1750–1830*, edited by Jacquline M. Labbe. Vol. 5 of *The History of British Women's Writing*, edited by Jennie Batchelor and Cora Kaplan, 29–46. Houndmills, UK: Palgrave Macmillan, 2010.

Lieberman, Marcia R. "'Some Day My Prince Will Come': Female Acculturation through the Fairy Tale." In *Sharing Literature with Children*, edited by Francelia Butler, 332–43. New York: David McKay, 1977.

Lipking, Joanna. "Fair Originals: Women Poets in Male Commendatory Poems." *Eighteenth-Century Life* 12, no. 2 (1988): 58–72.

Liu, Yu. *Seeds of a Different Eden: Chinese Gardening Ideas and a New English Aesthetic Ideal*. Columbia: Univ. of South Carolina Press, 2008.

Lovejoy, A. O., and G. Boas. *Primitivism and Related Ideas in Antiquity*. Baltimore: Johns Hopkins Univ. Press, 1935.

Lynch, Deidre Shauna. *The Economy of Character: Novels, Market Culture, and the Business of Inner Meaning*. Chicago: Univ. of Chicago Press, 1998.

MacArthur, Elizabeth J. *Extravagant Narratives: Closure and Dynamics in the Epistolary Form*. Princeton, NJ: Princeton Univ. Press, 1990.

Mac Cuarta, Brian. Introduction to *Ulster 1641: Aspects of the Rising*, 1–6. Edited by Brian Mac Cuarta. Belfast: Institute of Irish Studies, 1993.

Mackie, Erin. *Market à la Mode: Fashion, Commodity, and Gender in "The Tatler" and "The Spectator."* Baltimore: Johns Hopkins Univ. Press, 1997.

MacLeod, Emma V. "'Thinking Minds of Both Sexes': Patriotism, British Bluestockings, and the Wars against Revolutionary America and France, 1775–1802." In *Gender, War and Politics: Transatlantic Perspectives, 1775–1830*, edited by Karen Hagemann, Gisela Mettele, and Jane Rendell, 247–64. Houndmills, UK: Palgrave Macmillan, 2010.

Major, Emma. "The Politics of Sociability: Public Dimensions of the Bluestocking Millennium." In *Reconsidering the Bluestockings*, edited by Nicole Pohl and Betty A. Schellenberg, 175–92. San Marino, CA: Huntington Library Press, 2003.

Marlow, Joyce. *The Life and Times of George I*. London: Weidenfeld & Nicolson, 1973.

Marshall, Elizabeth. "Stripping for the Wolf: Rethinking Representations of Gender in Children's Literature." *Reading Research Quarterly* 39, no. 3 (2004): 256–70.

Marshall, Madeleine F. "Elizabeth Singer Rowe." In the *Dictionary of Literary Biography*. Vol. 95, *Eighteenth-Century British Poets, First Series*, edited by John Sitter, 248–56. Detroit: Gale Research, 1990.

———. "Teaching the Uncanonized: The Examples of Watts and Rowe." In *Teaching Eighteenth-Century Poetry*, edited by Christopher Fox, 1–24. New York: AMS Press, 1990.

Maslen, Keith. *Samuel Richardson of London, Printer: A Study of His Printing Based on Ornament Use and Business Accounts*. Dunedin, New Zealand: Univ. of Otago Press, 2001.

McArthur, Tonya. "Jane Barker and the Politics of Catholic Celibacy." *SEL* 47, no. 3 (2007): 595–618.

McCarthy, William. *Anna Letitia Barbauld: Voice of the Enlightenment*. Baltimore: Johns Hopkins Univ. Press, 2008.

McKeon, Michael. "The Pastoral Revolution." In *Refiguring Revolutions: Aesthetics and Politics from the English Revolution to the Romantic Revolution*, edited by Kevin Sharpe and Steven Zwicker, 267–89. Berkeley: Univ. of California Press, 1998.

Mee, John. "'Severe contentions of friendship': Barbauld, Conversation and Dispute." In *Repossessing the Romantic Past*, edited by Heather Glen and Paul Hamilton, 21–39. Cambridge: Cambridge Univ. Press, 2006.

Messenger, Ann. *Pastoral Tradition and the Female Talent*. New York: AMS Press, 2001.

Miller, Claire Cain. "Where Some Earn Loyalty, Jobs Won Affection." *New York Times*, 26 August 2011, B1.

Miller, Nancy K. *Subject to Change: Reading Feminist Writing*. New York: Columbia Univ. Press, 1988.

Mills, Rebecca M. "Mary, Lady Chudleigh (1656–1710): Poet, Protofeminist and Patron." In *Women and Poetry, 1660–1750*, edited by Sarah Prescott and David E. Shuttleton, 50–59. Houndmills, UK: Palgrave Macmillan, 2003.

Mitchell, Jane Tucker. *A Thematic Analysis of Mme. D'Aulnoy's "Contes de Fées."* University, MS: Romance Monographs, 1978.

Moi, Toril. *Simone de Beauvoir: The Making of an Intellectual Woman*. Oxford: Blackwell, 1994.

Moore, Lisa L. "Mary Delany and Her Circle, in the Museum and on the Page." *Eighteenth-Century Studies* 44, no. 1 (2010): 99–104.

———. "Queer Gardens: Mary Delany's Flowers and Friendships." *Eighteenth-Century Studies* 39, no. 1 (2005): 49–70.

———. *Sister Arts: The Erotics of Lesbian Landscapes*. Minneapolis: Univ. of Minnesota Press, 2011.

Moretti, Franco. *Graphs, Maps, Trees: Abstract Models for a Literary History*. London: Verso, 2005.

Mounsey, Chris. "Conversion Panic, Circumcision, and Sexual Anxiety: Penelope Aubin's Queer Writing." In *Queer People: Negotiations and Expressions of Homosexuality, 1700–1800*, edited by Chris Mounsey and Caroline Gonda, 246–60. Lewisburg, PA: Bucknell Univ. Press, 2007.

Myers, Sylvia Harcstark. *The Bluestocking Circle: Women, Friendship, and the Life of the Mind in Eighteenth-Century England.* Oxford: Clarendon, 1990.

Myrone, Martin. "The Society of Antiquaries and the Graphic Arts: George Vertue and His Legacy." In *Visions of Antiquity: The Society of Antiquaries in London, 1707–2007*, edited by Susan Pearce. Vol. III of *Archaeologia.* III vols. London: Society of Antiquaries, 2007.

Naess, Arne. *Ecology, Community and Lifestyle: Outline of an Ecosophy.* Translated and revised by David Rothenberg. Cambridge: Cambridge Univ. Press, 1989.

Napier, Elizabeth. "Elizabeth Singer Rowe." In *British Novelists, 1660–1800*, edited by Martin C. Battestin, 409–11. Vol. 39 of *Dictionary of Literary Biography.* Detroit: Gale Research, 1985.

Neisser, Ulric. "Five Kinds of Self-Knowledge." *Philosophical Psychology* 1 (1988): 35–59.

———. Introduction to *The Perceived Self: Ecological and Interpersonal Sources of Self-Knowledge*, edited by Ulric Neisser, 3–21. Cambridge: Cambridge Univ. Press, 1993.

Neuber, Wolfgang. "Poltergeist the Prequel: Aspects of Otherworldly Disturbances in Early Modern Times." In *Spirits Unseen: The Representation of Subtle Bodies in Early Modern European Culture*, edited by Christine Göttler and Wolfgang Neuber, 1–17. Leiden: Brill, 2008.

Nixon, Cheryl. "'Stop a Moment at This Preface': The Gendered Paratexts of Fielding, Barker, and Haywood." *Journal of Narrative Theory* 32, no. 2 (2002): 123–53.

Novak, Maximillian. *Daniel Defoe: Master of Fictions.* Oxford: Oxford Univ. Press, 2001.

———. "Defoe's Spirits, Apparitions and the Occult." *Digital Defoe* 2, no. 1 (2010): 9–20.

Novak, Maximillian, and Carl Fisher. "Publishing History and Modern Editions." In *Approaches to Teaching Defoe's "Robinson Crusoe,"* edited by Maximillian Novak and Carl Fisher, 3–5. New York: MLA, 2005.

Nurmi, Arja, and Minna Palander-Collin. "Letters as a Text Type: Interaction in Writing." In *Studies in Late Modern English Correspondence: Methodology and Data*, edited by Marina Dossena and Ingrid Tieken-Boon van Ostade, 21–49. Bern: Peter Lang, 2008.

Nussbaum, Felicity. "Women Novelists 1740s–1780s." In *The Cambridge History of English Literature, 1660–1780*, edited by John Richetti, 745–67. Cambridge: Cambridge Univ. Press, 2005.

O'Brien, Karen, "Imperial Georgic." In *The Country and the City Revisited: England and the Politics of Culture, 1550–1850*, edited by Gerald Maclean, Donna Landy, and Joseph P. Ward, 160–79. Cambridge: Cambridge Univ. Press, 1999.

O'Hara, David A. *English Newsbooks and Irish Rebellion, 1641–1649.* Dublin: Four Courts Press, 2006.

Palmer, Melvin. "*The History of Adolphus* (1691): The First French *Conte de Fée* in English." *Philological Quarterly* 49, no. 4 (1970): 565–67.

———. "Madame d'Aulnoy in England." *Comparative Literature* 27, no. 3 (1975): 237–53.

Palmer, Nancy, and Melvin Palmer. "English Editions of French *Contes de fées* attributed to Mme D'Aulnoy." *Studies in Bibliography: Papers of the Bibliographical Society of the University of Virginia* 27 (1974): 227–32.

———. "The French *Conte de Fée* in England." *Studies in Short Fiction* 11, no. 1 (1974): 35–44.

Palmer, Sally. "'I Prefer Walking': Jane Austen and 'The Pleasantest Part of the Day.'" *Persuasions: Journal of the Jane Austen Society of North America* 23 (2001): 154–65.

Paulson, Ronald. *Breaking and Remaking: Aesthetic Practice in England, 1700–1820.* New Brunswick: Rutgers Univ. Press, 1989.

Perceval-Maxwell, Michael. *The Outbreak of the Irish Rebellion of 1641.* Montreal: McGill Univ. Press, 1994.

Philips, Charles. *Kings and Queens of Britain's Modern Age: From Hanover to Windsor.* London: Southwater, 2008.

Pocock, J. G. A. *Barbarism and Religion.* Vol. 1, *The Enlightenments of Edward Gibbon, 1737–1764.* Cambridge: Cambridge Univ. Press, 1999.

Pointon, Marcia. "'Surrounded with Brilliants': Miniature Portraits in Eighteenth-Century England." *Art Bulletin* 83, no. 1 (2001): 48–71.

Potter, Tiffany. "'Decorous Disruption': The Cultural Voice of Mary Davys." *Eighteenth-Century Women* 1 (2001): 63–93.

Prescott, Sarah. "The Debt to Pleasure: Eliza Haywood's *Love in Excess* and Women's Fiction of the 1720s." *Women's Writing* 7, no. 3 (2000): 427–45.

———. "Elizabeth Singer Rowe: Gender, Dissent, and Whig Poetics." In *"Cultures of Whiggism": New Essays on English Literature and Culture in the Long Eighteenth Century,* edited by David Womersley, assisted by Paddy Bullard and Abigail Williams, 173–99. Newark: Univ. of Delaware Press, 2005.

———. "Elizabeth Singer Rowe (1674–1737): Politics, Passion, and Piety." In *Women and Poetry, 1660–1750,* edited by Sarah Prescott and David E. Shuttleton, 71–78. Houndmills, UK: Palgrave Macmillan, 2003.

———. "Provincial Networks, Dissenting Connections, and Noble Friends: Elizabeth Singer Rowe and Female Authorship in Early Eighteenth-Century England." *Eighteenth-Century Life* 25, no. 1 (2001): 29–42.

———. *Women, Authorship and Literary Culture, 1690–1740.* Houndmills, UK: Palgrave Macmillan, 2003.

Rabb, Melinda A. *Satire and Secrecy in English Literature from 1650 to 1750.* Houndmills, UK: Palgrave Macmillan, 2007.

Rack, Henry D. *Reasonable Enthusiast: John Wesley and the Rise of Methodism.* Philadelphia: Trinity Press International, 1989.

Radcliffe, David Hill. "Genre and Social Order in Country House Poems of the Eighteenth Century: Four Views of Percy Lodge." *SEL* 30, no. 3 (1990): 445–65.

Raven, James, and Antonia Forster. *The English Novel 1770–1829: A Bibliographical Survey of Prose Fiction Published in the British Isles.* 2 vols. Oxford: Oxford Univ. Press, 2000.

Reeves, Marjorie. *Pursuing the Muses: Female Education and Nonconformist Culture, 1700–1900.* London: Leicester Univ. Press, 1997.

Ribeiro, Aileen. *Fashion and Fiction: Dress in Art and Literature in Stuart England.* New Haven, CT: Yale Univ. Press, 2005.

Richetti, John. *The English Novel in History, 1700–1780.* London: Routledge, 1999.

———. *The Life of Daniel Defoe.* Oxford: Blackwell, 2005.

———. "Mrs. Elizabeth Rowe: The Novel as Polemic." *PMLA* 82, no. 7 (1967): 522–29.

———. *Popular Fiction before Richardson: Narrative Patterns, 1700–1739.* 1969. Reprint, Oxford: Clarendon, 1992.

Riley, Lindy. "Mary Davys's Satiric Novel *Familiar Letters*: Refusing Patriarchal Inscription of Women." In *Cutting Edges: Postmodern Critical Essays on Eighteenth-Century Satire,* edited by James E. Gill, 206–21. Knoxville: Univ. of Tennessee Press, 1995.

Rizzo, Betty. *Companions without Vows: Relationships among Eighteenth-Century British Women.* Athens: Univ. of Georgia Press, 1994.

———. "Equivocations of Gender and Rank: Eighteenth-Century Sporting Women." *Eigheenth-Century Life* 26, no. 1 (2002): 70–93.

———. "The Frances Greville Letters: An Edition, Part I." *Eighteenth-Century Women* 4 (2006): 313–62.

———. "Two Versions of Community: Montagu and Scott." In *Reconsidering the Bluestockings*, edited by Nicole Pohl and Betty A. Schellenberg, 193–214. San Marino, CA: Huntington Library Press, 2003.

Roach, Joseph. "Power's Body: The Inscription of Morality as Style." In *Interpreting the Theatrical Past: Essays in the Historiography of Performance*, edited by Thomas Postlewait and Bruce A. McConachie, 99–118. Iowa City: Univ. of Iowa Press, 1989.

Robert, Raymonde. *Le conte de fées littéraire en France de la fin du XVIIe à la fin du XVIIIe siècle*. Nancy: Presses Universitaires de Nancy, 1982.

Rothstein, Eric. *Gleaning Modernity: Earlier Eighteenth-Century Literature and the Modernizing Process*. Newark: Univ. of Delaware Press, 2007.

Roulston, Christine. "The Eighteenth-Century Ménage-à-Trois: Having It Both Ways?" *Journal for Eighteenth-Century Studies* 27, no. 2 (2004): 257–77.

———. "Having It Both Ways? The Eighteenth-Century Ménage-à-Trois." In *Queer People: Negotiations and Expressions of Homosexuality, 1700–1800*, edited by Chris Mounsey and Caroline Gonda, 274–98. Lewisburg, PA: Bucknell Univ. Press, 2007.

Rowe, Karen E. "Feminism and Fairy Tales." *Women's Studies* 6, no. 3 (1979): 237–57.

Rumbold, Valerie. "Rank, Community and Audience: The Social Range of Women's Poetry." In *Women and Poetry, 1660–1750*, edited by Sarah Prescott and David E. Shuttleton, 121–39. Houndmills, UK: Palgrave Macmillan, 2003.

Sabor, Peter. Introduction to *The Adventures of David Simple*. Edited by Peter Sabor. Lexington: Univ. Press of Kentucky, 1998.

Sairio, Anni. "Bluestocking Letters and the Influence of Eighteenth-Century Grammars." In *Studies in Late Modern English Correspondence: Methodology and Data*, edited by Marina Dossena and Ingrid Tieken-Boon van Ostade, 137–62. Bern: Peter Lang, 2008.

———. "Methodological and Practical Aspects of Historical Network Analysis: A Case Study of the Bluestocking Letters." In *The Language of Daily Life in England (1400–1800)*, edited by Arja Nurmi, Minna Nevala, and Minna Palander-Collin, 107–35. Amsterdam: John Benjamins, 2009.

Salaman, Malcolm C. *The Old Engravers of England in Their Relation to Contemporary Life and Art (1540–1800)*. London: Cassell, 1906.

Sale, William M. *Samuel Richardson: Master Printer*. Ithaca, NY: Cornell Univ. Press, 1950.

Saxton, Kirsten, and Rebecca Bocchicchio, eds. *The Passionate Fictions of Eliza Haywood*. Lexington: Univ. Press of Kentucky, 2000.

Schellenberg, Betty. "Bluestocking Women and the Negotiation of Oral, Manuscript, and Print Cultures." In *1750–1830*, edited by Jacqueline M. Labbe. Vol. 5 of *The History of British Women's Writing*, edited by Jennie Batchelor and Cora Kaplan, 63–83. Houndmills, UK: Palgrave Macmillan, 2010.

———. *The Conversational Circle: Rereading the English Novel, 1740–1775*. Lexington: Univ. Press of Kentucky, 1996.

———. "Putting Women in Their Place: Locating Women Novelists in the 1750s." In *Masters of the Marketplace: British Women Novelists of the 1750s*, edited by Susan Carlile, 242–58. Bethlehem: Lehigh Univ. Press, 2011.

Schofield, Mary Anne. *Masking and Unmasking the Female Mind: Disguising Romances in Feminine Fictions.* Newark: Univ. of Delaware Press, 1990.

Seifert, Lewis C. *Fairy Tales, Sexuality, and Gender in France, 1690–1715: Nostalgic Utopias.* Cambridge: Cambridge Univ. Press, 1996.

———. "Marie-Catherine le Jumel de Barneville, Comtesse d'Aulnoy (1650/51–1705)." In *French Women Writers: A Bio-Bibliographical Source Book,* edited by Eva Martin Sartori and Dorothy Wynne Zimmerman, 11–20. New York: Greenwood, 1991.

———. "On Fairy Tales, Subversion, and Ambiguity: Feminist Approaches to Seventeenth-Century *Contes de fées.*" In *Fairy Tales and Feminism: New Approaches,* edited by Donald Haase, 53–71. Detroit: Wayne State Univ. Press, 2004.

Sermain, Jean-Paul. *Le Conte de Fées: Du Classicisme aux Lumières.* Paris: Centre National du Livre, 2005.

Shagan, Ethan Howard. "Constructing Discord: Ideology, Propaganda, and English Responses to the Irish Rebellion of 1641." *Journal of British Studies* 36, no. 1 (1997): 4–34.

Shaw, Jane. *Miracles in Enlightenment England.* New Haven, CT: Yale Univ. Press, 2006.

Simms, Hilary. "Violence in County Armagh, 1641." In *Ulster 1641: Aspects of the Rising,* edited by Brian Mac Cuarta, 123–38. Belfast: Institute of Irish Studies, 1993.

Siochrú, Micheál O. "Atrocity, Codes of Conduct and the Irish in the British Civil Wars 1641–1653." *Past and Present* 195, no. 1 (2007): 55–86.

Skinner, John. *An Introduction to Eighteenth-Century Fiction: Raising the Novel.* Houndmills, UK: Palgrave, 2001.

Sowerby, Robin. *The Augustan Art of Poetry: Augustan Translation of the Classics.* Oxford: Oxford Univ. Press, 2006.

———. "Imagining the Woman Poet: Creative Female Bodies." In *Women and Poetry, 1660–1750,* edited by Sarah Prescott and David E. Shuttleton, 99–120. Houndmills, UK: Palgrave Macmillan, 2003.

Spacks, Patricia Meyer. *Novel Beginnings: Experiments in Eighteenth-Century English Fiction.* New Haven, CT: Yale Univ. Press, 2006.

Spencer, Jane. "Imagining the Woman Poet: Creative Female Bodies." In *Women and Poetry, 1660–1750,* edited by Sarah Prescott and David E. Shuttleton, 99–116. Houndmills, UK: Palgrave Macmillan, 2003.

———. *The Rise of the Woman Novelist: From Aphra Behn to Jane Austen.* Oxford: Blackwell, 1986.

Starr, George A. *Defoe and Casuistry.* Princeton, NJ: Princeton Univ. Press, 1971.

———. Introduction to *Serious Reflections during the Life and Surprising Adventures of Robinson Crusoe.* Edited by George A. Starr. Vol. 3 of *The Novels of Daniel Defoe,* edited by W. R. Owens and P. N. Furbank, 1–47. London: Pickering & Chatto, 2008.

———. "Sentimental Novels of the Later Eighteenth Century." In *The Columbia History of the British Novel,* edited by John Richetti, 181–98. New York: Columbia Univ. Press, 1994.

———. "Why Defoe Probably Did Not Write *The Apparition of Mrs. Veal.*" *Eighteenth-Century Fiction* 15, nos. 3–4 (2003): 427–50.

Staves, Susan. *A Literary History of Women's Writing in Britain, 1660–1789.* Cambridge: Cambridge Univ. Press, 2006.

Stecher, Henry F. *Elizabeth Singer Rowe, the Poetess of Frome: A Study in Eighteenth-Century English Pietism.* Bern: Herbert Lang, 1973.

Stedman, Allison. "D'Aulnoy's *Histoire d'Hypolite, comte de Duglas* (1690): A Fairy-Tale Manifesto." *Marvels and Tales: Journal of Fairy-Tale Studies* 19, no. 1 (2005): 32–53.

———. "Sacred Writings, Secular Identities: D'Aulnoy's Manipulation of the Psalm-Paraphrase Tradition." In *Intersections*, edited by Faith E. Beasley and Kathleen Wine, 347–56. Tübingen: Gunter Narr Verlag, 2005.

Stevens-Cox, James. *Elizabeth Rowe, 1674–1737: Poetess and Polemical Novelist, born at Ilchester, Somerset: With a Short Title Catalogue of Her Works and Specimens of Her Poems*. Guernsey: Toucan Press, 1991.

Sutherland, James. *Defoe*. Philadelphia: Lippincott, 1938.

Swenson, Rivka. "Representing Modernity in Jane Barker's *Galesia Trilogy*: Jacobite Allegory and the Patch-Work Aesthetic." *Studies in Eighteenth-Century Culture* 34 (2005): 55–80.

Talley, Mansfield Kirby. *Portrait Painting in England: Studies in the Technical Literature before 1700*. Guildford: Paul Mellon Centre for Studies in British Art, 1981.

Taylor, Barbara. Introduction to "Section 7: Feminism and Enlightened Religious Discourses." In *Women, Gender and Enlightenment*, edited by Sarah Knott and Barbara Taylor, 410–15. Houndmills, UK: Palgrave Macmillan, 2005.

Thomas, Keith. *The Ends of Life: Roads to Fulfilment in Early Modern England*. Oxford: Oxford Univ. Press, 2009.

———. *Religion and the Decline of Magic: Studies in Popular Beliefs in Sixteenth and Seventeenth Century England*. New York: Scribner, 1971.

Turner, Cheryl. *Living by the Pen: Women Writers in the Eighteenth Century*. 1992. Reprint, London: Routledge, 1994.

Turner, James Grantham. *The Politics of Landscape: Rural Scenery and Society in English Poetry, 1630–1660*. Cambridge, MA: Harvard Univ. Press, 1979.

Valenze, Deborah M. "Prophecy and Popular Literature in Eighteenth-Century England." *Journal of Ecclesiastical History* 29, no. 1 (1978): 75–92.

Vigué, Jordi. *Great Women Masters of Art*. New York: Watson-Guptill Publications, 2002.

Wakely, Alice. "Mary Davys and the Politics of Epistolary Form." In *"Cultures of Whiggism": New Essays on English Literature and Culture in the Long Eighteenth Century*, edited by David Womersley, 257–67. Newark: Univ. of Delaware Press, 2005.

Wall, Cynthia. *The Prose of Things: Transformations of Description in the Eighteenth Century*. Chicago: Univ. of Chicago Press, 2006.

Wallace, Anne D. *Walking, Literature, and English Culture: The Origins and Uses of Peripatetic in the Nineteenth Century*. Oxford: Clarendon, 1993.

Walmsley, Peter. "Whigs in Heaven: Elizabeth Rowe's *Friendship in Death*." *Eighteenth-Century Studies* 44, no. 3 (2011): 315–30.

Walsh, Elizabeth, and Richard Jeffree. *The Excellent Mrs. Mary Beale*. London: Inner London Education Authority, 1975.

Warner, Marina. *From the Beast to the Blonde: On Fairy Tales and Their Tellers*. New York: Farrar, Straus & Giroux, 1994.

Watson, Victor. "Jane Johnson: A Very Pretty Story to Tell Children." In *Opening the Nursery Door: Reading, Writing and Childhood 1600–1900*, edited by Mary Hilton, Morag Styles, and Victor Watson, 31–46. London: Routledge, 1997.

Watts, Richard. *Politeness*. Cambridge: Cambridge Univ. Press, 2003.

Webb, Dominic. "Inflation: the Value of the Pound 1750–2005." House of Commons Research Paper 06/09, 13 February 2006. House of Commons Library, UK.

Weinbrot, Howard. *Augustus Caesar in 'Augustan' England: The Decline of a Classical Norm*. Princeton, NJ: Princeton Univ. Press, 1978.

———. *Britannia's Issue: The Rise of British Literature from Dryden to Ossian.* Cambridge: Cambridge Univ. Press, 1995.

Wendorf, Richard. *Sir Joshua Reynolds: The Painter in Society.* Cambridge, MA: Harvard Univ. Press, 1996.

Whyman, Susan E. *The Pen and the People: English Letter Writers, 1600–1800.* Oxford: Oxford Univ. Press, 2009.

Williams, Abigail. "Patronage and Whig Literary Culture in the Early Eighteenth Century." In *"Cultures of Whiggism": New Essays on English Literature and Culture in the Long Eighteenth Century,* edited by David Womersley, assisted by Paddy Bullard and Abigail Williams, 149–72. Newark: Univ. of Delaware Press, 2005.

Williams, Raymond. *Marxism and Literature.* 1977. Reprint, Oxford: Oxford Univ. Press, 1988.

Williamson, Marilyn. *Raising Their Voices: British Women Writers 1650–1750.* Detroit: Wayne State Univ. Press, 1990.

Wilputte, Earla. "Harridans and Heroes: Female Revenge and the Masculine Duel in Jane Barker, Delarivier Manley and Eliza Haywood." *Eighteenth-Century Women* 4 (2006): 27–51.

Wilson, Carol Shiner, ed. *Galesia Trilogy and Selected Manuscript Poems of Jane Barker.* New York: Oxford Univ. Press, 1997.

Wilson, Sharon Rose. *Myths and Fairy Tales in Contemporary Women's Fiction: From Atwood to Morrison.* Houndmills, UK: Palgrave Macmillan, 2008.

Womersley, David, ed. *Augustan Critical Writing.* London: Penguin, 1997.

———. Introduction to *"Cultures of Whiggism": New Essays on English Literature and Culture in the Long Eighteenth Century,* 9–26. Edited by David Womersley. Newark: Univ. of Delaware Press, 2005.

Woodward, Caroyln. "Sarah Fielding's Self-Destructing Utopia: *The Adventures of David Simple.*" In *Living by the Pen: Early British Women Novelists,* edited by Dale Spender, 65–81. New York: Teachers College Press, 1992.

Wright, H. Bunker. "Matthew Prior and Elizabeth Singer." *Philological Quarterly* 24, no. 1 (1945): 71–82.

Zeeuw, Lyda Fens-de. "The Letter-Writing Manual in the Eighteenth and Nineteenth Centuries: From Polite to Practical." In *Studies in Late Modern English Correspondence: Methodology and Data,* edited by Marina Dossena and Ingrid Tieken-Boon van Ostade, 163–92. Bern: Peter Lang, 2008.

Zipes, Jack. *Beauties, Beasts, and Enchantment: Classic French Fairy Tales.* New York: New American Library, 1989.

———. "Of Cats and Men: Framing the Civilizing Discourse of the Fairy Tale." In *Out of the Woods: The Origins of the Literary Fairy Tale in Italy and France,* edited by Nancy L. Canepa, 176–93. Detroit: Wayne State Univ. Press, 1997.

———. *The Trials and Tribulations of Little Red Riding Hood.* New York: Routledge, 1993.

Zuk, Rhoda, ed. "'A Fairy Tale' Introductory Note." In *Catherine Talbot and Hester Chapone.* Vol. 3 of *Bluestocking Feminism: Writings of the Bluestocking Circle, 1738–1785,* edited by Gary Kelly, 123. London: Pickering & Chatto, 1999.

INDEX

Achinstein, Sharon, 1, 200, 228
Addison, Joseph, 14, 177, 179, 232; gardens, 98, 189–90, 264n87; influence on Rowe, 51, 73, 140, 174–75; plays, 121, 136; on spirits and fairies, 62–63, 86; style, 50, 178. *See also* *Spectator*
aesthetic: in fairy tales, 91–92, 97, 99, 101–2, 112, 114, 144–45; fiction, 41, 45, 67, 68, 201, 254n90; in Heaven, 97; landscape, 174–75; pastoral, 97–99. *See also* Rowe, Elizabeth Singer: intellectual, aesthetics
Akenside, Mark, 14
amatory fiction, 2, 44–45, 52–59, 68, 76, 82; pastoral, 192–96; revenge stories, 80; uses of, 40, 47, 56–57, 71, 200. *See also* patchwork fiction
Anderson, Misty, 72
Anne, queen of England, 12
apparition literature, 40, 47, 60–68, 244nn47–48, 245nn49–51; meeting in Heaven, 66–67, 172, 188
Arabian Nights, 84
Astell, Mary, 170, 212–13
Athenian Mercury, 8, 13, 129–30. *See also* Dunton, John
Aubin, Penelope, 2, 46, 122, 149; characteristics of fiction, 105, 111, 149, 153, 156, 158, 247n101; *Life of Charlotta Du Pont*, 68, 75, 125; *Life of Lady Lucy*, 52–53, 59, 64
Austen, Jane, 72, 104, 207

Baillie, Joanna, 119
Bakhtin, Mikhail, 93
Ballaster, Ros, 38, 56

Bannerman, Anne, 63, 118
Barbauld, Anna Laetitia, 60, 228, 232; Nonconformist, 7, 225; opinions, 118–19, 182–83, 221–22, 224–26; regarding Rowe, 6, 209, 217
Barber, Mary, 60
Barker, Jane, 2, 46, 68, 80, 111, 122–25; alternatives to marriage, 58, 76, 81, 154, 156; fairy tale, 85; *Patch-Work* novels, 47, 69–73, 114, 126, 152, 200; poetry, 133, 139; politics, 74–75
Beale, Mary, 14–17
Behn, Aphra, 13, 39, 40, 89, 142, 222; and amatory fiction, 53–56, 58, 73, 204; on discourse, 124, 162; influence on Rowe, 55–56, 135; *Love Letters between a Nobleman and his Sister*, 14, 123, 125–26; portraits, 23, 25
Bermingham, Ann, 174, 189
Bigold, Melanie, 47, 94, 96
bildungsroman, 114–15
Blackmore, Richard, 7, 14, 97
Bluestockings, 187, 193, 209–36; as counterpublic sphere, 201, 233–34; fairyland code, 191, 212, 222; knowledge of Rowe, 4, 44, 116, 191, 216–17, 224; letters, 170, 190, 213–14, 217; as models, 207, 222, 229–30
Boscawen, Frances, 210. *See also* Bluestockings
Bourdieu, Pierre, 159, 178
Bowerbank, Sylvia, 97, 141, 184, 187–88, 221
Bowers, Toni, 75
Brant, Clare, 48, 170, 180–81, 185, 190
Brewer, John, 97
Brooke, Frances, 92, 132, 192, 199, 200, 242n4
Brooke, Lady Mary Thynne, 10, 12, 16–17, 167

Browning, Elizabeth Barrett, 119–20
Buckingham, George Villiers, Duke of, 4, 127, 151
Bunyan, John, 13, 158, 205
Burney, Frances, 155, 162, 176, 177, 186, 224, 227
Byatt, A. S., 92–93, 120, 256n120

Caroline, Princess of Wales (then queen), 10, 11–12, 143
Carter, Elizabeth, 29, 191–93, 219–20, 222, 228–30, 233; imagining friends, 92, 191, 213–14; outdoors, 187, 219–20; reputation, 26, 207, 229; and Rowe, 5, 216–17, 224–25, 230, 269n64. *See also* Bluestockings
Cavendish, Margaret, 222
Centlivre, Susanna, 13
Chandler, Mary, 7
Chapone, Hester, 214–15, 224, 227, 229
Charles II, king of England, 12, 19, 79, 89
Chartier, Roger, 42, 150–53
Chetwood, William, 46. *See also* travel narratives
children's literature, 36–37, 52, 66, 88
Chudleigh, Lady Mary, 14, 177, 225
Cibber, Colley, 13
Clarke, Norma, 68, 201, 208; Rowe and passion, 6, 53, 55, 200, 224; Rowe's reputation, 1, 38, 208–9, 229
Cockburn, Catharine Trotter, 12
Collyer, Mary, 43, 192–98, 200, 203, 208, 227; and Bluestockings, 214; ideology in novels, 170, 192, 265n102; pastoral adventure, 196, 204, 206, 231
Colman, Benjamin, 9–10
Congreve, William, 12, 13, 141
Cook, Elizabeth Heckendorn, 48, 123, 146, 148, 171, 180, 190
Cooke, Charles, 29–31, 34, 36–37
coterie writing, 7, 10, 45, 71–73, 148–50, 186; edition of *History of Adolphus*, 83, 89–90
Cowley, Hannah, 88, 124
Cowper, William, 118
Cross, Peter, 16–17
Curll, Edmund, 4, 129

d'Aulnoy, Marie-Catherine Le Jumel de Barneville, Comtesse, 40–41, 83–107, 112–20, 140, 202; author of devotional meditations, 102, 254n68; characteristics of tales, 126, 145, 165, 231, 252n34; plot of *Isle of Happiness*, 90–91, 112, 142, 192; "White Cat," 99–100, 102, 104, 106, 109, 120, 141–42, 144–45
Davys, Mary, 2–3, 40, 46, 111, 122, 204; characteristics of fiction, 80–81, 125–26, 153; *Familiar Letters Betwixt a Gentleman and a Lady*, 47, 68–70, 74–80, 82; and Ireland, 74–79; and patriarchal order, 160; *The Cousins*, 47, 157
Day, Robert Adams, 48–49, 69, 82, 94, 102, 123, 171
Defoe, Daniel, 1–2, 7, 14, 40, 122, 139, 227; fictional forms, 46, 71–72, 156–57; practical divinity books, 49, 66, 179, 226; prose style, 49, 51, 64–65, 87, 126, 149, 171
Defoe, Daniel, works of: *Essay on the History . . . of Apparitions*, 60–64; *Moll Flanders*, 52, 71, 105, 153, 157; *Robinson Crusoe*, 1–2, 62, 125, 126, 157–58; *Roxana*, 58, 59, 71, 126, 153, 157
DeJean, Joan, 84–86
Delany, Mary, 212, 214, 218
Dennis, John, 14, 127
Divine Hymns and Poems, 5, 7, 151
Dixon, Sarah, 200
Donne, John, 136
Doody, Margaret, 98, 111, 118
Drayton, Michael, 73, 136–37, 154–55
Dryden, John, 7, 14, 73, 89, 142, 245–46n68; as playwright, 13, 79, 134, 214; on poetic style, 127
Duggan, Anne, 85, 99
Duncombe, John, 4; *Feminiad*, 4, 11, 209, 238n15
Dunton, John, 4, 8–10, 14, 30, 180

educational books, 36–37, 52, 116–17, 172, 192–93, 235
Egerton, Sarah Fyge, 14, 200
"elsewhere, an," 41, 92–93, 182, 188–92, 196, 201–2; alternate domestic space, 81, 161; and identity, 191, 222
enthusiasm, religious, 35, 61, 179, 226–27
epistolarity, 42–43, 48, 80, 132, 163–205; and the body, 162, 180–82; religious, 179, 181–82
epistolary fiction, 2–3, 40, 122–23, 139; catego-

ries of, 48–49, 69, 77, 173; collections of, 48–50, 122, 147; development of, 48–52, 75, 139–40, 227; mid-century form, 70–71, 82, 102, 132, 147, 162, 173–74, 202; popularity, 48, 152
Etherege, George, 89
Ezell, Margaret, 133, 139, 257n31

fairy tales, 40–41, 83–121, 165, 174, 251n28, 252n34; attitude toward, 114–17; commercial success of, 115, 250nn7, 16; definition, 40–41, 86–88, 103–4, 115; mid-century novels as, 194–95, 202–3; modern uses, 119–21
Farquhar, George, 13
Fielding, Henry, 56, 152, 155–56, 173, 202, 231
Fielding, Sarah, 43, 68, 116, 199, 216, 231; *David Simple*, 202–6, 266nn127, 133, 135; fairy tales, 83, 85, 111–16, 126; *Familiar Letters*, 112–14, 173–74, 205, 227, 234–35; influence, 116
Finch, Anne, Countess of Winchilsea, 4, 10–11, 14, 17, 117, 200; miniature of, 16–17; political, 22, 238n19; and Rowe, 5, 10
Finch, Heneage, 11–12, 16, 19, 22, 46, 145
Five Love Letters from a Nun to a Cavalier, 70, 82, 123
Foucault, Michel, 42–43, 163–64, 178, 184, 185; and subjectivity, 221–22
Frederick, Prince of Wales, 19
Friedman, Emily, 130, 203, 266nn126, 130

Gay, John, 14
gentility movement. *See* politeness movement
Gentleman's Magazine, 4, 5, 14, 29
George I, king of England, 12, 19, 77, 79, 167, 168, 169–70
Gildon, Charles, 2, 40, 47, 48, 68, 122–23; *Post-Boy Robb'd of his Mail* and *Post-Man Robb'd*, 69–70, 73, 77, 126, 152
Goldsmith, Oliver, 115–16, 199, 242n4
Gray, Thomas, 42, 51, 117
Green Book, 11, 12, 44, 216–17, 240n51
Greville, Frances, 117–18
Grey, Lady Jane Seymour, 19–22, 50, 132, 135–36
Griffith, Elizabeth, 155, 186, 200
Grove, Henry, 19
Guest, Harriet, 202–3, 224, 227, 229

Hamilton, Mary, 192
Hands, Elizabeth, 7
Harding, Elizabeth, 122
Hawkesworth, John, 86–87
Hayes, Mary, 227
Haywood, Eliza, 2, 46, 52–57, 59, 114, 156–58; *Betsy Thoughtless*, 15, 105, 109, 177, 186, 194, 196, 199, 204, 209; *British Recluse*, 57–59, 73, 111, 156; discourse, 72–73, 124, 132–33, 149, 196; fictional forms, 40, 68, 80, 105, 111, 122, 153, 156–60; *Fruitless Inquiry*, 46, 52–53; *Love in Excess*, 52–55; portraits of, 19, 24–26; reputation, 26, 39, 139
Heidegger, Martin, 107–8
heroic epistle, 19–22, 49, 135–39
Herrick, Robert, 117
Hertford. *See* Seymour, Algernon
Hertford, Frances Seymour, Countess of, 29, 61, 93, 150–52, 166–70, 180; biography, 10–12, 181, 184, 186–87, 210–16, 218–19; collaboration with Rowe, 94, 145, 148–49, 163, 175, 215–16, 232, 253n51; and Jane Grey, 19–22; *Inkle and Yarrico*, 21, 91, 215; reputation, 143, 151, 209; Rowe imagining her, 67, 83, 168, 172, 188–89, 213; tributes to, 11, 129, 143, 186, 209, 218; visits Rowe, 98–99
heteronormativity, 41, 47, 76
Hill, Aaron, 12, 34
Holt, Jane Wiseman, 85
Howard, Isabella Byron, 118
Hunter, J. Paul, 65, 84, 111, 159–60
Hutcheson, Francis, 179, 197

Jajdelska, Elspeth, 42, 126, 153
James II, king of England, 12, 19, 22
Janeway, James, 66, 179
Jobs, Steven P., 66–67
Johnson, Samuel, 4, 52, 82, 210
Jones, Mary, 44, 171, 200
Jonson, Ben, 85, 117

Ken, Thomas, 12–13, 22, 65
Killigrew, Anne, 22, 23, 25, 34
Kincade, Kit, 62, 64
King, Kathryn, 38, 47, 81, 227, 247n100; paradigms of authorship, 39, 45, 72, 227; political dimensions of fiction, 74–75, 128, 160
King, Sophia, 115

Kitchin, Thomas, 29
Kneller, Godfrey, 18–19

Lafayette, Marie-Madeleine Pioche de la Vergne, Comtesse de, 53, 85, 110–11
Landry, Donna, 196, 221
Lane, William, 30, 36, 115
Lanser, Susan, 132, 162, 265n124
Lee, Nathaniel, 13, 22, 89
Lennox, Charlotte, 229, 266–67n145; *Life of Harriot Stuart*, 109, 199, 209, 223–24, 226, 228–29
letters: importance of, 48; manuals, 49–50, 172; personal letters, 42–43. *See also* epistolarity
lifestyle: development of, 106–8, 110–11, 163–207; exemplary, 96–97, 104; expression of identity, 159–61, 206–7; single, respected, 47, 76, 81
Lintot, Bernard, 4, 30, 151
Little, Janet, 5
Locke, John, 14, 175, 178, 197, 219–20

Macaulay, Catherine, 165
Mackie, Erin, 49, 203, 266nn126, 130
Manley, Delariviere, 39, 53, 59, 68, 73, 222; prose style, 124, 126, 152
marriage, 57–59, 75–77, 105–11, 142, 156; alternate lifestyles, 47, 58, 76, 81, 109, 114, 156–57, 201–2; beautiful, 199–200; forced, 70, 109–10, 254n83
Marrow, Arabella, 9, 10, 186, 188, 246n76
Marvell, Andrew, 14
Mary, queen of England, 12, 19
Mary Queen of Scots, 50
Masters, Mary, 5, 44
McKeon, Michael, 38, 84, 98, 188
Millenium Hall. See Scott, Sarah
Miller, Lady Anne, 213
Miller, Nancy K., 41, 156, 222
Milton, John, 8, 13, 86, 96–98, 139; influence on Rowe, 117, 130–31; quoted in novels, 73, 96–98, 133–34, 192
miniatures, 14–17, 186, 216, 240nn63–64
Monkly, Nycky (nephew), 3
Monkly, Sarah Rowe (sister-in-law), 165, 169
Montagu, Elizabeth, 92, 188, 191–93, 210–15, 221–22, 227; dialogues, 60, 225; on lifestyle, 184, 229, 230. *See also* Bluestockings

Montagu, Lady Barbara, 213, 214, 216–17
Montagu, Lady Mary Wortley, 49, 171, 216
moral romance, 3, 43, 194, 202, 231
More, Hannah, 39, 97–98, 232
Murat, Henriette-Julie de Castelnau, Comtesse de, 84, 86
Murry, Ann, 119

Newbery, John, 115, 119
Nixon, Cheryl, 42, 81–82, 148, 153, 185
Nonconformist ideology, 7–8, 66, 109–10, 167–69, 221, 226, 270n97; women's church activity, 8, 239n35
novel: definition, 47; histories of, 84
Nussbaum, Felicity, 57

Opie, Amelia, 230
Otway, Thomas, 8, 13–14, 73, 134
Ovid, 73, 101, 127, 138–39, 141–42, 215

pastoral adventure, 3, 43, 204, 231
patchwork fiction, 40, 41, 47–48, 68–82; characteristics of, 68–69, 74, 81; political content, 74–79
Perrault, Charles, 83, 103, 250n8, 251–52n31; compared to d'Aulnoy, 87–89, 115–16, 119
Perry, Ruth, 104–5
Philips, Ambrose, 5
Philips, Katherine, 72, 133, 139, 170, 232; friendship poem, 134–35, 234; portrait, 22–23, 25
Piozzi, Hester Thrale, 60, 111, 225–26
Poems by Eminent Ladies, 6
poetry: in novels, 47, 72, 133; religious, 7. *See also under* Rowe, Elizabeth Singer
politeness movement, 3, 42–45, 161–92, 231–32, 262–63n43; in fairy tales, 119; gendered behavior, 198–99, 232–34; in novels, 52, 192–202, 206; in *Spectator*, 52; women's alternate, 44, 182, 198–99, 213, 217–18, 232, 234–35
Pomfret, Lady Henrietta Louisa Fermor, 148, 210–12, 216
Pope, Alexander, 4, 34, 36, 49, 69, 143; prints *On the Death of Mr. Thomas Rowe*, 5, 151, 223; quoted by Rowe, 73, 96, 121, 133–34; *Rape of the Lock*, 50–51, 121; Rowe's contemporary, 14, 19, 60, 127, 240n52

Portland, Lady Margaret Cavendish Harley, 211–12, 214–16, 218, 220, 222
Prescott, Sarah, 2, 6, 39, 52–53, 59
Prior, Matthew, 5, 7, 8–10, 19, 60

quest, modern, 162, 200–202, 231–32

Radcliffe, Ann, 85
readers, 51–52, 148–53, 158–62, 178–79; identifications with characters, 148–50, 185; reader communities, 52, 179, 203, 210–15, 266n131
reading revolution, 3, 42–43, 148–53, 203–4, 259n71
reason, 61–64, 222; rational religion, 35, 59, 166, 206, 209, 222–23, 225–29
Reeve, Clara, 119
register, 61, 98, 148, 169, 180, 226; defined, 41–42, 261n14; novelistic, 3, 165–66, 178
retirement, 143, 151–52, 167, 201
Richardson, Samuel, 38–39, 85, 170, 202, 210, 214; characteristics of fiction, 44, 53, 162, 180, 231–32; prints Rowe texts, 243n26; rewrites Rowe scene, 53–55, 67–68, 146
Richardson, Samuel, works of: *Clarissa*, 2, 57–58, 67–68, 87, 109–10, 123, 151–54, 158, 181–82, 197; *Pamela*, 57, 87, 123, 146–47, 156–57, 168–69, 181, 199, 260n103
Richetti, John, 37–39, 40, 52, 82, 85, 123–24; on style, 126
Robinson, Mary, 29
romances, 39, 52, 73, 111, 122, 203; French, 2, 68, 74, 76, 82, 86, 123, 141, 174; literary, 133, 141; modern mass market, 53–54, 121
Rosse, Susannah-Penelope, 14–17
Rothstein, Eric, 42, 43, 153, 155, 158
Roulston, Christine, 57–58, 81, 161
Rowe, Elizabeth Portnell (mother), 7–8
Rowe, Elizabeth Singer, biographical: birth and early life, 7–14; courtships and marriage, 8–10; death, 3, 34, 36; lifestyle, 3–4, 184, 186–87, 214–19, 239n36; political experiences, 7–8, 74–75, 79; portraits of, 14–34; pseudonyms, 4–5; reading, 8, 11–12, 50, 147, 174–75, 179, 184, 214
—reputation, 4, 9, 26–40, 139, 142, 151, 161, 164–65, 185, 229; after death, 11, 142–44, 208–10, 234–36; anthologized, 49, 172; as educational writer, 36–37, 235; modern, 1–2; tributes to, 5–6, 35; *On the Death of Mr. Thomas Rowe*, 5, 26, 36, 143, 151, 223
Rowe, Elizabeth Singer, intellectual
—aesthetics: of death, 59, 68, 176; from fairy tales, 41; of Heaven, 97, 101–2; lifestyle, 159, 174–82
—ideology: creating, 96, 124–25, 158–60, 178–80, 229–30; fiction as, 161–62, 184
—views and attitudes of: mysticism, 61, 179, 226–27; Nonconformist, 7–8, 50, 66, 109–10, 128, 160, 163, 165, 170, 221; religious tolerance, 226; toward rank, 167–70; unity of earth and Heaven, 80, 97–98, 101–2, 108, 135–36, 158–59, 177–92
Rowe, Elizabeth Singer, lifestyle model: influential, 2–4, 41, 153, 161, 207–10; and "liberty," 43, 110–11, 176, 182, 185–92, 200–201, 231; as single, independent woman, 81, 104–9, 206–7, 227–30; of technologies of the self, 43–44, 158–62
Rowe, Elizabeth Singer, personality: characteristics of, 1, 9–10, 29; passionate, 223–24; sensuality, 108–9, 130–31, 135, 138, 145, 180, 228
Rowe, Elizabeth Singer, writing: aesthetics of production and reception, 42, 140–45, 161, 178–81, 185; authority of, 132–33, 139–41, 144, 147–48, 150–53, 185; characteristics of, 64–65, 148–49, 182–92, 223–24; domestic, 59, 144–45; inspiration for, 12, 13, 19–22, 51–52, 65; and periodical essay, 39; prose style, 50–52, 121, 124–62, 178–82, 231; publishers, selection of, 4–5
—*Miscellaneous Works in Prose and Verse*, 3–4, 44, 61, 227; dialogues, 60, 129; letters in, 165–74, 180, 217; "Life," 4, 35–36, 81, 164–65, 207, 209; portrait in, 17–19; revised poetry in, 129–31
—strategies: creating alternate worlds, 92–93, 99, 101–2, 167, 188–89
—subjects: death, and letters left for friends, 246n76; death, scenes of, 59, 66–68, 71, 166; death, and Wilmot, Earl of Rochester, 65; erotic love, 106, 199–200, 228; reason, 58, 61, 79, 103, 158, 165–66, 205–6
Rowe, Elizabeth Singer, works, devotional: *Devout Exercises*, 29–30, 35–36, 152, 225, 235

Rowe, Elizabeth Singer, works, fiction: amatory, 52–59, 71, 231; apparition, 60–68; fairy tales, 86, 90–121; familiar letters used in, 11, 12, 145; heroine's quest, 3, 41, 43, 57, 92, 162, 183–90, 200, 231; new subjects, 153–62; patchworks, 70–82, 171
—*Friendship in Death . . . To which are added, Letters Moral and Entertaining*: biblical allusions, 149; characteristics of, 3, 70–72, 124–25, 139–53, 171–72; contemporary classification, 40; contemporary references in, 12, 65, 71, 86; contents, 8, 70–71, 152–53, 183–84; editions, 1–2, 29–30, 35–36, 46–47, 235, 237n4; influence on modern novels, 40, 43, 44, 82, 121, 227, 231–32; Laura story, 57, 71, 93–94, 101–4, 107–9, 120–21, 149–50, 184, 193; manual similarities, 49; Melinda story, 58, 93, 100, 104–5, 120–21, 144–47, 157, 178; Melissa story, 94–96, 106, 109, 132, 144, 154, 157, 160, 202; Rosalinda story, 36–37, 55–57, 71, 88–89, 93, 96, 98–110, 129, 134, 140–41, 144–45, 149–50, 154–57, 165, 176, 192–95; Silviana story, 100–101, 105–7, 140–42, 146, 157, 224–25
Rowe, Elizabeth Singer, works, poetry: characteristics, 2, 4–7, 127–39; experimental, 42, 127; revised, 129–31, 136–37; varied, 35–36, 127–28; verse epistles, 135–39, 154–55
—in *Athenian Mercury*, 129; Canticles, 35–36, 55, 129–31, 138–39, 199–200, 228; *History of Joseph*, 35–36, 64, 129, 151, 180; in *Letters*, 42, 73–74, 128–29, 131–39; *Philomela*, 4, 129; *Poems on Several Occasions*, 4, 8, 129–30
Rowe, Nicholas, 5, 8, 22, 154
Rowe, Sarah (niece), 169
Rowe, Sarah (sister-in-law). *See* Monkly, Sarah Rowe
Rowe, Theophilus (brother-in-law), 68, 246n76
Rowe, Thomas, 10, 29, 167, 169, 228, 257n20; *On the Death of Mr. Thomas Rowe*, 5, 26, 36, 143, 151, 223
Rowe, Walter, 7–10
rural adventure, 194–95
Sappho, 3; reference to, 6; woman poets as, 29
Savage, Mary, 213
Savage, Richard, 11–12, 46, 214

Schellenberg, Betty, 199, 206, 217, 254n90, 268n51
Scott, Sarah, 184, 206, 212, 216–17, 226–27, 229, 233; *Millenium Hall*, 58, 161, 200–202, 206, 215–17, 227, 265n124
secret histories, 2, 48, 77, 122–23
Sedley, Charles, 13
Seifert, Lewis, 88–89
self, 174–75, 178; conceptual, 43, 163, 178, 183–85, 191, 206, 223, 256n4; expressions of, 221–25; steadfast, 200–201, 203–7
Sermain, Jean-Paul, 85–86, 110–11
Seward, Anna, 3, 15, 26, 29, 213, 232
Seymour, Algernon, Earl of Hertford, 10, 19–21, 46, 134
Seymour, Frances. *See* Hertford, Frances Seymour, Countess of
Shaftesbury, Anthony Ashley Cooper, Earl of, 175, 187, 192–94, 202, 232; benevolence, 204–5; and Collyer, 192, 197–98; and politeness movement, 43–44, 171, 232; Rowe reading his work, 8, 162–65
Shakespeare, William, 85, 86, 90, 111, 117
Shenstone, William, 14, 143
Sheridan, Frances, 185, 186, 200, 227
Sherwood, Martha Mary, 115
Sidney, Philip, 133
Smith, Charlotte, 124, 133
Smollett, Tobias, 162, 165, 199
Spectator, 49–52, 62–63, 69–70, 161, 189, 215; prose style, 50–52, 69, 123, 126–27, 172, 178; recommended reading, 52, 192–93, 226–27; Rowe adapts, 51, 140, 165, 167. *See also* Addison, Joseph
Spencer, Jane, 38, 84
Spenser, Edmund, 85, 90, 117, 192
Starr, George A., 61–62, 222–23
Staves, Susan, 6, 39, 53, 193, 207, 210
Steele, Richard, 14, 147, 227
style: masculine, 123–24; modern novelistic, 124–25; novelistic, 122–62; women's, 123–24. *See also* register
Swift, Jonathan, 4, 13, 14–15, 77, 122, 199; reading fairy tales, 86

Talbot, Catherine, 67, 214–16, 225, 229; fairy tale, 116–17, 216; philosophy, 187–88, 191–92, 207. *See also* Bluestockings

Tasso, Torquato, 8, 39, 73, 92; translated by Rowe, 102, 134, 211
Tate, Nahum, 13, 256–57n16
Thomas, Elizabeth, 24–26, 48, 170
Thomson, James, 8, 14, 175–76, 186, 202, 214; and Hertford, 11–12, 143, 218; quoted in novels, 11, 98, 133, 140, 175, 192
Thynne, Frances. *See* Hertford, Frances Seymour, Countess of
Thynne, Grace, 8–11, 19, 29, 166–67
Thynne, Henry, 8, 10, 16
Thynne, Thomas, 8–10, 12–13, 16
Tollet, Elizabeth, 122
Tonson, Jacob, 4–5, 9, 30, 138, 151, 238n16
travel narratives, 2, 46, 48
Tuite, Lady Eliza, 50, 102

Vanbrugh, John, 5
Vandergucht, Michael, 18–19, 22, 25
Vertue, George, 17–29
Vesey, Elizabeth, 191, 210, 213–14, 220, 222, 230. *See also* Bluestockings

walking, 184, 187–89, 206, 218–21, 228, 232, 269nn59, 62; gendered, 219
Walmsley, Peter, 97, 239n41, 245n61
Walsh, Octavia, 177–79, 238n16
Watts, Isaac, 9, 13, 73, 133, 143, 151, 228
Wesley, John, 63
Wharton, Anne, 138–39
William III, king of England, 12, 19, 75, 109, 128
Williams, Helen Maria, 7, 29
Wilmot, John, Earl of Rochester, 14, 65
Wollstonecraft, Mary, 228, 256n12
Worrall, Thomas, 46–47
Wroth, Mary, 141
Wycherley, William, 12

Young, Edward, 89, 121, 149–51, 192; characters reading, 121, 149; dedication to, 83, 147, 151; reputation, 11, 46, 240n52, 249n1

Zipes, Jack, 87–88, 109, 119–20

PR 3671 .R4 Z58 2013
Backscheider, Paula R.
Elizabeth Singer Rowe and
the development of the